AF553463

DECEMBER 13
Terror over Democracy

DECEMBER 13
Terror over Democracy

Nirmalangshu Mukherji

Foreword Essay
Manipulation of Fear
by
Noam Chomsky

PROMILLA & CO., PUBLISHERS
in association with
BIBLIOPHILE SOUTH ASIA

NEW DELHI & CHICAGO

Published by
PROMILLA & CO., PUBLISHERS
in association with
BIBLIOPHILE SOUTH ASIA
URL : www.biblioasia.com

C-127, Sarvodaya Enclave
New Delhi 110 017, India

First published 2005

ISBN : 81-85002-54-1 (Pb.)
ISBN : 81-85002-57-6 (Hb.)

Typeset in AGaramond
Layout and processing by Tarun Beri, New Delhi

Printed and bound in India by Uthra Print Communications, New Delhi

Acknowledgement

This work grew out of detailed conversations, spread over many meetings, with Prashant Bhushan, Uma Chakravarti, Ali Javed, Svati Joshi, Neeraj Malik, Nivedita Menon, Nandita Narain, Gautam Navlakha, Madhu Prasad, Ashim Roy, Arjun Prasad Singh, Kumar Sanjay Singh, Vijay Singh, Tripta Wahi, and many other academicians, lawyers and activists, especially friends in Peoples Union for Democratic Rights (PUDR) and other organizations. Despite crushing international schedule, Noam Chomsky gave his unfailing support to the project with his powerful foreword. It is an honour to be associated with people who are actively engaged in the protection of civil and human rights in the face of growing attacks on democracy often initiated for reasons of state.

I am especially grateful to Vasanthi Raman, Ashim Roy, and Vijay Singh for their friendly support during the execution of this project. Thanks to Nandita Haksar, Basharat Peer, and PUDR for allowing me to include their work in the Annexures. Most sincere thanks to Ashok Butani of Bibliophile South Asia for agreeing to publish this book with much affection under a severe deadline; to Tarun Beri and B.D. Diwan for setting everything aside for this project. I am also indebted to an unusually large number of reviewers who have read the manuscript with care and have made valuable suggestions. However, the author takes full responsibility for the facts stated and the opinions expressed in this work.

N.M.
Delhi, January 2005

By convicting innocents, you cannot suppress emotion. Peace comes with justice. Without justice there will be no democracy; it is Indian democracy that is under threat.

— *Syed Abdul Rehman Geelani*

After he was sentenced to death by the special court for consipiring to attack the Indian Parliament

Contents

FOREWORD ESSAY ix-xvii
Manipulation of Fear *by Noam Chomsky*

CHAPTER ONE :
An Attack on Democracy
- Terrorism and Preventive Measures 1
- Windows of Opportunity 5
- Role of the Media 13
- Court Documents 30
- Notes and References 33

CHAPTER TWO:
Who Attacked Parliament?
- Prosecution Story 38
- Story Disputed 47
- Incredible Features 52
- Acquittal of Geelani 63
- Arrest Memos 70
- 'Procured' Witnesses 80
- A Surrendered Militant 85
- Unfair Trial 93
- An Appeal for Parliamentary Inquiry 96
- Notes and References 103

ANNEXURES

1. The Charge Sheet 109
2. Confession of Mohammad Afzal 138
3. Confession of Shaukat Hussain Guru 145
4. Statement u/s 313 Cr.P.C. S.A.R. Geelani (Extracts) 149
5. Statement u/s 313 Cr.P.C. Mohammad Afzal 151
6. Statement u/s 313 Cr.P.C. Shaukat Hussain Guru 184
7. Deposition by Geelani's wife (Extracts) 205
8. Transcript of media trial by police (Extracts) 208
9. Letter from Amnesty International 211
10. Letter to Chief Justice of India by university teachers 225
11. Special Court Judgment (Extracts) 229
12. *Trial of Errors:* First PUDR Report 256
13. *Victims of December 13*: Basharat Peer 301
14. *A Presumptuous Judgment:* Nandita Haskar 315
15. Statements from Delhi University Teachers and Noam Chomsky 333
16. High Court Judgment (Extract) 337
17. *Balancing Act:* Second PUDR Report 354
18. *A Wife's Appeal For Justice* : Tabassum 369

Index 373

Foreword Essay
Manipulation of Fear

The resort to fear by systems of power to discipline the domestic population has left a long and terrible trail of bloodshed and suffering, which we ignore at our peril. Recent history provides many shocking illustrations.

The mid-twentieth century witnessed perhaps the most awful crimes since the Mongol invasions. The most savage were carried out where Western civilization had achieved its greatest splendors. Germany was a leading center of the sciences, the arts and literature, humanistic scholarship, and other memorable achievements. Prior to World War I, before anti-German hysteria was fanned in the West, Germany had been regarded by American political scientists as a model democracy as well, to be emulated by the West. In the mid-1930s, Germany was driven within a few years to a level of barbarism that has few historical counterparts. That was true, most notably, among the most educated and civilized sectors of the population. In his remarkable diaries of his life as a Jew under Nazism – escaping the gas chambers by a near miracle – Victor Klemperer writes these words about a German Professor friend whom he had much admired, but who had finally joined the pack:

> If one day the situation were reversed and the fate of the vanquished lay in my hands, then I would let all the ordinary folk go and even some of the leaders, who might perhaps after all have had honourable

> intentions and not known what they were doing. But I would have all the intellectuals strung up, and the professors three feet higher than the rest; they would be left hanging from the lamp posts for as long as was compatible with hygiene.

Klemperer's reactions were merited, and generalize to a large part of recorded history.

Complex historical events always have many causes. One crucial factor in this case was skillful manipulation of fear. The "ordinary folk" were driven to fear of a Jewish-Bolshevik conspiracy to take over the world, placing the very survival of the people of Germany at risk. Extreme measures were therefore necessary, in "self-defense." Revered intellectuals went far beyond. As the Nazi storm clouds settled over the country in 1935, Martin Heidegger depicted Germany as the "most endangered" nation in the world, gripped in the "great pincers" of an onslaught against civilization itself, led in its crudest form by Russia and America. Not only was Germany the prime victim of this awesome and barbaric force, but it was also the responsibility of Germany, "the most metaphysical of nations," to lead the resistance to it. Germany stood "in the center of the Western world," and must protect the great heritage of classical Greece from "annihilation," relying on the "new spiritual energies unfolding historically from out of the center." The "spiritual energies" continued to unfold in ways that were evident enough when he delivered that message, to which he and other leading intellectuals continued to adhere.

The paroxysm of slaughter and annihilation did not end with the use of weapons that may very well bring the species to a bitter end. We should also not forget that these species-terminating weapons were created by the most brilliant, humane, and highly educated figures of modern civilization, working in isolation, and so entranced by the beauty of the work in which they were engaged that they apparently paid little attention to the consequences: significant scientific protests against nuclear weapons began in the labs in Chicago, after the termination of their role in creation of the bomb, not in Los Alamos, where the work went on until the grim end. Not quite the end. The official US Air Force history relates that after the bombing of Nagasaki, when Japan's submission to unconditional surrender was certain, General Hap Arnold "wanted as big a finale as possible," a 1000-plane daylight raid on defenseless Japanese cities. The last bomber returned to its base just as agreement to unconditional surrender was formally received. The Air Force chief, General Carl Spaatz, had preferred that the grand finale be a third nuclear attack on Tokyo, but was dissuaded. Tokyo was a "poor target," having already been incinerated in the carefully-executed firestorm in March, leaving perhaps 100,000 charred corpses in one of history's worst crimes.

Such matters are excluded from war crimes tribunals, and largely expunged from history. By now they are hardly known beyond circles of activists and specialists. At the time they were publicly hailed as a legitimate exercise of self-defense against a vicious enemy that had reached the ultimate level of infamy by bombing US military bases in its Hawaiian and Philippine colonies.

It is perhaps worth bearing in mind that Japan's December 1941 bombings – "the date which will live in infamy," in FDR's ringing words – were more than justified under the doctrines of "anticipatory self-defense" that prevail among the leaders of today's self-designated "enlightened states," the US and its British client. Japanese leaders knew that B-17 Flying Fortresses were coming off the Boeing production lines, and were surely familiar with the public discussions in the US explaining how they could be used to incinerate Japan's wooden cities in a war of extermination, flying from Hawaiian and Philippine bases — "to burn out the industrial heart of the Empire with fire-bombing attacks on the teeming bamboo ant heaps," as retired Air Force General Chennault recommended in 1940, a proposal that "simply delighted" President Roosevelt. Evidently, that is a far more powerful justification for bombing military bases in US colonies than anything conjured up by Bush-Blair and their associates in their execution of "preemptive war" — and accepted, with tactical reservations, throughout the mainstream of articulate opinion.

The comparison, however, is inappropriate. Those who dwell in teeming bamboo ant heaps are not entitled to such emotions as fear. Such feelings and concerns are the prerogatives only of the "rich men dwelling at peace within their habitations," in Churchill's rhetoric, the "satisfied nations, who wished nothing more for themselves than what they had," and to whom, therefore, "the government of the world must be entrusted" if there is to be peace — a certain kind of peace, in which the rich men must be free from fear.

Just how secure the rich men must be from fear is revealed graphically by highly-regarded scholarship on the new doctrines of "anticipatory self-defense" crafted by the powerful. The most important contribution with some historical depth is by one of the leading contemporary historians, John Lewis Gaddis of Yale University. He traces the Bush doctrine to his intellectual hero, the grand strategist John Quincy Adams. In the paraphrase of the *New York Times*, Gaddis "suggests that Bush's framework for fighting terrorism has its roots in the lofty, idealistic tradition of John Quincy Adams and Woodrow Wilson." We can put aside Wilson's shameful record, and keep to the origins of the lofty, idealistic tradition, which Adams established in a famous state paper justifying Andrew Jackson's conquest of Florida in the first Seminole war in 1818. The war was justified in self-defense, Adams argued. Gaddis agrees that its motives were legitimate security concerns. In Gaddis's version, after Britain sacked Washington in 1814, US leaders recognized that "expansion is the path to security" and therefore conquered Florida, a doctrine now expanded to the whole world by Bush — properly, he argues.

Gaddis cites the right scholarly sources, primarily historian William Earl Weeks, but omits what they say. We learn a lot about the precedents for current doctrines, and the current consensus, by looking at what Gaddis omits. Weeks describes in lurid detail what Jackson was doing in the "exhibition of murder and plunder known as the First Seminole war," which was just another phase in his project of "removing or eliminating native Americans from the southeast," underway long before 1814. Florida was a problem both because it had not yet been incorporated in the expanding American empire and because it was a "haven for Indians and runaway slaves ... fleeing the wrath of Jackson or slavery."

There was in fact an Indian attack, which Jackson and Adams used as a pretext: US forces drove a band of Seminoles off their lands, killing several of them and burning their village to the ground. The Seminoles retaliated by attacking a supply boat under military command. Seizing the opportunity, Jackson "embarked on a campaign of terror, devastation, and intimidation," destroying villages and "sources of food in a calculated effort to inflict starvation on the tribes, who sought refuge from his wrath in the swamps." So matters continued, leading to Adams's highly regarded state paper, which endorsed Jackson's unprovoked aggression to establish in Florida "the dominion of this republic upon the odious basis of violence and bloodshed." These are the words of the Spanish Ambassador, a "painfully precise description," Weeks writes. Adams "had consciously distorted, dissembled, and lied about the goals and conduct of American foreign policy to both Congress and the public," Weeks continues, grossly violating his proclaimed moral principles, "implicitly defending Indian removal, and slavery." The crimes of Jackson and Adams "proved but a prelude to a second war of extermination against [the Seminoles]," in which the remnants either fled to the West, to enjoy the same fate later, "or were killed or forced to take refuge in the dense swamps of Florida." Today, Weeks concludes, "the Seminoles survive in the national consciousness as the mascot of Florida State University" – a typical and instructive case.

Weeks also stresses that Adams' forceful endorsement of Jackson's crimes shifted the power to make war from Congress to the Executive, in violation of the Constitution, a principle that remains in force, not troubling strict constructionists. He points out that Adams's rhetoric also established the "presidential 'rhetoric of empire' designed to marshal public and congressional support for its policies, ... a durable and essential aspect of American diplomacy inherited and elaborated by successive generations of American statesmen but fundamentally unchanged over time." The rhetorical framework rests on three pillars: "the assumption of the unique moral virtue of the United States, the assertion of its mission to redeem the world" by spreading its professed ideals and the 'American way of life,' and the faith in the nation's divinely ordained destiny." The theological framework undercuts reasoned debate, and reduces policy issues to a choice between Good and Evil, thus reducing the threat of democracy. Critics can be dismissed as "anti-American," an interesting concept borrowed from the lexicon of totalitarianism. And the population must huddle under the umbrella of power, in fear that its way of life and destiny are under imminent threat.

The issue of defense against Britain never remotely arose: British Minister Castlereagh was so eager to cement Anglo-American relations that he even overlooked Jackson's murder of two innocent British citizens, which Adams defended for its "salutary efficacy for terror and example." Adams was heeding the words of Tacitus, his favorite historian, Weeks suggests: that "crime once exposed had no refuge but in audacity."

The goal of Adams' diplomacy was not security, but territorial expansion, to the Pacific. That was achieved, though the British threat was not entirely overcome. British military force barred the conquest of Canada and Cuba, which, Adams predicted, would drop into US hands like a "ripe fruit" by the laws of political gravitation, once the US succeeded in subduing its British enemy. By the end of the century, the laws of political gravitation had shifted, as Adams had predicted, and the US was able to intervene to bar Cuba's liberation from Spain, turning it into a "virtual colony" until 1959. Since the early days after the long-delayed liberation in 1959, the island has been the target of unremitting terror and economic strangulation, because of its "successful defiance" of policies tracing back to the days of grand strategist Adams, we learn from declassified documents of the Kennedy-Johnson years. It is also the site of the infamous Guantanamo torture chamber, on land effectively stolen from Cuba and kept by the leader of the enlightened states in part to prevent Cuban economic development.

Filling in the blanks, the picture supports Gaddis's judgment about the precedents for the Bush doctrine and its implementation. As for the expansion of the precedent to the entire world, others may judge for themselves. But keeping to the present theme, within the culture of enlightenment virtually any action, however horrendous, is justified by fear, which is legitimate if there is any possibility, however remote, that something might interfere with the goals of the rich men living at peace within their ample habitations — goals that are necessarily noble, as the intellectual classes soberly explain, though occasionally some light breaks through. Churchill revealed his grasp of reality in internal debate in Parliament in 1914, when he was urging an expanded military budget:

> we are not a young people with *an innocent record and* a scanty inheritance. We have engrossed to ourselves ... an *altogether disproportionate* share of the wealth and traffic of the world. We have got all we want in territory, and our claim to be left in the unmolested enjoyment of vast and splendid possessions, *mainly acquired by violence, largely maintained by force*, often seems less reasonable to others than to us.

The italicized phrases are those that Churchill omitted when he published these words years later. The meaning of the phrases need not be explained in India. They are not part of the internalized history of the "enlightened states." They are dispatched to the same oblivion as other exercises of the "the lofty, idealistic tradition" by which the "rich men ... engrossed to [them]selves an altogether disproportionate share of the wealth and traffic of the world," and must retain it, in "unmolested enjoyment," resorting to justified self-defense if they perceive any potential challenge, mobilizing their population by the traditional and well-practiced device of fear.

There is no need to review how the people of the most powerful country of the world have been driven to desperate fear for their survival in recent years, and what measures their leaders have taken to allay these fears. To be sure, the fears are not manufactured from nothing. Even the most vulgar propaganda must have some basis in reality. In this case the threat of terror of the doctrinally admissible kind – *their* terror against *us* – is very real. It is hard to overestimate the potential dangers of the Jihadist terror that was organized for traditional reasons of state by the current incumbents in Washington and their immediate mentors, along with their associates. Sooner or later it is likely to be united with WMD, as was known long before 9-11. The threat is being consciously escalated by global leaders. Bush and Blair were well aware that the invasion of Iraq would be likely to enhance the threat of terror, as it did, but terror does not rank high among their priorities, as this and many other examples illustrate.

The US population is overwhelmingly opposed to the use of force except in self-defense against ongoing or imminent attack. Three-quarters of Americans believe the government had no right to invade Iraq if it was not developing WMD or co-operating with al-Qaeda. Half believe that the invasion was justified. There is no contradiction. Rather, the numbers reveal, once again, the enormous effectiveness of manipulation of fear. Even after official inquiries have completely undermined government-media propaganda about Saddam's WMD and links to al-Qaeda, half the population continue to believe the charges, and thus support not only the invasion – the "supreme international crime differing only from other war crimes in that it contains within itself the accumulated evil of the whole," in the wording of the Nuremberg Tribunal – but also the ongoing war crimes that are depicted without shame on the front-pages of the world's greatest newspaper, always in self-defense against evil forces threatening us with destruction.

We cannot underestimate the threat of terror, or the cynicism of centers of power in pursuit of their own often despicable ends, or the murderous violence to which they will resort if authority is granted to them by a frightened population.

It is within this context that we should, I believe, consider the terrible events of 13 December, the reaction to them on the part of the government and media, and the detailed investigation carried out in this important and careful study. And it is within the same context, I think, that the people of India should respond constructively to the call for a serious parliamentary inquiry into what actually happened and its roots. Indian democracy is one of the triumphs of the twentieth century, but a fragile one. The plant has to be protected and nurtured, or it can all too easily wither, with consequences that are sure to be grim.

Noam Chomsky
Massachusetts Institute of Technology

Chapter One

An Attack on Democracy

Terrorism and Preventive Measures

Five armed persons entered the Parliament complex in New Delhi on 13 December 2001 at about 11.30 A.M. in a white Ambassador car when Parliament was in session. On being challenged near the motorcade of the Vice-President of India, they opened fire. "For half an hour, a fierce battle raged outside the building; inside, around 200 trapped and terrified politicians listened to gunfire and grenade explosions. By noon, it was all over" (Annexure 13, p. 302). All five persons died on the spot before they could enter inside the Parliament building. Nine other people, including some members of the security forces, died in the attack while sixteen persons from the security forces were injured. A much larger catastrophe was barely averted. In terms of the scale of the attack and its symbolic significance, it was perhaps the most daring terrorist assault on the Indian soil in recent years.

Since the attack took place just a few months after the terrorist outrage in New York and Washington on 11 September 2001, comparison with those events are inevitable. Speaking at the Annual Convocation of Visva Bharati University, Prime Minister Atal Behari Vajpayee likened the attack on December 13 to the September 11 attack in US. In this connection, Vajpayee suggested that "the phenomenon of terrorism has many dimensions and the strategy to counter it will have to be implemented across many fronts."[1] We will see later how the Indian state in fact reacted to the event.

In a similar vein, Noam Chomsky wrote, while commenting on the judgment of the lower court in the Parliament attack case, "terrorism is a serious matter, and merits careful attention and scrupulous preventive measures and response" (Annexure 15). Citing the work of Jason Burke and others, Chomsky has suggested more recently that "there is a broad consensus of specialist opinion on how to reduce the threat of terror – keeping here to the subcategory that is doctrinally acceptable, *their* terror against *us* – and also on how to incite further terrorist atrocities, which, sooner or later, may become truly horrendous."[2]

Apart from measures to improve intelligence and other law-enforcing mechanisms, two preventive measures of a more general and transparent character come immediately to mind: *public inquiry* and *protection of rights*. In fact, for reasons that follow, the ability of the law-enforcing arm of a state to prevent terrorist assaults depends heavily on the credibility of its democratic institutions. An authoritarian state only provides further fuel to terrorism even though it boasts of ruthless law-enforcing mechanisms.

Terrorist attacks, especially of the scale of September 11 and December 13, are designed, among other things, to cause deep injury to the psyche of a people. In the aftermath of such attacks, people are likely to suffer from a sense of diminishing control over their lives, especially in complex urban centers where people have less command on their lives anyway. The combination of fear and helplessness may then promote both a loss of confidence in open, democratic procedures and an increased dependence on the preremptory features that any state has.

As Chomsky illustrates in graphic detail in his Foreword to this book, instead of securing the confidence of its people, even "democracies" often use the opportunity to enforce the obedience of its people by fanning – in fact, *promoting* – fear. Adam Curtis observes: "In an age when all the grand ideas have lost credibility, fear of a phantom enemy is all the politicians have left to maintain their power."[3] Allowed to grow, the paranoia may eventually lead to suspicion of specific communities, resulting in ugly division of people. The spiraling cycle of distrust, violence and loss of democracy only helps the terrorist.

As the reactions to both September 11 and December 13 illustrate, people are not naturally inclined to rush into such closed states of mind. In the December 13 event, unarmed and ill-equipped security people gave their lives to prevent harm to the building and the persons, including the Members of Parliament, working inside it. The rest of the nation, instead of bursting into uncontrolled rage, simply expressed grief in the loss of lives with admirable restraint and waited for the government to take appropriate measures.

As for 9/11, there is some evidence that the passengers of at least one hijacked plane forced it to crash in a field; they died in saving some major national institutions. Policemen and firefighters of New York rushed in immediately to help the people caught up in the twin towers — saving many and dying in the process. Apart from a few and isolated incidents of attack on members of a minority community, the American people in general showed exemplary restraint. There were many reports of white Americans protecting the Arabs, and queuing up in Arab restaurants to promote their business.

This world continues to be livable because people, even in the face of extreme provocation, generally act with wisdom. This is the reason why terrorists of all shades work in small groups, and hide from the masses. It is the duty of a state to take measures that help sustain this resilience of people. After calamitous terrorist outrages, a responsible democratic state is expected to help people regain their full confidence in transparent, democratic procedures, thereby pulling the rug from below the terrorist.

One of the measures a government can take in that direction is to order a full-fledged inquiry by an institution that functions with transparency and has wide legitimacy with the general public. There is no doubt that the problem of terrorism is serious and complex. As such, any probe into terrorist outrages demands skills of management and deliberation of a high order, especially with respect to sharing and dissemination of information. As long as the institution is able to display an over-all transparency and human concern, the general public itself will appreciate the constraints under which the institution is compelled to function. The task is not easy, but it must be undertaken to secure the confidence of people.

A related measure is the preservation of rights. It is widely recognized that protection of civil and human rights is a significant preventive measure and response against terrorism. It could well be that terrorist groups in fact welcome the enactment of measures that infringe upon civil rights. As civil rights are curbed, as in an authoritarian state, the space for open democratic expression of dissent shrinks, while dissent itself grows because of the application of the measures themselves. The terrorist hopes, with some justification, that some of this unexpressed dissent will flow to swell their ranks and legitimize their goals in the general population.

Kofi Annan, the Secretary General of the United Nations, observed that "we should all be clear that there is no trade-off between effective action against terrorism and the protection of human rights. On the contrary, I believe that in the long term we shall find that human rights, along with democracy and social justice, are one of the best prophylactics against terrorism." Similarly, Mary Robinson, former UN High Commissioner for Human Rights, urged states "to ensure that any measures restricting human rights in response to terrorism strike a fair balance between legitimate national security concerns and fundamental freedoms that is fully consistent with their international law commitments."[4] Thus, in the context of the terrorist attack on Parliament on December 13, Chomsky hoped that "Indian democracy and its legal system will rise to the challenge, ... and ensure that human and civil rights are properly protected" (Annexure 15).

With respect to December 13 then, the envisaged commission of inquiry could have been entrusted with the task of addressing the following questions:

- *Who attacked Parliament?*
- *What exactly was the conspiracy?*
- *How could the attackers nearly succeed in blowing up the building itself?*
- *What are the domestic and international ramifications of this event?*
- *What steps have been taken to bring the real perpetrators to justice?*
- *Have the accused been given a fair trial and their human rights protected?*

No commission of public inquiry was ever instituted at any level.[5]

Windows of Opportunity

In contrast, what followed December 13 not only thwarted the composition of a commission of inquiry, it led to further erosion in democracy and social justice. As Chomsky observed, this is a general phenomenon in recent times: "the atrocities of 9-11 were exploited in a vulgar way by governments all over the world." Thus, Chomsky found it "disgraceful" that, in the name of war on terrorism, "the authentic threat of terrorism [is often] exploited as a window of opportunity for intolerable actions." Chomsky listed several ways in which such intolerable actions are promoted (Annexure 15):

— by escalating massive crimes on the pretext of "combating terrorism"

— by implementing repressive legislation to discipline their own citizens with no credible connection to preventing terrorist threats

— by carrying out programmes that had not the remotest connection to terrorism and might even enhance it and that were opposed by the majority of the population.

The implicit reference here is to the actions of the US government following September 11 — actions which illustrated each of the concerns Chomsky raised. We will see later how the actions of the Indian government matched those of US.

As Michael Moore documented in his film *Fahrenheit 9/11*, the newly-elected Bush administration was fast losing ground by September 2001: the scandal of the Florida vote won't go away; the President could not get his cabinet nominations approved by the Congress; the economy was worsening with unprecedented rise in unemployment; for a new President, Bush's ratings fell to an all-time low. Moore's unconcealed suggestion is that state policy quickly took advantage of the carnage in New York as a fresh opportunity for aggression in the third world, thereby turning the attention of the nation away from its domestic failures. In other words, as the complex and time-consuming issue of how to bring the perpetrators of 9/11 to justice in accordance with civil norms and international law engaged political thinking in the world, the US pre-empted any consolidation of world opinion by a massive attack on the entire nation of Afghanistan.[6]

It is well known that immediately after 9/11, the Taliban government in Afghanistan not only condemned the attacks, they offered to join the international community in addressing the grave menace of terrorism. In particular, they offered to hand over Osama Bin Laden and his colleagues to a neutral country for interrogation and trial, provided the US supplied the evidence it claimed to possess of Bin Laden's links to 9/11. By any rational standard, the Taliban offer was perfectly legitimate. If a sovereign state is asked to hand over one of its subjects, it has the right to examine preliminary evidence to decide whether the person ought to face judicial procedure at all. Satisfied, it has the right to ensure his justice and security. The Taliban could have claimed, as they did initially, that their own judicial system is adequate for the purpose. But, on the possible objection that they could be viewed as a party, they agreed to hand over Bin Laden to a judicial system that is not a party to the conflict. In effect, they asked for parity.[7]

The US rejected the Taliban offer and demanded the handing over of whomsoever it wanted unconditionally. When the Taliban justifiably failed to oblige, the US responded by mounting a full-scale war on the people of Afghanistan, ignoring all appeals of restraint from the international community. In the process, the US adopted methods that killed thousands of civilians,[8] turned fertile agricultural land into desert,[9] demolished hospitals, schools and power stations with high-tech gravity and cluster bombs,[10] prevented food-aid from reaching millions of starving people,[11] armed mercenaries and warlords to teeth, and filled an entire country permanently with mines, spies and special forces. Most of the world, including a vast majority of people in the US, opposed this war.

Violating the norms set by the Geneva Convention, the prisoners of war from Afghanistan were taken to the inhospitable island of Guantanamo Bay, and were subjected to atrocities of an unprecedented scale. Flushed with its apparent military success against a hapless foe, the US not only ignored the Geneva Convention and UN resolutions on terrorism, it walked out of the Kyoto protocol on the environment, the ABM treaty, and the biological warfare convention, among others.[12]

At home, illegal surveillance and detention of people from the Arab countries were supplemented by several enactment of the "Patriot Act" that infringed upon the civil rights of US citizens. These intolerable actions continued in an even larger scale with the invasion of Iraq. The planned "Domestic Security Enhancement Act of 2003" extends "powers of surveillance without court authorization, permits secret arrests, and further protects the state from the scrutiny of citizens," among other things.[13]

Not surprisingly, these actions have led to a manifold increase in terrorism in the regions most affected by US actions. Surveying a range of recent work, Chomsky reports: "Middle East expert Fawaz Gerges found that 'It's simply unbelievable how the war has revived the appeal of a global jihadi Islam that was in real decline after 9-11.' Recruitment for the al-Qaeda networks increased, reaching more 'menacing' sectors, while Iraq itself became a 'terrorist haven' for the first time, also suffering its first suicide attacks since the 13th century. Suicide attacks worldwide for the year 2003 reached the highest level in modern times. Substantial specialist opinion believes that the war led to proliferation of weapons of mass destruction (WMD), also as predicted."[14] Arundhati Roy explains: "In a strange sense, the U.S. government's arsenal of weapons and unrivalled air and fire power makes terrorism an all-but-inescapable response. What people lack in wealth and power, they will make up for with stealth and energy."[15]

Turning to the Indian scene, the actions of the government of India in the aftermath of December 13 matched US actions almost point by point, except for the scale — understandable, due to the vast differences in the economic and military might of US and India. The National Democratic Alliance (NDA) government led by the right-wing *Bharatiya Janata Party* (BJP) came back to power in 1999. By September 2001, it had lost virtually every regional and civic election, often by a wide margin. Its façade of clean governance stood exposed in a series of massive scams involving the Defence Minister George Fernandes in particular.[16] The Defence Ministry was charged with buying metal coffins for soldiers who had died in the Kargil war at prices many times higher than those prevailing in the market. Further, a confidante of the Defence Minister was caught on videotape accepting bribe for the sale of defence equipment in the house of the minister himself.

Some sections of the electorate, who had supported the BJP earlier on its claims of *swadeshi* ('nationalism'), felt betrayed with the regime's record of surrender to global corporate interests that led to neoliberal economic policies and an unprecedented impoverishment of the masses, especially in the rural sector.[17] The BJP also began facing resistance from its own more ideologically adamant sections such as the *Bharatiya Majdoor Sabha* (BMS) and the *Swadeshi Jagaran Manch* – the labour and the economic forums – for its capitulation to foreign capital. The growing discontent resulted in a series of demonstrations by trade unions, including the BMS, culminating in the impressive hold-out for months by the workers of the recently privatized Bharat Aluminium Company, just prior to 9/11.

In fact, in its attempts to preserve the NDA, the government failed even to deliver to its most loyal constituency, namely, the militant Hindu fundamentalists in *Rashtriya Swayamsevak Sangh* (RSS), *Bajrang Dal, Viswa Hindu Parishad, Akhil Bharatiya Vidyarthi Parishad,* etc., collectively known as the "*Sangh Parivar.*" In frustration, these forces began taking actions, such as intimidating and often murdering people from the minority communities (Graham Steins' case, nun's case, etc.), and issuing ultimatums on the Ayodhya temple issue. The resulting appeasement of these forces by the government exposed the diabolical character of the BJP even further. Its meek attempts to revive its fundamentalist agenda by tampering with educational and cultural institutions met with strong resistance from virtually all sections of the society. The election results clearly illustrated this array of exposures.

As it was forced to fall back on some populist measures – pushed primarily by the worried non-BJP allies in the NDA – to regain some credibility, it began to lose the strong corporate support that was one of the key elements of its ascendancy to power. Its failure to push through the labour 'reforms,' urged by the chambers of commerce and resisted by all trade unions including the BMS, illustrated its problems.[18] In sum, by September 2001, nothing was working in its favour.

Not surprisingly, 9/11 and then December 13 gave the BJP the fresh lease it desperately needed. Almost immediately after 9/11, the government adopted a belligerent posture towards its Islamic neighbour Pakistan. Even before December 13, General Musharraf had called the Indian Prime Minister to express his concern about the ghastly terrorist attack on the legislative assembly in Srinagar in October 2001; he had also urged the resumption of dialogue at the highest level.

The Indian government not only refused talks, it demanded an immediate stop to what it called "cross-border terrorism;" further, it gave a list of twenty "terrorists" to Pakistan with the demand that they be handed over to India unconditionally. It does not require great political acumen to understand that if Pakistan agreed to the Indian demands, then there was very little for it to negotiate with, especially on Kashmir. Assuming that the government of India understood this as well, the demands in effect amounted to a refusal to negotiate.[19] Pakistan repeated its concern and offered a joint probe immediately after December 13; India once again rejected the offer.

Instead, the government proposed – and the opposition agreed to – the adjournment of the winter session of Parliament *sine die* after the attack. Holding Pakistan responsible for the attack, the government mounted a massive military offensive that brought India and Pakistan to the brink of war with fingers on the nuclear trigger. Several thousand crores of rupees were spent and hundreds of soldiers died in the war-effort. Reportedly, over one hundred children died and many farmers lost their livelihood due to heavy mining in the border areas. However, the actual war never took place because the US did not want its own plans of global violence to be disturbed by the Indian effort.[20] It is difficult to believe that the Indian government was unaware of the US position that a war at that stage simply would not be allowed; yet, a frenzied war-effort was sustained for nearly a year. The war-effort was finally withdrawn as expected, and dialogues with Pakistan resumed, without any of the earlier demands being met.

Furthermore, in the name of assisting the civilized world in its fight against terrorism, the government of India sided with the US military and economic interests with a straight face, and won back its corporate and media support. Having thus appeased the US and its neoliberal support in India, it returned to its basic communal-fundamentalist agenda in the atmosphere of unconcealed Islamophobia that engulfed the non-Muslim world after 9/11.[21] What the US aggression and the accompanying propaganda machine enabled the *Sangh Parivar* to do is to claim not only moral legitimacy, but also some form of international solidarity for its attacks on minorities, especially the Muslims.[22] Exploitation of this "window of opportunity" paid handsome dividends for both the right wing, jingoist governments in India and US.[23]

Prior to the attack, the government had failed to get the draconian Prevention of Terrorism Act (POTA) passed in Parliament despite repeated efforts. After the attack, the Prevention of Terrorism Ordinance (POTO-I) was first reissued as POTO-II and was duly converted to an Act in March 2002 in a joint session of the parliament.[24] It has now been exhaustively documented that this draconian law, instead of addressing the menace of terrorism, has been widely used to target the minorities, the poor, the dalits, and inconvenient political opponents, among others.[25]

In Gujarat, the Muslim population was subjected to horrendous atrocities such as rape, murder, and pillage in an unprecedented scale by Hindu mobs during the communal carnage of February-March 2002; while over 2000 Muslims lost their lives, several hundred thousand were forced to take shelter in ill-equipped refugee camps for years.[26] Yet, POTO-II and then POTA were used "with great precision"[27] so that out of the 287 persons booked under them in Gujarat till 2003-end in nine different categories, one is a Sikh and the rest 286 are Muslims.[28]

December 13 was India's 9/11 as the actions of governments in each case generated a sense of helpless fear resulting in heightened prejudice against the Muslim community. In the Indian case, these factors, coupled with the enactment of POTA and the prospect of an imminent war with Pakistan, plunged the nation virtually into a state of emergency. As a result, the BJP won handsomely in the elections that followed in some major provinces. Subsequently, elections were also held in Gujarat where the BJP was returned to power with overwhelming majority despite the involvement of the *Sangh Parivar* in the pogrom of Muslims in February-March 2002. Basharat Peer explains: "This victory lengthened the shadow of Hindu religious violence and Islamic terror attacks that loomed over India throughout 2002. In Gujarat, the fear of Muslim-sponsored terrorism consolidated effectively the Hindu nationalist votes" (Annexure 13, p. 313).[29]

In sum, the fear and the prejudice already generated by 9/11 grew rapidly after the Parliament attack; the fear drove people to close their minds and huddle under state power, as elsewhere in the world.[30] The period between December 13, 2001 and May 2004, when the BJP-led government was finally thrown out of power, could well be viewed as the darkest phase in post-independence India, outweighing perhaps the dark days of Emergency imposed by Indira Gandhi in 1975. Ironically then, even though the terrorists failed to destroy the Parliament building itself, their action left a gaping hole in Indian democracy in terms of the consequences that followed.

Role of the Media[31]

Apart from the general case for a transparent inquiry as a response to terrorism discussed above, the actions of the government in the aftermath of December 13 precipitated an additional need for inquiry. Soon after the attack on Parliament, the government declared war on Pakistan on the ground that it had sufficient proof of Pakistan's involvement in the attack. As noted, this led to a massive build up of troops along the border, death of many soldiers and civilians, and a huge dent in the exchequer. Yet within a month, the chances of an actual war fell to less than 5%, according to none other than the President of Pakistan General Musharraf himself. What happened to the "proof" of Pakistan's involvement? Was it the pressure from the Americans alone as the US Secretary of State Colin Powell had boastfully claimed?[32] Then why was the massive war-effort launched in the first place and *maintained for nearly a year*?

These concerns were further substantiated by the High Court judgment of 29 October 2003 which directly linked the war-effort with the Parliament attack case. The Court held two individuals accused of conspiring in the crime, Mohammad Afzal and

Shaukat Hussain Guru, as guilty under section 121 of the Indian Penal Code (IPC) — waging of war against the Indian state. "After the unfortunate incident," the Court observed, "this country had to station its troops at the border and large scale mobilization of the armed forces took place." As "the clouds of war with our neighbour loomed large for a long period of time," "the nation suffered not only an economic strain but even the trauma of an imminent war." With these words, the High Court enhanced the sentence of life imprisonment awarded by the Special Court[33] u/s 121 IPC to death sentence to these two accused (Annexure 16, para 448).

However, the Special Court found the accused guilty only in December 2002 when the *de*mobilization of troops was nearing completion after a year of "the trauma of an imminent war." It follows once again that the government must have had definite proof of the conspiracy to attack Parliament as soon as the accused were arrested so that the mobilization of troops could begin immediately after the attack. What was that proof? What if the accused were found *not guilty* later? In other words, did the government itself encourage a violation of the cardinal principle of natural justice that one is innocent until found guilty? How else do we explain the stunning fact that the Prime Minister and the Home Minister *endorsed* a film that portrayed just the prosecution side of the story even before the Special Court delivered its judgment? (see p. 27)

In a massive failure of democratic institutions in India, no mainstream political party, no group of prominent individuals, and none of the influential print or visual media ever raised the issue of an inquiry into these obvious questions. In an incisive article, the lawyer-activist Nandita Haksar points out that "(n)o one questioned the government's story that the attack was the handiwork of Pakistan-based terrorists belonging to the Lashkar-e-Toiba and Jaish-e-Mohammad." This is because the "media, in a willing suspension of disbelief, published whatever the police and investigating agencies put out." Having swallowed the stories put out by the media, "the public no longer felt the need for a 'judicial trial' ... where was the need for formal proof."[34]

As with other intolerable actions in the global war on terrorism, the role of the Indian media converged with that of most of the "democracies." The political commentator for the BBC, Adam Curtis observes: "the suspiciously circular relationship between the security services and much of the media since September 2001: the way in which official briefings about terrorism, often unverified or unverifiable by journalists, have become dramatic press stories which – in a jittery media-driven democracy – have prompted further briefings and further stories. Few of these ominous announcements are retracted if they turn out to be baseless: 'There is no fact-checking about al-Qaida.'"[35]

Since the issue is crucially linked to the absence of demand for inquiry into the Parliament attack case, a survey of the role of the media is needed at this point to examine how exactly the suggested complicity between the police and the media worked in India. We restrict our attention only to some samples from the print media — essentially, national English dailies, with one exception with which we begin.

The media coverage of S.A.R. Geelani's role in the attack is particularly revealing. As we will see, the prosecution's case against him was at best "absurd and tragic,"[36] and, as it turned out, the High Court acquitted him from all charges with adverse remarks that could not have been pleasing to the police (see 'Acquittal of Geelani'). After his arrest, leading national newspapers reported on Geelani's role in the attack with impressive detail within two days.

Sujit Thakur of *Rashtriya Sahara* captioned his Hindi write-up of 17 December 2001, GEELANI SOWED THE SEEDS OF TERRORISM FROM ALIGARH TO ENGLAND. Citing police sources, Thakur reported that, from what Geelani had "disclosed," it was "clear" that the Jaish-e-Mohammad had an elaborate plan of securing the support of the intelligentsia around the world; Geelani was assigned this task for India. To that end, he contacted students and teachers in several colleges and universities in India and abroad, including Aligarh Muslim University and the London School of Economics. In fact, Geelani was in close touch with a dreaded terrorist called "Ahmad Umar Saeed Sheikh" who was a student of LSE and was linked to the hijacking of IC-814.[37] However, the police failed to list these very specific charges in the chargesheet (Annexure 1). In any case, we will see that Geelani never disclosed anything or confessed to anything, although he was forced to sign on some blank sheets (Annexures 4, 7). Apart from police "sources," the only other evidence Thakur cited for the preceding portrait of Geelani was (a) he had said to have watched a film titled "Destruction of a Nation" several times, and (b) he had read a book on the assassination of John F. Kennedy titled "Portrait of an Assassin." Thakur failed to cite the sources from which he gathered these facts.

Sutirtho Patranobis of *Hindustan Times* titled his piece of 17 December 2001, DON LECTURED ON TERROR IN FREE TIME. Patranobis wrote his piece after an interview with the Principal of Zakir Hussain College in Delhi where Geelani teaches Arabic. Throughout the interview the Principal made only nice remarks on Geelani: "a seven member team has selected him after going through his academic records and interviewing him", "students liked him", "seldom took very long leaves", "I have also not heard any colleague complain about his behaviour", "mixed around as any other professor", "nothing extraordinary in his character", etc. However, without citing any source at all, Patranobis concluded his piece with the following words: "In his free time, behind closed doors, either at his house or at Shaukat Hussain's, another suspect to be arrested, he took and gave lessons on terrorism." This is of course what the police claimed in their briefings to justify Geelani's arrest.

Devesh K. Pandey of *The Hindu* began his piece of 17 December 2001 with the heading VARSITY DON GUIDED 'FIDAYEEN'. As with the other reporters cited above and below, Pandey dispensed with routine qualifiers such as "allegedly" or "believed to have" or "reportedly" to assert that three of the four persons who supplied logistic support and provided a safe haven to the five 'fidayeen' studied at the prestigious Delhi University, one of whom turned out to be a highly qualified lecturer. Geelani had "disclosed" that he was in the know of the conspiracy since the day the 'fidayeen' attack was planned. Pandey could report this with confidence because, according to him, "intelligence agencies had been tapping Geelani's telephone for sometime as he had contacts in Pakistan." Unfortunately, the "intelligence agencies" failed to submit the intercepted conversations as evidence before the court.

Rajnish Sharma of *Hindustan Times*, 17 December 2001, reported on HUNT FOR TEACHER'S PET IN JUBILEE HALL. Exploring Geelani's "international contacts," Sharma learnt about a Jordanian doctoral student of Delhi University in Astrophysics who knew Geelani. Sharma reports that they spent long hours together; also, lengthy phone-calls were made to West Asia from booths located in the Delhi University campus.[38] In a box situated in the middle of his write-up, Sharma listed PROFESSOR'S PROCEEDS in a suggestive deductive chain: Geelani recently purchased a house for Rs. 22 lakhs in West Delhi; Delhi police are investigating how he came upon such a windfall; the terrorists who planned the operation were flush with funds; before carrying out the attack on Parliament, the terrorists had sent back to Srinagar Rs. 10 lakhs of unspent money and a laptop. Sharma failed to mention the address of the house purchased by Geelani; also, the report did not carry either a photograph of the house or a copy of the sale-deed. In subsequent coverage, Sharma failed to follow up on the police investigation into the "windfall." Both Nandita Haksar and Basharat Peer reported on the difficulties faced by Geelani's family in finding even modest rented accommodation in Delhi.[39] Mohammad Abdullah, Geelani's father-in-law said, "A news report said Geelani bought a house worth 22 lakhs. If someone can find the house the family can move there in these difficult times."[40] All this was reported within two days after the arrests, as noted.

The media coverage reached newer heights in "willing suspension of disbelief" with the dramatic event on 20 December 2001, exactly a week after the attack. On that day, the investigating officer in charge of the case, ACP Rajbir Singh, organized a press meet. In that meet, only one of the accused, Mohammad Afzal, was "brazenly paraded before the press" (Annexure 16, para 139). By then, Afzal was projected by the police as the principal link between Jaish-e-Mohammad and Lashkar-e-Toiba commanders in Kashmir and the terrorist operation in Delhi. During the parade, Afzal admitted to his active participation in the conspiracy. In what follows, we will not discuss the credibility of this "confession" since it had no legal validity; it was meant only for public consumption. We focus only on the media's role in this sordid affair.

Commenting on the incident, the Amnesty International wrote that "parading accused before national media during which they are made to incriminate themselves violates their right to be presumed innocent until convicted according to law in the course of fair proceedings and their right not to be compelled to testify against themselves or to confess guilt. These rights are provided in

Articles 14(2) and 14 (3) (g) of the ICCPR respectively" (Annexure 9, p. 215). These are well established norms that the media in a democratic set up are likely to know and follow. In that sense, the fact that the police allowed this meet to take place at all should have been of major concern to the media.[41] But the media not only asked for it, they attended and reported the interview *en masse*.

In the interview, although Afzal admitted to his involvement in the crime, he categorically exonerated Geelani from any involvement. In full view of the assembled press, the investigating officer ACP Rajbir Singh reprimanded Afzal for mentioning Geelani despite his orders to the contrary. The ACP then asked the press not to report Afzal's exoneration of Geelani. The whole thing was recorded on videotape which was submitted as evidence in the court by the defence (Annexure 8).

By any measure, this was big news. The "varsity don" who "sowed the seeds of terrorism from Aligarh to England" and who "guided the 'fidayeen'" was exonerated from any involvement in the attack by the self-confessed principal operator in custody. It follows either that Afzal's admission before the media was worthless, or, that the police (and the media) stories about Geelani's involvement handed out for the past week were false. Moreover, Rajbir Singh's reprimand to Afzal suggested that Afzal's "confession" could have been dictated by the police. Why should the police take this recourse unless at least parts of the case against Afzal were fabricated? Finally, Rajbir Singh's "request" to the press not to make Afzal's statement public indicated that the police was trying to use the media to propagate a possibly suspect story. In sum, large sections of the police story announced so far began to collapse with this singular utterance from Afzal.

We would expect any self-respecting media to at least pick up the issue and tell the country that something was wrong somewhere. We would have expected headlines such as AFZAL ABSOLVES GEELANI FROM ANY INVOLVEMENT and PARLIAMENT ATTACK CASE TURNS MURKY to dominate the front-pages the next day. The demand for a full-fledged public inquiry on the entire sequence of events, including the conduct of the police, would have been the next logical step.

Instead, the entire media, with an interesting exception discussed below, simply followed the ACP's order by suppressing the utterance. The channel Aaj Tak showed the interview with Afzal on the same evening without the utterance; the channel showed the full interview 100 days later (Annexure 8). By then the 'truth' about the Parliament attack was firmly established in the public mind and the attention of the nation had shifted to the carnage in Gujarat and the impending war with Pakistan.

However, the chargesheet was still two months away. An alert media, including Aaj Tak itself, could have pounced upon the unedited tape, and highlighted the momentous utterance with the disturbing implications that follow from it. Needless to say, the entire matter was shelved in silence until the defence brought it up in court many months later. Reportedly, one of the journalists involved with the case justified his silence on the ground that he could not afford to disobey Rajbir Singh as the ACP was a "very good" source of police information.[42]

The reports that appeared on the next day, 21 December 2001, continued the tirades against Geelani. Under the title TERROR SUSPECT FREQUENT VISITOR TO MISSION, Swati Chaturvedi of *Hindustan Times* cited "authoritative sources" to report that Geelani had visited the High Commission of Pakistan on two different social gatherings: an iftaar party and a national day celebrations. Chaturvedi failed to mention whether officials of the Indian government, politicians, film stars, journalists and prominent citizens of Delhi, including some from the academia, also attended these functions. When contacted by the paper, a senior officer of the high commission had reportedly said, "we will have to go over our records," since a large number of people are invited to these occasions. As for Geelani in particular, the officer said, "we do not know him and Pakistan has nothing to do with him." Chaturvedi found these responses "non-committal;" she also reported that the "security sources" did not "buy this argument." In the very next paragraph, Chaturvedi reverted to Geelani's (earlier) "admission" that he was in touch with militants of the Jaish-e-Mohammad based in Pakistan. The two paragraphs thus created a 'montage' that suggested a reason for Geelani's "frequent" visits to the "Pak mission."

However, shedding new light on the issue, Chaturvedi also reported Geelani's admission that he had been provided with funds by the Jaish to buy two flats for the militants to operate from. As it turned out later during the trial, none of the 80 prosecution witnesses ever mentioned Geelani's affiliation with any terrorist organization (Annexure 14, p. 325). Moreover, the chargesheet mentioned only Afzal and Shaukat who were allegedly responsible for *renting* some rooms in Delhi to be used as hideouts by the militants.

This seems to be a persistent problem with much of the reporting on this case: the AMU and the LSE connections, the house worth 22 lakhs, the two flats, the Jordanian angle, the guidance to the 'fidayeen' etc. The "information" ascribed variously to "authoritative sources," "security sources," "intelligence agencies", etc., were not used by these agencies themselves in subsequent proceedings. It is questionable, therefore, whether these "sources" in fact passed on such information to Chaturvedi and other reporters. We return to this.

Neeta Sharma's 6-column headline report in *Hindustan Times* of the same day – PAK USES FANATICS TO SPREAD TERROR

IN INDIA – was placed below coloured photographs of Afzal, Shaukat and Geelani, in that order from left to right. The photographs were cumulatively captioned CONFESSION TIME, and each photograph was accompanied by some remarks apparently made by the person whose photograph it was. The artwork gave the impression that these remarks are snippets from the "confessions" made by each of them individually. In reality, as noted, only Afzal made an admission before the media, and the official confession under POTA of Shaukat was to take place only later on the 21st itself; Geelani neither disclosed nor confessed anything. These factual details are further obliterated by Sharma's opening sentence: "The Delhi Police on Thursday allowed four people held in connection with the attack on Parliament to go public with their version of how it was planned and how terrorists operate."

Embedded in the piece was a box with three headings in colour: "Perfectly Disguised" reported on Afzal's portrayal of the terrorists; "Inside Story of IC-814" reported, via Afzal, that one of the terrorists was also one of the hijackers; "The Elusive Gazi Baba" described the secretive Pakistani terrorist with many aliases who would not be easy to catch. The rest of Sharma's piece need not detain us since she basically repeated what we have already covered. However, we must emphasize that the story is false in at least two respects: (a) "four people" did not "go public", only Afzal did, (b) the Delhi Police did not "allow" Afzal to go public, it directed him to.

The point of interest about this story, and many similar stories across the country, is that it had all the features of settled truth. The country now knew who the terrorists and conspirators were, how they looked like, and what were their backgrounds. The country also knew from the horses' mouth how the operation was planned and executed. All that remained to be done was to catch Ghazi Baba — not an easy task, the author warned. All this within a breathtaking period of a week. The judicial trial became virtually redundant: "where was the need for formal proof," Haksar lamented.

The Times of India also reported Afzal's confession on 21 December 2001 under the heading TERRORISTS WERE CLOSE-KNIT RELIGIOUS FANATICS. The report is interesting in a variety of ways. The report focused entirely on Afzal and on the politico-ideological aspects of the attack on Parliament, rather than on its operational and conspiratorial aspects. Afzal narrated the religious influence of Masood Azhar, the leader of Jaish-e-Mohammad, and explained the geo-political goals of Pakistan. He described the mental profiles of the terrorists in detail: religious fanatics given to regular prayers, totally focused on their job, attired in Western clothes to deceive the police, etc.; it is difficult to miss the suggested resemblance with the alleged attackers of 9/11. Thus, a complete and reassuringly familiar picture of Islamic terrorism was superimposed on the factual details of conspiracy and attack already settled by police investigation.

Interestingly, in apparent violation of the ACP's order, *The Times of India* story did actually report Afzal's exoneration of Geelani, but in the following words: "Afzal was also quick to point out that while he may have been guilty of abetting in the crime, his co-accused, Shaukat Hussain and Syed AR Geelani, had nothing to do with the attack."[43] While applauding this exception to the rule, we also note:

- The statement was buried in the fourth column of the report carried in the inside pages devoted to regional news and was placed under "DELHI."
- Afzal did not exonerate *both* Shaukat and Geelani; he absolved just Geelani when asked specifically by a correspondent. By falsely mentioning both the co-accused, the report gave the impression that Afzal was merely engaged in a general amiable

gesture to save his friends; hence, Afzal's statement lost factual weight.

- During the trial, Afzal stated that in the interview he had said that Geelani was "innocent" (Annexure 8). During the said interview, he had also stated "I have never shared any of this information with him." Without these qualifications, just the indefinite phrase "had nothing to do with the attack" leaves open the possibility that, even though Geelani did not directly participate in the planning and the execution of the attack itself, he was broadly aware and supportive of the militants' goals.
- The preceding apprehension was immediately borne out by the rest of the report in the same paragraph of the story: "According to [the police] all those arrested were in the know of the plan to attack which itself is sufficient ground to proceed against them."[44] The wording of this statement not only diluted the effect of Afzal's statement as noted, it also gave the police the last word in the sense that the police had merely asked "to proceed" after giving "sufficient ground" for arrest.
- Finally, the reporter failed to mention the utter contradiction between mere knowledge of the plan to attack and the tons of grave charges – "guiding the 'fidayeen'," "buying two flats for the militants," "keeping in touch with terrorists based in Pakistan," etc. – which emanated apparently from police sources for full one week.

In sum, Afzal's statement was couched in such a way that its far-reaching implications would not be seen. No wonder nothing happened after this report.

As a net effect of the campaign and the verdict by the media, the Parliament attack case gradually disappeared from the media and the public view within weeks. As the entire country bayed for their blood, the four accused, charged under POTA, languished in jail; as recent documents suggest, some of them were subjected to torture, humiliation and sexual abuse.[45] Shaukat's wife, co-accused Afsan, gave birth to their child in prison. The trauma of the past months broke her spirits and she developed psychotic symptoms. The young wives of Afzal and Geelani, both with small children, traveled long distances in hostile territory and waited for hours at the jail to meet their "high-risk" husbands in handcuffs, praying desperately for competent legal defence and fair trial.[46] The children dropped out of school as the families moved from one shelter to another;[47] the eye-treatment of Geelani's little daughter had to be discontinued. Except for some occasional coverage in the Kashmir press, the national media largely ignored the human tragedy.

The lack of interest from the media persisted during the trial of the case that "has come to be something of a marker in the national psyche."[48] Basharat Peer reports: "I had expected a crowd of reporters at what seemed to me the most high-profile legal case in India, but was surprised to see very few there"(Annexure 13, p. 308). A handful of gallant human rights activists, such as N. D. Pancholi and Gautam Navlakha, worked hard to secure proper defence for the accused. Very few lawyers were willing to oblige: most "did not want to be associated with the Parliament attack case."[49] The defence was often insufficient with lawyers dropping out in succession. Moreover, since the Hon'ble judge of the Special Court had ordered a "fast-track" trial in this immensely complex case, the defence was always running short of time to gather and examine evidence; most importantly, *crucial documents and depositions were admitted without cross-examination of witnesses.*

Even then, as we will see in much detail, huge cracks appeared in the case: some of the arrest memos looked forged; the accused were 'identified' by shopkeepers, landlords, etc., without identification parades; crucial physical evidence was found not to be sealed; call records from phone companies did not match the times recorded by the police; questions arose about the credibility of the evidence related to a laptop computer allegedly used by the terrorists; intercepted conversations were widely misinterpreted; SIM cards and transcripts of telephone conversations were either missing or were not made available, and much else as we will see (Annexures 12, 14). Much of this was either barely mentioned or not reported at all, not to speak of subjecting them to incisive analysis.

Finally, with the arduous effort of some individuals, a high-profile national defence committee for S.A.R. Geelani was formed with Rajani Kothari as the chairperson. Over 200 teachers from Delhi and Jawaharlal Nehru universities signed a petition to the Chief Justice of India pointing out problems with the trial and asking for fair trial, especially for Geelani. With sustained campaign by the committee, at least the Geelani-part of the trial began to appear in bits in a few newspapers, notably *The Hindu* and *The Indian Express*.[50] Afzal's and Shaukat's trials remained essentially unexamined by the media.

In fact, in some write-ups pleading for Geelani's innocence, there was a conscious attempt to separate Geelani's case from those of Afzal and Shaukat. After a brief review of the Parliament attack case, the senior journalist Prem Shankar Jha, known for his concerns about civil rights and democratic values, criticized the police in fairly strong terms: "The police have become a law unto themselves and don't feel obliged to avoid disrupting a suspect's life and reputation without good prima facie cause … they now believe in arresting people first and wringing a confession out of them, … This is the true face of the democracy of which we were once so proud." Thus, in his review of the case, Jha asked, "why has [Geelani's] life been destroyed and why are the police desperately attempting to prove a case that doesn't exist?" However, Jha also stated, "the case presented by the police against Afzal looks prima facie to be fairly strong."[51] Jha failed to note that the act of "arresting people first and wringing a confession out of them" applies to Afzal, if at all, since Geelani never made a confession.

While these reports were few and far between and were carried in English papers with lesser reach, even this modest critical effort was massively confronted by the Zee television network. Just before the Special Court judgment was to be delivered, it repeatedly telecast a film on the Parliament attack case, entitled *December 13*. The film was not only a re-enactment of the chargesheet, Nandita Haksar wrote, "it in fact made allegations against Geelani that went far beyond the prosecution case:" for example, "the film portrayed Geelani as the mastermind and showed scenes of him talking to the five dead attackers and planning the attack."

"The film was shown to the Prime Minister and then the Home Minister, and the media recorded their approval of the film," Haksar reports.[52] Although the defence secured a stay from the High Court restraining the broadcast of the film, the Supreme Court of India vacated it on the ground that judges could not be influenced. Thus, the 'whole truth' that was placed before the general public only in dribbles in print before, was now presented with the full vigour and the authority of the visual media. There are now reports of "uncanny resemblances" between the Zee film and a Bollywood film titled *Dil Se*, released in 2000.[53]

On the day the Special Court announced the verdict, "the courtroom was for once crowded with reporters," Basharat Peer reported. "Led by Singh," Peer described, "personnel from the Delhi police's anti-terrorism wing, who had arrested Geelani and conducted the investigation, filled the courtroom. The policemen, who were usually unshaven and shabbily clothed, were dressed in expensive suits, with matching neckties. They would look good in the newspaper photographs tomorrow, I thought."(Annexure 13, p. 311)

As the verdict sentencing Afzal, Shaukat and Geelani to death and Afsan Guru to five years' R.I was announced, "the members of the Special branch, in pressed suits and polished shoes, could not stop smiling; they had become national heroes."[54] Except for a very few restrained editorials, jubilation engulfed the media; there was all-out praise for a judgment in a trial the media had not really attended. With the sentencing, Afsan's condition deteriorated while Afzal, Shaukat and Geelani were shifted to the death row.

We skip another prolonged period of indifference shown by the media and move straight to the High Court judgment of October 29, 2003. The court confirmed the death sentences of Afzal and Shaukat while it acquitted Geelani and Afsan. At least one newspaper thought that the acquittals showed "the ineffectiveness of our intelligence agencies" and "the inadequacy of the judiciary's vertebrae."[55] The same newspaper also directly complained against the judgment: "the fact that Geelani had admitted his involvement to the police cannot be wished away."[56]

However, most newspapers welcomed the judgment. *The Hindu* thought the "judgment is a welcome reflection of the strength of the judicial process, particularly its capacity for self-correction."[57] According to the *Indian Express*, the judgment "highlights ... the eternal quest for justice."[58] *Hindustan Times* admitted, "when the Delhi police announced that they had come across evidence beyond doubt Geelani was guilty, many including this news paper, made the mistake of believing them."[59]

We recall some of the "evidence" against Geelani, discussed in detail above, that *Hindustan Times* "made the mistake of believing": in his free time, behind closed doors, Geelani took and gave lessons on terrorism; Geelani recently purchased a house for Rs. 22 lakhs in West Delhi; Geelani admitted that he was in touch with militants of the Jaish-e-Mohammad based in Pakistan; Geelani also admitted that he had been provided with funds by the Jaish to buy two flats for the militants to operate from, etc. All of this was reported between December 16 and 21, 2001.

The chargesheet was finally filed in May 2002. In the chargesheet, none of the preceding evidence that the police "came across" was mentioned, as noted. Even then, the newspaper kept quiet, not to speak of making the effort to visit the house and the flats that pointed to Geelani's guilt "beyond doubt." The silence was maintained throughout the trial. The judgment of the Special Court, sentencing Geelani to death, was hailed by the same newspaper when it, for one, knew very well that the police had used the newspaper by passing on straight and horrendous lies about Geelani. The admission from the newspaper came only on 31 October, 2003 – full 18 months later – unaccompanied by any apology to Geelani and his family.

Furthermore, by any rational standard, the acquittal of Geelani and Afsan was expected to unleash a burst of investigative journalism. The defence lawyers Nitya Ramakrishnan and Nandita Haksar asked the most obvious questions about the police and the judiciary within hours of the High Court judgment. Ramakrishnan asked: "Why had the police, with the best legal advice and in such a high-profile case, not paused to consider if it had sufficient evidence to prosecute the case?" Haksar commented: "the question that remains to be answered is how did any court sentence a man to death on no evidence at all?"[60]

The issue is simple: the grievous miscarriage of justice in the Special Court for Geelani and Afsan cast an extensive shadow on the very credibility of the functioning of the police and the judiciary, notwithstanding a partial amelioration of the judiciary in the High Court judgment. Why should we now believe in the prosecution's story for the rest of the case? In particular, what justifies the underlying assumption that, although the police, the prosecution and the Special Court have been horribly wrong in one part of the case, they have been vindicated for the other parts?

With Geelani out of the way, who was the guide, the local mastermind of the terrorists? Once we know that Afzal falsely implicated Geelani in his confession, why should we continue to believe the rest of his confession, especially the parts where he described the transborder conspiracy to attack Parliament, and for which the investigating agencies failed to submit any independent evidence? What are the implications of the disturbing fact that Afzal is a past militant of the Jammu and Kashmir Liberation Front (JKLF) who surrendered to the Border Security Force in 1993?[61]

As we saw, there were many moments in the Parliament attack case where an honest and unbiased media could have initiated the process of public inquiry by its own investigative efforts. Instead, it thwarted the process itself by either propagating the police stories or by maintaining silence during crucial junctures. As a result, the urgent issue of inquiry never reached the public domain. The High Court judgment was yet another occasion for the media to re-examine the intricate joints of this case, and to demand a comprehensive public inquiry to settle all doubts. The media failed the country once again.

Court Documents

An interesting aspect of the Parliament attack case is that, apart from the role of the media, the demand for comprehensive inquiry never engaged the public mind because, in a sense, the issue was taken over by the courts of law. As indicated already in connection with the sentencing in the case, the court proceedings themselves may be viewed as serving the purpose of an indirect inquiry, since, as it turned out, the courts of law largely upheld the police story. Thus, in effect, as the Parliament attack case took a legal turn, the trial by the media merged into a trial by the courts. The phenomenon arose as follows.

Terrorist acts are usually shrouded in mystery. The attack on Parliament appears to be a singular exception. Although there were initial reports of a sixth terrorist escaping from the scene, the Delhi police claimed to have shot down all the terrorists, numbering five, on the spot. The terrorists not only did not blow themselves up, they left behind a thick trail of unused arms and ammunition, mobile phones supposedly used during the attack, addresses, phone numbers, and much else. Within days, the Delhi police traced and arrested four alleged local conspirators: Mohd. Afzal, Shaukat Hussain Guru, Afzan Guru, and S.A.R. Geelani. Afzal allegedly identified the dead terrorists, the hideouts, and the shops from where chemicals, mixer, the attack vehicle etc. were purchased. Finally, the police pieced together the entire story from the confessions made by Afzal and Shaukat. With the help of an obliging media, as documented, the Delhi police announced to the nation that the case has been solved. Also, the abundance of evidence enabled the state to frame chargesheets against the accused.

The case went on trial in May 2002 in the Special Court for POTA in Delhi and, following a "fast-track" trial, a judgment *upholding* the prosecution's case was delivered in December 2002. The judgment was sent to the High Court in New Delhi which also delivered its judgment on 29 October 2003; this court also broadly *upheld* the prosecution's case. As per law, the Courts were not formally assigned the task of explaining the event; their only task was to decide whether the prosecution's case against the accused was valid in law.

However, the four accused were *not* charged with actually carrying out the attack; they were charged only with conspiring, planning and abetting the attack. Therefore, by proving the role of the accused in the conspiracy, the prosecution has deemed to have shown, at least in a broad outline, which terrorist acts and waging of war were planned and executed by whom. In other words, the proof of guilt in this case is also an explanation of the event. By parity of reason, if there are doubts about the proof, the explanation of the event remains incomplete to that extent.

The court judgments and the related material are the only official documents available to citizens who are anxious to learn the truth about the attack on Indian Parliament. In the absence of any other official paper, we are thus compelled to enter into an unfamiliar territory.

We are aware that the Parliament attack case currently rests with the Hon'ble Supreme Court of India.[62] We have no intention or interest in interfering with the judicial process; if anything, our intention is to co-operate with it. As indicated, we will be exploring aspects of the events surrounding the attack on Parliament that do not even directly fall under the jurisdiction of the courts; they fall under the jurisdiction of an inquiry commission that was never instituted. We are only marginally interested in questions of law, admissibility of evidence and the propriety of verdicts; needless to say, we do not judge the guilt or the innocence of the accused. As the angle and the style of presentation of this study will show, our only concern is to examine whether the legal documents contain a plausible explanation of the attack on Indian democracy.

As we will see, the story presented by the prosecution has too many grey areas to be credible. This is not to deny the possibility that it was indeed a genuine terrorist attack, perhaps masterminded by some terrorist organization across the border. Our only claim is that the story that appears in the court documents does not enable us to draw any inference either way.

Hence, despite the indirect inquiry conducted in the courts, the demand for a direct inquiry stands.

Just to give a flavour of how we will proceed from now on, the argument will consist of the following broad steps. We will enumerate more detailed steps after presenting the prosecution's case in the next chapter.

- First, we will present an outline of the prosecution's case by piecing together elements of the chargesheet (Annexure 1) and related documents such as the confessions by Mohd. Afzal and Shaukat Guru (Annexures 2 and 3). This will serve as the 'text' in which a complete story of the conspiracy planned and executed by the accused – dead and alive, in custody or at large – is told.
- Second, we will examine this text from a variety of directions, focusing especially on those aspects of the text which claim to offer an *explanation* of the event, to see how much of the prosecution's story actually stands, notwithstanding the 'truth' proclaimed by the police and the media. We will show in some detail that there are serious flaws in almost every aspect of the prosecution story. These flaws are of a character and gravity that raise disturbing questions about the very functioning of investigating agencies and the judiciary, especially when it concerns questions of national security addressed under POTA.
- Finally, following the analysis, we will briefly sketch a number of possible and conflicting scenarios. Only a full-fledged, transparent, and public inquiry into the entire affair is required for selecting one of the scenarios, if at all, as the truth about the Parliament attack.

Notes & References

1. "Terrorism dominates PM's convocation speech", *The Times of India*, Kolkata, 16 December 2001.

2. Noam Chomsky, "Afterword" to *Hegemony and Survival*, 2004.
3. Adam Curtis, cited in Andy Beckett, "The making of the terror myth", *The Guardian*, 15 October, 2004. Also, Noam Chomsky, *Hegemony or Survival: America's Quest for Global Dominance*, Henry Holt, New York, 2003, p. 115-21.
4. Statements from Kofi Annan and Mary Robinson are cited in Nandita Haksar, *A Presumptuous Judgment; A New Concept of Democracy*? A critique on the lower court judgment on Dec 13 Parliament attack, All India Defence Committee for Syed Abdul Rehman Gilani, 2003. (Annexure 14)
5. This is not to rule out the possibility that some internal inquiry on this matter may have been conducted by the government in secret.
6. See my "The moment of global support," *Socialist Alliance*, 30 September 2001.
7. See my "Offers of peace", *South Asean Citizens Wire* #2, 17 October 2001; also, Edward S. Herman and D. Petersen, "Who terrorizes whom?", *Zmag.org*, October 2001.
8. William Blum, "Civilian casualties: theirs and ours", *Counterpunch*, 17 December 2001 at http.//www.counterpunch.org/blumcasualties.html for figures of civilian casualties in the Afghan war.
9. A. C. Thomson, "War without end", *The Nation* (USA), 2 December 2001, for environmental destruction of Afghanistan.
10. Human Rights Watch report on the types of bombs used in the Afghan war at http.//www.hrw.org/backgrounder/arms/cluster-bck1031.html.
11. Chomsky, *Hegemony or Survival: America's Quest for Global Dominance*, Henry Holt, New York, 2003, p. 128-9.
12. Richard Du Boff, "Mirror mirror on the wall, who's the biggest rogue of all?", *Znet*, 7 August 2003, for a comprehensive list of recent violations of international treatise by US.
13. Chomsky, *Hegemony or Survival: America's Quest for Global Dominance*, Henry Holt, New York, 2003, p. 27.
14. Chomsky, "Afterword" to *Hegemony and Survival*, 2004. See the notes in this citation from Chomsky for extensive references.
15. Arundhati Roy, "Public power in the age of empire", *Frontline*, 22 October 2004, p.15.
16. See my "A parliament adjourned", *Economic and Political Weekly*, 29 December 2001. Also, "Attack takes heat off Fernandes", *Times News Network*, 16 December 2001.
17. For a study of Andhra Pradesh, see George Monbiot, "This is what we paid for: Britain's foreign aid has been used to bankroll a programme for

mass starvation," *The Guardian*, 18 May 2004. Also, Utsa Patnaik, *The Republic of Hunger*, Sahmat, 2004.

18. It is well-known that the success of a labour movement is directly proportional to the viciousness with which it is portrayed in the corporate-controlled media. See, for example, the lead Editorial of *The Times of India*, 28 April 2001.
19. See my "Offers of peace", *South Asean Citizens Wire* #2, 17 October 2001.
20. See my "Manufacturing peace", *South Asean Citizens Wire* #1, 3 January 2002.
21. Vaskar Nandy, "War against terrorism: perspective on protests", *Economic and Political Weekly*, 27 October 2001. Also, Mahmood Mamdani, *Good Muslim, Bad Muslim: America, the Cold War and the Roots of Terror*, Pantheon Books, 2003. For the Australian scene, see Iain Lygo, "Who will be charged under terrorism laws?" *Znet*, 23 October 2004.
22. See my "Gujrat and the world order", *Znet South Asia Watch*, June 2002.
23. See Vidya Subrahmaniam, "Two gods, one message," *The Hindu*, 11 November 2004.
24. See my "Teachers and war on terrorism", *Economic and Political Weekly*, 25 October, 2003.
25. *The Terror of POTA and other security legislation: A report on the People's Tribunal on the Prevention of Terrorism Act and other security legislation*, Ed. Preeti Verma, Human Rights Law Network, New Delhi, March 2004.
26. *Crime Against Humanity: An Inquiry into the Carnage in Gujarat*, Concerned Citizen's Tribunal, published by Anil Dharkar for Citizens for Peace and Justice, 2002. Also, *State Sponsored Genocide: Factsheet Gujarat 2002*, CPI(M) Publications, 2002.
27. V. Venkatesan, "A reality check," *Frontline*, 13 August 2004, p.80.
28. Zakia Jowher, "POTA and the terrorized minority community in Gujarat", in *The Terror of POTA and other security legislation: A report on the People's Tribunal on the Prevention of Terrorism Act and other security legislation*, Ed. Preeti Verma, Human Rights Law Network, New Delhi, March 2004.
29. See Ashim Roy, "Gujarat genocide: the passage to fascism," *Revolutionary Democracy*, Vol.8, No.2, September 2002, p. 3-15, for an incisive analysis of the phenomenon.
30. Chomsky, *Hegemony or Survival: America's Quest for Global Dominance*, Henry Holt, New York, 2003, pp.115-21.
31. Full texts of most of the media statements cited in this section are posted at www20.brinkster.com/sargeelani.
32. Amit Baruah, "Now, a third party to the talks?", *The Hindu*, 22 October 2004.

33. This court is also known as the Trial Court, Sessions Court, Special Court for POTA, and POTA Court.
34. Haksar, "The many faces of nationalism", *Seminar 533*, January 2004, p.96. Also, Nandita Haksar, "Tried by the media: the S A R Geelani trial," *Crisis/Media: Sarai Reader 04*, Center for Studies in Developing Societies, Delhi, February 2004.
35. Adam Curtis, cited in Andy Beckett, "The making of the terror myth", *The Guardian*, October 15 2004.
36. These words were used by Delhi University Teachers In Defence of SAR Geelani in their press statement of 18 September, 2003. Some of this statement was subsequently reported in the *Statesman*, *The Hindu*, *Navbharat Times*, *Asian Age*, and other papers on 19 September. These words were also used by Noam Chomsky in his statement (Annexure 15).
37. Readers aware of the profiles of terrorists allegedly involved in 9/11 cannot miss the resemblances.
38. The sordid case of the said Jordanian student with relentless harassment by the police and his ultimate deportation from India without any cause is discussed in Tripta Wahi, "Qays' deportation case," *Revolutionary Democracy*, Vol.10, No.2.
39. Haksar, "The many faces of nationalism", *Seminar 533*, January 2004, p. 99. Peer, "Victims of December 13", (Annexure 13, p. 307).
40. "Geelani's family in dire straits," *Milli Gazette*, 1-15 February, 2002.
41. The issue was mentioned near the end of Neeta Sharma's colourful report in *The Times of India*, 21 December 2001, but only after all the damage to the accused had been done. The report is discussed below.
42. "Press, police suppressed information in Dec. 13 Case", *The Hindu*, 11 October 2002.
43. The TOI correspondent was also a defence witness in the court.
44. Ten months later, in a piece titled "Press, police suppressed information in Dec. 13 Case", *The Hindu*, 11 October 2002, reported, "Mr. Afzal stated that another of the accused, S.A.R. Geelani, had nothing to do with the attack and had no knowledge of it."
45. Haksar, "The many faces of nationalism", *Seminar 533*, January 2004, p. 97. Haksar, "Tried by the media: the S A R Geelani trial," *Crisis/Media: Sarai Reader 04*, Center for Studies in Developing Societies, Delhi, February 2004, p.162. "Complaint to the National Human Rights Commission on torture and discrimination of detainees and prisoners in the high risk cells of Tihar Jail," by Syed Abdul Rahman Geelani, forwarded to the NHRC by All India Defence Committee for Syed Abdul Rehman Gilani, January 8, 2004.

46. Nandita Haksar and K. Sanjay Singh, “December 13,” *Seminar 521*, January 2003, p.123.
47. Archana Jyoti, “Geelani children have no school to study in Delhi,” *Asian Age*, 10 January 2003.
48. “Justice speaks”, Editorial, *The Indian Express*, 30 October 2003.
49. Nandita Haksar and K. Sanjay Singh, “December 13,” *Seminar 521*, January 2003.
50. “Pota under trial in Dec. 13 Case”, *Indian Express*, 25 July 2002; “”Parliament attack accused complain of unfair trial”, *The Hindu*, 6 August 2002; “I’ve been framed, alleges Geelani”, *Indian Express*, 17 September 2002; “Fair trial sought for Geelani”, *The Hindu*, 30 September 2002; “Holes in the Dec. 13 attack case”, *The Hindu*, 10 October 2002; “Press, police suppressed information in Dec. 13 Case”, *The Hindu*, 11 October 2002; “Police misinterpreted phone conversation”, *The Hindu*, 12 October 2002, etc.
51. Prem Shankar Jha, “A lecturer in prison”, *Outlook Magazine*.
52. Haksar, “Tried by the media: the S A R Geelani trial,” *Crisis/Media: Sarai Reader 04*, Center for Studies in Developing Societies, Delhi, February 2004, p.161.
53. Deposition by Shuddhabrata Sengupta in Public Hearing on ‘Media Trials’ in the context of the ‘War Against Terrorism,’ SARAI, Delhi, 13 September 2004.
54. Haksar, “The many faces of nationalism”, *Seminar 533*, January 2004, p. 97.
55. Chandan Mitra, “Go ‘home’, Geelani & friends”, *The Pioneer*, 30 October 2003.
56. “Go on appeal”, Editorial, *The Pioneer*, 31 October 2003.
57. “Justice done,” Editorial, *The Hindu*, 31 October, 2003.
58. “Justice speaks”, Editorial, *The Indian Express*, 30 October, 2003.
59. *The Hindustan Times*, Editorial of 31 October, 2003.
60. Anjali Mody, “Geelani, Afsan Guru acquitted in the Parliament attack case”, *The Hindu*, 30 October, 2003. Also, Nandita Narain and Neeraj Malik, “The Parliament attack case: no redress for wrongly accused”, *The Times of India*, 15 January 2004.
61. Haksar, “The many faces of nationalism”, *Seminar 533*, January 2004, p. 101.
62. We have not incorporated the *new* submissions and arguments currently being heard at the Supreme Court. However, most of the submissions and arguments have been carried over from the hearings at the Session and High courts.

CHAPTER TWO

Who Attacked Parliament?

The Prosecution Story

According to the prosecution, the conspiracy begins with Maulana Masood Azhar, the leader of Jaish-e-Mohammad based in Pakistan, instructing, at the instance of ISI, one Ghazi Baba, the Supreme Commander of the outfit in Kashmir, to carry out actions on important institutions of the Indian nation. To that end, Ghazi Baba directed one Tariq Ahmed to arrange for an operation. Tariq got in touch with Mohd. Afzal and motivated him to join the jehad for liberation of Kashmir. Subsequently, Afzal met Ghazi Baba and the plan was worked out. It was going to be a joint operation of Jaish-e-Mohammad and Lashkar-e-Toiba. Beginning with one Mohammad, Afzal arranged for several militants – Haider, Hamza, Raja and Rana – to bring huge quantities of arms, explosives and a laptop computer to Delhi in pre-arranged hideouts. In Delhi, the team got in touch with Afzal's cousin Shaukat Hussain Guru, Shaukat's wife Afsan Guru and S.A.R. Geelani, a lecturer of Arabic in Delhi University.

Afzal helped the militants buy the required chemicals and a Sujata mixer-grinder for making explosives. He was also actively involved in the purchase of a white ambassador car, a magnetic red light used by VIPs, and a motorcycle for recee. In the beginning, the terrorists had their options open between Delhi Assembly, UK and US embassies, Parliament and the Airport; recee was conducted accordingly. However, Ghazi Baba instructed them over satellite telephone to settle for Parliament. Once the details of the attack were firmed up, the explosives were duly made in the hide-outs and the car was fitted with some of them. The laptop was used, among other things, to prepare a "Home Ministry" security sticker and identity cards for each of the terrorists. In a final meeting on the night of 12 December 2001, the militants handed over Rs. 10 lacs to Afzal, Shaukat and Geelani for their part in the conspiracy; they also handed over the laptop to be returned to Ghazi Baba.

The militants started off in the car towards the Parliament complex at about ten in the morning of December 13. Just before the attack, the militants got in touch with Afzal over mobile phones repeatedly to instruct him to watch television to find out the presence and location of VVIPs inside Parliament. Afzal failed to do so as he was in the Azadpur market where there was no electricity; so, he instructed Shaukat to do so. However, the militants started their operation without waiting for this information. Once they went inside the complex after clearing security with the "Home Ministry" sticker and the VIP light on their car, they tried to park the car near Gate No. 11 of the complex, which is used by the Vice-President of India. As the car was reversing, it hit the main car of the Vice-President's motorcade. In the ensuing commotion, the terrorists got out of the car, started shooting indiscriminately and attempted to run towards the building. As the security forces assigned to the complex got alerted, exchange of fire started. All the five terrorists and nine other people including some from the security forces died on the spot; sixteen persons from the security forces were injured. The event was over in less than half an hour.

Subsequently, Shaukat met Afzal at Azadpur. Together they started off for Srinagar in a truck registered under the name of Shaukat's wife, Afsan. The police picked them up on 15 December 2001 along with the laptop with accessories, a mobile phone and Rs. 10 lacs. The police could trace them in Srinagar because, once the attack was over, the police found mobile phones and slips of paper with phone numbers written on them as well as a large quantity of unused arms, ammunitions, explosive devices, identity cards, etc.

They found that mobile 98114-89429, a Delhi number, was given as contact number in all the identity cards. From the call records of this number they found that it was in touch with the mobile numbers found on the dead terrorists as well as with two other Delhi numbers 98115-73506 and 98100-81228. The number 98114-89429 and the numbers found on the dead terrorists were in touch with satellite phones in Kashmir; the mobiles found on the terrorists were also in touch with numbers in Pakistan, Dubai, and Switzerland. Out of all the prominent numbers only one mobile number 98100-81228 was found to be a regular mobile card of AIRTEL, which stood in the name of Sayed Abdul Rehman Geelani, resident of 535, Mukherjee Nagar, Delhi. As the mobile 98114-89429 was found switched off, they intercepted 98115-73506 and 98100-81228.

On 14 December, they located an incoming call from Kashmir to the mobile 98100-81228 in which the receiver of the call said things in Kashmiri to the effect that he supported the attack. On that basis, Geelani was arrested from his house on 15 December. Later in the evening of 14 December, they located another incoming call from Kashmir, this time to the mobile 98115-73506. Upon his arrest, Geelani admitted to his knowledge and participation in the crime; he also told the police that the mobile 98114-89429 belonged to Mohammad Afzal and 98115-73506 to

Shaukat Hussain Guru. The police located Shaukat's house at Geelani's instance.

In the house, the police found Shaukat's wife Afsan Guru alongwith the mobile 98115-73506. They found another mobile no. 98104-46375. Afsan admitted to her knowledge of the attack and named her husband and Mohammad Afzal as conspirators. She also clarified that the call from Kashmir the previous evening was from Shaukat. Once the police learned about Afzal and Shaukat and their location in Srinagar, they informed the police in Kashmir who arrested Afzal and Shaukat and seized the laptop, Rupees 10 lacs and a mobile phone *without* its SIM card assumed to be bearing the number 98114-89429.

Once they were brought back to Delhi, they made disclosure statements which led to the hideouts, the shops and the seizure of chemicals, detonators, etc. Also, Afzal identified each of the five dead militants lying in the morgue. Finally, Afzal and Shaukat made detailed confessions on 21 December 2001 after sections of POTA were introduced into the case on 19 December 2001. From these confessions, the police put together the conspiracy theory as summarized above. The seizure of a sticker with "we hate India" write-up, mention of huge sums of hawala money in Afzal's confession, and Shaukat's admiration for Osama Bin Laden mentioned in his confession added telling touches to the story.

On the basis of this story, the Special Court awarded death sentences to Mohd. Afzal, Shaukat Hussain Guru and S.A.R. Geelani, while Ms. Afsan Guru was given rigorous imprisonment (R.I.) for five years.

Planning and operational parts: We will examine this conspiracy theory from a variety of directions in this work. For now, we note a significant division between two broad parts of the theory. The first part consists of the sequence of events that begins in Pakistan at the instance of the ISI and Maulana Masood Azhar, proceeds via Ghazi Baba and Tariq Ahmed to the recruitment of individual terrorists from JeM and LeT, and ends with the five terrorists moving into pre-arranged shelters in Delhi with arms, ammunition and explosive material brought from Kashmir. For convenience, we call this the *Planning Part*. The second part consists of the preparations for the attack from these shelters. This part includes the survey of targets, purchase of additional explosive material, car and motorcycles, uniforms and other items, preparation of ID cards and stickers, and, finally, the attack itself. For convenience, we call this the *Operational Part*.

This division is significant because, as we will see ('A surrendered militant'), *the only evidence for the Planning Part is Afzal's confession under POTA*. As noted in the prosecution story, the police did claim to recover mobile phones from the dead terrorists which were allegedly used to communicate with numbers in Pakistan, Dubai, Kashmir and Switzerland. Arguably, an investigation into these call-records could have given the police some indication of the Planning Part independently of Afzal's confession. The police claimed to have made two efforts to secure this information; both the efforts failed.

First, to secure the details of communication between mobiles used by the dead terrorists (via the Internet) and numbers in Kashmir, "a request was made to the 'AIRTEL' for getting the details in this regard but the AIRTEL could not furnish the same due to technical non-feasibility" (Annexure 1, p. 129-30). Second, "a request for obtaining the call details of the International telephone numbers and satellite phone numbers, which have figured during the investigation of the case, has been made to INTERPOL, but the report is still awaited" (Annexure 1, p. 130). However, no report from the Interpol or any other relevant international agency was ever submitted as evidence. In the absence of any other corroborating evidence, the entire weight of the Planning Part thus rests on the credibility of Afzal's confession.

In particular, Afzal's confession is the only evidence regarding the identity of the five dead terrorists: their names and the terrorist organizations they belonged to. Obviously, since all the attackers died during the attack, the attack itself cannot be linked to any prior conspiracy without this crucial information. The problem is that Afzal himself denied any knowledge of the identity of the dead terrorists subsequently in his statement u/s 313 Cr.P.C.: "I had not identified any terrorist. Police told me the names of terrorists and forced me to identify" (Annexure 5, p. 165). Statements of the accused are recorded in court u/s 313 Cr.P.C when the accused get the final chance to reply to questions put by the court. It is important to emphasize that this statement, unlike confession under POTA, is made by an accused before the court rather than before a police officer; also, this statement is made when an accused is in judicial custody, not in police custody. We return to this statement and the confession.

In search of some 'independent' evidence on this crucial matter, the Special Judge of the Sessions Court claimed that the dead persons were Pakistanis since no Indian came forward to claim their bodies (Annexure 11, para 220)! As a matter of fact, neither did any Pakistani through the good offices of the Government of Pakistan. Outside the judicial proceedings, the then Home Minister L.K. Advani volunteered an 'evidence' in Parliament with his statement that "the dead men looked like Pakistanis." "Does Advani look like a Pakistani? Musharraf like an Indian? We need Toba Tek Singh to decide," Nandita Haksar and Kumar Sanjay Singh suggested.[1]

The Operational Part in contrast was flooded with alleged material evidence to which the police had independent access at the scene of the attack itself. It is not unreasonable to expect, therefore, that with proper investigation the police might have been able to find witnesses from among the shopkeepers, landlords, and the like, to locate the hideouts and the incriminating material stored there. In fact, according to the police, the car dealer, who sold the attack vehicle to the terrorists, came forward within hours of the attack after he learnt about it from television (Annexure 1, p. 115-16). From such investigation, the police might have been able to piece together much of the Operational Part without help from Afzal. To that extent, Afzal's disclosure and confession only made the task easier for the police.

However, a construction of just this part of the story would have fallen far short of an *explanation* of the event, for, it would have missed details about meetings, motivation, source of funding, etc., without which an explanation would have remained essentially incomplete. *These details can only be reached from the testimony of at least one of the participants.* In that, the construction would have failed to link the attack to international terrorism.

For example, the construction could have simply meant that five unidentified and deranged young persons, inspired by sundry films, were out on a dark adventure for instant fame and a large sum of ransom money.[2] The sheer amateurishness of the attack – discussed below in 'Incredible features' – could be a pointer in that direction. In that sense, Mohammad Afzal's testimony turned a possibly mindless criminal adventure into an awesome terrorist attack. Mohammad Afzal is central to the prosecution story.

Plan of examination: Given the distinction between the planning and the operational parts, and the pivotal role of Mohd. Afzal's confessional statement in the prosecution story, we will examine the story as follows.

1. *Grave Charges*: In 'The story disputed,' we will show that, despite the apparent abundance of evidence against the accused produced by the prosecution, a team of very eminent lawyers challenged almost every aspect of both the investigation and the trial in severely critical terms. The charges ranged

from fabrication and concoction of evidence to palpable mistrial. The gravity of the charges suggests at least that the prosecution story can not be taken for granted. We are thus led to examine both the over-all coherence of the story and the validity of its major parts.

2. *Implausible Explanation*: Next, in 'Incredible features,' we show with concrete examples that even if we grant validity to the individual parts of the story, these parts just do not cohere as a plausible explanation of the attack. This suggests that significant parts of the story can not be true. The suggestion is strengthened by the fact that, in each case of incredibility, a credible explanation is available if we assume, *pace* defence, that much of the evidence is fabricated. Combining the effect of (1) and (2), we are led to study the more significant individual pieces of evidence.
3. *Poverty of Evidence*: In 'Acquittal of Geelani,' we show that the judgment of the High Court itself contains a direct critique of the evidence produced against the accused. Although S.A.R. Geelani was found guilty on eleven counts and was awarded death sentences by the Special Court, the High Court *acquitted* him of all charges by summarily dismissing each piece of evidence produced against him. We discuss the Special Court judgment to illustrate the absurd features of evidence with which Geelani was sentenced to death. Geelani's trial raises grave doubts about the rest of the trial.
4. *Fabricated Documents*: In 'Arrest memos,' the basic issue is that, given the centrality of Mohd. Afzal, the prosecution needs to document the chain of evidence which led from the scene of attack to the arrest of Mohd. Afzal. As noted, some mobile phones and call-records, allegedly linking the accused with the terrorists, enabled the police to organize a sequence of arrests culminating in Afzal. We show in detail that each piece

of evidence, including the arrest and the recoveries themselves, are seriously questionable; in fact, and as noted by the High Court, parts of this sequence are certainly fabricated and/or illegal. In particular, the credibility of police witnesses is questionable. This part of the prosecution's story linking Mohd. Afzal to the terrorists collapses.

5. *Dubious independent evidence*: The credibility of the prosecution story thus depends on the material evidence recovered from the hideouts, and on the veracity of the confessions. Keeping to the former, the police allegedly recovered large quantities of incriminating material from the hideouts, and traced them to the shops from where these were allegedly purchased. Almost the entire weight of this set of evidence depends on the credibility of public witnesses such as landlords and shopkeepers. In, 'Procured witnesses', we show in detail that crucial safeguards were routinely violated by the police. Further, there are palpable incredibilities and contradictions in the depositions of almost every public witness, giving rise to the possibility that they were deposing under duress.
6. *Forced Confessions*: Thus, not only that the confessions are not supported by independent evidence, the entire weight of the prosecution's case in fact depends on the veracity of these confessions, especially Afzal's. In 'A surrendered militant,' we note first that these confessions were deliberately recorded under POTA before a police official, rather than before a judicial magistrate. Next, we raise a series of queries and corroborating evidence to suggest that the confessions were extracted under torture. Further, the confessions are flatly in contradiction with the statements u/s 313 Cr.P.C. made by the same accused. We show that Afzal's 313 is largely credible in that (a) the courts admitted some of the statements, (b) the statements suggest honesty and truthfulness, and (c) the statements lend much

credibility to an otherwise incredible story. Finally, parts of Afzal's 313, when conjoined and interpreted, raise dark issues about the complicity of the security agencies in the conspiracy.

7. *Vitiated Trial*: The cumulative effect of the preceding problems is that the entire proceedings were patently unjust for the accused. In addition, it is pointed out that (a) Mohd. Afzal never had proper legal representation at the trial stage, (b) effectively, he was never given a chance to narrate his side of the story, although the court mechanically recorded his statement 313.

It follows not only that the prosecution story is essentially unproven, large-scale fabrication, concoction and denial of natural justice characterized the proceedings.

The Story Disputed

The prosecution's case and the Special Court judgment did not go unchallenged. Despite the heap of evidence noted above, two very senior lawyers, Mr. Ram Jethmalani and Mr. Shanti Bhushan, both former Union Ministers of Law, agreed to defend S.A.R. Geelani and Shaukat Guru respectively in the High Court without charging any fees; the noted lawyer Mr. Colin Gonsalvis defended Afzal. Lawyers of the stature of Ms. Kamini Jaiswal, Ms. Nitya Ramakrishnan, and Ms. Nandita Haksar assisted the senior lawyers in the High Court; Ms. Ramakrishnan also appeared for Afsan Guru. Here we record only some of the general observations on the Special Court trial by some of these eminent lawyers and others to give a sense of the broad issues that arose from this trial. Specific objections, as detailed in Annexures 12, 14 and 17, will be discussed later as we proceed.

In his submission before the High Court on behalf of the appellant S.A.R. Geelani, Ram Jethmalani contended: "This is a case of no evidence. The law of evidence has been treated as non-existent. The provisions of the Code of Criminal Procedure and Evidence Act have been flagrantly violated. Serious objections remain undisposed of." Elaborating, Jethmalani held that "the cognizance of the various offences charged has been taken without the sanctions required by Section 196 of the Code of Criminal Procedure or Section 5 of POTA or Section 7 of the Explosive Substances Act." As a result, "the evidence discloses total non-application of mind and an unforgivable frivolity of attitude when the law enjoins careful and serious analysis and appraisal of evidence before granting the sanctions." Hence, "the purported sanctions are void and the trial totally without jurisdiction and a nullity."

Commenting on the investigation, Jethmalani argued that it "is riddled with illegality. The evidence discloses concoction and fabrication. All these have been grossed one and have resulted in a grave miscarriage of justice." About the charges, the senior counsel held that they are "illegal." In fact, "some charges are so ridiculous that the proceedings are deprived of the solemnity of a serious criminal trial ... All the charges of offence under Chapter VI of the Indian Penal Code are bad in law."

About the legal defence available to the accused, Jethmalani observed that "in capital cases particularly those that arouse public prejudice and anger against the accused making it difficult for them to arrange for their own defense, it was the duty of the Court to provide adequate defence at State expense." However, "this duty was not performed and the record discloses that the accused never got proper and adequate legal assistance."

In sum, "the howlers including callous and gross carelessness, the irregularities, the illegalities at every stage and exhibitions of prejudice and hostility against the accused at every step place the trial court and its conduct of the trial far below the standards required by Article 21. This whole trial is unconstitutional, illegal and void."[3]

In his submission on behalf of Shaukat Hussain Guru, Shanti Bhushan contended that his client "has been falsely implicated in the conspiracy case by the investigating agency." The agency has not only "gone out of its way in concocting evidence," it "had even gone to the extent of forging and fabricating important documents for framing the appellants and police officials had clearly given perjured evidence." "In fact," the senior counsel emphasized, "even according to the findings recorded by the Special Judge himself the investigating officers had clearly fabricated documents and given perjured evidence."

According to the Senior Counsel, "the investigating officials have clearly committed offences punishable imprisonment with life under Section 194 and 195 of I.P.C." "When such a serious offence has been committed by the investigating officials," Shanti Bhusan continued, "it is only by having them punished that such fabrication of documents and the giving of perjured evidence can be stopped by the Court." Furthermore, since "the investigating officials were prepared to forge and fabricate documents against the appellants," it follows that "the only evidence on which reliance could still be placed by the Court would be evidence totally independent of these investigating officers."[4]

In their meticulous review of the trial at the Special Court, the Peoples Union for Democratic Rights (PUDR) worked through the case file to observe that the trial "brings out several anomalies, discrepancies, inconsistencies and misconstructions in vital areas of evidence which undermine the conclusions arrived at in the judgment." After a careful analysis of the evidence against the accused, PUDR reached the conclusion that "the combined effect of all the above goes a long way in demolishing the prosecution's case against the accused": "there is no evidence which unerringly implicates them or whose authenticity is beyond reproach." Thus, they noted that "the judgment claims a degree of certainty in its conclusions, which does not in fact exist."

Reflecting specifically on the fact that the Parliament attack case was the first trial under POTA, PUDR observed that the "anti-democratic" character of this law "became more evident in the course of the trial." Linking the law to the uncertain character of the evidence produced against the accused, PUDR thought that "it is perhaps inherent in a trial under POTA that the accused is disabled to a point where rules of evidence become pliable and conjecture can take over and death sentences become easy to award." Moreover, "in the present political and ideological atmosphere, where the very act of applying POTA prejudges the action, the rights of the accused are treated as an especially dispensable commodity." As a result, a combination of "an unjust law and unfair trial" has "in all probability ended up committing a grievous error sentencing three men to death and a woman to five years of RI on dubious evidence and shoddy investigations" (Annexure 12, p. 300).

Focusing on the Special Court Judge S.N. Dhingra, Nandita Haksar observed that "one is struck by the fact that he makes so many presumptions, all of them in favour of the investigating agencies and against the accused" (Annexure 14, p. 317). For example, concerning the objection that the police did not follow procedures and may have tampered with the evidence, the judge remarked: "There is no reason to disbelieve the testimony of any of the police officers as none of police officers were having any kind of enmity against any of the accused persons" (Annexure 11, para 179). With respect to the contention of the defence that the witnesses produced by the police, such as the shopkeepers, were "procured witnesses," the judge asserted that it "has not been shown that any of the shopkeeper had any kind of enmity against the accused and wanted to implicate him in false case" (Annexure 11, para 113).

"None of the presumptions made by Shri S.N. Dhingra," Haksar comments, "are either sanctioned under the ordinary criminal law or even under the POTA. The judge justifies the violation of rules, regulations and procedures by the police by reference to the seriousness of the offence and denies the accused their rights under the law. Implicit in his reasoning is that the accused are enemies of the Government of India and therefore they have no right to the protections and safeguards provided under the law or under the Constitution." In this, Haksar notes, "the Judge is coming close to the way US President Bush and his lawyers are trying to characterize 'terrorists' as 'unlawful combatants' who are not entitled to the protection of the Bill of Rights. This reasoning has been criticized on the ground that it defeats the entire concept of fair trial." (Annexure 14, p. 318).

The judgement, Haksar concludes, "is chilling reading." The Special Judge "has shown scant respect for the principles and ideals of human rights enshrined in our Constitution by the Founding Fathers." "If his judgement is upheld," Haksar fears, "it would lay the foundation for a police state where every citizen would be a potential victim of institutionalized repression" (Annexure 14, p. 332).

To summarize, the following general concerns about the trial arose:

— some documents were forged
— some evidence was fabricated and concocted
— some sanctions were frivolous and unauthorized
— vital procedures were not followed
— the investigation was shoddy, often callous
— the trial judge was biased and prejudiced, and
— the human, constitutional and legal rights of the accused were violated

Our concern is that, with such grave complaints against almost every aspect of the investigation and the trial, it is unlikely that the prosecution's story is wholly true. If the story is false even in parts, it is of utmost importance to find out whether the remaining (true) parts, if any, amount to a satisfactory explanation of the event. In other words, we simply cannot take the prosecution's conspiracy theory for granted.

Incredible Features

A preliminary problem with the story is that, even if we take the individual pieces of the evidence offered to support it to be valid, the cumulative effect of some of the evidence looks incredible from considerations of truth and coherence. Notice that these concerns do not fall under the jurisdiction of the courts; their only concern is to see that the chain of evidence as presented by the prosecution stands unrefuted, and that it proves the guilt of the accused beyond reasonable doubt. The courts did not raise concerns of overall credibility; hence, they were not raised at all since there was no commission of inquiry, and the media followed the police. Yet, concerns like these are immensely significant for reaching a plausible explanation of the event. We will illustrate these points as we proceed. We will study three examples.

Example one: Consider some of the features of the attack itself. By any measure, the attack was so embarrassingly flawed that the police had to come up with some explanation of why it failed. Thus, according to a very senior police officer, "clearly the militants were inexperienced, especially the driver of the Ambassador." This is illustrated by the fact that, first, the militant-driver alerted the guards as he drove "too fast;" then he mistook a "vacant area" for a parking lot. On being challenged by the Security Guards, "he lost his nerve, took a U-turn to return to the main carriage way and in doing so rammed into one of the cars in Vice President Krishan Kant's convoy."[5]

"Thankfully," the officer continued, "the impact loosened the wires of the detonator in the Ambassador which was to be used to blow up the porch of Parliament," thereby turning the "wired-up car" into "a dud." This observation clearly suggests that the "wiring-up" of the car with explosive material was a job poorly done such that a mild collision loosened the entire detonating system. "With their plan going awry," the officer hypothesized, "the suicide squad panicked," jumped out and started firing, "thus revealing their deadly game prematurely." Moreover, "they made the mistake of splitting up, becoming easy targets." The official concluded that "they obviously didn't have a pre-determined plan and started spraying bullets in all directions"; in fact, "they had no fall-back plan either." Finally, although the terrorists were laced with explosives, they did not blow themselves up as they died, enabling the police to recover active mobile phones, identity cards and paper slips with phone numbers written on them.

The plan fell apart because, according to the same officer, "much of the lack of coordination was caused by the extreme secrecy and the delay in selecting the target ... The militants had prepared two plans — of attacking either the airport or Parliament ... Mohammad got the message to head for Parliament just minutes before the attack." Is this explanation credible in view of the rest of the story?

First, according to Afzal's confession (which is the only evidence at issue), the attack on Parliament was supposed to be a joint operation of two dreaded terrorist organizations, Jaish-e-Mohammad and Lashkar-e-Toiba, under the overall guidance of ISI (Annexure 1, Annexure 2). We can form some idea of the sophistication in planning and operation of these organizations by recalling the hijacking of IC-814 in December 1999. That extremely complex operation involving four states (India, Pakistan, Nepal and Afghanistan), several airports, management of hundreds of passengers and crew, and nerve-racking negotiations conducted for weeks in biting cold, virtually brought the Indian state down to its knees as the Union Minister Jaswant Singh was compelled to accompany the terrorist Masood Azhar to Kandahar.

It is not unreasonable to guess that the Parliament attack was designed to be perhaps the most ambitious terrorist action contemplated by these organizations. In fact, according to Afzal again, one of the terrorists, Mohammad (also known as "Burger"), who was the alleged leader of the Parliament attack team, was involved in the IC-814 operation as well (Annexure 1, p. 131). Yet, according to the senior officer, the militants, who "didn't have a predetermined plan", were "clearly" inexperienced in that they "panicked" and revealed their "deadly game prematurely" by "spraying bullets in all directions."

Furthermore, the explanation that the plan went astray because "Mohammad got the message to head for Parliament just minutes before the attack" does not match either Afzal's confession or what the police itself stated in the chargesheet. According to the chargesheet, a lot of people knew about the plan to attack Parliament much in advance. For example, Geelani was said to have stated that "meetings were held in the house of Saukat in Mukharjee Nagar and in these meetings Shaukat Hussain and Mohd. Afzal along with all the deceased terrorists used to be present and discuss the plan to carry out attack on Parliament House." Even Afsan allegedly stated that "she was aware of the plan of terrorist to attack Parliament House because a number of meeting were held in her house." In fact, "Afzal purchased a black Yamaha motorcycle No. HR-51E-5768" apparently exclusively "to conduct recee of Parliament House ... They conducted repeated recee of Parliament House and the areas around it" (Annexure 1, p. 122).

In his confession under POTA, Afzal did say, as noted above, that several targets were surveyed in the beginning. However, "after conducting recee of all the targets, Mohammad informed Ghazi

Baba who told him that they must strike at the Parliament." Accordingly, "a trial meeting was held in the house of Shaukat in which all were present and the plans for attack on Parliament House was finalized." Only then was the Ambassador car, the attack vehicle, was purchased on 11.12.2001 — two days before the attack. Finally, in the night meeting on 12.12.2001, Mohammad told Afzal that "they are going to conduct a Fidayeen attack on the Parliament House on 13.12.2001" (Annexure 2, p. 143).

We must conclude, therefore, that if the chargesheet and Afzal's confession are valid, then the idea that Mohammad got the message to head for Parliament "just minutes before the attack" is a figment of police's imagination just to placate the general public in view of the palpable amateurishness of the operation. If the explanation given by the police is false, then the attack just does not square up with the profile of the terrorist organizations at issue.

As an aside, we just note, for what it is worth, that Maulana Masood Azhar, the leader of Jaish-e-Mohammad, reportedly denied any involvement with the attack soon after the event. Quoting reports that mounds of explosives were brought to be used in the attack, he said it was impossible for the militants to transport such a huge quantity of explosives.[6] On the other hand, General Javed Ashraf Qazi, the former chief of Pakistan's ISI, reportedly told a joint sitting of Pakistani Parliament more than two years later that "we must not be afraid of admitting that Jaish was involved in the deaths of thousands of innocent Kashmiris, bombing the Indian Parliament, (journalist) Daniel Pearl's murder and attempts on President Musharraf's life."[7]

What took Qazi so long to say this? What does it mean for Qazi to "admit" that Jaish was involved? Was Qazi's selective list of terrorist outrages just a statement of fact or was it politically aligned to the changed circumstances involving India, Pakistan, the US and the Iraq war? Recalling that the Delhi police, via Afzal, claimed that Lashkar-e-Toiba was equally involved, why didn't Qazi implicate Lashkar-e-Toiba with the Parliament attack when he did mention Lashkar-e-Toiba's "harmful" role in Kashmir in the same speech? What is the truth?[8]

Before we proceed, note that the issues of amateurishness and inexperience do not concern the courts of law. As long as there is evidence, admitted and proven under the law, that some people committed a crime and that these people were conspiratorially linked to some other people, the case is upheld. From the legal point of view, it does not matter if the commission of the crime showed signs of naivete or if the actions of the criminals do not match the presumed profile of the organization they belong to. However, they do matter for establishing the truth.

Example two: The absence of a "pre-determined plan" seemed to have affected other aspects – such as communication between the attackers and co-conspirators – of the terrorist operation as well. As noted, the terrorists allegedly got in touch with Afzal over mobile phones just prior to and during the attack. According to Afzal's confession, when the terrorists were "in the vicinity" of Parliament House, they wanted him to find out "about the presence of various VVIPs inside Parliament House." Afzal failed to do so since he was in the Azadpur market where there was no electricity!! After 25 minutes, Mohammad called again with the same demand. Only then Afzal informed Mohammad about the lack of electricity and asked for some more time. At that point Afzal instructed Shaukat to watch TV and call him back with the information. However, Shaukat states in his confession that by the time "I switched on the TV I received another call from Afzal that the mission is on." Apparently then the terrorists had decided to go ahead with the attack even before they received the information they were insisting upon.

Just what was the relevance of this piece of information for the terrorists just minutes before the attack? Why should they bother about this detail when they were allegedly planning to secure the entire Parliament which was in session in any case? Could Afzal (or Shaukat) have gleaned this specific information on demand from TV? What was Afzal doing in Azadpur market at a time like this? Why wasn't this supposedly crucial task pre-arranged? Finally, if the information was so crucial for the success of the attack, why did the terrorists go ahead without it?

Example three: Afzal and Shaukat were found guilty of conspiring in a terrorist act and waging of war of horrendous proportions. According to the High Court judgment, Mohd. Afzal was a part to the conspiracy to attack Parliament when it was in session, he was instrumental in the smuggling of arms and ammunitions, he had actively purchased the chemicals (Annexure 16, para 400). Shaukat Guru's involvement was more than mere knowledge, acquiescence, carelessness, indifference or lack of concern, there is clear and cogent evidence of informed and interested co-operation, simulation and instigation (Annexure 16, para 402). Both were accused of working in close co-operation with a group of hardened foreign terrorists with the aim to cause damage to the sovereignty and integrity of India. These words suggest a certain criminal profile of the accused. Now, according to the police, they behaved as follows.

Afzal and Shaukat drove out of Delhi in an easily identifiable vehicle, namely, a truck registered in the name of Shaukat's wife, to reach Kashmir via the difficult mountain roads filled with the slush and snow of winter. Were these plausible choices of vehicle and immediate destination for terrorists escaping from such a high-profile crime? Since the news was immediately on TV, Afzal and Shaukat knew that the attack had failed and the terrorists had been found intact and dead. So, there was every likelihood for the police to recover the mobiles, trace the numbers and post surveillance.

However, instead of disappearing in thin air, they continued onwards towards Kashmir in that truck. Not only that. On completion of the journey, Shaukat called his wife 36 hours after the attack to tell her that he had reached Srinagar safely. We reproduce the entire conversation that the police claimed to have intercepted at Annexure 16 (para 341).

The veracity of this conversation was much discussed in the courts. However, everyone seemed to agree that, if the conversation is true, then it showed that Afsan was scared and that she was concerned about Shaukat's safety; the Hon'ble judges of the High Court also thought that Afsan and Shaukat were "talking between the lines" (Annexure 16, para 342). In what follows, we do not concede the veracity of the call; we simply assume that the said conversation took place.

The point of interest – not discussed so far – is that, apart from the amazing fact that Shaukat had called his wife at all, he continued the conversation even after being warned by Afsan; in fact, he advised Afsan to call him back later in the night. Moreover, even after being warned by Afsan at about 8.00 in the evening, they did not flee but stayed put in the Srinagar Mandi for the whole night. In the morning, they drove out of the Mandi in the same truck with the laptop, the mobile and the huge sum of money, and proceeded onwards presumably to meet Ghazi Baba when they were picked up near a police station.

How can these parts of the evidence be valid and the story they generate so incredible at the same time? Moreover, if these parts of the total body of evidence make the narrative incredible, why should the rest of the parts of the evidence be viewed as credible? We emphasize again that these concerns about credibility do not fall under the jurisdiction of the courts; if Afzal and Shaukat behaved like overconfident fools, it was their problem. Yet, concerns like these are immensely significant for reaching a plausible explanation of the event: how can organizations like the Jaish recruit such overconfident fools for their most ambitious terrorist operation?

An alternative perspective: The incredibility factors of these examples get immediately removed if we adopt an alternative perspective. In that perspective, let us imagine that the evidence and the interpretation produced by the police in these examples are in fact *false*, although the evidence is *needed* by the police for sealing crucial joints of a preferred conspiracy theory.

This perspective assumes obviously that the police is capable of massive fabrication to meet its own ends, rather than serving the law. It is unlikely that the courts of law will routinely adopt this alternative perspective, unless specifically asked to do so. The courts may – and often do – reprimand investigating agencies for shoddy work, not adhering strictly to the law, minor fabrications etc. But, *other things being equal*, they are not likely to adopt the alternative perspective to question the entire functioning of an agency in a particular case. The investigative agencies, even under nomal circumstances, are themselves viewed as arms of the law; hence, the police and the courts form a natural mutuality.[9] The mutuality is likely to tighten in *abnormal* circumstances such as terrorism and national security. The entire burden in these circumstances is then on the defence to show that other things are not equal. In case of large-scale fabrication in abnormal circumstances, the task is nearly impossible given heightened mutuality, and the vast powers of the police over instruments of intimidation and repression. This is where a commission of inquiry takes precedence over a court of law.

Returning to the incredible features of the examples discussed above, suppose that a group of amateurs carried out the attack (at whose instance we do not know); that is, suppose that five unidentified and deranged young persons, inspired by sundry films, were out on a dark adventure for instant fame and a large sum of ransom money. It will then be false that JeM and LeT were behind the attack, notwithstanding Afzal's confessional statement. However, the police needed this part of Afzal's statement to portray the attack as a familiar international terrorist operation. More importantly, from the police point of view, the ascription of the attack to JeM and LeT via Afzal's confession *closes the case around Afzal.*

Again, suppose that the terrorists never made those phone-calls to Afzal regarding the VVIPs; that is, suppose either that the relevant call-records produced by the police are false or that the evidence linking Afzal to the mobile no. 98114-89429 is false or both. Then the incredibility of the content of those calls disappears simply because these calls wouldn't have been made. However, the police needed this evidence to link Afzal and, in turn, Shaukat directly to the attack itself, rather than depending wholly on questionable witnesses and confessional statements.

Incidentally, PUDR questioned the call-records of two calls that might be viewed as relevant for their timing for the issue in hand. PUDR observed that "the Call Detail Record (CDR) shows that at 11.19.14 am on December 13, two calls were made simultaneously from the same calling number 89429 (Afzal's) to the same called number 73506 (Shaukat's) but were made on handsets with different IMEI numbers. The same phenomenon was repeated at 11.32.40 the same day. The IMEI number is a unique number each cellular handset has and which is transmitted each time the phone is operated. It is therefore impossible for this phenomenon to occur unless the Call Detail Records have been doctored" (Annexures 12, p. 283). In a later report published after the High Court judgment, PUDR maintained the observation

(Annexure 17, p. 362). Are these the two calls Afzal supposedly made to Shaukat regarding the presence of VVIPs in Parliament?

Finally, suppose it is false that Afzal and Shaukat were *conspirators* fleeing from the area of the crime. Then it is perfectly intelligible that they made a routine trip between the Azadpur and the Srinagar wholesale markets as part of their regular fruit-trade (supposing of course that they made the trip together or individually at all). This also explains the phone call: husband calling wife after reaching another city. We emphasize once again that the argument that follows is entirely conditional: we interpret the call as produced by the police *assuming* its veracity. As we will see, there is much evidence to suggest that the entire call-record is fake; in fact, there are reasons to believe that the mobile phone, including the said SIM card, was planted in Afsan's hand.

Turning to the content of the call, unknown to Shaukat, Afsan was already in custody; hence, she was compelled to say things which in turn were construed as knowledge of conspiracy. Let me explain. We will see that the time of Afsan's arrest is in dispute ('Arrest memos' below). According to the police, Afsan was arrested on 15 December morning at Geelani's instance (Annexure 1, p. 119). According to Afsan, corroborated by Geelani's wife, she was in fact arrested around 6.00 P.M. on the 14th itself (Annexure 7). Thus, she could have received the call while in custody. Interestingly, the prosecution itself cited the following part of Afsan's statement u/s 313 Cr.P.C. to assert that she received the phone call from her husband: "It is correct. I enquired as to what has been brought in truck. *I talked to him in police custody*" (Annexure 16, para 248 (c), emphasis added).[10]

No wonder she was scared and she wanted to save her husband by "talking between the lines."[11] *Ignorant of all this*, Shaukat didn't quite get the message, and wanted her to call back later in the night. Notice that this interpretation of the conversation between Shaukat and Afsan not only removes the concerned incredibility, it in fact lends additional weight to (a) Shaukat's innocence, and (b) Afsan's arrest on the 14th itself. In fact, *it suggests Afzal's innocence as well* since Shaukat was hardly likely to accompany Afzal innocently if Afzal was escaping from the crime.

Furthermore, there is another feature of the call that could indicate Afzal's innocence. Near the end of the call, Afsan asked, "Reached safely?" to which Shaukat replied, "Yes Yes." Then Afsan asked, "And Chotu?" to which again Shaukat replied "Yes Yes" (Annexure 16, para 341). "Chotu" happens to be Afzal's byname. Now, if Afzal and Shaukat were travelling *together* in the truck, Afsan's query sounds pointless; it makes sense if they were travelling separately. In his statement u/s 313 Cr.P.C., Afzal stated that he left his apartment in Delhi on 12.12.2001 with some bags after handing over the keys to the landlady, and telling her that he would bring his family after Id (Annexure 5, p. 168-69). In his statement, he also said that he went to Srinagar alone by bus. A natural inference is that he left for Srinagar on 12.12.2001 itself, i.e., *the day before the attack.* Since he was supposed to have reached Srinagar already by himself, Afsan's separate query as to whether Chotu had (also) reached safely makes sense.

Recall that Mohammad Afzal – in fact, the confession extracted from him – was central to the prosecution story. Once the police was able to explain how they reached him, the rest of the theory fell in place by the sheer weight of a single testimony. In order to reach Afzal, therefore, *beginning* with the regular mobile-holder Geelani who allegedly took them to Afsan, the police was compelled to construe an otherwise innocuous trip as principal conspirators escaping from the area of crime. In other words, what was needed had to be superimposed on what actually transpired. Under the perspective in hand, a series of falsities thus ensued — calls from terrorists to Afzal, Geelani's arrest, Afsan's arrest, interpretation of the phone-call, Afzal and Shaukat's arrests, recovery of material including the mobile, etc. — to protect the original falsity that Afzal and Shaukat were conspirators, rather than regular fruit-traders. We return to this ('Arrest memos' below).

The massive conflict between the incredible police story and the credible alternative perspective – when read with the stringent criticism of every aspect of the trial by eminent lawyers and PUDR – gives rise to the new apprehension that the prosecution story is not only likely to be partly false, but false in crucial respects.

Acquittal of Geelani

The deep problems with the character and quality of evidence produced by the prosecution in the Parliament attack case was officially illustrated in the trial of S.A.R. Geelani, the lecturer in Arabic in Delhi University. On 29 October, 2003, the Indian judicial system added a feather to its cap when the Hon'ble High Court *acquitted Geelani of all charges*. The Special Court had earlier found him guilty of "conspiracy to attack the parliament, wage war against the government of India, murder and grievous hurt," and had awarded him two death sentences among other punishments. In the trial, the prosecution produced three crucial pieces of evidence against Geelani.

Confession of co-accused: The first piece concerned the confessions of the co-accused Afzal and Shaukat both of whom implicated Geelani, as noted; Shaukat in fact implicated his wife, pregnant with their first child. However, in contrast to the earlier anti-terrorist legislation TADA, confession of an accused is not admissible against the co-accused in POTA (Annexure 16, paras 376, 377). Thus the High Court set the evidence aside (Annexure 16, para 411). Yet, despite the well-known provision of POTA, both the police and the prosecution used the confessions of Afzal and Shaukat against Geelani.

It is interesting that the Special Court judge used the confessions against Geelani if only "to lend assurance to other circumstantial evidence." For example, he held that even though whether Geelani attended some meetings with the terrorists the night before the attack "cannot be inferred" from the confessional statements, the statements apparently "lend assurance" to a phone-call he had allegedly made around that time showing that "Geelani was very much alive to the preparations going on for attack" (Annexure 11, para 230). In effect, disputes about the content and veracity of alleged phone-calls (see below) was settled against the accused by drawing on the confessional statements of co-accused.

Conversation with half-brother: The second piece concerned a telephonic conversation in Kashmiri, which the police intercepted, between Geelani and his half-brother in Kashmir in the afternoon of 14 December 2001. The handling of this piece of evidence gives a telling indication of how the trial was conducted in the Special Court; hence, we will study this evidence in some detail. According to the transcript of this conversation produced by the prosecution, the half-brother had asked, "What have you done in Delhi?", to which Geelani had allegedly replied, "This was necessary." According to the prosecution, this conversation revealed Geelani's involvement in the attack.

The defence raised a variety of objections. The police version was based on a verbal translation into Hindusthani done by Rashid, a fifth class pass Kashmiri fruit-seller, which was then written down by a policeman; the transcript of the original Kashmiri conversation was never submitted. These facts need to be kept in mind in what follows.

In any case, there were serious problems with the quality of the tape: the expert witness produced by the prosecution observed that the "voice was inaudible due to high interfering background noise"; the High Court, who called for the original tape, remarked that "the voice was so inaudible that we could not make head or tail of the conversation" (Annexure 16, para 346). Rashid listened to the tape 2-3 times in an ordinary cassette player inside a noisy police station. Significantly, Rashid insisted that there were no English words in the conversation.

The defence produced two expert witnesses: Sanjay Kak, a Kashmiri and a film-maker and, thus, an audio-visual expert; Sampat Prakash, a noted trade union leader in Kashmir, part of his job is to transcribe speeches and writings back and forth between Kashmiri and other languages. The defence witnesses had to listen to the tape very carefully for nearly a dozen times to ascertain its content. According to these witnesses, the Kashmiri equivalent of "This was necessary" does not occur in the original tape at all, but the English words "syllabus and prospectus" clearly do. According to the transcript produced by the two defence witnesses, the part of the conversation mentioned above ran as follows.

Caller (brother): What has happened?
Receiver (Geelani): What, in Delhi?
Caller: What has happened in Delhi?
Receiver: Ha! Ha! Ha! (laughing)

As the defence explained the whole conversation, Geelani's half-brother had called because he wanted Geelani to send some syllabus and prospectus for medical entrance examinations in Delhi. During the call, the stated portion of the conversation took place because the brother had heard of a mild rift between Geelani and his wife regarding their visit to Kashmir for Id (Annexure 4). Geelani's wife testified in court that, since Geelani had refused to go as he did not have holidays, she had complained over phone to her mother-in-law (Annexure 7). Geelani avoided a discussion of a personal issue with his brother, much younger than him, by simply laughing the matter away (Annexures 12, 13, 14). The half-brother wouldn't have imagined that his mild curiosity would lead to death sentences for his elder brother.

The Special Court judge thought otherwise. First, he admitted the credibility of the fruit-seller since Kabir, Tulsidas and others were famous literary figures without being formally educated. In fact, he held that it is a graduate or a post-graduate, "who after acquiring knowledge of English starts forgetting his mother tongue and can speak only in Hinglish, Chinglish or Kashinglish" (Annexure 11, para 204). Second, he rejected the contention of the expert witnesses produced by the defence that the Kashmiri equivalent of "What has happened in Delhi?" could be a reference to anything, including a quarrel between Geelani and his wife over the cancellation of the trip to Srinagar for Id. Recall that the testimony of Geelani's wife to the effect that she had a quarrel with her husband gave a natural interpretation to the conversation between Geelani and his half-brother (Annexure 7). Without giving any reasons, the judge held that "She is not a trustworthy witness at all and her testimony cannot be relied" (Annexure 11, para 237).

Instead, according to the learned judge, the query "What has happened in Delhi?", "only relates to the incident in Delhi." He even brought in his personal knowledge in this regard: "This court had no knowledge of Kashmiri language and had to take some lessons in Kashmiri language" (Annexure 11, para 202). Third, he viewed both the defence witnesses as "interested witnesses." Sanjay Kak did not qualify because he is a member of the "All India Defence Committee for fair trial of SAR Gilani;" Sampat Prakash failed to qualify since he was "known to one Mr. Balraj Puri," a Convenor of Peoples Union for Civil Liberties (Annexure 11, 202). Thus, a membership or any other connection with civil rights organizations committed to defend the rights of accused persons disqualifies a person from being a (disinterested) witness.

Nandita Haksar explains the issue: "None of these people are 'interested' witnesses as ordinarily understood in criminal law. They have an impeccable reputation for integrity and patriotism. They are not related to the accused," and Kak and Prakash did not know Geelani personally; in fact, Kak and Prakash did not even know each other before the case. "They are textbook disinterested witnesses. The definition of a disinterested witness is: Impartial, fair-minded; unbiased. A disinterested witness is one 'who has no personal interest in the case being tried or the matter at issue and is legally competent to give testimony'" (Annexure 14, p. 330). Both Sanjay Kak and Sampat Prakash eminently qualify under these guidelines.

The High Court deliberated on the said conversation as follows. First, "the prosecution witness, Rashid, who prepared a transcript of the tape is fifth class pass and it was not his profession to prepare transcript of taped conversation. The possibility of his being in error cannot be ruled out. Benefit of doubt must go to the defence" (Annexure 16, para 346). Second, regarding the disputed portion of the conversation cited above, the judges held: "This part of the talk is undoubtedly in colloquial style. The conclusion drawn by the prosecution can hardly be contended, much less accepted" (Annexure 16, para 348).

Third, and most important, "even assuming the prosecution version to be correct, [we had] come to the conclusion that there was nothing which could incriminate Gilani as far as the conversation is concerned" (Annexure 16, para 408). Suppose for the sake of argument that Geelani did utter "This was necessary" and it related to the Parliament attack. But for this utterance to imply that Geelani *participated* in the attack, the knowledge of Geelani's participation has to be ascribed to his half-brother for him to ask the *relevant* question, which in turn implicates the half-brother as well. However, it was never the prosecution's case that the half-brother was also involved; hence, no inference about Geelani's participation in the attack can be made. For this reason, we are refraining from reproducing the three versions of the said conversation.

The Special judge, however, not only held that "This conversation confirmed the involvement of the accused in the conspiracy," he did not limit his observation to the Parliament attack case since, according to the learned judge, Geelani "considered that such kind of attacks were necessary from time to time" (Annexure 11, para 237).

Acquaintance with co-accused: The third piece of evidence concerned some telephonic conversation between Geelani, Afzal and Shaukat during the presumed period of conspiracy. Geelani never denied his acquaintance with Afzal and Shaukat since they all came from the Baramulla district of Kashmir, and were fellow students at Delhi University. Geelani had conducted the 'nikah,' the Muslim marriage ceremony, between Shaukat and Afsan. This explains why Geelani and Shaukat might have called each other first once they acquired their phones (Annexure 16, para 405).

Further, the period under consideration was also the period of Ramzan when Muslims get in touch with each other to plan religious programmes. Thus, if the said midnight call did take place, there could be a perfectly legitimate explanation for it: it was the night of Shab-e-Kadr when Muslims call on each other to pray for their well-being. The judges observed that mere acquaintance, even during this period, does not prove complicity in the conspiracy (Annexure 16, para 405). Therefore, with respect to this "only piece of evidence" against Geelani, the Hon'ble judges contended that "this circumstance ... do not even remotely, far less definitely and unerringly, point towards the guilt of the accused" (Annexure 16, para 412).

Each piece of evidence brought against Geelani by the prosecution was thus summarily dismissed by the High Court. In this connection, it is tempting indeed to recall the words of Ram Jethmalani: "This is a case of no evidence," "the evidence discloses total non application of mind and an unforgivable frivolity of attitude." The 'frivolity of attitude' was further illustrated in what the Special judge thought of Geelani.

Role of Geelani: It is important to recall that according to the police and the obliging media, Geelani was thought to be the local mastermind, the intellectual leader of the conspiracy ('Role of the media' above). Although *this charge was not specifically mentioned in the chargesheet or by the prosecution*, the Special judge reached a similar view of Geelani. Interestingly, as noted, this 'mastermind' image of Geelani was also portrayed at length in the film *December 13* telecast by Zee TV three days before the judgment was announced. The learned judge seemed to have developed this view in two broad steps.

He argued first, essentially on the basis of an ill-written 'love letter,' that the deceased terrorists were "hardly educated" (Annexure 11, para 42).[12] Then the judge referred to a "very neatly prepared" note found with the deceased terrorists that gave the topography of Parliament. This suggested to him that the terrorists were getting "active help" from the other co-accused, and Geelani was "the most educated among them" (Annexure 11, para 238). Also, according to the learned judge, "it is a matter of common knowledge that terrorists are able to hire and convince even best brains also for jehad" (Annexure 11, para 239). So a lecturer of Arabic and scholar of Urdu poetry was "hired" to prepare the topography of Parliament "very neatly."

Second, he furnished his own account of the phone-call allegedly made by Geelani "on the night intervening 12th and 13th Dec.01": "so he made this call ... to know the final result of the meeting, as to whether the next date is the target date or not," even though "this call has not been explained by accused Geelani" (Annexure 11, para 230). How could Geelani "explain" a call when he was never told its content? Yet, the judge somehow knew why Geelani made that call! Having thus established Geelani's active role in the conspiracy, the judge offered his own unsupported explanation of why Geelani refused to visit Kashmir: "It seems that the programme of going to Eid was cancelled by accused Gilani not because of paucity of holidays but because he was hopeful that the five terrorists would succeed in capturing parliament and he had envisaged a role for himself thereafter" (Annexure 11, para 236). That is why perhaps Geelani was so eager to learn about the outcome of the decisive meeting: "he had envisaged a role for himself thereafter."

With his outright acquittal, not on technical grounds, but on sheer lack of evidence, a hole appears in the case insofar as Geelani's role in the conspiracy – as ascribed to him by the Special judge – is concerned.

Arrest Memos

Notwithstanding the views of the Special judge and the media on Geelani's role, the fact remains that neither the chargesheet nor the prosecution assigned any specific role(s) to Geelani in the conspiracy to attack Parliament; the same holds for Afsan Guru. In that sense, the acquittals of Geelani and Afsan by the High Court did not make any substantive difference to the conspiracy theory advanced by the prosecution. Moreover, the evidence discussed so far in connection with the Geelani trial in the preceding section did not give rise to any momentous concern about concoction and fabrication of evidence,[13] although the study of that trial did show the prosecution and the judge in poor light.

No doubt, the conduct of the Geelani trial is enough ground for skepticism about the trials of Afzal and Shaukat as well. Since the police, the prosecution and the Special Court have been horribly wrong in one part of the case, why should we now believe that they have been vindicated for the other parts? Nonetheless, the skepticism needs to be supported with more direct empirical argumentation.

Significantly, the trial of Geelani also brought out at least one direct instance of fabrication of crucial evidence by the investigating agency that has a large bearing on the conspiracy theory. According to the Hon'ble judges of the High Court themselves, "a very disturbing feature pertaining to the arrest of the accused persons has been noted by us" (Annexure 16, para 250, 255). They observed that "the prosecution stands discredited qua the time of arrest of accused S.A.R. Geelani and accused Afsan Guru" (Annexure 16, para 251).

The issue is this. According to the prosecution, Geelani was arrested first on 15 December 2001 at about 10 A.M., Afsan Guru was subsequently arrested at about 10.45 A.M., and Afzal and Shaukat were arrested at Srinagar at 11.30 A.M. on the same day. Thus, as noted earlier, the police finally reached Afzal through this sequence of arrests beginning with Geelani, whom the police could trace first because he held a registered mobile phone. Obviously, the sequence had a bearing on how the police came to learn of the conspiracy. Each of these arrests were vigorously contested by the defence.

It is a mandatory requirement that an arrest memo is prepared upon the arrest of a person. The memo needs to be signed by a public witness or a near relative and attested by the arrestee. As PUDR documented in detail, the requirement was violated for *each* of the arrests (Annexure 12, p. 272-73):

— In the case of Afzal and Shaukat's arrest in Srinagar, it is indeed curious that the J&K police chose not to arrest them at the Parampura fruit mandi, where they were first located by the police, and where plenty of witnesses would be available. They were arrested later from an area where there were no public witnesses.

— In other cases viz. Gilani and Afsan, it is also quite surprising that the police did not find witnesses, even when the locality where the two lived is densely populated and the houses were inhabited by other tenants as well.

— Curiously, neither of the two sub-inspectors who live in the same building as Shaukat and Afsan were called during the arrests or search of premises or to identify anyone suspected to be part of the conspiracy. Moreover, Geelani's house was not even searched, which is odd, for someone suspected of participating in this kind of conspiracy.

In Geelani's case, the defence counsel Ram Jethmalani pointed out that the arrest memo for Geelani was not produced (Annexure 16, para 247(c)). According to Geelani's statement u/s 313 Cr.P.C., he was arrested on the afternoon of 14.12.2001 after being dragged out of a bus near Khalsa College on the Mall Road in North Delhi (Annexure 4). Subsequently, he was taken to an undisclosed location and tortured; later he was made to sign on blank papers. This was corroborated by Geelani's wife, Arifa, who testified that she, alongwith her two children and her brother, were also picked up by the police in the evening of 14.12.2001. In the police station, Arifa saw her husband with injuries showing torture. She also stated that Geelani's brother, Bismillah, was also in custody by that evening and was forced to sign papers (Annexure 7).

The High Court judges note that, after they "perused the case diaries," they found that the arrest memos of Geelani, Afzal and Shaukat were attested by Bismillah since "Mohd. Afzal's and

Shaukat's arrest memos have been prepared at Delhi" after they were picked up by the J&K police in Srinagar on 15.12.2001 and brought back to Delhi by the Delhi police. Thus, the witness to the arrests was himself in "illegal confinement" when he was forced to "sign papers" (Annexure 16, para 251).

Another fact that seems to support Geelani's arrest on 14.12.2001 is that Geelani's mobile phone was found switched off since 1.03 P.M. of that day. A natural explanation is that the phone was with the police. However, the Special judge held that "the accused had smelled about the surveillance and taken care not to make any call" (Annexure 11, para 79). If Geelani was guilty, we would expect him to switch off his phone as soon as he knew on 13.12.2001 itself that the attack had failed and active mobiles and phone numbers had been seized from the terrorists. Given his "best brain", why should he wait for over a day until he "smelled about the surveillance?" Taking all of Geelani's statement, Geelani's wife's statement, Afsan's statement, Bismillah's illegal confinement, and the switched off mobile, two facts seem to stand out: (a) Geelani was illegally arrested on 14.12.2001; (b) his arrest memo for 15.12.2001 was fabricated.

As noted earlier, Afsan also stated that she was arrested on 14.12.2001 at about 6.00 in the evening. This was not only corroborated by Arifa who saw Afsan in the police car in which Arifa and her children were taken away on 14.12.2001 (Annexure 7), her presence in custody on 14.12.2001 lends a natural interpretation to the telephonic conversation with her husband, as we saw ('Incredible features' above). It follows that the police version of Afsan's arrest was false as well, as noted by both the Special Court and the High Court.

The facts around the arrests of Afzal and Shaukat are more complicated. The defence pointed out that the Delhi police's version of their arrests at Srinagar at about 11.30 A.M. on 15.12.2001, *after securing information from Afsan at 10.45 A.M. about their location*, must be false. This is because, according to the J&K police, they received information from Delhi police at about 5.45 in the morning of 15.12.2002; thereafter, the truck was located at about 8.00 A.M., and Afzal and Shaukat were arrested at about 11.00 A.M (Annexure 12, p. 275). In other words, it is false either that the truck was located upon securing information from Afsan or that Afsan was reached only at about 10.30 A.M. at Geelani's instance.

However, the preferred sequence can still be resurrected by admitting that Geelani was arrested first on 14.12.2001 afternoon; Afsan was arrested next the same evening at the instance of Geelani; Afzal and Shaukat were arrested last when crucial recoveries (the laptop, Rupees Ten lacs, mobile phone, etc.) were made. This seems to be the prosecution's revised position that retains the sequence of arrests while changing their timings (Annexure 16, para 248). The are several problems with this position.

First, it is unclear as to how the police reached Geelani in the first place. As Basharat Peer reports, "Geelani's lawyer pointed out that the phone records" from AIRTEL "cited by the police" that allegedly enabled them to locate Geelani "were dated December 17, 2001. It left many wondering how the police could arrest the accused teacher two days before it got the phone records that "led" them to him. The prosecution had no explanation to offer" (Annexure 13, p. 310). However, as the PUDR complained, the High Court judges gave the benefit of doubt to the prosecution by ruling that the "date of 17.12.2001 on the Air Tel letter was a typographical error" (Annexure 17, p. 359). We will see later ('A Surrendred militant') that this AIRTEL letter also contradicted the official claim that POTO was introduced in the case only on 19.12.01, since the letter dated 17.12.01 cited POTO clauses in reference (see p.86). The suggestion that the date was a typographical error does not explain both the points simultaneously. If the letter was actually written after 19.12.01, it saves the POTO issue, but then the arrest issue gets even murkier, and vice-versa.

Second, it is questionable how the police reached Afsan. PUDR states: "Gilani's disclosure memo – the first statement given by an accused when arrested – ... makes no mention of any mobile phones let alone the identification of their owners. He reiterated the same in his statement under 313 Cr.P.C (the accused's response to questions put by the court). Gilani also denied having led the police to Shaukat's house, he has also rejected the prosecution's claims that when confronted by the evidence of certain calls on his cell phone, he told the police that 9811489429 belonged to Afzal and 9811573506 belonged to Shaukat. Significantly, the disclosure statement bears out the above since there is no reference to any mobile phone or their alleged owners" (Annexure 12, p. 275-6).

This part of Geelani's disclosure appears to be corroborated from a totally different direction. It seems incredible that the five terrorists carried only three mobile handsets among themselves although there were six SIM cards available, four of them with Mohammad alone! Could it be that there in fact were five handsets as expected, but two of them were not shown and 'placed' in the hands of Afsan and Afzal? If that is so, then Geelani could not have recognized the two numbers presented to him.

Third, if Afsan was already in custody between 6.00 P.M. and 7.00 P.M. on 14.12.2001, the police could not have reached her by dint of the call from Shaukat that came only at 8.15 that evening. As Afsan said, she received the call while in custody. The call, as we will presently see, and in fact the ownership of mobile 9811573506, as just noted, are suspect.

In any case, there are two further problems with this call. Since 9811573506 was operated on a cash card, that is, it was not a regular connection, it is hard to see how the police could locate Afsan or anyone else on the basis of the call alone. Moreover, there is a serious problem with the veracity of this call. As the High Court judges pointed out, there is a discrepancy between the duration of the call in the call-records and the duration of the conversation in the tape produced by the police. The expert witness to whom the taped conversation between Shaukat and Afsan was sent for analysis testified that the conversation itself lasted 74 seconds. According to the call records, the entire call lasted 49 seconds only. This led the judges to conclude that "this call has to be ignored" since the "discrepancy was not explained by the prosecution even during oral arguments at the bar" (Annexure 16, para 340).[14] Significantly, in the same tape, the expert was also sent extensive voice samples taken from the accused where the accused were made to utter expressions that were found in the transcript produced by the police. In any case, if Geelani did not disclose and if the call "has to be ignored," how did the police reach Afsan?

Fourth, the prosecution claimed that Afsan was arrested at about 10.45 A.M. on 15.12.2001. It claimed further that immediately the information about the truck was flashed to J&K police, who tracked the truck and arrested Afzal and Shaukat by 11.30. A.M. — in 45 minutes flat. If true, this ought to be counted as impressive police action. However, on the revised scenario, Afsan was arrested sometime during the evening of 14.12.2001. Yet, the J&K police was informed about the truck only at 5.30 A.M. — some ten hours later. What took them so long in a case like this? What was the source of their assurance, if any, that the alleged fugitives will stay on at the market for the whole night? Moreover, the J&K police took another six hours to arrest them ostensibly on the ground that they did not want to make the arrests in a market-place.

Fifth, Afzal and Shaukat also denied the prosecution's story of their arrests in their statements recorded u/s 313 of Cr.P.C. According to Afzal, he was arrested alone at a bus stop in Srinagar; Shaukat claimed that he was arrested near his house on the evening of 14 December 2001 (Annexures 5, 6). What do we make of these claims? As noted, their arrest memos were prepared in Delhi and the witness himself was in illegal confinement. Thus, the entire weight of the prosecution's case depends on the depositions by the J&K police, PW-61 and PW-62. As noted also, there is material contradiction between these depositions and the claim of the Delhi police regarding the time when the J&K police was alerted by the Delhi police. The prosecution explained the discrepancy as follows: "PW-61 and PW-62 were overzealous in their testimony and it was natural human conduct to take credit" (Annexure 16, para 248 (f)). If J&K police was "overzealous," and Delhi police was preparing illegal arrest memos, how do we ascertain when Afzal and Shaukat were arrested?

With little to go by, we can only conjecture. We noted Afzal's claim in his statement u/s 313 that he traveled alone to Srinagar, perhaps leaving Delhi on 12.12.2001. Suppose he was visiting Kashmir on his own errand as an agent of medical equipment, and to bring his family to Delhi after Id. Once Shaukat reached Srinagar Mandi with his load of bananas (Annexure 6, p. 193), he could have inquired about Afzal either directly from Afzal or from some common acquaintance. This gave a natural explanation of Afsan's query about Chotu, thereby raising the credibility of Afzal's statement 313. In this statement, he also said that he was picked up by J&K police alone from a bus stop from where he was planning to go to Baramulla to meet his family. Given that Afzal and Shaukat had *separate* errands in Kashmir, this statement sounds credible. Following this line of conjecture, Shaukat was also arrested alone perhaps with his truck somewhere in Srinagar. Once they were separately arrested, they were brought to the police station, and the rest of the story followed.

The conjecture is somewhat obfuscated by the fact that in his statement u/s 313, Shaukat denied that he went to Srinagar at all, and that he was picked up near his house in Delhi in the evening of 14.12.2001 at a time he did not remember (Annexure 6, p. 186). Now, this statement is false *if* it is true that he made that phone-call from Srinagar, on 14.12.2001.[15] Supposing it to be false, the senior counsel Shanti Bhusan explained it as follows: "It is well known that even an innocent accused person is many a time inclined to deny facts which he thinks might create suspicion against him and such conduct has always been regarded as normal conduct even from an innocent person."[16] Thus, other things being equal, there is no immediate need to revise the conjecture proposed above.

Unless new evidence is brought up, the cumulative effect of the five problems with the prosecution's story of arrests does give the impression that four persons were picked up separately without any delineable sequence. In other words, if these arrests weren't made at random, they seem to be *pre-planned* rather than based on a chain of leading evidence — the "evidence" following after the decision to arrest them had already been made.

Two very disturbing consequences follow from the preceding line of thinking. An explanation of how the police reached Afzal – the central character in the conspiracy theory offered by the police – at the said bus stand becomes an enigma. Since Afzal's confessional statement under POTO serves as the only basis for the *planning part* of the prosecution's story (see 'Prosecution story' above), a plausible explanation of how the police reached him is a significant requirement for the sustenance of the prosecution's case. With doubts accumulating as above, it is no longer possible to take this part of the case for granted.

Also, notice that the line of thinking finds Afzal alone at the bus stand, and Shaukat alone with his truck. This separation of the truck from Afzal raises doubts as to the alleged seizures from the truck — the laptop, Rs. 10 lacs, and the mobile phone among other things. According to the police, as noted, the circumstance of these seizures coincides with the circumstance of the arrests of Afzal and Shaukat in the truck.

No doubt the arrest of a person and recoveries made from him are distinct facts (Annexure 16, para 255). But in this specific case, the two facts seem to be so intimately glued that the falsity in one respect raises doubts about the truth of the other. For example, is it credible that Afzal would leave Shaukat alone with all that incriminating material in his truck? Alternatively, is it credible that Afzal himself was carrying the laptop, audio video camera, CD adaptor, digital audio and video recorder, memory stick and instruction manuals alongwith 23 wads of currency amounting to Rupees 10 lacs on his person? Who was carrying what and how?[17]

These doubts are compounded by the fact that (a) the seizure memos were not attested by any public witness, (b) serious doubts remain as to whether the laptop computer was tampered with (Annexure 12, p. 288-9), (c) the SIM card of the mobile phone allegedly belonging to Afzal was never found. In addition, except for his confessional statement, there is no direct evidence that links Afzal with this crucial mobile number. In his statement 313 Afzal denied all these recoveries from him, including the recovery of the mobile (Annexure 5, p. 152).

Pursuing (c), the mystery of this mobile, PUDR pointed out that "The story of this significant telephone number gets even more curious, if one looks at the testimony of Kamal Kishore (PW 49) who claims to have sold a Motorola phone and SIM of 9811489429 to Afzal on 4.12.01. He had no record of any kind relating to the sale receipt to show what he had sold, if anything, to Afzal. The call records for the number, however, show that the phone had been in use since 6 November 2001! Which is to say that the card was sold a month after it came in to use! Since this number is the key link that implicated Afzal and through him the others, the contradiction between the prosecution witness's claimed date of sale, and the person it was sold to, and the date of activation raises a question about the credibility of this witness" (Annexure 12, p. 284-5). In turn, the evidence against Afzal regarding phone calls allegedly made from and received in this instrument, especially to and from the terrorists, stands discredited.

In any case, the Hon'ble judges note that the instrument allegedly recovered from Afzal was frequently in the hands of the terrorists themselves (Annexure 16, para 399/5). As a consequence, we can no longer trace the phone-calls made from this instrument, notably, the calls made and received from satellite phones in Kashmir, phones in Dubai, Pakistan, Germany, etc., to Afzal himself. Furthermore, as noted, it is incredible that, in a terrorist operation of this scale, only three of the five terrorists carried mobile handsets, although six SIM cards – four with Mohammad alone – were recovered from the site. In sum, (i) the mobile can not be definitively placed with Afzal, (ii) the mobile was frequently used by the terrorists, (iii) Afzal denied ownership of the mobile. Whose mobile was this?

'Procured' Witnesses

The preceding examination of the arrests and the related recoveries raise serious questions about the credibility of police witnesses in Delhi and in J&K. We also know that there are other serious problems with the prosecution's case: (1) there is an apprehension of foul-play in the conduct of the investigation, (2) much of the evidence makes crucial joints of the story incredible. What then remains of the prosecution's case except for the confessions?

The prosecution of course produced a series of independent evidence in the form of seizure memos supported by exhibits, pointing memos, records of phone calls, police witnesses, expert witnesses and other public witnesses, to prove the case. Although we did cast doubt already on much of the evidence concerning seizures, phone-calls, police witnesses, etc., we have no space and competence for discussing this body of evidence in full. Nonetheless, much of the credibility of independent evidence depends on the credibility of public witnesses who testified about the alleged hideouts, meetings, purchases and recoveries. Some indication of the general picture regarding the credibility of public witnesses may be reached by drawing inferences from an adverse comment on the police recorded in the High Court judgment.

The Hon'ble judges note the "disturbing feature" of trial by the media in which Mohd. Afzal was "brazenly paraded before the press" (Annexure 16, para 139). During the parade, Afzal confessed to his active participation in the conspiracy, but exonerated Geelani from any involvement, as noted. The whole thing was recorded on videotape. In full view of the assembled press, the investigating officer ACP Rajbir Singh castigated Afzal for absolving Geelani. Next day, as noted, Afzal implicated Geelani in the conspiracy. We have discussed the role of the media in this affair. In addition, it is important to note that not only was Afzal made to 'confess' before the media, the accused were shown repeatedly on television since their arrest, with the police proclaiming that they had solved the case.

But why did the police take this route? Was it "overzealousness," acts for "taking credit," or was there an attempt by the police, led by ACP Rajbir Singh, to influence the prosecution witnesses? The Hon'ble judges of the High Court observed as follows:

"Accused persons are exposed to public glare through T.V. and in case where Test Identification Parade or the accused person being identified by witnesses (as in the present case) arise, the case of the prosecution is vulnerable to be attacked on the ground of exposure of the accused persons to public glare, weakening the impact of the identification" (Annexure 16, para 139).

This is partly a technical issue on which we have no competence. However, sheer commonsense dictates that if an accused is presented repeatedly in the entire mainstream visual media as guilty, not only are the viewers likely to 'retain' the face in their memory, they will associate the face with the crime. PUDR, who had examined the issue in depth, observed, "when people have been described by the police as implicated, the natural psychological tendency is to then 'recognize' them as involved."

The problem is aggravated when "given the prevalent stereotypes about Islamic, especially Kashmiri terrorism, witnesses are very likely to be biased" (Annexure 17, p. 361). In this connection, it is important to recall the mass hysteria that ensued after the attack on Parliament. We discussed in detail the role of the media in fomenting this hysteria ('Role of the Media' above). As noted, India was nearly at war with Pakistan and POTA became the law of the land.

Given this prejudicial atmosphere, would it have been possible for hapless landlords and petty shopkeepers to withstand pressures, if any, brought against them by the police? PUDR observed: "While theoretically the witnesses should have no reason for falsely implicating the accused, no one can deny that the police in India wield tremendous power and the public – especially, shopkeepers – would feel it unwise to go against the police" (Annexure 17, p. 361). If you are a landlord and you are told that terrorists had been hiding in your premises, what options do you have except obey orders? If you are a petty shopkeeper selling bomb-making ingredients such as ammonium nitrate and aluminium powder to all and sundry, perhaps without proper trade documents, can you refuse to testify falsely if you are told that otherwise you may be charged with supplying incriminating material to terrorists?[18] How difficult would it be for the police to fabricate each of these links in the story?

If the police scrupulously maintained the required procedures for identification, some of the general problems noted above might have been addressed in part. For example, PUDR argued that "the depositions of the vendors make it clear that Afzal was brought to them for identification, and introduced as someone connected with the attack on Parliament. In other words, they were not called in to the Special Cell and asked to identify him on their own, which would have made the identification foolproof" (Annexure 12, p. 270-1). That is, instead of organizing the required Test Identification Parades, "The 15 witnesses who identified the accused were provided prior knowledge of the identity of the accused as those involved in the attack on the Parliament" (Annexure 12, p. 268). With this general picture in mind, we document some of the disturbing facts involving public witnesses recorded by PUDR (Annexure 12, p. 268-71).

1. SAR Gilani's landlord PW 39 Naresh Gulati ... identifies Afzal and Shaukat in court as persons who "used to visit the house of SAR Gilani." It is significant that this witness goes on to say that several other people including lecturers and students visited Geelani and that he "might have seen Afzal and Shaukat visiting Jalani [sic] 2-3 times during the period he stayed in my house" (i.e. almost eleven months).
2. We recall once again the testimony of Kamal Kishore (PW 49) who claims to have sold a Motorola phone and SIM card of 9811489429 to Afzal on 4.12.01. He had no record of any

kind relating to the sale receipt to show what he had sold, if anything, to Afzal. The call records for the number, however, show that the phone had been in use since 6 November 2001! Which is to say that the card was sold a month after it came in to use!

3. In his first statement to the police on the 16 December 2001 under 161 CrPC (the first statement by a witness to the police in which he or she is bound to tell the truth and which the police is bound to record truthfully), Mr. Malhotra (landlord at Gandhi Vihar) claimed simply that on 13th morning he saw five boys (not named) getting into a white ambassador and driving off. Seven months later in court, he claimed "On 13.12.01, Mohammad Afzal, Shaukat and four more persons had left the premises around 10 am."
4. Photos of the dead militants (with mutilated faces) were shown to two witnesses (PW 34, Subhash Chand Malhotra, landlord of the Gandhi Vihar house and PW 45, Tejpal Kharbanda, Shaukat and Afsan's landlord in Mukherjee Nagar). While showing of photographs of the dead is legitimate, the point is that in order to lend authenticity to the identification the witnesses must select the photographs from a pack and the prints must be clearly showing the face. There was, however, no attempt at identification here since only photographs of the deceased were shown to the witnesses. Thus only affirmation was demanded of the witnesses. But what is even more unusual is that the witnesses were then asked whether the persons found in the photos were seen in the company of the accused. When Tejpal Kharbanda (PW 45), Shaukat's landlord, was first shown photos of the dead men on the 17th, he 'recognizes' them but makes no mention of seeing them at Shaukat's house *two-three days prior* to Parliament attack. Yet nine months later, his memory seems to have improved to the

extent that he recalls them as having accompanied Afzal to Shaukat's house during those critical days before the attack.

5. Motorcycle salesman, Sushil Kumar (PW 29) identified Shaukat on 18.12.01. In his statement under Cr.P.C 161 that day, Sushil Kumar said that on the day Afzal and others came to the shop to purchase the motorcycle, Shaukat was standing at a distance. Eight months later, during his court deposition on 16.7.02, he identified Shaukat unambiguously as one of the three men who came to purchase the motorcycle. Sushil Kumar's identification of Afsan Guru in the Special Cell as one of the four persons who came to his shop to purchase the motorcycle does not hold ground since TIP procedure was not followed. Moreover, later in the court Sushil Kumar expressed inability in identifying Afsan as the woman among the four, stating that the woman was standing at some distance.

The list goes on: the defence argued that all public witnesses presented by the prosecution were "procured."

A Surrendered Militant

We have already cited extensively both from Afzal's confessional statement under POTA (Annexure 2) and his statement u/s 313 Cr.P.C. (Annexure 5). We saw that, in the absence of any independent evidence, the *planning part* of the prosecution's case depends entirely on this confession. We also saw that, in the absence of or the questionable character of evidence produced for some of the *operational part* as well, the prosecution depended ultimately on this confession. For example, the issues of the phone-calls made by the terrorists to Afzal before and during the attack, Afzal and Shaukat travelling together to Srinagar in the truck, their arrests and the attendant recoveries, and much else, were ultimately settled in favour of the prosecution by dint of Afzal's confession. Finally, we also saw that the confession and the statement 313 massively contradict each other. Thus, we need to examine these two documents closely with an eye towards their truth.

Consider first the credibility of the confessions. As noted, Afzal's confession enabled the police not only to nail him down, but also to fill all the blanks of an otherwise incomplete story; Shaukat's confession is essentially contained in Afzal's confession (Annexure 16, para 368). In his confession, Afzal told a full story of how he got acquainted with the terrorists, his meetings with Ghazi Baba and Tariq, his determination to help the cause of Jehad, his knowledge of what the terrorists were upto, the guidance from across the border, etc. Interestingly, although he did not take part in the attack itself, he was not only made privy to, he in fact remembered the exact number of arms and ammunitions brought by the terrorists from Kashmir in their holdall: 4 AK Rifles, 12 loaded magazines, 1 grenade launcher, 3 pistols with spare magazines, 15 hand grenades, 15 grenade shell, two packs of electronic detonators, two transreceivers and radio active detonation devices and explosives. These statements of the confession, *not proved by any independent evidence*, complete the chain of evidence for the prosecution.

It is important to note that the charges under POTA (then POTO) were officially introduced only on 19 December 2001, that is, six days after the event, and the confessions under POTO were recorded on 21 December 2001. "Officially" because the defence showed that the provisions of POTO were in use from the very beginning. For example, the AIRTEL letter of 17 December 2001 "responding to a police request for the call records, refers to Section 3/4/5/21/22 POTO. It is inconceivable that AirTel would make up these sections on their own" (Annexure 17, p. 358). Could it be that, although POTO was in *de facto* use, it could not be introduced *de jure* because most of the safeguards sanctioned under POTO were violated (Annexures 17)? Why then was POTO needed at all at a later date?

The police had already gathered most of the alleged facts of the case before 19 December. These included identification of the terrorists by Afzal in the morgue, disclosure of the hideouts by Afzal, seizure of chemicals, detonators etc. from these premises, pointing of the shops by Afzal from where the chemicals, Sujata mixer etc. have been bought, pointing of the agencies from where the attack vehicle and the motorcycle for recee were purchased, as well as the material on telephone conversations.

Moreover, displaying incredible loquacity, both Afzal and Shaukat had poured out everything they knew about the conspiracy in their disclosure statements immediately after their arrest. Also, experts had already been assigned the task of analyzing the chemicals seized from the premises and the scene of attack, and securing information from the laptop seized on 15 December 2001 when Afzal and Shaukat were allegedly arrested in Srinagar. In sum, the confessions themselves did not contain anything that was not already available to the police on independent investigation based on the earlier disclosures.

Why then were the confessions, allowed by POTO, needed? Could it be that the confessions provided the necessary link to complete the chain of evidence which was otherwise lacking at that stage from independent evidence alone? In fact, could it be that the confession was the only method available to the police to lend credibility to what was claimed to be independent evidence, as we saw in some cases above? In any case, there are several reasons for doubting the credibility of the confessions.

As the Hon'ble judges of the High Court note, confessions are also admissible under general law provided that they are recorded before a designated magistrate. Since Afzal and Shaukat allegedly expressed their willingness to confess to everything in their disclosures of 16 December, why wasn't general law used in the present case to rule out the charge of fabrication and involuntariness in the extraction of confessions repeatedly raised by the defence and by civil rights organizations? Specifically, why did the police *wait* for POTA to be introduced on 19 December and confessions under POTA recorded on 21 December? Could it be that the immensely significant chain of events detailed in the confession, which tell the *only* narrative of the attack on Parliament, and without which the case against the accused is less than complete, could not have been procured without the convenience of POTA that allows the recording of confessions before a police officer of a certain rank? In particular, could it be that the confession the police wanted to secure could not have passed the strict safeguards before a designated magistrate?

The possibility that the confessions were extracted under torture arises from another direction. The Deputy Commissioner of Police, Special Cell, Mr. Ashok Chand, who was empowered to record the confessions, gave a written order to his subordinate Assistant Commissioner of Police, Special Cell, Mr. Rajbir Singh to produce the accused before the DCP at 11.30 A.M. on 21 December 2001. As such, Mohammad Afzal, Shaukat Guru and SAR Geelani were produced at the appointed time. However, Geelani refused to make a confessional statement, and his statement to this effect was recorded by 11.55 A.M.

Then, instead of producing the next accused before the DCP for confession, they were taken away and brought back over three hours later when the recording of Shaukat's confession started at 3.30 P.M.; recording of Afzal's confession started at 7.10 P.M. A plausible explanation is that, after Geelani refused to confess, the other two accused were subjected to further torture so that they fell in line before the recordings were resumed.[19] As for the credibility of the DCP who recorded the confessions, Geelani says in his statement u/s 313 Cr.P.C. that he was tortured after his illegal arrest by the ACP Rajbir Singh in the presence of the DCP Ashok Chand (Annexure 4). In any case, as the head of the Special Cell, DCP Ashok Chand was obviously in the know of the case, and was familiar with the history of the accused. In effect, the investigating official also acted as a "judge" for recording the confessions of the accused brought before him by his colleague in office.

The PUDR reports (Annexures 12, 17) contain stringent criticisms of procedures that allow extraction of confessions under POTA: "It is in the Court's acceptance of the confessions made by Afzal and Shaukat that we see the challenge posed by POTA to the very concept of a fair trial. ... The gravest danger of POTA is that it gives free rein to police torture in order to extract suitable 'confessions'" (Annexure 17, p. 364). There is growing evidence that investigating agencies often use the provisions of POTA to fit fabricated evidence with confessions extracted under torture.[20] Why should the Delhi police be exempted from this charge given their proven record of concoction of evidence in this case itself? The defence also raised this issue repeatedly, but the courts chose to accept the confessions presumably because of the heightened mutuality discussed earlier ('Incredible features' above).

As discussed earlier ('Role of the media' above), the High Court judges noted a palpable discrepancy in the confession. The day before the confession, Afzal had said, in full view of the media, that S.A.R. Geelani was not a party to the conspiracy (Annexure 16, para 113). Yet, in his confession recorded the next day, Afzal held Geelani responsible, a palpably false statement in view of what transpired later in the proceedings. From this the defence justly inferred that the confession was made under duress. Was Afzal a free agent during those early turbulent days right after the attack when he was in police custody before *and* after the making of the confession? Could he afford to refuse the recording of his confession at that stage when he had already done the rounds with the police, allegedly incriminating himself in everything that the police wanted?

These queries are compounded by the fact, as repeatedly noted in the judgment, that Afzal is a surrendered militant (e.g., Annexure 16, para 368). A surrendered militant, especially in the context of terrorism in Kashmir, is a person who is likely to be compelled to do things against his will. Unfortunately, in the High Court judgment, we have not been told either about the circumstances of his surrender and the arrangements, if any, that he entered into with the security forces to buy his survival. Even then, at the very least, the confession of such a person ought to be viewed in a light different from that applicable to a 'normally' accused person. As noted, this aspect of the maker of the confession has not been looked into by the Hon'ble judges.

Be that as it may, the location of statements, concerning Afzal's militant past, in the judgments is most interesting. Both the Special and High Court judgments, as well as the chargesheet, record the fact that Afzal is a surrendered militant. Now this statement appears in Afzal's confession as well as in his statement u/s 313 Cr.P.C. As noted, this statement, unlike confession under POTA, is made by an accused before the court rather than before a police officer; also, it is made when an accused is in judicial custody, not in police custody.

It is interesting that the Special Court judgment also recorded the fact that "a surrendered terrorist has to mark his attendance with regular intervals at the STF, J&K" (Annexure 12, para 222). "STF, J&K" stands for Special Task Force, Jammu and Kashmir, a shadowy counter-insurgency outfit of the state. To our knowledge, this fact is stated *only* in Afzal's statement u/s 313 Cr.P.C. In the same paragraph, the judgment also used this statement to record the fact that Afzal called Shaukat from Kashmir to hire a room, although the judge failed to mention that in this statement Afzal wanted Shaukat to hire a room for *Afzal* so that he could bring his family to Delhi after Id. With these citations, therefore, the Special Court judgment lend credibility to the statement u/s 313 Cr.P.C. In fact, the Special Court cited this statement fairly frequently – and selectively, as in the above – whenever it suited his argument.

Furthermore, there are manifest instances of honesty and truthfulness in Afzal's statement 313. For example, Afzal did not shy away from admitting the possibly incriminating fact that he accompanied Mohammad when the latter purchased a second-hand Ambassador car. When his lawyer attempted to deny this fact during the trial, Afzal intervened to insist that he indeed accompanied Mohammad.

Pursuing the relevant paragraph of this statement then, we learn about the circumstances of Afzal's surrender in 1993 in detail. Afzal states:

- he was frequently asked by the STF to work for them
- he often paid large sums of money to the STF to avoid and/or escape detention; he was detained as late as in 2000
- he was asked to become a Special Police Officer, which is an euphemism for "Police Informer"
- he met one Tariq *in the STF camp*
- this Tariq was already working for the STF and he wanted Afzal to join the force as well
- Afzal was introduced to one Mohammad by Tariq *also in the STF camp*
- Tariq persuaded him to take Mohammad to Delhi from where Mohammad was planning to go abroad. But Afzal denied that he arranged any residence for Mohammad.

Recall that Afzal admitted to bringing one of the terrorists, Mohammad, to Delhi from Kashmir in his confession as well.

A number of disturbing consequences follow. First, Afzal was in close touch with the security agencies throughout the period 1993 to at least 2000. Second, three of the persons allegedly involved in the attack – Tariq, Afzal, Mohammad: *the mastermind, the link, the leader of the attack* – originated from the STF camp itself. Third, if the statement u/s 313 is true, the confession is false except for those few claims that occur in the statement as well. Recall that several statements of the confession were found to be incredible while many statements from the statement 313, that contradicted the relevant statements of the confession, added to credibility in the alternative perspective ('Incredible features' and 'Arrest memos' above).

In the rest of his statement 313, Afzal denied every aspect of his involvement in the conspiracy to which he had allegedly confessed earlier. For example, as noted, he stated that "*I had not identified any terrorist. Police told me the names of terrorists and forced me to identify.*" If Afzal is telling the truth, either the names of the terrorists announced to the nation are fictitious or the police knew the terrorists. Needless to say, Afzal also stated that the police made him sign the disclosure and the confession under torture. For example, he stated that the accused were not presented before the designated magistrate at all for the verification of the confessions; they were made to sit in the police van outside while the investigating officer went inside to get the seal of approval to the pre-written documents.

Let us recount again what the nation had been told exclusively in Afzal's voice: the names of five unidentified dead persons kept in the morgue, that they were Pak nationals, that they were members of JeM and LeT, that they came to Delhi for a 'fidayeen' attack under the command of one Ghazi Baba, that the plan was supervised by one public offender Tariq, that the five terrorists brought the huge cache of arms and ammunition for the said purpose — **the planning part.** *All this because Afzal says so.* There is not an iota of independent evidence supporting any of these crucial links of the narrative. Afzal denied everything in his statement 313.

Unfair Trial

In sum, it is difficult to resist the conclusion that almost every part of the prosecution's case is seriously flawed. Charges of fabrication (call-records) and concoction of documents (arrest memos), possible tampering with (laptop, tapes) and planting of physical evidence (laptop, Rs. ten lacs, mobiles), intimidation of witnesses (Bismillah, landlords, shopkeepers), forced extraction of disclosure and confessional statements (Afzal, Shaukat), and the like, seem to get progressively substantiated as we look deeper into the case. In the process, the rights of the accused were irrepairably harmed.

In addition, their rights were damaged in the conduct of the trial itself. We consider just two examples among many.[21] Mohammad Afzal's trial was especially vitiated because, although his case was the most complex, he never had proper legal representation at the Special Court. "In capital cases," Ram Jethmalani observed, "particularly those that arouse public prejudice and anger against the accused making it difficult for them to arrange for their own defence, it was the duty of the Court to provide adequate defence at State expense." Afzal in fact submitted a list of lawyers he wanted for his defence. "The Court instead appointed an 'amicus'. This is not known to our law and practice." Afzal expressed his dissatisfaction with his lawyer repeatedly. The amicus, Neeraj Bansal, did not even pay a visit to his client: "his presence and participation have caused confusion and prejudice vitiating the trial," Jethmalani complained.[22]

In a moving statement pleading for fair trial for her husband, Afzal's wife Ms. Tabassum says, "The court appointed a lawyer who never took instructions from Afzal, or cross examined the prosecution witnesses. That lawyer was communal and showed his hatred for my husband. When my husband told Judge Dhingra that he did not want that lawyer the judge ignored him. In fact my husband went totally undefended in the trial court. Whenever my husband wished to say something the judge would not hear him out and the judge showed his communal bias in open court." "I believe," Tabassum complains, "that no one has heard my husband's story."

The story Tabassum tells "is the story of many young Kashmiri couples. Our story represents the tragedy facing our people." "Like thousands of other youth," Afzal went to Pakistan for training and stayed there for a little while. However, "he was disillusioned by the differences between different groups and he did not support pro-Pakistani groups." "My husband wanted to return to normal life and with that intention he surrendered to the BSF." In 1997, Afzal started a small business of medicines and surgical instruments in Kashmir; in 1998, Afzal and Tabassum were married. Afzal was 28, Tabassum just 18. Soon they had a child whom they named "Ghalib."

However, "throughout the period that we lived in Kashmir the Indian security forces continuously harassed Afzal and told him to spy on people they suspected of being militants. One Major Ram Mohan Roy of 22 Rashtriya Rifles tortured Afzal and gave him electric shocks in his private parts." "Another time he was taken to the STF (State Task Force) camp Palhalan Pattan. Some days later they took him to the Humhama STF camp. In that camp the officers, DSP Vinay Gupta and DSP Darinder Singh demanded Rs one lakh. We are not a rich family and we had to sell everything, including the little gold I got on my marriage to save Afzal from the torture. Afzal was kept in freezing water and petrol was put into his anus. One officer Shanti Singh hanged my husband upside down for hours naked and in the cold. They gave electric shocks in his penis and he had to have treatment for days." "Afzal wanted to live quietly with his family but the STF would not allow him."

On Afzal's decision to move to Delhi, Tabassum states, "It was under these conditions that forced Afzal to leave his home, family and settle in Delhi. He struggled hard to earn a living and he had decided to bring me and our four-year old son, Ghalib, to Delhi. Like any other family we dreamed of living together peacefully and bringing up our children, giving them a good education and seeing them grow up to be good human beings. That dream was cut short when once again the STF got hold of my husband in Delhi. The STF told my husband to bring one man Mohammad to Delhi from Kashmir. He met Mohammad and one other man Tariq there at the STF camp. He did not know anything about the men and he had no idea why he was being asked to do the job" (Annexure 18).

Significantly, Tabassum's report substantiates Afzal's statement u/s 313 Cr.P.C. In that sense, Afzal's story had in fact been "told" on paper, but, as Tabassum states, "the court chose to believe half his statement about bringing Mohammad but not the bit that he was told to do so by the STF" (see Annexure 11, para 224). We saw that the statement 313 of the accused should have played a crucial role in the case in the sense that this provision of law enables the accused to display his mind with a high degree of voluntariness. Yet, these statements hardly played a role in the actual proceedings since the courts decided to rely mostly on the confessions which these statements refute. Speaking of Afzal, Nandita Haksar asked: "If he can be sentenced to death on three counts on the basis of his own confession, why can we not believe the other part of his story recorded in the court under section 313 of the Criminal Procedure Code?"[23]

In fact, senior counsel Ram Jethmalani pointed out that "the most vital safeguard for the accused is Section 313 of the Code." Yet, he said, "circumstances which ought to have been put to the accused were never put to him for his explanation and if necessary cross-examination of witnesses and leading of defence evidence."[24] "Instead," Jethmalani complained, "non-existing circumstances were put to him." "Principles of natural justice," he concluded, "have been thrown to the winds resulting in miscarriage of justice."[25]

Appeal for Parliamentary Inquiry

It is a source of great concern that a long series of doubts seems to naturally arise after a perusal of the prosecution's case. Until these grave doubts are addressed to the satisfaction of the nation, we do not yet know who attacked Parliament on that fateful day. Could it be that the real culprits are still at large? In fact, when these doubts are read with proven acts of fabrication of evidence on the part of the police, it is difficult to dispel the apprehension of an elaborate scheme to restrict the case exclusively to the four accused, with Mohd. Afzal as the main link.

The alleged terrorists died on the spot; their alleged mastermind in Kashmir, one Ghazi Baba, reportedly also died in a recent encounter, and the dead don't speak: where is Tariq? Was there a real Ghazi Baba at all with his "camp" deep in the mountains of Kashmir guarded by scores of heavily-armed militants, or was the terrifying image "constructed" only for the purpose of the case, to be dismantled when the purpose was served? Is there an attempt here to *close* the story around Afzal, a past militant, and thus a natural suspect?[26] If these conjectures are true, is it possible for the concerned officers of the investigating agency to come up with this extraordinary attempt on their own without directions from higher authorities?

The biggest problem with the Parliament attack case is that the simplest and the most familiar explanation of the event isn't likely to be true. *Any other explanation is fraught with immensely disturbing consequences for the functioning of the Indian state and, hence, for the health of Indian democracy.*

The simplest explanation of course is the prosecution story that some well-known international terrorist organization with known grouse against India planned a dramatic terrorist attack not only to boost its image, but also to cause severe damage to Indian democracy. To that end, they organized some local support, brought in arms and ammunition, and carried out the attack.

It can be argued that this story is essentially true even if it was accompanied by shoddy and callous investigation, prejudice against the accused, and compulsions of the climate. This argument *does not* exonerate the law enforcing system from further scrutiny, especially in view of the massive violation of rights of the accused. Even if the investigation and the trial were merely shoddy and callous, they were so at a scale that raises serious questions on the fairness of the justice system. Still, it will be immensely reassuring if this argument broadly holds. Does it hold?

As our analysis has brought out, our suspicion is that the prosecution's story is unlikely to hold in major respects from what we currently know. What we saw did not seem to amount merely to "shoddy and callous" investigation. It gave the impression of an elaborate scheme of fabrication and concoction on the part of the investigating agency. To recall a few cases: *each* arrest memo was fabricated, *no* recoveries were attested by reliable public witnesses, *no* public witness was asked to identify the accused on the basis of proper methods of identification, *every* disclosure and confessional statement was likely to have been secured under torture. The only explanation of this display of chilling arrogance is that the investigating agency must have thought that it can get away with anything in the prejudicial atmosphere created largely by the State in the name of "war on terrorism." In fact, it did get away with awesome lies through two successive judicial proceedings.

To be explicit, once we set the prosecution story aside, it is difficult to escape the thought that the investigating agencies themselves planned and executed their own conspiracy at least for a part of the case. On one extreme, this could mean just that the investigating agencies took advantage of a genuine terrorist attack by falsely incriminating the accused to bolster their own image, and to close the case which they could not have otherwise solved from their resources. But, on the other extreme, reminiscent of the infamous *Reichstag Fire* in Nazi Germany,[27] it could also imply the stunning prospect of the state actually planning the attack itself. Virtually, an indefinite number of possibilities obtain in between. We just do not know.

In a recent interview, the eminent lawyer Shanti Bhusan complained that the government "pushed us to the brink of a nuclear war" following the attack on Parliament. However, "the police failed to crack the case" as "all the five militants died in the attack." So the police, Shanti Bhusan suggested, "framed people" in order "to create a conspiracy case." Later in the interview, Shanti Bhusan observed that "an inquiry commission is instituted when the government does not know the real truth of some incident, when there are different versions, and in order to get correct information."[28]

Since the "police failed to crack the case," we do not "know the real truth." In fact, Shanti Bhusan is suggesting that it seems most likely that the absence of "real truth" was attempted to be filled up with an imaginary conspiracy case. According to Shanti Bhusan's criterion, it follows that the Parliament attack case demands an inquiry commission on two counts:

(a) the law-enforcing system failed to ascertain the truth, and

(b) a false conspiracy theory was used instead to push the country to "the brink of a nuclear war."

The Parliament attack case, thus, cries out for a comprehensive inquiry. To our knowledge, there have been exactly two demands for inquiry into the attack, both far removed from the mainstream.[29] On December 17, 2001, that is four days after the attack, the Hurriyat Conference organized a public demonstration in Kashmir, protesting against the arrest of four Kashmiris and demanding a full-fledged inquiry.[30] More recently, after reviewing the High Court judgment on the Parliament attack case, the lawyer-activist Nandita Haksar has raised this demand eloquently in a little magazine:

> We must demand that the government table a full report on the facts relating to the attack on Parliament. We have a right to know who actually attacked our Parliament. Why have we not made this demand? Out of a sense of nationalism? Are matters of national security best left to the state, no matter what its character?[31]

The point to note is that Haksar, who has been closely associated with the Parliament attack case since the beginning, has reasons to believe, even after the High Court judgment in the case nearly two years later, that we do not know "who actually attacked our Parliament." Yet, as noted, this historical question basically remained unasked. As documented in this essay, except for a handful of individuals and human rights forums, the general response to the Parliament attack case illustrates massive failure of institutions in India committed to democratic and secular values of our Constitution: the media, the judiciary, the executive, the human rights commission, and the political parties. What accounts for this failure of probity on a national scale?

Haksar's phrase "a sense of nationalism" explains the phenomenon. For our purposes here, the phrase may be understood with the following example. It is well-known that the media in India gave full support to the US invasion of Afghanistan; television channels actually designed "war rooms" from where the daily bombings and other atrocities were gleefully covered. But this did not prevent democratic and anti-imperialist individuals and groups, including the parties of the left, from joining the rest of the world in impressive anti-war demonstrations, despite almost total blackout of these events by the media. Dozens of writer-activists simply shifted to alternative media to express their anger with the US, and their solidarity with the people of Afghanistan. Many authors protested against the abject violations of human rights in Afghanistan and in Guantanamo Bay. In fact, these anti-war protests continued well into the period in which all democratic voices fell silent when it came to the Parliament attack case.

The only explanation is that the US, after all, is a state distinct from ours; it is easy to condemn the US. So, we signed, demonstrated and marched in protest against US aggression on the rest of the world. We wrote and circulated papers on the lies about al-Queda connections and weapons of mass destruction. We examined the extraordinary facts unraveled in the Butler commission report on the war on Iraq, and the Ken commission report on 9/11, and criticized both for the failure to draw the unsavoury conclusions from these facts that stare in the face.[32] However, when a terrorist attack is perceived to be directed against "our nation," universal norms of dissent are forfeited in favour of concerns about "sovereignty" and "national security." As Haksar pointed out, we left "matters of national security" to the state, "no matter what its character" even when extraordinary facts stared in the face.

Under the circumstance, it is not surprising that the capitulation of liberal-democratic sections paved the way for the right-wing forces to disseminate a malignant version of "nationalism" virtually unopposed. It also enabled these forces to brand the handful of individuals, who stood up against the wall of silence, as terrorists and foreign collaborators. When the death sentences were announced by the Special Court in December, 2002, V.K. Malhotra, the spokesperson of the BJP, recommended punishment under POTA for those who had opposed the death sentence on the grounds that they were agents of Pakistan's spy agency, the Inter-Services Intelligence (Annexure 13, p. 313). When Ram Jethmalani agreed to defend Geelani in the High Court, Shiv Sena activists vandalised his office, burnt his effigy as a "traitor," and threatened him with "consequences" if he honoured his promise.

After the High Court acquitted S.A.R. Geelani and Afsan Guru from all charges, an editorial in a prominent newspaper stated: "In this context, the unconcealed glee with which some of this country's self-proclaimed champions of human rights have reacted to the acquittals leaves a foul taste in the mouth. One wonders what matters most to them, the security and the integrity of the country or the well-being of people accused of undermining both."[33] Notice that the editorial continued to accuse Geelani and Afsan Guru libelously of "undermining" the security and the integrity of the country after they were acquitted by the court.[34] No one, not even the left, made any public protest, not to speak of taking the newspaper to the courts.

Stupefied by the troubling issue of terrorism, erstwhile institutions of democracy allowed – perhaps even encouraged – the police and the related agencies of the state to play havoc with the system of justice, preparing the ground thus for further erosion of democracy, and the consequent growth of fascism and terrorism. The only civilized method of reversing this trend is to subject these institutions and agencies to a just critique. It "is beyond hypocritical," Arundhati Roy writes, to talk of "justice without unmasking the institutions and the systems that perpetrate injustice."[35] "We surrender both democracy and humanity," observes

John Pilger, "if we refuse to question and probe the hidden agendas and unaccountable secret power structures at the heart of 'democratic governments'."[36]

These disturbing concerns do not pertain to the Supreme Court where the Parliament attack case currently rests, as noted. Hence, the new government will do well to initiate the long-delayed inquiry into them. The inquiry is best conducted by a joint parliamentary committee for at least two reasons:

1. Since the attack concerned Indian Parliament itself, the highest forum of Indian democracy, it is fitting that Parliament examines the entire gamut of issues from its own resources. Parliamentary committees enjoy the maximum transparency, support and representation of the people of India.
2. The inquiry ought to cover every aspect of the functioning of each institution that was involved with the case: the media, the police, the executive and the judiciary – especially the functioning of investigating agencies, and Special Courts in POTA cases. Hence, for the sake of transparency, the inquiry *can not* be left in the hands of the "watchdogs" of these institutions such as the Human Rights Commission, Law Commission, Police Commission, and Press Council.

We mentioned earlier that, under the extreme right-wing government led by the BJP, the period between September 2001 and May 2004 was perhaps the darkest period in contemporary India in terms of erosion of democratic institutions and rights, assaults on the basic livelihood of people, and violent attacks on the minorities. Despite unconcealed support to this government by the Indian elite and the media, the people of India voted out this government in the general elections of May 2004. The vote was widely seen as a verdict for democracy, communal harmony and social justice.

In response to the will of the people, the new United Progressive Alliance government, in its Common Minimum Programme, has promised to "preserve, protect and promote social harmony and to enforce the law without fear or favour to deal with all obscurantist and fundamentalist elements who seek to disturb social amity and peace." It has also pledged to the people of this country "to provide a government that is corruption-free, transparent and accountable at all times, to provide an administration that is responsible and responsive at all times."[37] Specifically, the Union Home Minister, Mr. Shivraj Patil, has asserted in Parliament that the main tools of the UPA Government in dealing with terrorism would be dialogue, good governance, social justice, economic growth and the cooperation of the people.[38]

After the judgment of the Special Court, a committee of teachers of Delhi University warned that the Parliament attack case is a "test case for the Indian legal system and its ability to deliver justice. In fact, Indian democracy itself is on trial" (Annexure 15). The trial of democracy continues even after the High Court judgment. Whether the "trial" finally culminates in the delivery of justice, or leads to even further erosion of democracy, will depend on how the new government upholds its solemn pledges to the people of India.

Notes & References

1. Nandita Haksar and K. Sanjay Singh, "December 13," *Seminar 521*, January 2003, p. 121.
2. We are reminded of the boy in US who, in a bid to emulate the terrorist attack on 9-11, drove a single-engine plane into a building, and died in the process.

3. Written Submissions on behalf of S.A.R. Gilani, Murder Reference 1 of 2003, presented by Shri Ram Jethmalani, Senior Advocate.
4. Written Submissions on behalf of Shaukat Hussain Guru, In Murder Reference 1 of 2003 & Criminal Appeal 36 of 2003, presented by Shri Shanti Bhushan, Senior Advocate.
5. "Terrorists panicked, gave the game away," *Times News Network*, 17 December 2001.
6. "Jaish denies hand in attack on Parliament," *The Times of India*, 17 December 2001.
7. "Ex-ISI head accepts Jaish hand in Parliament attack", *Rediff.Com*, 6 March 2004.
8. On this crucial question, the media simply followed the police version, as with the rest of the case. For example, in "Kandahar gave Qaida a boost", *The Times of India*, 5 February 2004, the senior journalist Siddharth Varadrajan states, without citing any source, that the "December 13, 2001 attack on Parliament" was "the handiwork of the JeM."
9. See, for example, the citation from Supreme Court judgment 613, 2000 (vii) A.D. Government of NCT of Delhi Vs. Sunil in Annexure 16, para 259.
10. This statement does not amount to Afsan's admission of the phone-call. As the defence clarified later, she was mentioning her talking to her husband in person inside the custody.
11. Obviously, she wouldn't have been allowed by the police to report that she was in custody.
12. In fact, the "We hate India" sticker found at the scene of attack does not fare much better (Annexure 11, para 5). Why didn't the terrorists take Geelani's help in composing this momentous note for posterity?
13. With the possible exception of tampering with the tape with respect to the Kashmiri equivalent of "It was necessary," as noted.
14. However, the judges proceeded to discuss the conversation to show that, even if the conversation was valid, it did not implicate Afsan (Annexure 16, paras 341, 342, 419).
15. Also, Shaukat's signature was allegedly found on disclosure memos prepared by J&K police at Srinagar. Should we depend on these documents anymore? Recall that we did not concede the veracity of this call.
16. Written Submissions on behalf of Shaukat Hussain Guru, In Murder Reference 1 of 2003 & Criminal Appeal 36 of 2003, presented by Shri Shanti Bhushan, Senior Advocate, p. 46.
17. The seizure memo, listing items recovered from the personal search of Afzal, records the following: a pocket diary containing some phone num-

bers, a key, a wrist-watch, some negatives of photographs, an identity card, and Rupees 2500/-. Interestingly, the phone numbers and the key were not subjected to further investigation.

18. No doubt Ammonium Nitrate and Aluminium powder can be mixed in the right proportion with some other chemicals to produce high explosives. But individually these are harmless, common chemicals which can be purchased in any quantity from the open market without a permit, and without even a proper record of the transactions (Annexure 16, para 62). Aluminium powder is widely used in paints (Butani, *Dictionary of Science*, p. 13), while Ammonium Nitrate is the "most common nitrogenous component of artificial fertilizers" (*Encyclopedia Britannica, Micropedia* I, p. 319). These common uses of the said chemicals were also noted in the judgement of the Sessions Court (Annexure 11, paras 102, 106).
19. See my "Confessions were forced in the Dec. 13 Case", *South Asian Citizens Wire*, 17 October 2004.
20. Vijay Nagaraj, Amnesty International (India), in *Blurred Lines*, a film by Sujata Venkateswaran and Ruksh Chatterjee. Also, "Use of POTA against Dalit and Adivasi's in District Sonbhadra, U.P.", UP Agrarian Reform & Labour Rights Campaign Committee – both presented before People's Tribunal on POTA, New Delhi, 13 March 2004.
21. See Annexures 12, 14, 17 for more.
22. Written Submissions on behalf of S.A.R. Gilani, Murder Reference 1 of 2003, presented by Shri Ram Jethmalani, Senior Advocate.
23. Nandita Haksar, "The many faces of nationalism", *Seminar 533*, January 2004, p.101.
24. For example, once Afzal claimed that he left his flat in Delhi on 12.12.2001, he was never asked to detail his whereabouts during the period between his leaving the flat and getting arrested at a bus stop on 15.12.2001.
25. Written Submissions on behalf of S.A.R. Gilani, Murder Reference 1 of 2003, presented by Shri Ram Jethmalani, Senior Advocate.
26. On other hand, it is incredible that a renegade, with close links with the STF, would be trusted by terrorist organizations for such an important action. Tabassum states, "You will not perhaps realise that it is very difficult to live as a surrendered militant in Kashmir" (Annexure 18).
27. See Alan Bullock, *Hitler: A Study in Tyranny*, Pelican, 1962, p. 262-77.
28. *Tehelka: The People's Paper*, 16 October 2004, p. 21.
29. Most recently, the demand was also raised in my "Who attacked Parliament?", *Revolutionary Democracy*, Vol. X, No.2, September 2004.

30. *Rediff.com*, 17 December 2001.
31. Nandita Haksar, "The many faces of nationalism", *Seminar 533*, January 2004, p. 101.
32. John Pilger, "Iraq: the unthinkable becomes normal," *New Statesman*, 15 November 2004.
33. "Go on appeal", Editorial, *The Pioneer*, 31 October 2003.
34. The same newspaper had much else to say about "Human Rightswalas" that are essentially unprintable; see Chandan Mitra, "Go 'home', Geelani & friends", *The Pioneer*, 30 October 2003.
35. Arundhati Roy, "Peace", *Znet*, 7 November 2004.
36. John Pilger, "Iraq: the unthinkable becomes normal," *New Statesman*, 15 November 2004.
37. For the full text of the Common Minimum Programme, see *The Hindu*, 28 May, 2004.
38. *The Hindu*, 7 December 2004.

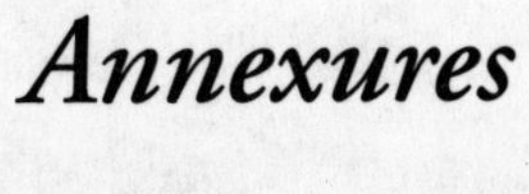

Annexures

ANNEXURE 1

Parliament Attack (Dec. 13, 2001)
The Charge Sheet

District New Delhi _____________________Charge Sheet No.____________________Date__________

Police Station______Parliament Street__________________FIR No.__417/2001___________________Date___13/12/2001

Name address and occupation of complainant or informant	Name and address of accused persons not sent up for trail, whether arrested or not arrested, including Absconders	Name and address of accused persons sent for trial		Property (including weapons) found with particulars of where, when and by whom found and whether forwarded to magistrate	Name and address of witnesses	Charge or information – Name and offence and circumstances connected with it, in concise detail, and under what section of the law charged. U/s 3/4/5/20/21/22 POTA 121/121A/122/124/120B/ 186/353/332/333/302/307 IPC, 3/4/5/6 Explosive Substances Act & 25/27 Arms Act.
		In Custody	On bail or recogni-zance			
1	2	3	4	5	6	7
SI Shyam Singh, Vice President Security, New Delhi.	1. Mohd. Masood Azhar –Pak National. 2. Ghazi Baba @ Abu Jehadi @ Saqlain-Pak National 3. Tariq Ahmed-Pak National 4. Mohammad, 5. Haider 6. Hamza 7. Raja & 8. Rana (Accused Serial No. 4 to 8 are deceased terrorists and all are Pak nationals).	1. Mohd. Afzal S/o Late Habibu-llah R/o Vill. Seer Jagir, PS Sopore, Distt. Baramullah, J&K. 2. Shaukat Hussain Guru		Memos attached	List Attached	Sir, The brief facts of the case are as under.- On 13.12.2001 at 11.45 AM, upon receiving the wireless message regarding firing in Parliament House, Inspr. G.L. Mehta, SHO/Pt. Street along with SI Rajender Singh, SI YR Dogra, SI Sanjeev Verma, HC Sukhbir No. 73/ND, Ct. Mohan 799/ ND, CT Rajesh 845/ND reached the spot i.e. Parliament House. On reaching Parliament House Inpr. G.L. Mehta got the Gate No.2 opened and he along with staff and senior officers, who had reached the spot, entered Parliament House premises and inspected the scene. There after he recorded the

1	2	3	4	5	6	7
	6. Hamza 7. Raja & 8. Rana (Accused Serial No. 4 to 8 are deceased terrorists and all are Pak nationals).	S/o Abdul Sattar Guru R/o Vill. Doabga, Sopore, Distt, Baramullah, J&K. At Present- 1021, Ist Floor Mukherjee Nagar, New Delhi. 3. Sayed Abdul Rehman Geelani S/o Sayed Abdul Wali Geelani R/o 535 2nd Floor, Mukherjee Nagar, New Delhi. 4. Navjot Sandhu @ Afshan Guru W/o Shaukat Hussain Guru R/o 1021, Ist Floor, Mukherjee Nagar, New Delhi.				statement of SI Shyam Singh No. D-3075, Vice President Security, Delhi Police, regarding the incident, in Hindi and the English version of the same is as under "I am posted as Sub Inspector in Delhi Police and I have been performing duties in Vice President House Security for last one year. Today i.e. 13.12.2001, I was performing my duties in the Pilot car of Vice President's Carcade from 8.00 AM. Today at about 10.25 AM the movement of Vice President took place for the Parliament House and the Carcade of Vice President reached the Parliament House at about 10.35 AM. After about 15 minutes, on

receiving orders from Shri S.S. Manan, ACP, PSO to Vice President to get the carcade ready we positioned the carcade in front of Gate No.11, facing Gate No. 1 and waited there. After about 15-20 minutes, a white Ambassador car No. DL-3C J-1527 fitted with VIP Red Light came speedily towards our carcade. The car was being chased by Sh. Jagdish Yadav of Watch & Ward Staff, who was shouting and waving to stop the car. Meanwhile that car took a left turn and came on to the sand dust road (bajri wala road). And immediately while reversing, the car hit the right front side of the main car of Vice President. On this, Shekhar, the driver of Vice President's car alighted from his car and approached the driver of that Ambassador car in order to talk to him about his driving. In the meantime, I along with ASI Jeet Ram and ASI Nanak Chand of VP carcade headed towards that Ambassador car to enquire. Meanwhile, without any delay the occupant terrorists alighted from all the four doors of that car and they appeared to be commandos, armed with AK-47 Rifles. They started firing indiscriminately in all directions. Owing to this firing, we tried to take safe positions but ASI Jeet Ram, Driver Rampal and ASI Nanak Chand received bullet injuries. One of the terrorists ran back towards Gate No. 1, simultaneously firing indiscriminately, whereas, rest of the terrorists ran towards Gate No. 12 after scaling the wall. Meanwhile, the security personnel posted on that place got alert on firing and fired in defence. The terrorist, who ran towards Gate No.1, fired at Sh. Jagdish Yadav of Watch & Ward Staff also. The firing continued from both the sides. When the firing stopped, we came to know that driver Ghanshyam (Escort car), Driver ASI Rampal (Escort car) of our carcade and ASI Nanak Chand have died in the firing. ASI Jeet Ram also got injured in the firing and HC Om Prakash who was also on Escort duty, also died. Sh. Jagdish Yadav (Watch & Ward) also died in the firing and a gardener who was watering in front, also died. Later on I came to know that the security personnel have gunned down all the terrorists. Many people also got injured during the indiscriminate firing by the terrorists, who are being shifted to the hospital in Ambulance vans. I have heard my statement and it is correct". The statement was read over to SI Shyam Singh who signed it after admitting as correct. On this Insp./ SHO GL Mehta endorsed, as follows-On preliminary inspection, a terrorist was spotted lying dead in the porch of Gate No.1 of Parliament House building, whose right arms and both legs were severely damaged due to explosion. Some ammunition and wires were found scattered near the body of this terrorist. In the porch of Gate No.5 of the building, a body of another terrorist was found, beside which one AK-47 rifle with attached grenade-launcher was found lying. In the porch of Gate No.9 of the building, dead bodies of three terrorists were found lying side-by-side. Some explosive material was suspected on the bodies of the terrorists. An Ambassador car No. DL 3C J-1527 was found parked in front of building Gate No.11, which was reportedly used by the terrorists. A large quantity of explosive material was suspected in it. And some wires were seen extending out of the car. One IED was found on the scene, which was kept covered by security personnel near Iron Gate No.1, which was later defused by the BDS. Blood, fired cartridges and hand grenades were found scattered between Gate No.5 and Gate No.11 of the Parliament House Building. Few cars with bullet marks and broken glasses were also found parked on the spot. Bullet marks were also found at different places of the Parliament House Building. Various Ambulance vehicles shifted the persons injured in the firing to the hospital. Since explosive was suspected on the dead bodies and in the car, they were cordoned off to safety. Teams of NSG/BDS, Crime, BDS District, Dog Squad, Crime teams, Photographers, Video-graphers, CFSL, Lodhi Road and FSL, Malviya Nagar were summoned at the spot for the examination. From the contents of the statement of SI Shyam Singh, circumstances, preliminary site inspection and information received from RML Hospital, it was found to be a planned terrorist act to disrupt the sovereignty, unity and integrity of India with the intention to kill the VVIPs, MPs, Security Personnel and the Govt. officials present in the Parliament House and to cause destruction in the Parliament House building; the Suicidal Squad of terrorists, equipped with deadly arms and explosive materials in large quantity, have caused explosions and fired indiscriminately thereby causing loss of life and property and disrupting the legal and official discharge of duties of Govt. officials, committed offences punishable under section

121/121A/122/124/120B/186/332/353/302/307/ IPC, 3/4/5/ Explosives Substances Act & 25/27 Arms Act. Insp. G.L. Mehta, SHO/Parliament Street sent the ruqqua through HC Sukhbir No. 73/ND, got the said case registered at PS Parliament Street and took up the investigation.

Meanwhile, the team of NSG, BDS (National Security Guard, Bomb Disposal Squad) reached the sport for Rendering Safe Procedure (RSP) and removed some of the explosive materials from the spot and also diffused some of it at the spot for safety purpose. From near gate No. 1 of Parliament House, team of NSG, BDS collected explosive substance (hand grenades, rifle grenades, and explosive contained in steel containers – after diffusal in-situ). This team also collected explosive substance (hand grenades, rifle grenades, detonators and explosive contained in steel containers) recovered from deceased terrorists from gate No.9 of Parliament House. From near gate No.5 of Parliament House this team collected 2 hand grenades and from Ambassador car No. DL-3CJ-1527, this team of NSG BDS collected explosive material-30 Kg (approx), one Kg RDX and 4 electric detonators concealed in a cylindrical container. The official photographer reached the spot and took the photographs of the spot. After that Insp. G.L. Mehta along with staff inspected the scene of crime and prepared the site plan (without scale). The scaled site-plan was also got prepared later on during the course of investigation.

Meanwhile, I along with the team of Special Cell Lodhi Colony, New Delhi also reached the spot and joined the investigation as per the direction of senior officers. Accordingly, Insp./SHO GL Mehta along with staff conducted the spot investigation whereas Insp. Mohan Chand Sharma of Special Cell conducted the investigation relating to mobile numbers and Insp. HS Gill of Special Cell examined some of the eyewitnesses.

Exhibits from the spot were seized by different Police Officers through seizure memos. From the body of deceased terrorist found lying near Gate No.1 (Later identified as Mohammad - a Pak national) and from near the body/gate No.1, SI Yograj Singh of PS Parliament Street seized the arms/ ammunition (one 9mm pistol along with 1 broken magazine, 2 magazines of AK-47 rifle, 20 empty cartridges of AK-47,5 empty cartridges of 9mm and 29 live cartridges of AK-47), a pin of hand grenade, batteries, one mobile phone make Sony CMO, J-70 (IMEI NO. 35066834011747/2) with number - 98105-11085, bag, cloths (including burnt and semi-burnt), cash, two I-cards of Xansa Websity Computer Education in the name of Rohail Ali Shah & Rohail Sharma, and one I-card of Cyber Tech Computer Hardware in the name of Ashiq Hussain Khan (all bearing the photograph of deceased terrorist Mohammad), one slip having details regarding topography of the Parliament House, one paper slip bearing five mobile numbers - 98105-10816, 98105-11085, 98115-44860, 98103-02438 & 98110-59315, one slip bearing two phone numbers of Dubai - 0097150-5516899 & 0097150-7683340, three SIM cards of mobile number 98106-93456, 98115-44860 & 98105-65284, one I card of Satyam i-way and blood sample of deceased terrorist Mohammad, etc. through seizure memos.

From the body of deceased terrorists lying near gate No.5 of Parliament House and later identified as Haider, SI Rajinder Singh of PS Parliament Street seized arms (one AK-56 rifle along with 2 magazines), hand grenade lever, one bag, one I-card of Xansa Websity Computer Education in the name of Sanjay Kaul (bearing the photograph of deceased terrorist Haider) etc. through seizure memo.

From gate No.9 of Parliament House, SI Sanjeev Kumar Verma of PS Parliament Street seized arms/ ammunition (one AK-47 along with 3 magazines, one .38 bore pistol, 57 live cartridges of .38 bore and 15 live cartridges of AK-47), one bag, nylon rope, one I-card of Xansa Websity Computer Education in the name of Anil Kumar (bearing the photograph of one of the deceased terrorists) etc. from deceased terrorists lying near gate No.9 and later identified as Hamza. From this place SI SK Verma also seized arms/ ammunition (one AK-47 rifle along with 2 magazines and 12 live cartridges of AK-47), nylon rope, one I-card of Xansa Websity Computer Education in the name of Raju Lal (bearing the photograph of one of the deceased terrorists), one paper slip bearing five mobile numbers-98105-10816, 98105-11085, 98115-44860, 98103-02438 & 98110-59315 & two phone numbers of Dubai-0097150-5516899 & 0097150-7683340 and one mobile phone make Motorola (IMEI No. 449269219639010) with SIM card of mobile No. 98105-10816 etc. from another deceased terrorist lying near gate No.9 and later identified as Raja. He also seized arms (one AK-47 rifle along with 2 magazines), one bag nylon rope, one I-card of Xansa Websity Computer Education in the name of Sunil Verma (bearing the photograph of one of the deceased terrorists), one paper slip bearing five mobile numbers-98105-10816, 98105-11085, 98115-44860, 98103-02438 & 98110-59315 & two phone numbers of Dubai – 0097150-5516899 & 0097150-7683340 and one mobile phone make Motorola (IMEI No. 449269405808650) with SIM card of mobile No. 98103-02438 etc. from another deceased terrorist), lying near gate No.9 and later identified as Rana. He also seized 48 empty cartridges of AK-47 scattered around Gate No.9 of Parliament House. SI SK Verma prepared the seizure memo of the above articles.

On the same day Insp. G.L. Mehta, seized ammunition (used as well as live ones) of AK-47 rifle scattered over different places from the spot through seizure memo. One Harpal Singh S/o Sh. Gurcharan Singh R/o H.No. 344-345, I Floor, Mantola, Pahar Ganj, Delhi, a car-dealer having his office in Karol Bagh by the name "Lucky Motors" and has mediated in the sale of Ambassador car No. DL-3C-J-1527, came to the spot after watching the news on TV. He also identified deceased terrorist lying at Gate No.1 of Parliament House as the person who had bought this Ambassador car on 11.12.2001 from him. He also produced relevant documents relating to this purchase and the same were seized by Inspector G.L. Mehta through seizure memo. The documents also included the original delivery receipt bearing the photograph of deceased terrorist (Mohammad) as buyer in the name of Ashiq Hussain Khan.

Ins. G.L. Mehta recorded statement of Harpal Singh. He also stated that one more person has accompanied the deceased terrorist during the purchase of this car and that person signed as a witness on the delivery receipt. The Ambassador car was found registered in the name and address of Infrastructure Leasing & Finance Services Ltd., Core 4B, 4th Floor, India Habitat Center, Delhi. Statement of this company's Executive (Admn.) Shri Mathew George revealed that the car was sold to Shri Dhiraj Singh, another employee of the company. Dhiraj Singh further sold the car to one Satbir Singh who in turn sold it to Raghubir Singh @ Veera. One Harish Chander Jaggi and his business partner Harpal Singh of Lucky motors jointly purchased the car from Raghubir Singh @ Veera, and was later sold to deceased terrorist by Harpal Singh. Insp. HS Gill also recorded statements of all these persons.

On 13.12.2001, SI Yograj Singh, SI Rajinder Singh and SI SK Verma also conducted the Inquest-proceedings u/s 174 CrPC, of all the five deceased terrorists lying near gates No.1, 5 & 9, respectively.

From the Ambassador car No. DL-3CJ-1527, arms/ammunition, binoculars, batteries and dagger etc. were recovered and the same were seized along with the car by Insp. G.L. Mehta, through seizure memo on 14.12.2001. Insp. G.L. Mehta also seized documents regarding the ownership of car, map of Delhi and some other documents through separate seizure memo. From the spot, he also seized ammunition (damaged/deformed parts and particles of bullets empty catridges) pieces of white metal chips, concrete pieces from the spot where craters were formed due to the blasts of the grenades, burnt/broken pieces of plastic material and some black smoked substance through separate seizure memo. He also seized blood samples from gate No. 1 and 5 to 12 of Parliament House; and damaged Ambassador car No. DL-1C-F-5330, DL 1C F-5355 & DL-1C F-1249, through separate seizure memos. These three Ambassador cars have been released on Supurdari. On the same day, seized the video cassettes of CCTV unit installed in parliament House.

On 15.12.2001, Insp. G.L. Mehta, also seized sticker bearing the title of 'Ministry of Home Affairs' from Ambassador car No. DL-3CJ-1527 and sample soil from this car through separate seizure memos.

Insp. Mohan Chand Sharma of Special Cell, Lodhi Colony was assigned for investigation regarding the mobile numbers recovered from the deceased terrorists. Deceased terrorists were found in possession of three mobile instruments and six SIM cards. Mobile numbers of 6 SIM cards were found to be 98105-11085, 98106-93456, 98105-65284, 98115-44860 (all four recovered from deceased terrorist Mohammad), 98103-02438 (recovered from deceased terrorist Rana), 98105-10816 (recovered from deceased terrorist Raja). Mobile number 98114-89429 has been given as the contact number in all the fake I-Cards of 'Xansa Web City' recovered from the deceased terrorists. Call details of all the mobile numbers were obtained. Detail of 98114-89429 (later found out that accused Mohd. Afzal was using this mobile number) showed that this number was in contact with mobile numbers 98106-93456 (recovered from deceased terrorist

Mohammed), 98115-73506 (Later found that accused Shaukat Hussain Guru was using this card) and 98100-81228 (later found that accused S.A.R. Geelani was using this card). This number was also found receiving calls from Ghazi Baba (Satellite Mobile No. 008821651150059). From the study of printouts it also came to notice that all these mobile numbers were also in contact with each other just before the attack on Parliament on 13.12.2001. The location parameter (Cell ID) of all the mobile numbers recovered from the deceased terrorists and that of mobile members 98114-89429, 98115-73506 & 98100-81228 was found to be that of Mukherjee Nagar for most of the time. Out of all the prominent numbers only one mobile number 98100-81228 was found to be a regular mobile card of AIRTEL, which stood in the name of Sayed Abdul Rehman Geelani r/o H No. 535, Mukherjee Nagar, Delhi. The subscriber was also found to have made the payments to the Mobile Company through his SBI card, which also had the same address as revealed from the report received from the SBI.

Interception of these mobile telephone numbers along with other relevant international numbers was taken. Mobile No. 98114-89429 was found switched off. On 14.12.2001 an incoming call from Srinagar was intercepted on mobile No.98100-81228 and during the conversation the user of this mobile (accused S.A.R. Geelani) while talking in Kashmiri language, supported the attack on Parliament. The transcription was translated in Hindi. On the same day an incoming call from Srinagar was intercepted on mobile No.98115-73506. During this intercepted conversation one lady (later found to be accused Smt. Afsan Guru @ Navjot Sandhu) while talking to accused Shaukat Hussain Guru asked about the well being of Shaukat and Chhotu (accused Mohd. Afzal). The recorded conversations along with the transcriptions were seized through seizure memos.

Meanwhile, the team of Special Cell, Lodhi Colony headed by Insp. Mohan Chand Sharma mounted surveillance at the residence of S.A.R. Geelani in Mukherjee Nagar and on 13.12.21001 (sic) Sayed Abdul Rehman Geelani was apprehended from his house. On interrogation, he told that he had the knowledge of the attack on Parliament and that mobile No. 98114-89249 was being used by Mohd. Afzal r/o Vill. Seer Jagir, Sopore, Distt. Baramullah, J&K and mobile No. 98115-73506 was being used by Shaukat Hussain presently residing in H. No. 1021, Ist floor, Mukherjee Nagar, Delhi. A mobile phone instrument make Alkatel having SIM card of mobile No.98100-81228 recovered from him was seized through seizure memo by Insp. Mohan Chand Sharma of Special Cell, Lodhi Colony. He further told that he along with Mohd. Afzal & Shaukat Hussain were involved in the conspiracy to attack the Parliament House on 13.12.2001 and he had been in touch with the deceased terrorists and that Mohd. Afzal is the main coordinator of Jaish-e-Mohmmad, militant outfit, in Delhi. He further stated that meetings were held in the house of Saukat in Mukharjee Nagar and in these meetings Shaukat Hussain and Mohd. Afzal along with all the deceased terrorists used to be present and discuss the plan to carry out attack on Parliament House. After interrogation Sayed Abdul Rehman Geelani was arrested in the case by Insp. Mohan Chand Sharma.

At the Instance of accused Sayed Abdul Rehman Geelani, immediately, a raid was conducted at Shaukat Hussain's house No. 1021, Ist floor, Mukherjee Nagar, Delhi. Smt. Afsan Guru @ Navjot Sandhu (Shaukat Hussain's wife) was found present in the house. A mobile phone instrument make Sony with SIM card of mobile No.98115-73506 was recovered from her possession. Call received/ dialed list of recovered mobile number was checked and telephone numbers 9810081228, 9811489129, 0194492610 were found. She told that her husband Shaukat Hussain had called her on the recovered mobile on 14.12.2001 night from the landline No. 0194492610 of Srinagar which appeared in the list of received calls and that Mohd. Afzal @ Chhotu was also with him in Srinagar. The mobile phone along with the SIM card was seized through seizure memo. Two photographs of Shaukat Hussain, Mohd. Afzal and Afsan Guru were also seized from her house at her instance through seizure memo. On interrogation she further stated that she was aware of the plan of terrorist to attack the Parliament House because a number of meeting were held in her house. Also that after the incident on 13.12.2001, Shaukat Hussain and Mohd. Afzal had left for Sri Nagar in truck No. HR-38-E-6733. Another mobile phone instrument make Ericsson with IMEI No.490174612116430 and SIM card No. 8991100102-009283792 (corresponding to mobile number 98104-46375) was also recovered from the house and seized through seizure memo. After interrogation Smt. Afsan Guru @ Navjot Sandhu was arrested in the case by Insp. Mohan Chand Sharma.

Immediately, the information about Shaukat Hussain and Mohd. Afzal was shared with intelligence agencies, who communicated it to the concerned Police Officials in Srinagar. On the same day, Srinagar police located the truck and apprehended Mohd. Afzal and Shaukat Hussain Guru. A laptop Computer along with its attachment/accessories, one mobile phone instrument make Nokia with IMEI (Instrument Manufacturer's Equipment Identity) number 350102209452432 and Rs. 10 lakhs were also recovered from them. Simultaneously a team of Special Cell comprising of SI Hridaya Bhushan, SI Sharat Kohli and others, reached Srinagar. SI Hridaya Bhushan along with some team members took the custody of Shaukat Hussain and Mohd. Afzal & the recovered articles and brought them (except the truck) back to Delhi on the same day. The truck No. HR 38 E-6733 was later brought to Delhi by SI Sharat Kohli and other team members. On interrogation Mohd. Afzal and Shaukat Hussain Guru confessed their involvement in the Parliament House Complex attack on 13.12.2001. After interrogation both of them were arrested in the case by Insp. Mohan Chand Sharma.

All the accused persons were subjected to intensive interrogation and their disclosure statements were recorded vide separate Disclosure Memos by Insp. Mohan Chand Sharma. Their disclosure statements revealed that accused Mohd Afzal joined militancy after completing his schooling from Government School, Sopore, Baramullah and he joined JKLF in 1990. He crossed over to Pakistan and underwent training for 2½ months at a training camp at Muzzafarabad (Pak Occupied Kashmir) which was run by Pak ISI. After completion of training he was smuggled into India in 1990, by his handlers. Due to pressure of security forces, he came to Delhi and started residing with accused Shaukat Hussain, (his cousin) at Mukherjee Nagar, Delhi and pursued his studies. In 1993/1994 he surrendered before BSF and also handed over arms and ammunition brought from Pakistan. In February 2001 he was contacted in Srinagar by Tariq Ahmed – a Pak national and terrorist of Jaish-e-Mohammad outfit who motivated him to join Jaish-e-Mohammad. Tariq Ahmed took him to Ghazi Baba @ Doctor – Pak national and Supreme Commander of Jaish-e-Mohammad in India, who has his base in Adu hills, Pahalgam (J&K). Ghazi Baba told Mohd. Afzal that on directions from Pak ISI, a Fidayeen attack should be undertaken in Delhi. Ghazi Baba motivated Mohd. Afzal to go to Delhi and set up a base. Consequent to that, Mohd. Afzal came to Delhi and motivated accused Shaukat Hussain and S.A.R. Geelani, to be part of conspiracy for conducting & Fidayeen attack in Delhi. In the month of October 2001 Ghazi Baba introduced him to another Jaish-e-Mohammand terrorist by the name of Mohammad, a Pak national. Mohammad was to lead the Fidayeen attack in Delhi. Mohd. Afzal brought

Mohammad to Delhi along with a laptop and Rs. 50,000/-. Meanwhile Shaukat Hussain arranged a safe hideout in Delhi in Christian Colony, Mukherjee Nagar. Mohd. Afzal left Mohammad in the hide out and after a week proceeded back to Sri Nagar. Meanwhile Shaukat Hussain had also arranged another safe hide out in Gandhi Vihar, Mukherjee Nagar. During his visit to Sri Nagar Mohd. Afzal met Tariq. He introduced him to two more Jaish-e-Mohammad terrorists – Raja and Haider both Pak nationals. He brought them to Delhi in November 2001. He took them to the hide out at Gandhi Vihar. After a week Mohd. Afzal again went back to Sri Nagar and there again he met Tariq, who introduced him to two more terrorists – Rana and Hamza both Pak nationals. They came to Delhi in the beginning of the first week of December 2001. They brought with them two holdalls which contained 4 AK rifles, 3 pistols, 12 magazines, I grenade launcher, 15 shells, 15 grenades, two packets of detonators, Rado activated devices and two wireless sets. In order to conduct recee of the Parliament House Afzal purchased a black Yamaha motorcycle No. HR-51E-5768 from a dealer in Karol Bagh for Rs. 20,000/-. They conducted repeated recee of the Parliament House and the areas around it. They also purchased 5 Mobile phones, 6 SIM cards, 5 cargo trousers, 5 T-shirts, 5 jackets and 5 Shoes from Tibetan Market, Civil Lines, Delhi, 5 knapsacks from Chandni Chowk and 3 police uniforms from Kingsway Camp. In order to prepare Improvised Explosive Devices they purchased 30 Kgs of Ammonium Nitrate, 4 Kgs Sulphur and 4 Kgs Aluminum powder from Tilak Bazaar, Khari Baoli. They also purchased a container of 30 Kgs capacity and five small containers to prepare IEDs. They then arranged fake I.D. cards and a parking label sticker, downloaded from Internet, for entering the Parliament House complex. On 11.12.2001, they purchased a white Ambassador Car from a dealer in Karol Bagh. They fitted it with tinted glasses and a VIP Red light. On 13.12.2001 accused Mohd. Afzal and Shaukat Hussain Guru met deceased terrorists Mohammad and others at Gandhi Vihar and then Mohammad (the Fidayaeen leader) handed over the laptop and Rs. 10 lakhs to Mohd. Afzal, with the directions to keep the money for their use and to hand over the laptop to Ghazi Baba. The heavily armed 5 terrorists then left for Parliament House, Mohammad called Afzal on this mobile phone asking him to watch the proceedings in the Parliament House on Television and inform him on his mobile regarding the presence of VVIPs in the House. In turn Afzal called accused Shaukat Hussain for this purpose. However when Mohd. Afzal could not respond promptly, Mohammad decided to enter the Parliament House. In the ensuing shoot out all the five terrorists were killed. All the deceased terrorists along with accused Mohd. Afzal, Shaukat Hussain Guru and Afsan Guru @ Navjyot Sidhu (wife of Shaukat Hussain Guru) held meetings in the house of Shaukat Hussain to discuss the conspiracy. Accused Shaukat Hussain Guru also confessed to have received calls on his mobile phone from Ghazi Baba's satellite telephone.

Insp. Mohan Chand Sharma obtained the Police Custody remand of all the four accused persons from the Court. On 16.12.2001 at the instance of accused Mohd. Afzal and Shaukat Hussain, the hide out of the deceased terrorist i.e. H.No. A-97, 2nd Floor Gandhi Vihar, Timarpur, Delhi was identified and explosives substance, one mixer grinder, explosive containers, batteries, timepieces, police-uniforms, map of Delhi, Motor cycle No.HR-51-E-5768 make Yamaha etc. were recovered from there in the presence of landlord of this house namely Sh. Subhash Chand Malhotra and seized through seizure memos. Sh. Subhash Chand Malhotra also identified the accused Mohd. Afzal and the photographs of all the five deceased terrorists, whereas property dealer Sh. Devender Pal Kapoor who helped accused Mohd. Afzal in getting this accommodation correctly identified him. Their statements were recorded in this regard by Insp. HS Gill. On the same day another hideout of the deceased terrorists i.e. H.No.281, 2nd Floor, Indira Vihar, Mukherji Nagar, Delhi was also identified at the instance of accused Mohd. Afzal and Shaukat Hussain. Explosive substance, explosive containers, Motorcycle No. DL-1S-K-3122 make Yamaha etc. were recovered from there in the presence of landlords of this house namely Sh. Jagdish Lal and seized through seizure memos. Sh. Jagdish Lal identified the accused Mohd. Afzal and the photographs of all the five deceased terrorists, whereas property dealers Sh. Balraj Singh and Akhil Singh who had helped accused Mohd. Afzal in getting this accommodation, also correctly identified him. Their statements were recorded in this regard by Insp. HS Gill. Accused Mohd Afzal also identified another hideout i.e. Room No. 5, Yamuna Hostel, B-41, Christain Colony, Delhi. Landlord of this accommodation namely Sh. Prem Chand @ Kale correctly identified accused Mohd Afzal, Shaukat Hussain Guru and photograph of deceased terrorists Mohammed, whereas property dealer Sh. Rajnish Kumar who had helped accused Mohd. Afzal and Shaukat Hussain Guru in getting this accommodation correctly identified him. Their statements were recorded in this regard by Insp. HS Gill.

The statements of Sh. Tejpal Kharbanda and Smt. Usha Kharbanda, the landlord/landlady of H. No, 1021, Dr. Mukherjee Nagar, Delhi in which accused Shaukat Hussain Guru and Smt. Afshan Guru was staying as tenant, were recorded by Insp. HS Gill. In their statements they identified accused Mohd. Afzal, SAR Geelani and all the five deceased terrorists. The statement of Sh. Naresh Gulati, the landlord of H No. 535, Dr. Mukharjee Nagar, Delhi in which accused SAR Geelani was staying as tenant, was also recorded by Insp. HS Gill. In his statement he identified accused Mohd. Afzal and Shaukat Hussain Guru, who used to visit accused SAR Geelani.

On 17.12.2001, in the mortuary of LHMC accused Mohd. Afzal identified deceased terrorists as 1) Mohammad r/o Punjab, Pakistan – found lying near Gate No 1, Parliament House Complex and from whose possession I-cards in the name of Rohail Sharma and Ashiq Hussain & bearing his photograph were recovered. 2) Haider r/o Punjab, Pakistan – found lying near Gate No.5, Parliament House Complex and from whose possession I-Card in the name of Sanjay Kaul & bearing his photograph, was recovered. 3) Raja r/o Punjab, Pakistan – found lying near Gate No.9, Parliament House Complex and from whose possession I-Card in the name of Raju Lal & bearing his photograph, was recovered. 4) Rana r/o Punjab, Pakistan – found lying near Gate No.9, Parliament House Complex and from whose possession I-Card in the name of Sunil Verma & bearing his photograph, was recovered. 5) Hamza r/o Punjab, Pakistan-found lying near Gate No.9, Parliament House Complex and from whose possession I-Card in the name of Anil Kumar & bearing his photograph, was recovered. Identification memo (Fard Shankht) was prepared accordingly by Insp. HS Gill.

On 17.12.2001 accused Mohd. Afzal identified the shop No. 657, Swan Dry Fruit and Kirana Store, Fatherpuri Chowk, Delhi and its shopkeeper from where he along with the deceased terrorist Rana had bought the dry fruits. He also identified the shop No.990, Gali Teliyan, Tilak Bazar, Delhi and its shopkeeper from where he along with the deceased terrorist Hamza had bought the Ammonium Nitrate for making explosive device. He also identified the shop No.141, Tilak Bazar, Delhi and its shopkeeper from where he along with the deceased terrorist Mohammad had bought the Silver powder for making explosive device. He also identified the shop No. 1/2628, Hamilton Road, Kashmiri Gate, Delhi and its shopkeeper from where he along with the deceased terrorist Mohammad had bought the VIP red light which was used on the recovered Ambassador car No. DL-3C-J-1527 for entering the Parliament House. He also identified the shop No. 6504, RD Store Fatehpuri, Delhi and its shopkeeper from where he along with the deceased terrorist Mohammad had bought the mixer-grinder for mixing the explosive ingredients in order to make explosive device.

Shri Harpal Singh of "Lucky Motors" who had mediated in the sale of Ambassador car No. DL-3C-J1527 to deceased terrorist who was found lying at Gate No.1 of Parliament House (Later identified as Mohammad) identified accused Mohd. Afzal as the one who had accompanied deceased terrorist Mohammad during the purchase of this car.

On 18.12.2001 accused Mohd. Afzal also identified the Shop No 26, Gaffar Market, Karol Bagh, Delhi and its shopkeeper from where he had bought Mobile Phone hand set make Sony and the Magic SIM card – later used in the Parliament attack. He also identified the shop No.1731/56, Naiwalan, Karol Bagh, Delhi and its shopkeeper from where he had bought Motor Cycle No. HR-51-E-5768, which was used for conducting racee of Parliament House. Delivery receipt "Bill book" and Commission Book produced by the shopkeeper to this effect on 19.12.2001 were seized through seizure memo.

On 19.12.2001 accused Mohd. Afzal also identified the shop No. B-10, Model Town–II, New Delhi and its shopkeeper from where he along with accused Shaukat Hussain had bought Mobile Phone handset make Motorola and the SIM cash card. When the bill book of the shopkeeper's distributor namely Sanjay Jain was checked, Mobile speed card 98114-89429 (bought by accused Mohd. Afzal from the shopkeeper Kamal Kishore) was found sold to Shri Kamal Kishore on 21.09.2001. The bill book was accordingly seized through seizure memo by Insp. HS Gill.

The statements of all the shopkeepers/salesmen who accordingly identified accused Mohd. Afzal, Shaukat Hussain Guru and the photographs of deceased terrorists Mohammad, Rana and Hamza were recorded by Insp. HS Gill who conducted this part of the investigation.

The Manager of "Xansa India Ltd.", Okhla, New Delhi, namely Shri Sanjay Maini and franchise holders "Xansa Websity Computer Education" functioning at 37, Bunglow Road, Kamla Nagar, New Delhi namely Sh. Jaswinder Singh and Sh. Sandeep Singh were examined by Insp. Mohan Chand Sharma. They stated that they have never issued I-cards to any of the student enrolled with their institute and that no student with the names as mentioned in the recovered I-cards has ever enrolled with their institute. An original I-card of Xansa Websity Computer Education was seized as sample and it is found to be visibly different from the recovered ones.

Subsequently, provisions of POTA were added in the case on 19.12.2001 and accordingly I took up the investigation.

During Police custody remand accused Mohd. Afzal, Shaukat Hussain Guru, Sayed Abdul Rehman Geelani had offered their willingness to give their confessional statements to the Deputy Commissioner of Police. Accordingly on 20.12.2001, a request in this regard was made to DCP/Special Cell. On 21.12.2001, confessional statements of accused Mohd. Afzal and Shaukat Hussain Guru were recorded u/s 32 of POTA by Shri Ashok Chand, DCP/ Special Cell; however accused Syed Abdul Rehman Geelani refused to give any confessional statement to DCP/ Special Cell. Accused Muhammad Afzal confessed that the Parliament attack was a joint action by the militant outfits Jaish-e-Mohammad and Lashkar-e-Tayyaba (LeT). Copies of the confessional statements of accused Mohd. Afzal and Shaukat Hussain Guru and the refusal of accused Sayed Abdul Rehman Geelani were obtained from the

DCP/Spl. Cell. On 22.12.2001, the original confessional statements (sealed by DCP/ Spl. Cell) along with the accused persons were produced before the Hon'ble Court of Shri V.K. Maheshwari, ACMM who after examing the accused persons confirmed the confessional statements and recorded the proceedings to this effect. The copies of the court proceedings and the statements of accused persons recorded in the court were obtained.

Accused Mohd. Afzal had disclosed that after attack on parliament on 13.12.2001, he destroyed the SIM card of Mobile No.98114-89429, which he was using in the mobile phone instrument make Nokia recovered from him. The call details revealed the use of mobile number 98114-89429 in this Nokia phone with corresponding IMEI number (Instrument Manufacturer's Equipment Identity — a unique number of mobile phone instrument). This number (98114-89429) was found mentioned on the I-cards recovered from the deceased terrorists and was in regular contract with deceased terrorist Mohammad.

The call details of telephone number 98115-73506 (used by accused Shaukat Hussain Guru) revealed its regular contact with accused Mohd. Afzal and S.A.R. Geelani. It also revealed contact with both of them just prior to and after the attack on Parliament House Complex. The call details of telephone number 98104-46375 (corresponding to the SIM card recovered from the house of accused Shaukat Hussain Guru at the instance of accused Navjot Sandhu) revealed his contact with satellite phone of Gazi Baba.

The call details of the mobile numbers of the deceased terrorists have also revealed their connection with Pakistan. Afzal had disclosed that in the evening of 12.12.2001, deceased terrorist Raja had used deceased terrorist Mohammad's mobile number 98105-65284 for calling his parents in Karachi, Pakistan. Then from the same phone deceased terrorist Rana spoke to his father in Pakistan on a landline telephone number. After that Mohammad called Karachi from the same phone. This was also corroborated by the call details showing contact with telephone numbers 0092215883479 & 0092212813015 (Karachi numbers) and 00924522396328 Liyaqatabad (Pakistan).

Call details of Mobile number 98105-11085 (IMEI No. 350668340117870), which was also recovered from deceased terrorist Mohammad revealed its frequent contact with telephone numbers of Dubai besides that of Pakistan. On 13.12.2001 at 11:39:01 (Date and time when terrorists attacked the Parliament House) this number called 00971505516899, a Dubai mobile number. This number has also received calls from 8821651150178 (A GSM cum Satellite Phone). As per the disclosure/confessional statements of accused Mohd. Afzal and Shaukat Hussain Guru this phone was being used by Ghazi Baba – Supreme Commander of Jaish-e-Mohammad in India who coordinated the Parliament attack.

Call details of another mobile number 98106-93456, found in the possession of deceased terrorist Mohammad revealed frequent contact with 491722290100, a telephone number of Switzerland and another OSM cum Satellite Phone Number 8821651150059. This phone was also used by Ghazi Baba. As per the information extracted from the website www.thuraya.com, the two GSM cum Satellite phone are called "Thuraya" and having its Head Quarter in Dubai. Details of mobile number 98115-73506, used by accused Shaukat Hussain Guru and found in the possession of the wife accused Afsan Guru @ Navjot Sandhu has also revealed its contact with Thuraya Satellite cum Mobile numbers 8821651150059 and 8821651150178 (used by Ghazi Baba). The call details of mobile number 98106-93456 of deceased terrorist Mohammad also revealed its use to access Internet through Internet service of Airtel named 'TANGO'. A request was made to the 'AIRTEL' for getting the details in this regard but the

AIRTEL could not furnish the same due to technical non-feasibility. The Mobile number was also found used on mobile phone instruments corresponding to IMEI numbers 449269219639010, 449269405808510, 350668340117470 and 35010220-9452430 which were recovered from deceased terrorist Raja, Rana, Mohammad and accused Mohd. Afzal respectively.

Call details of mobile phone number 98105-10816 (IMEI No. 449269219639010) recovered from deceased terrorist Raja revealed that this mobile phone instrument was earlier used by mobile number 98114-89429 which was also used on mobile phone instrument with IMEI No. 449269405808650, recovered from deceased terrorist Rana. The mobile number 98105-10816 was also found in contact with Thuraya phone number 88216-51150178 (used by Ghazi Baba).

A request for obtaining the call details of the International telephone numbers and satellite phone numbers, which have figured during the investigation of the case, has been made to INTERPOL, but the report is still awaited.

The Laptop computer along with its attachments/accessories recovered from accused Mohd. Afzal and Shaukat Hussain Guru was initially got examined by private Computer expert, Shri Vimal Kant Arora of Orion Convergence Ltd., A-357, Defence Colony, New Delhi, in order to extract maximum information at the earliest which could be useful for investigation purpose. Shri Vimal Kant Arora after detailed examination, handed over his report on 29.12.2001. According to the report the recovered Compaq Presario laptop had accessed Internet through Pakistan based ISPs (Internet Service Providers). There are video clippings of news items showing political leaders with the Parliament House in background down loaded from the television through video camera, besides I-cards, MHA sticker, code table, e-mail addresses, chat room for their on line chatting, still and moving phtotographs etc. Designed sticker of Ministry of Home Affairs (same as recovered from ambassador car No.DL-3C-J-1527 used by deceased terrorists), incomplete identity card of Indian Army and Scanned images of identity cards of (1) Ashiq Hussain Khan s/o Ab. Rashid Khan r/o Khwaja Gilgit (Sopore) District Baramullah, (2) Cyber Tech Computer Hardware Solution in the name of Ashiq Hussain with phtograph of deceased terrorist Mohammad, (3) Xansa Websity Computer Education, 37, Bunglow Road, Kamla Nagar, New Delhi- 110007 in the name of Anil Kumar s/o Vinod Kumar r/o 120-A, Adarsh Nagar, Delhi, Date of issue 15.10.2001 (same as recovered from deceased terrorist Hamza), (4) Xansa Websity Computer Education, 37, Bunglow Road, Kamla Nagar, New Delhi-110007 in the name of Sunil Verma s/o Kailash Verma r/o 120-A, Adarsh Nagar, Delhi Date of issue 15.10.2001 (same as recovered from deceased terrorist Rana), (5) Xansa Websity Computer Education, 37, Bunglow Road, Kamla Nagar, New Delhi-110007 in the name of Raju Lal s/o Ram Lal r/o 120-A, Adarsh Nagar, Delhi Date of issue 15.10.2001 (same as recovered from deceased terrorist Raja) and (6) similar I-Cards of Xansa Websity Computer Education and Cyber Tech Computer Education issued in different names, were also found stored in the files of Laptop. The print outs of MHA sticker and the I-cards etc. were taken out. Statement of Shri Vimal Kant Arora was recorded.

E-mail addresses in the name of 'burger' were also found. Accused Mohd. Afzal has disclosed that deceased terrorist Mohammad was also involved in the hijacking of the Indian Airlines flight No.IC-814 in December-1999 and during that hijacking Mohammad was code-named as 'Burger'. He identified the photograph of Sunny Ahmed Quasi @ Burger @ Mansoor, one of the accused persons of that case as deceased terrorist Mohammad.

In the shoot-out with the terrorist on 13.12.2001, the following Police personnel and other persons were killed – (1) Lady Constable Kamlesh-CRPF, (2) ASI Rampal-DP, (3) ASI Nanak

Chand-DP, (4) HC Ghanshyam-DP, (5) Jagdish Prasad Yadav-Watch & Ward staff of Parliament House, (6) Desh Raj-CPWD & (7) HC Om Prakash-DP on 13.12.2001; whereas (1) Matwar Singh Negi-Watch & Ward staff and (2) HC Vijendar Singh-DP succumbed to the gun shot injuries in the Hospital on 16.12.2001 and 18.12.2001 respectively. Their autopsy was got conducted in Lady Harding Medical College and the PM reports along with the exhibits were collected. In all the PM reports the cause of death has been opined as the injuries caused by firearms. The autopsy of all the five deceased terrorists was also got conducted in Lady Harding Medical College and the PM reports along with the exhibits were collected. In PM report of deceased terrorist Mohammad the cause of death has been opined as the multiple injuries resulting from blast including pellet injuries. In PM reports of other deceased terrorists namely Raja, Hamza, Rana and Haider, the cause of death has been opined as the injuries caused by firearms. Efforts were made to identify the deceased terrorist but none has come forward as yet to claim the relationship with the dead bodies of any of the five deceased terrorists.

In the shoot-out with the terrorists on 13.12.2001, the following Police personnel and other persons received gunshot/splinter injuries – (1) Purshotam Singh, Assistant Commandant, CRPF, (2) HC Kamal Singh-DP, (3) HC Y.B. Thapa-CRPF, (4) Constable Rakesh Kumar-CRPF, (5) Driver Hans Raj-CRPF, (6) Constable Sukhvinder Singh-CRPF (7) HC Samar Singh-Delhi Police, (8) Constable Mahipal Singh-CRPF, (9 Constable Arjun Ram Siyare-CRPF, (10) Vikram Singh, (11) N.M.S. Nair, (12) Sanjeev Kumar @ Sanju, (13) Purshottam Pandey, (14) Constable Rajat Bisht, (15) ASI Jeet Ram-Delhi Police and (16) Sh. Anand Jha-Asst. Commdt. CRPF. Their MLCs have been collected and it has been opined by the doctor that they received bullets/ splinter injuries. The statements of all the injured persons were recorded during the investigation.

The explosives seized by NSG BDS from the spot on 13.12.2001 was got examined from CFSL Chandigarh by the NSG. The CFSL report No. CFSL/538/01/01 dated 01.01.2002 in this regard has been collected from the NSG. It has been opined in the report that the exhibits contained Ammonium Nitrate, Potassium Nitrate, Aluminum Sulphar and PETN. The remnants were collected from NSG and seized through seizure memo. The destruction certificate regarding the rifle grenades and hand grenades recovered by the NSG BDS from the sport on 13.12.2001 has been obtained from NSG. The Destruction Certificate regarding the 11 Electric Detonators seized by the NSG from the spot has also been obtained from the NSG. After Action Report on neutralization of IEDs planted in Ambassador Car No. DL-3C-J-1527 and recovered from the bags of the deceased terrorists has been obtained from the NSG. Some more articles recovered and seized by the BDS, NSG from the possession of deceased terrorists/ spot, i.e. 3 stainless steel dollu, 1 stainless steel cylindrical container (20 ltrs), Flexible wire (35 meters), 1 Sunea battery, 2 alarm clocks (broken), 1 remote bell, 1 shouldering iron and 1 shoulder bag were collected from the BDS, NSG and deposited in the "Malkhana."

According to the report of Major P Patnaik of NSG (dated 26.12.2001), the recovered hand grenades have the marking–HE (Spl HGr-84 Gren ARGES, HE 7 93 002). According to report received from Republic of Austria, an Austrian firm had sold machine and tools used in the production of "ARGES" hand grenades to a firm in Pakistan.

A report regarding the recovered MHA sticker was also obtained from the Ministry of Home Affair which stated that no parking sticker had been issued for ambassador car No.DL-3C-J1527 and that recovered sticker is entirely different from the original one.

The exhibits (explosives arms and ammunitions, clothes of deceased terrorist and other persons, documents etc.) seized from the spot and the explosives substance etc. recovered from the hide-outs of Gandhi Vihar and Indira Vihar have been deposited in CFSL, Delhi for examination.

Part-CFSL Result relating to ballistic opinion i.e. Report, No.CFSL-2002/F-0066 dated 01.04.2002 has been obtained from the CFSL, Delhi. As per the CFSL report-1) the three assault rifle, 9 mm pistol and .38 pistol used by the deceased Pak terrorists in carrying out the attack on parliament House are "Fire-Arms" as defined in the Arms Act-1959 and are in working order. 2) The opinion regarding the live cartridges is in affirmative. The recovered cartridge cases, fired bullets and jacket pieces of fired bullets were opined to have been fired from the recovered arms. 4) The opinion regarding the live detonators recovered from the terrorist's hideout is in affirmative. 5) Aluminum powder, Sulphur and Ammonium Nitrate was detected in the respective exhibits recovered from the terrorist's hideout and that these chemicals can form the components of "Improvised Explosive Device/s" and are therefore, explosive substances as defined in the "Explosive Substances Act-1908". 6) Presence of "PETN" based high explosive was confirmed in the exhibits taken from the spot and as such the high explosive is therefore, explosive substances as defined in the "Explosive Substances Act-1908".

CFSL Reprot No. CFSL-2002/F-130 dated 30.04.2002 regarding the seized Mixer Grinder has also been obtained from CFSL, Delhi. As per the report Ammonium Nitrate was also detected in the Mixer Grinder.

Specimen handwriting of accused Mohd. Afzal was obtained and has been sent to CFSL, Delhi for comparison with the signatures on the delivery receipt of the Ambassador car used by terrorists.

The print outs of MHA sticker and the I-cards down loaded from the recovered Laptop have been deposited in the CFSL for comparison with the sticker/I-cards recovered from the ambassador car of deceased terrorists.

The specimen voice samples of accused Sayed Abdul Rehman Geelani, Shaukat Hussain Guru and Smt. Afsan Guru @ Navjot Sandhu were recorded and seized through seizure memo. The same along with the intercepted conversation recorded on 14.12.2001 has been deposited in CFSL for comparison.

The laptop computer along with the attachments/accessories has been deposited in Government Examiner of Question Document, B.P.R&D, Hyderabad for further detailed examination. Remaining results from CFSL/GEQD (Hyderabad) are still awaited. The same would be collected later and filed in the Court.

Motorcycle No. DL-1S-K3122 which was recovered from the terrorist's hideout at Indira Vihar was found registered in the name of accused Shaukat Hussain Guru. The recovered truck No.HR-38-E- 6733 was found registered in the name of Navjot Sandhu @ Afsan Guru. Motorcycle No. HR-51-E-5768 which was recovered from the terrorist's hideout at Gandhi Vihar was found registered in the name of one Ram Niwas of Faridabad. Shri Ram Niwas stated to have sold the Motor Cycle to one Jeeva Ram of JJ Colony, Shakoor Pur, who in turn sold it to another person Salim Malik, of Old GT Karnal Road, Delhi. Shri Salim Malik stated to have sold it to one Babu Khan of Gandhi Vihar, who in turn sold it to Shri Sushil Kumar who had finally sold the Motorcycle to accused Afzal. Statements of these persons were recorded by Insp. HS Gill.

The Confessional/ Disclosure statements of accused Mohd. Afzal and Shaukat Hussain Guru have revealed the involvement of Mohd. Masood Azhar (Chief of Jaish-e-Mohammad, militant outfit), Ghazi Baba @ Abu Jehadi @ Saqlain and Tariq Ahmed – all Pak Nationals in the case. It was revealed that the conspiracy to attack Parliament House was hatched in Pakistan at the instance of Pak ISI and it was a joint terrorist action of the two militant outfits i.e. JeM and LeT. Ghazi Baba planned and coordinated for the execution in India. Their portrait-parle was got prepared on the descriptions given by accused Mohd. Afzal. However, they are yet to be arrested in the case despite best efforts and they are evading their arrest. Therefore, proceeding u/s 82/83 Cr.P.C. were initiated against these accused persons and the Court declared them as proclaimed offenders.

With intent to threaten the unity, integrity, security and sovereignty of India, to strike terror in the people; deceased terrorists – Mohammad, Raja, Rana, Hamza & Haider in conspiracy with the accused Mohd. Afzal, Shaukat Hussain Guru, Sayed Abdul Rehman Geelani and Navjot Sandhu @ Afshan Guru (Column No.3) and Mohd. Masood Azhar, Ghazi Baba @ Abu Jehadi @ Saqlain and Tariq Ahmed – all three Pak Nationals (Column No 2) entered the Parliament House and have used explosive substances, bombs & deadly firearms: thereby causing death & injuries to several persons including security personnel and causing damage to government property. All the deceased terrorists and accused Mohd. Afzal, Shaukat Hussain Guru, Sayed Abdul Rehman Geelani and Navjot Sandhu @ Afshan Guru and the absconding three Pak nationals are also members of terrorist organization "Jaish-e-Mohd" and have also supported to further the terrorist act of "Jaish-e-Mohd" & another terrorists organization "Lashkar-e-Tayyaba" (LeT).

From the investigation conducted so far and statements of the witnesses, there is sufficient evidence against accused 1. Mohd. Afzal, 2. Shaukat Hussain Guru, 3. Sayed Abdul Rehman Geelani and 4. Navjot Sandhu @ Afshan Guru (Column No 3) to prosecute them u/s 121/121A/122/124/186/332/333/353/307/302 IPC read with section 120B IPC; u/s 3/4/5/6 of the Explosive

Substance Act & section 3/4/5/20/21/22 of POTA read with section 120B IPC. There is sufficient evidence to prosecute the accused persons namely Mohd. Masood Azhar, Ghazi Baba and Tariq Ahmed – all Pak nationals (Column No.2) – under the said offences of IPC, POTA and Explosive Substance Act as mentioned above, who had hatched a conspiracy with the accused persons mentioned in column No.3 and also with the deceased terrorist namely Mohammad, Haider, Hamza, Raja and Rana mentioned in column No.2.

Therefore the challan against the accused persons has been prepared. Accused persons (Column No.3) arrested in the case are in judicial custody. Prosecution sanctions u/s 196 Cr.P.C., 50 POTA & Explosive Substances Act have been received from the competent authorities. The challan against the accused persons is being filed in the court, may kindly be tried. Further investigation in the case u/s 173.8 Cr.P.C. is still continuing.

ACP/Special Cell
New Delhi Dated : 12.05.2002.

ANNEXURE 2

Confessional Statement of Mohammad Afzal

PW 60/7&8

Date : 21.12.2001
Place : 11, Alipur Road, Go'S Mess, Delhi
Time : 7.10 P.M.

Accused Mohd. Afzal @ Chotu s/o Late Habibullah Guru r/o Vill Seerajagir Tehsil and P.S.Sopore, Dist Baramullah J&K has been arrested in case FIR No. 417 dt. 13.12.2001 u/s 302/307/186/353/332/121/121A/122/124 IPC and 120/B IPC and 25/27 Arms Act, 3/4/5 Explosive Substances Act and 3/4/5/20/21/22 POTO, P.S. Parliament Street, New Delhi. He has been produced before me by the IO Shri Rajbir Singh ACP for recording of a confessional statement u/s 32 of POTO at the Gazetted Officers Mess, 11, Alipur Road, Delhi.

Now, I have asked ACP/Shri Rajbir Singh to leave the room where the proceedings are being conducted. He has since left the room and myself and accused Mohd. Afzal Guru are present only. I have now warned and explained to accused Mohd. Afzal Guru that he is not bound to make a confessional statement and that if he does so, it can be used against him as evidence during trial in the court of law.

I am not under any duress. I am ready to give my confessional statement.

Sd/-
21.12.2001

PW 60/9

Despite warning the accused Mohd. Afzal has stated that he wants to make a confessional statement voluntarily. I am satisfied that the accused is not under duress or pressure to make a confessional statement. I therefore proceed to record his confessional statement, which is as under:-

I was born in the year 1969 and completed my schooling from Govt. School Sopore in the year 1988. In the year 1989-90 on the motivation of yasin Mallick and Hamid Shah of Jammu and Kashmir Liberation Front, I joined their militant outfit for the purpose of Jehad and liberation of Kashmir. I alongwith several JKLF militants crossed over the Muzffarabad in Pakistan occupied Kashmir where we were camped at an old matchbox factory for about 2 ½ months and were given basic training in handling arms, ammunition and insurgent activities by one Zainulubdin, a retired Pak Army Officer. After completing my training I alongwith 80 trained militants crossed border to India through Trigam sector in Kupwara. I brought along with me one AK 47 with three loaded magazines and were also paid Rs.10,000 in Indian currency. On reaching India we were tasked to destroy communication network, educational institutions and important bridges in Jammu and Kashmir. However soon after my return security forces were tipped off and in order to escape the security forces my family sent me to Delhi alongwith my cousin Shaukat Hussain, R/o Doabgan, Sopore who was pursuing his studies in Delhi since 1988. After reaching Delhi I started doing odd jobs and also completed my graduation from Delhi University in 1993-94, while studying in Delhi University I met Abdul Rehman Gilani of Baramullah who was also pursuing his post graduate course from Delhi University. During the summer of 1993/94, I went to Srinagar and on the advice of my family, I surrendered before BSF and also handed over arms and ammunition brought from Pakistan. Thereafter, I again turned back to Delhi and earned my livelihood by working in various private companies and also doing private tuition upto 1996. In 1996 I returned back to Sopore where I started working as commission agent for medical and surgical goods. About eight months ago while I had gone to delivery surgical good at a shop in Lal Chowk, Srinagar I came across one Tanq [Tariq?] who introduced himself as a doctor residing in that area of Anantnag district. We had a discussion for half an hour residing the current state of affairs and also discussed about militancy in Kashmir. Thereafter, I met Tanq on two more occasions. Two months after the first meeting with Tanq when I had gone to offer Namaz at Batoraloo masjid in Srinagar, Tanq met me and disclosed that he was on a militant of Jaise-e-Mohammad outfit. He also motivated me to join the Jehad for liberation of Kashmir and for the cause of Muslim Qaum and also assisted me of financial support. When I expressed my unwillingness to work for Jaish-e-Mohammad, Tanq further introduced me to one Ghazi Baba who is the Supreme Commander of Jaish-e-Mohammad in Kashmir. The camp of Ghazi Baba in Kashmir consisted of about 60 heavily armed militants of Jaish-e-Mohammad. Ghazi Baba was also equipped with wireless sets, satellite phone and other means of communication. Ghazi Baba further motivated me and also gave me audio cassette and satellite containing provocative preachings of Maulana Mazood Azar, I was directed to contact Tanq after 6 weeks at the appointed here. I met Tanq who again took me to Ghazi Baba at his training camp who instructed me that he has been told by Maulana Masood Azhar that we must carry out actions on important institutions of Indian nation. Like the Indian Parliament and US and UK Embassies as also action in Kashmir has not led to the desired results. He told me that the action in Delhi would be a joint action of Jaish-e-Mohammad and Lashkar-e-Toiba. I was tasked to provide a safe hideout for the Fidayeen in Delhi. During this meeting Ghazi Baba introduced me to Mohammad Haider, Pak national and Militants of Jaishe-e-Mohammad. In the month of October I rang up Shaukat and asked him to arrange a rented accomodation for myself and Mohammad. In the first week of November, I brought Mohammad to Delhi. Who brought alongwith him a laptop and Rs.50,000/-. On reaching Delhi we went to Shaukat house who took us to the prearranged accomodation in Christian Colony, Room No.5, Boys Hostel. I introduced Mohammad to Shaukat as a resident of Doda, Kashmir. However Shaukat was not convinced. I then told him that Mohammad is a Pak national and Militant of Jaise-e-Mohammad and has come to Delhi to carry out Fidayeen attack. After about a week I arranged another safe hideout at A-97, Gandhi Vihar, Timarpur. Mohammad through Hawala collected Rs.20.00 lacs and gave me Rs. 5 lacs to give it to Tanq in Srinagar. I went to Srinagar and gave the money to Tanq. Tanq then told me to take two more militant of the Jaise-e-mohammad, Raja and Haider both Pak national to Delhi from Srinagar, & brought them to Delhi and took them to the hideout in Gandhi Vihar. To complete the task given by Ghazi Baba, I along with Mohammad went to Khari Baoli area in Delhi from where Mohammad bought 60 Kgs. of Ammonium Nitrate, 10 Kgs. Aluminum powder and 5 Kg sulphur. Mohammad told me that these chemicals when mixed in the ratio of 7:2:1 could make a high explosive. After about a week Mohammad again gave me Rs. 5 lacs and sent me to Srinagar where I handed over the money to Tanq. In the first week of December, I again met Tanq who asked me to take two more Jaish-e-Mohammad militants, Rana and Hamza both Pak nationals to Delhi. Rana and Hamza were carrying a holder which contained 4 AK rifles, 12 loaded magazines, 1 grenade launcher, 3 pistols, with spare magazines, 15 hand grenades, 15 grenade shell, two packs of electronic detonators, two transreceiver and radio active detonation devices and explosives. We came from Srinagar to Jammu by bus and from Jammu to Delhi by train. On reaching Delhi I took them to the Gandhi Vihar hideout. After reaching Delhi I arranged for another accomodation at 281, Indira Vihar in the area of Mukherjee Nagar. Mohammad had also purchased mobile phones and Sim cards from Ghaffar Market and Palika Bazar and received direction from Ghazi Baba from a satellite phone. During my visits to Delhi I used to meet Shaukat and SAR Geelani and motivate them for Jehad in Kashmir. Shaukat provided his motor cycle for conducting recee. Meetings were also held in the house of Shaukat for deciding future courses of action. In these meetings Geelani and Shaukat, Afsan also used to be present. In the meetings the targets that were discussed was Delhi assembly, UK and US Embassies and Parliament and Airport. Another motor cycle was also purchased by one from Karol Bagh which was also used for conducting recee. After conducting recee of all the targets, Mohammad informed Ghazi Baba who told him that they must strike at the Parliament. A trial meeting was held in the house of Shaukat in which all were present and plans for attack on Parliament House were finalized. As per plan on 11.12.2001 I alongwith Mohammad went to hucks motors in Karol Bagh and bought a second hand Ambassador car for Rupees 1 lakhs ten thousand. On 11th I alongwith Mohammad went to Kashmere Gate and purchased a magnetic GP red light to facilitate entry into the parliament house. Mohammad also got prepared sticker of MHA and identity cards through his laptop. Mohammad alongwith other militants prepared IED's after grinding and mixing the chemicals and put them in a container brought from Chandni Chowk. This IED was fitted in the car for carrying explosion. On the night of 12.12.2001 I alongwith Shaukat and Gilani went to the hideout in Gandhi Vihar, Timarpur where all the five Pak militants were prepared. Mohammad gave me the laptop and Rs. 10 lacs. He told me to take the laptop to Ghazi Baba and told me that Rs.10 lacs is for me and my friends Shaukat and Geelani. Mohammad told me that they are going to conduct a Fidayeen attack on the Parliament House on 13.12.2001. Myself Shaukat and Gilani then left the Gandhi Vihar hideout. We were in touch with each other on mobile phones and on 13.12.2001 at 10.40 a.m. I received a call on my mobile no. 98114-89429 from Mohammad's phone number 98106-93456 that I should watch TV and tell about the presence of various VVIPs inside Parliament house. They told me that they were in the vicinity of Parliament House and were awaiting for my reply. At that time I was at Azadpur Mandi but since there was no electricity I could not watch TV. After about 25 minutes, I again received a call from Mohammad regarding the presence of VVIPs in the house. I informed him that due to no electricity I could not watch TV and to give me some time. I contacted Shaukat on his mobile number 98115-73506 and asked him to watch TV and inform him. Thereafter I had talked to Shaukat. Mohammad called me and told me that he is going ahead with the attack on parliament. I then again called Shaukat and told him that the mission has started. Shaukat then came and met me at Azadpur Mandi and both of us went to Geelani's house and gave him Rs. 2 lacs as his share but Gilani told to take the money and give it at his house in Kashmir. Then myself and Shaukat left for Srinagar in Shaukat's truck HR-38E-6733. We reached Srinagar and were apprehended by the police on the 15th. The police recovered from us laptop alongwith attachment and Rupees ten lacs. We were brought back to Delhi and at Delhi I got recovered explosive and other material from the hideouts. I feel repentant for my actions.

Sd/-
21.12.2001

The recording of the confessional statement has been concluded.

Ashok Chand
DSP/Spl.Cell
21.12.2001
Time: 10.45 p.m.

ANNEXURE 3

Confessional Statement of Shaukat Hussain Guru

Date : 21.12.2001
Place : 11, Alipur Road, ___ Delhi
Time : 3.30 P.M.

Accused Shaukat Hussain Guru @ Shaukat s/o Abdul Sattar r/o Village Doabgar, Tehsil and P.S. Sopore, Dist. Baramullah J&K has been arrested in case FIR No. 417 dt. 13.12.2001 u/s 302/307/186/353/332/121/121A/122/124 IPC and 120/B IPC and 25/27 Arms Act, 3/4/5 Explosive Substances Act and 3/4/5/20/21/22 POTO, P.S. Parliament Street, New Delhi. He has been produced before me by the IO Shri Rajbir Singh ACP for recording of a confessional statement u/s 32 of POTO.

Now, I have asked ACP/Shri Rajbir Singh to leave the room where the proceedings are being conducted. He has since left the room and myself and accused Shaukat Hussain Guru are present only. I have now warned and explained to accused Shaukat Hussain Guru that he is not bound to make a confessional statement and that if he does so, it can be used against him as evidence during trial in the court of law.

I am not under any duress. I am ready to give my confessional statement.

Despite warning the accused Shaukat Hussain Guru has stated that he wants to make a confessional statement voluntarily. I am satisfied that the accused is not under duress or pressure to make a confessional statement. I therefore proceed to record his confessional statement, which is as under:-

I was born in the year 1967. I completed my schooling from Sopore in 1988 and in the same year, I came to Delhi to pursue higher studies. I completed my graduation in 1992. During this period I also came across Abdul Rehman Gilani of Baramullah (J&K) who was doing his post graduation in Arabic language from Delhi University. After graduation I also did some professional courses and simultaneously worked in various private companies. In 1997 I started fruit business and I used to buy fruits from Sopore and then supply in Delhi, Jammu and Calcutta during fruit season i.e. July to December. But I suffered a loss of Rs. 4-5 lakhs in this business and I could not compete with heavy transportation charges. I got married to a Sikh girl Navjot Sandhu in the year March 2000. After marriage Navjot Sandhu converted herself to Islam and her name was changed to Afsan Guru. With the help of my in-laws who gave me Rs. 4 lakhs I got financed a truck having number HR-38E-6733 in the name of Afsan in June/ July 2000 and started transport business. Mohd. Afzal, s/o late Habibullah, r/o Seerjagir, Sopore, Baramullah J&K surrendered JKLF militant and who happens to be my cousin also did his graduation with me from Delhi University in early 1990. During this period he also got acquainted with Abdul Rehman Gilani. During Afzal's visits to Delhi he used to motivate Gilani and me for joining the Jehad in Kashmir. I was very much influenced by Osama Bin after the US attack on September 11 this year. On October 2001, Afzal called me from J&K and asked to arrange a rented house for himself and one of his militant associates who would look after the flow of funds to the militants in J&K. Motivated by Afzal and the attack on US, I agreed and arranged for a rented accomodation in Room no.5, Private Boys Hostel, Christian Colony. On the first week of November 2001, Afzal and his associate militant Mohammed came to Delhi and met me at my house in 1021, Mukharjee Nagar. Initially, Afzal introduced Mohd. as a native of Doda, J&K, but when I got suspicious about Mohd. being a Kashmiri, Afzal disclosed that Mohd. is a Pak national and belongs to Jaish-e-Mohd. militant outfit and that he had come for carrying a Fidayeen attack in Delhi. During this period I also discussed about Jehad and Qaum with Abdul Rehman Gilani who agreed to work for Jehad and offered his help in carrying out the fidayeen attack. Meanwhile Afzal went to Srinagar to deliver money received in Delhi through Hawala to Gazi Baba @ Doctor, Supreme Commander of Jaish-e-Mohd. in Kashmir. During these visits he also brought 4 more Pak nationals and Jaish-e-Mohd. militant Raja, Rana, Hyder @ Tufail and Hamza to Delhi. Afzal arranged another accomodation at A-97 Gandhi Vihar, Timarpur. On the first week of December when Afzal brought Rana and Hamza to Delhi, they brought along with them arms and ammunitions and explosives etc. In order to execute the fidayeen attack, Afzal and Mohd. bought new mobile phones, Sim cards and explosive material. During this period, I also changed my mobile number from 9810446375 to 9811573506 as a precautionary measure, since I had been talking to Ghazi Baba, Mohd. and Afzal from my previous number 98104-46375. Afzal and Mohd. also used my yamaha motorcycle for conducting recee of the targets. Meetings were also held at my house for discussion and execution of the plan and my wife was also in the knowledge of our plans. According to the plan Afzal and Mohd. bought a second hand white ambassador car having no. DL-3C-J1527. Prior to the purchase of the car Afzal took another rented accomodation in Indira Vihar, Mukharjee Nagar. On 12.12.2001 night I along with Afzal and Gilani met Mohammad and other Pak militants at their Gandhi Vihar hideout. Mohd. gave laptop computer along with the attachments and Rs. 10 lacs to Afzal with the direction to hand over the laptop to Gazi Baba and the money was to be distributed among Afzal, Gilani and myself. Mohd. told that the next day i.e. 13.12.2001 they would carry out fidayeen attack on Parliament House. Myself, Afzal and Gilani then left the Gandhi Vihar hide-out on 13.12.2001 at about 11.20 A.M. Afzal called me from his mobile number 98114-89429 and asked me to watch TV and inform about the latest position of the VVIP in Parliament. By the time I switched on the TV I received another call from Afzal that the mission is on. After the incident I met Afzal at Azadpur Mandi and both of us went to Gilani's house to give him Rs. 2 lakhs as his share. Instead Gilani told to take the money and give it at his house in Kashmir. I along with Afzal left for Srinagar in my truck the same day. We were apprehended on reaching Srinagar on 15.12.2001. The laptop along with the attachments and Rs. 10 lacs were recovered from us by the police and later on brought to Delhi.

The recording of the confessional statement has been concluded.

Ashok Chand
DSP/Spl.Cell
21.12.2001
Time: 5.15 p.m.

ANNEXURE 4

Extract from Statement of SAR Geelani Under Section 313

Q: Why this case against you?

Ans: After I was picked up I was tortured by A.C.P. Rajbir Singh and other police officials in presence of D.C.P. Ashok Chand and I told them that I shall proceed against them in N.H.R.C. and I also told that they have caught a wrong person and I was innocent. Then I was told by them that they were framing me in this case. So I have been falsely implicated in this case.

Q: Why the witnesses deposed against you?

Ans: The witnesses have deposed against me due to fear of the police.

Q: Do you have anything else to say?

Ans: On 14th Dec. 2001 after I was arrested as already told by me I was blind folded and taken to some place which was like farm house. At that farm house tea was ordered by the police officials and on the sugar sachles Ashoka Countryside was written. At the farm house I was made naked and tortured and I was hanged upside down. I was forced to make confessional statement but I made no confessional statement as I was not involved. Thereafter I was threatened if I made no confessional statement my family members would be eliminated. On 14th Night I was brought to special cell Lodhi Colony where I found my wife, my two children, my brother, my brother-in-law and one another relative at the special cell. They had already been arrested. I saw Afasan Guru also at special cell at that time. Afsal in his interview given to media has categorically stated that I have no involvement. My conversation with my half brother on telephone was tampered. In the conversation where my brother had asked "Ya Kaya Keya" this question he asked about family matter as I was having some programme to go to Kashmir on Id. However due to business in the college I could not make programme for going to Kashmir and due to this, dispute arose between me and my wife also, who was insisting for going to Kashmir. My wife talked to my mother and my mother when inquired, as to why we were not going to Kashmir, then my wife told my mother that she should ask her son (me). It was for this reason that my half brother felt that there was some 'Garbar' and he might have asked that 'Yeh Kaya Kiya'. I did not say 'Yeh Jaroori Hota Hai'. My relationship with Shaukat and Afzal were of mere aquaintance.

Ques: Will you lead defence evidence.

Ans: Yes.

RO & AC Designated Judge
17.09.02

Note: The above extract is as it is recorded by the court.

Annexure 5

Statement of Mohammad Afzal Under Section 313

In the Court of Shri S. N. Dhingra, ASJ, N. Delhi
S/V Afzal Guru & Others FIR 417/01

Statement of accused Mohd. Afzal son of late Habibullah r/o village Seerjagir, Distt. Baramullah, J&K, under Section 313 Cr.P.C. without oath.

Q. It is in evidence against you that on 13th Dec. 2001 at about 11.40-11.45 a.m. a terrorist attack was done by the terrorist at Parliament House when Parliament was in session and Vice President of India, Ministers, M.Ps, V.I.Ps and V.V.I.Ps were in the Parliament. In this attack five Pakistani trained militants got killed at the hands of the security staff. 9 persons from security staff and other agencies also got killed. 15 persons were injured. In the attack explosive substances, hand grenades, AK 47 Rifles and pistol were used by the terrorists. What you have to say?

Ans. **I don't know.**

Q. It is in evidence against you that on the checking of 5 slain terrorists, fake identity card of Websity Xansa Computer Education were recovered which are Ext. PW 4/2, PW 4/4, PW 3/3, PW 2/3, PW 2/4 and PW 2/5 and on these I.Cards photographs of the terrorist with fake name and phone No. 98114 89429 was found written. What you have to say?

Ans. **I do not know.**

Q. It is in evidence against you that on the persons of 5 slain terrorists 5 mobile phone and slips containing certain mobile phone numbers were recovered. Slips are Ext. PW 2/16, PW 4/6, PW 4/7. What you have to say?

Ans. **I don't know.**

Q. It is in evidence against you that cell phone number 98114 89429 was cell number of your mobile phone which was being used by you. What you have to say?

Ans. **It is wrong.**

Q. It is in evidence against you that you were arrested by the police at Srinagar, alongwith your co-accused Shaukat Hussain Guru in truck No. HR 38E 6733 and in possesion of both of you one laptop alongwith accessories and cash amounting to Rs. 10 Lakhs was recovered. What you have to say?

Ans. **I was arrested alone from Srinagar & nothing was recovered from me.**

Q. It is in evidence against you that you were brought to Delhi by Delhi Police and arrested in this case and your disclosure statement Ext. PW 64/1 was recorded on 16-12-2001. What you have to say?

Ans. **I was brought to Delhi, but police recorded stt. itself after torturing me.**

Q. It is in evidence against you that you desire to make confessional statement before D.C.P. voluntarily. What you have to say?

Ans. **It is wrong.**

Q. It is in evidence against you that on 21.12.01 at about 7.10 p.m. you were produced before Shri Ashok Chand, DCP Spl. Cell by IO of this case ACP Rajbir Singh, for the purpose of recording your confessional statement and you were explained by DCP Ashok Chand that you were not bound to make any confessional statement but you expressed your willingness to do so by recording your willingness Ex. PW 60/7 is in your own hand. What have you to say?

Ans. **It is wrong.**

Q. It is further in evidence that warning given to you by DCP Ashok Chand was drawn in proceedings as Ex. PW 60/8 and thereafter your disclosure statement Ex. PW 60/9 was recorded by the said DCP. What have you to say?

Ans. **It is wrong. I only signed blank papers. I made no stt.**

Q. It is further in evidence that you had signed your confessional statement at point C and thereafter, it was sealed in an envelope Ex. PW 60/10 and carbon copy of the same was supplied to IO ACP Rajbir Singh on application moved by him in this regard. What have you to say?

Ans. **I made no stt. so I don't know.**

Q. It is in evidence against you that you recorded in your disclosure statement Ex. PW 60/7 that in the year 1989-90, on the motivation of Yasin Malik & Hamid Shah of Jammu & Kashmir Liberation Front you joined this militant outfit for the purpose of Jehad and you alongwith several JKLF militants crossed over to Muzaffarabad in Pak Occupied Kashmir. What have you to say?

Ans. **It is correct.**

Q. It is further in evidence that you were given basic training for about 2½ months, in handling arms and ammunition and insurgent activities by one Zainuluddin, a retired Pak army officer. What have you to say?

Ans. **I was not given proper training. The place was full of militants. I was told few things. After going there I found different atmosphere.**

Q. It is further in evidence that after completing your training, you alongwith 80 trained militants crossed back to India through Trigam sector in Kupwara and you had brought one AK 47 with three loaded magazines and Rs.10000/- in Indian currency paid to you by the militant outfit. What have you to say?

Ans. **It is wrong. I was not having ammunition, others were having ammunition who had crossed along with me. There were militants of different terrorist org. who crossed border with me.**

Q. It is further in evidence that on reaching India, you were tasked to destroy communication network, educational institutions and important bridges on J&K. What have you to say?

Ans. **It is correct.**

Q. It is in further evidence that soon after your return to India, security forces were tipped off and in order to escape security forces, you came to Delhi alongwith your cousin brother Shaukat Hussain. What have you to say?

Ans. **After coming from Muzfrabad, I stayed at my house for 25 days & then came to Delhi to my cousin Shokat.**

Q. It is further in evidence against you that you started doing odd jobs in Delhi and also completed your graduation from Delhi University in 1993-94. What have you to say?

Ans. **It is correct.**

Q. It is further in evidence against you that during summer of 1993-94, you had come to Srinagar and surrendered before BSF and had also handed over the arms and ammunitions brought by you from Pakistan. What have you to say?

Ans. **It is correct that I surrendered before BSF. Two more boys has surrendered with me & they also gave their arm & ammunition. I did not give arm & ammunition.**

Q. It is further in evidence that you had further disclosed that about eight months ago from 12.01, when you had gone to deliver surgical goods at a shop in Lal Chowk, Srinagar, you came across one Tariq who introduced himself as a doctor residing in Anantnag and you discussed with him about the current affairs and militancy in Kashmir. What have you to say?

Ans. **In summer of yr 2000, I was picked up by STF & confined for 21 days. I met Tariq during confinement. Tariq was in**

medicine business. At that time I had no discussion with him. I had to daily attend STF camp.

Q. It is further in evidence that you, thereafter, met Tariq on two more occasions and two months after the first meeting, when you had gone to offer Namaz at Batmallo Masjid, Tariq met you and disclosed that he was an active militant of Jaish-e-Mohammad outfit and you were motivated by Tariq to join Jehad for liberation of Kashmir and for the cause of Muslim community. What have you to say?

Ans. **Tariq was not a militant, however we used to talk about militancy. Tariq did not motivate me for Jehad. He used to ask me about my Delhi business.**

Q. It is further in evidence that Tariq had assured of financial support and you agreed to work for Jaish-e-Mohd. What have you to say?

Ans. **It is wrong.**

Q. It is further in evidence against you that you disclosed in Ex. PW 60/7 that Tariq further introduced you to one Ghazi Baba, the Supreme Commander of Jaish-e-Mohd. in Kashmir. What have you to say?

Ans. **It is wrong.**

Q. It is further in evidence that you further disclosed that Ghazi Baba's Company in Kashmir consisted of about 60 heavily armed militants of Jaish-e-Mohd. (JeM) and Ghazi Baba was also equipped with wireless sets, satellite phones and other means of communication. What have you to say?

Ans. **It is wrong.**

Q. It is further in evidence that Ghazi Baba further motivated you and also gave you audio cassette and literature containing provocative preachings of Maulana Masood Azhar and you were directed to contact Tariq after 6 weeks at the appointed time. What have you to say?

Ans. **It is wrong.**

Q. It is further in evidence against you that you met Tariq as directed, who again took you to Ghazi baba at his training camp, who instructed you that he had been told by Maulana Masood Azhar that they should carry out action on imporatant institutions of Indian nation like Indian Parliament and US & UK embassies, as their action in Kashmir had not led to the desired results. What have you to say?

Ans. **It is wrong.**

Q. It is further in evidence against you that you had further disclosed as per Ex. PW 60/7 that Ghazi Baba had told you that action in Delhi would be a joint action of JeM and Lashkar-e-Tyabba (LeT) and you were tasked to provide a safe hideout for the Fidayeens, in Delhi and you were also introduced by Ghazi Baba to Mohammad and Haider, Pak nationals and militants of JeM. What have you to say?

Ans. **It is wrong.**

Q. It is further in evidence against you that in the month of October, 01, you rang up co-accused Shaukat for arranging a rented accomodation for yourself and Mohammad in Delhi. What you have to say?

Ans. **It is wrong.**

Q. It is further in evidence against you that in the 1st week of November, you brought Mohammad to Delhi, who brought alongwith him a laptop and Rs.50000/- and on reaching Delhi, you both went to the house of Shaukat, who then took you and Mohammad to the pre-arranged accomodation in Christian Colony, Room No.5 of Boy's hostel. What have you to say?

Ans. **I was to come to Delhi, Tariq told me that Mohammad has to go to Delhi, I should take him to Delhi. He would stay in Delhi for some days & he has to go abroad. So Mohd. came with me, he himself arranged accomodation.**

Q. It is further in evidence that you introduced Mohammad to Shaukat as a resident of Doda, Kashmir and when Shaukat was not convinced, you told him that Mohammad was a Pak national and militant of JeM and had come to Delhi to carry out a fidayeen attack. What have you to say?

Ans. **It is wrong.**

Q. It is further in evidence against you that after about a week thereafter, you arranged another hideout at A-97, Gandhi Vihar, Timarpur. What have you to say?

Ans. **It is wrong.**

Q. It is further in evidence that Mohammad through Hawala collected Rs. 20 lakhs and gave Rs. 5 lakhs to you for giving it to Tariq in Srinagar, you went to Srinagar and gave the said money to Tariq. What have you to say?

Ans. **It is wrong.**

Q. It is further in evidence against you that at the asking of Tariq, you brought two militants of JeM, namely Raja and Haider, both Pak nationals to Delhi from Srinagar and took them to the hide-out in Gandhi Vihar. What have you to say?

Ans. **It is wrong.**

Q. It is further in evidence against you that you also disclosed as per Ex. PW 60/7 that in order to complete the assignment given by Ghazi Baba, you alongwith Mohammad went to Khari Baoli, Delhi, from where Mohammad purchased 60 Kgs. of Ammonium Nitrate, 10 Kgs. Aluminium powder and 5 Kgs. of sulphur. What have you to say?

Ans. **It is wrong.**

Q. It is further in evidence that Mohammad told you that these chemicals when mixed in the ratio of 7:2:1, would make a high explosive. What have you to say?

Ans. **It is wrong.**

Q. It is further in evidence that after about a week, Mohammad again gave you Rs. 5 lakhs and you went with that money to Srinagar and handed over the same to Tariq. What have you to say?

Ans. **It is wrong.**

Q. It is further in evidence that in the first week of December 01, you again met Tariq and at his instructions, brought two Pak nationals and militants of JeM, namely Rana and Hamja to Delhi. What have you to say?

Ans. **It is wrong.**

Q. It is further in evidence against you that you also disclosed before the DCP in Ex. PW 60/7 that said Rana and Hamja were carrying AK rifles, 12 loaded magazines, 1 grenade launcher, 3 pistols with spare magazines, 15 hand grenades, 15 grenade shells, two packs of electronic detonators, two transreceivers and explosives etc. What have you to say?

Ans. **I do not know.**

Q. It is further in evidence that you alongwith above-named persons had come from Srinagar to Jammu by bus and from Jammu to Delhi by train. On reaching Delhi you took them to hideout in Gandhi Vihar. What have you to say?

Ans. **It is wrong.**

Q. It is further in evidence that at Delhi, you had arranged another accomodation at 281, Indira Vihar, Mukherji Nagar area. What have you to say?

Ans. **I had rented this accomodation for myself as I was to come to Delhi after Eid.**

Q. It is in evidence against you that your co-accused Mohammad (slain) terrorist had purchased mobile phone and Sim cards from Gaffar Market and Palika Bazar in your company and had received directions from Ghazi Baba on the cell phone from satellite phone. What have you to say?

Ans. **It is wrong.**

Q. It is in evidence against you that during your visit to Delhi you used to meet Shaukat Hussain Guru and S.A.R. Geelani and motivate them in Jehad in Kashmir. What you have to say?

Ans. **It is wrong.**

Q. It is in evidence against you that accused Shaukat Hussain Guru provided his motor cycle to you and slain terrorist for taking recee? What you have to say?

Ans. **It is wrong.**

Q. It is in evidence against you that meeting of slain terrorists also used to be held in the house of Shaukat Hussain Guru for discussing further course of action and in this meeting accused SAR Geelani, accused Shaukat Hussain Guru and his wife Afsan Guru also used to be present. What you have to say?

Ans. **It is wrong.**

Q. It is in evidence against you that in these meetings of terrorists, you and other co-accused, targets to be chosen for terrorist attack were discussed as Delhi Assembly, U.K and U.S.A. Embassy, Parliament House and Airport. What have you to say?

Ans. **It is wrong.**

Q. It is in evidence against you that one more motor cycle was purchased by you from Karol Bagh which was also to be used for taking recee. What you have to say?

Ans. **It is wrong.**

Q. It is in evidence against you that after taking recee of all aforesaid targets, slain terrorist Mohammad informed Ghazi Baba and Ghazi Baba told you that they must strike at Parliament. What you have to say?

Ans. **I don't know.**

Q. It is in evidence against you that final meeting was held at the house of Shaukat Hussain Guru in which all of you (all accused persons and slain terrorists) were present and plans for attacking of Parliament was finalised. What you have to say?

Ans. **It is wrong.**

Q. It is in evidence against you that as per plan on 11-12-2001 you alongwith slain terrorist Mohammad went to Karol Bagh for purchasing a second hand Ambassador car for a sum of Rs. 1,08,000/- was purchased from Lucky Motors. What you have to say?

Ans. **Mohd. had expressed desire to purchase a car & he requested me to accompany him. I went along with him to Karol Bagh & he purchased a second hand car.**

Q. It is in evidence against you that on 11.12.2001 you alongwith Mohammad went to Kashmiri Gate and purchased a Magnetic VIP Red Light to facilitate entry of car into Parliament House. What you have to say?

Ans. **It is wrong.**

Q. It is in evidence against you that slain terrorist Mohammad got prepared sticker of M.H.A. and fake I.Cards through laptop. What you have to say.

Ans. **I don't know.**

Q. It is in evidence against you that Mohammad alongwith other militants prepared IEDs for grinding and mixing of chemical and put them in container brought from Chandni Chowk. What you have to say.

Ans. **I don't know.**

Q. It is in evidence against you that I.E.D. was fitted in the car for causing explosion. What you have to say?

Ans. **I don't know.**

Q. It is in evidence against you that on the night of 12-12-2001 you alongwith accused Shokat and S.A.R. Geelani went to hideout at Gandhi Vihar Timarpur where all the five Pak militants were present. What you have to say?

Ans. **It is wrong. I had not met Gilani six months prior to 13.12.01.**

Q. It is in evidence against you that Mohammad (slain terrorist) gave you laptop and Rs. 10 Lakhs and he told you to take laptop to Ghazi Baba and told that Rs. 10 Lakhs was for you and your friend Shaukat Hussain Guru and for S.A.R. Geelani. What you have to say?

Ans. **It is wrong.**

Q. It is in evidence against you that Mohammad (slain terrorist) told you that they were going to attack and fidayeen attack on Parliament House on 13.12.2001. What you have to say?

Ans. **It is wrong.**

Q. It is in evidence against you that you & your co-accused Shaukat Hussain Guru and S.A.R. Geelani left Gandhi Vihar hideout and continued in touch with each other on mobile phone. What you have to say?

Ans. **It is wrong.**

Q. It is in evidence against you that on 13.12.2001 at about 10.40 a.m. you received a call on your mobile phone 98114 89429 from Mohammad from his mobile phone 98110693456 and he asked you to watch TV and tell him about presence of various V.V.I.Ps inside the Parliament House and they told you that they were near the Parliament House and awaiting your reply. What you have to say?

Ans. **It is wrong.**

Q. It is in evidence against you that at that time you were in Azadpur Mandi. There was no electricity there and you could not watch T.V. After about 25 minutes you again received a call from Mohammad regarding the presence of VVIPs in the Parliament House and you informed him that due to electricity being not there, you could not watch the T.V. and you asked him to give you some more time. What you have to say?

Ans. **It is wrong.**

Q. It is in evidence against you that thereafter you contacted Shaukat Hussain Guru at his mobile phone no. 98115 73505 and asked him to watch TV and inform him (Mohammad). What you have to say?

Ans. **It is wrong.**

Q. It is in evidence against you that after you had talked to Shaukat Hussain Guru, they again called you and told you that they were going ahead with the attack on Parliament House.

Ans. **It is wrong.**

Q. It is in evidence against you that you then again called Shaukat and told him that mission has started. What you have to say?

Ans. **It is wrong.**

Q. It is in evidence against you that Shaukat Hussain Guru thereafter came and met you at Azadpur Mandi and both of you went to S.A.R. Geelani's house and gave him Rs. 2 lakhs as his share but Geelani told you that you should take his money and gave it at his house in Kashmir. What you have to say?

Ans. **It is wrong.**

Q. It is in evidence against you that after this you and Shaukat Hussain Guru left for Sri Nagar in truck No. HR 38E 6733 which belonged to Shaukat Hussain Guru and you reached Sri Nagar on this truck. You and Shaukat Hussain Guru were apprehended by the police in Sri Nagar. What you have to say?

Ans. **It is wrong. I went to Srinagar by bus.**

Q. It is in evidence against you that you made supplementary disclosure statement to ACP Rajbir Singh on 20-12-2001. What you have to say?

Ans. **It is wrong.**

Q. It is in evidence against you that your disclosure statement was recorded. In pursuance of your disclosure statement you and your co-accused Shokat led police party to a hideout of slain terrorists at A-97 Gandhi Vihar at second floor and got recovered from there three electronic detonators with yellow wire, two silver powder packs, ½ bucket of prepared explosive, two packs of sulphur, TCL, 2 cartons containing 20 sealed packs of aluminium nitrate purified, one carton containing 20 empty packs of aluminium nitrate and one empty pack of sulphur. All these articles were seized vide seizure memo Ext. PW 34/1 and the articles are Ext. P 60/1, 2, 3 and P 61 to P 71. Samples were taken out from the explosive substances and chemical and separately sealed with the seal of HSG and form C.F.S.L. was filled. What you have to say?

Ans. **It is wrong & false.**

Q. It is in evidence against you that you and co-accused Shaukat Hussain Guru had led police party to premises No. A-97 Gandhi Vihar, P.S. Timarpur and from you both got recovered police uniform shirts in Khaki colour 3 in number, police uniform pant in Khaki colour four in number, police uniform card black three in number, police berret cap 2 in number, electronic time piece 6 in number (two attached with wire), transistor make Kehibo one in number, volta meter with leads black one in number, 9 volt battery with wire one in number, battery cell (small) 12 in number, black starter one in number, battery caps with wire 3 in number, screw driver one in number, ear phone with leads two in number, wire pieces black 3 in number, Sujata mixer grinder with three jars used for mixing explosives. All these articles were seized by the police vide seizure memo Ext. PW 34/4 and Sujata mixer and its jar were sealed with the seal of HSG. What you have to say?

Ans. **It is wrong.**

Q. It is in evidence against you that you led police to A-97 Gandhi Vihar, New Delhi second floor and from there you got recovered one piece of paper having specimen stamp of "Cyber Tech Computer education Software Managing Director", one piece of paper bearing map of Chanakya puri, one blank I.Card, two Airtel magic cards, some photographs and some other papers and one map of Delhi which were seized by the police vide seizure memo Ext. PW 34/3. The seized papers/documents are collectively marked as Ext. P79. What you have to say?

Ans. **It is wrong.**

Q. It is in evidence against you that you also got recovered alongwith your co-accused Shaukat Hussain one motor cycle No. HR 51E 5768 standing near the house No. A97 Gandhi Vihar, Delhi which was seized by the police vide seizure memo Ext. PW 34/2. Motor cycle is Ext. P76. What you have to say?

Ans. **It is wrong.**

Q. It is in evidence against you that you and your co-accused Shaukat Hussain led police to 281 Indira Vihar second floor and this premises was found locked and after breaking the lock police entered it and recovered three electronic detonators attached with yellow colour wire, six pressure detonators, 2 silver powder packets each of one kg., two boxes of sulphur for TCL, one carton of Ammonium Nitrate containing 25 packs of Ammonium Nitrate and other house hold articles which were seized vide seizure memo Ext. PW 32/1 and articles are Ext. P 47 to P 57. What you have to say?

Ans. **The house was taken on rent by me for my family. The key was given by me to landlady. Nothing was recovered from this house except house hold articles.**

Q. It is in evidence against you that you and your co-accused Shaukat Hussain Guru also got recovered one motor cycle bearing number DL-1S-K3122 near the gate of house No. 281 Indira Vihar Delhi. What you have to say?

Ans. **The M/Cycle belongs to Shaukat & was at house of Shaukat. Police has wrongly shown it recovered from 281 Indira Vihar. Police picked up bike from Shaukat's house.**

Q. It is in evidence against you, you in custody of police went to mortuary and identified deceased terrorists from whom fake I.Card of Rohail Sharma and Ashiq Hussain were recovered, who was Mohammad r/o Punjab, Pakistan. Identification memo is Ext. PW 76/1 and photographs of deceased terrorist Mohammad is Ext. PW 29/5. What you have to say?

Ans. **I had not identified any terrorist. Police told me the names of terrorists & forced me to identify them.**

Q. It is in evidence against you that you led police party to shop No. 990 Gali Lothian Tilak Bazar Kashmiri Gate where from you and your associate Hamza (deceased terrorist) had purchased 50 kg Amonium Nitrate. The pointing out memo of the shop and identification of the person from whom this Amonium Nitrate was purchased is Ext. PW 40/1. What you have to say?

Ans. **It is wrong.**

Q. It is also in evidence against you that you led police party to shop No. 1/2628 Hamilton Road, Kashmiri Gate, New Delhi and pointed out the shop from where you and your associate Mohammad had purchased VIP red light for using on Ambassador car DL-3C-J1527. You identified Vijay Anand as shop owner from whom light was purchased. Identification and pointing out memo is Ext. PW 26/5. What you have to say?

Ans. **It is wrong.**

Q. It is in evidence against you that you led police party to the shop No. 343 Joshi Road Karol Bagh and identified Harpal Singh where from you had purchased alongwith your co-accused Mohammad Ambassador car No. DL-3C-J1527 for a sum of Rs. 1,08,000/-. The pointing out and identification memo is Ext. PW 20/9. What you have to say?

Ans. **It is wrong.**

Q. It is in evidence against you that you led police to shop No. 657 Sawan Dry Fruit and Kirana Store Fatehpuri, and pointed out the shop and owner where from you along with your co-accused Mohammad (deceased terrorist) had purchased dry fruits. The pointing out memo is Ext. PW 41/1. What you have to say?

Ans. **It is wrong.**

Q. It is in evidence against you that you took police to shop No. 151 Tilak Bazar, Kashmiri Gate, Delhi and identified the shop owner from whom you and your co-accused Mohammad had purchased silver powder for preparing IED. The pointing out and identification memo is Ext. PW 42/1. What you have to say?

Ans. **It is wrong.**

Q. It is in evidence against you that you led the police to shop No. 6504 R.D. Store, Fatehpuri, Delhi and identified the owner wherefrom you, alongwith your co-accused Mohammad, had purchased Sujata Mixer Grinder for mixing the chemical to prepare IED. The pointing out and identification memo is Ext. PW 76/2. What you have to say?

Ans. **It is wrong.**

Q. It is in evidence against you that you led police party to shop No. 1731/56 Naliwala Karol Bagh and pointed out the shop where from motor cycle No. HR-51E-5768 was purchased for a sum of Rs. 20,000/- and Rs. 560/- was given as commission. Memo in this respect is Ext. PW 29/1. What you have to say?

Ans. **It is wrong.**

Q. It is in evidence against you that you led the police party to shop No. 26 Gaffar Market, Karol Bagh, New Delhi, and told from this shop you had purchased mobile phone handset (Sony) and pre paid coupon from this shop. The memo in this respect is Ext. PW 44/1. What you have to say?

Ans. **It is wrong.**

Q. It is in evidence against you that you led the police party to shop No. B 10 Model Town II and pointed out the shop wherefrom you in company of Shaukat Hussain Guru has purchased one mobile phone handset Motorola from this shop with Sim card.

The pointing out memo in this respect is Ext. PW 49/1. What you have to say?

Ans. **It is wrong.**

Q. It is in evidence against you that police seized bill book containing entry of speed card of mobile phone No. 98114 89429 vide seizure memo Ext. PW 49/2. The bill book is Ext. P 82. What you have to say?

Ans. **I don't know.**

Q. It is in evidence against you that the laptop recovered from you was got examined from Orion Convergence Limited by Special Cell Delhi Police and report of the observation of the laptop is Ext. PW 72/1. As per this observation the laptop was using Pakistan based ISP named micro-net-PK. The internet and scanner was accessed on 5th Dec. 2001. ID Card file were edited on 12th Dec. 2001. Laptop contained file showing Zee News T.V. channel news item of 3 alleged Pakistani terrorist killed in Lucknow and news clipping showing interview of Mr. George Fernandes in front of Parliament House. News clipping showing proceeding of Parliament. News clipping showing Arun Jaitly, Minister on the gate of Parliament building, Mulayam Singh Jadav, Ex. Defence Minister entering the gate of Parliament building and news clipping of Arun Jaitley addressing the press and entering the gate of Parliament and news clipping of some minister of India entering the gate of Parliament and some minister standing near the gate of Parliament. News clipping of interview of Mr. Vijay Kumar Malhotra in front of Parliament House. News clipping of some people who are coming out of the gate of Parliament and another news clipping showing the long shot of building which look like Parliament of India and Supreme Court of India. What you have to say?

Ans. **I do not know.**

Q. It is in evidence against you that PW 29 Susheel Kumar identified you as a person who had come to purchase motor cycle

No. HR 51E 5768 alongwith other three persons from his shop on 8-12-01 in the morning and stated that motor cycle was sold to you for Rs. 20,000/- in the evening of 8-12-01. What you have to say?

Ans. **It is wrong.**

Q. It is in evidence against you that PW 29 also stated that you had filled the portion A to A and B to B of delivery receipt Ext. PW 29/2 and signed it at the time of taking delivery of the motor cycle. What you have to say?

Ans. **It is wrong.**

Q. It is in evidence against you that you got house No. 281 Indira Vihar second floor on rent of Rs. 4000/- p.m. on 9.12.01 through property dealer Balraj (PW 31) and he identified you and you paid him Rs. 1000/- as advance. What you have to say?

Ans. **It is correct.**

Q. It is in evidence against you that owner of house No. 281 Indira Vihar, namely Jagdish Lal, PW 32, identified you as the person who had taken the house on rent and you had paid him balance advance of Rs. 7000/- on 10-12-01 and taken possession of the floor. He put a condition that you can live in the house with your family. You told him that you will bring your family later on. What you have to say?

Ans. **It is correct.**

Q. It is in evidence against you that on 11-12-01 you alongwith 5-6 persons were seen going upstairs by PW 32 and he came to second floor and told you that he had given the flat for living with your family and you had brought those persons with you. You then told him that those persons were your friends and they would leave. What you have to say?

Ans. **It is wrong.**

Q. It is in evidence against you that on 12-12-01 you left the premises with some bags and locked it and told PW 32 that you would bring your family and children after Id. What you have to say?

Ans. **It is correct.**

Q. It is in evidence against you that on 16-12-01 you and your co-accused Shaukat Hussain Guru in police custody came to house No. 281 Indira Vihar and went to the premises under your possession and police broke the lock and police found some incriminating articles lying in the house which were seized by the police vide seizure memo Ext. PW 32/1 and they were sealed with the seal of HSG. What you have to say?

Ans. **It is wrong. The lock was opened by landlady. It was not broken.**

Q. It is in evidence against you that police showed photographs of the terrorists at the time of attack on Parliament and PW 32 identified them as those persons who were sitting with you in the premises on 11-12-01. The photographs of the terrorists identified by PW 32 are Ext. PW 1/20 to PW 1/24. What you have to say?

Ans. **I was alone in the house. Landlord has wrongly stated so at instance of police.**

Q. It is in evidence against you that police also seized one motor cycle DL-1S-K 3122 Yamaha make from the above premises vide seizure memo Ext. PW 32/2. PW 32 had told the police that motor cycle belonged to you people and was standing down stairs. What you have to say?

Ans. **It is wrong.**

Q. It is in evidence against you that Davinder Pal Kapoor (PW 33) has identified as a person you had gone to him in Nov. 2001 and wanted some house on rent. He got second floor of the house of Subhash Malhotra A 97 Gandhi Vihar, Delhi and rented out to you at Rs. 1200/- per month. What you have to say?

Ans. **It is wrong.**

Q. It is in evidence against you that you introduced yourself to Subhas Malhotra as Masood and told him that you were student of Kirori Mal College at the time of taking the house No. A 97 Gandhi Vihar, Delhi on rent. What you have to say?

Ans. **It is wrong.**

Q. It is in evidence against you that accused Shaukat Hussain Guru and 3-4 more boys visited you in the premises. What you have to say?

Ans. **It is wrong.**

Q. It is in evidence against you that you and your co-accused Shaukat Hussain Guru led the police to this house on 16-12-01 and police told your name as Mohd. Afzal to PW 34 who had known you as Masood, and police went to the second floor of the premises which was in your tenancy and broke open the lock and recovered several incriminating articles which were seized by the police vide seizure memo Ext. PW 34/1. The articles were sealed with the seal of HSG. The articles included one Sujata Mixer and other chemicals and explosive mixture in a plastic bucket. What you have to say?

Ans. **It is wrong.**

Q. It is in evidence against you that police also seized one motor cycle No. HR 51 E 5678 vide seizure memo Ext. PW 34/2. They also seized certain papers from the room via seizure memo Ext. PW/3 and seized some house hold articles vide seizure memo Ext. PW 34/4 in the presence of this witness. What you have to say?

Ans. **It is wrong.**

Q. It is in evidence against you that PW 34 had seen you, Shaukat Hussain Guru and 4 more persons leaving the premises around 10. A.M. on 13.12.01 in a Ambassador car. All of you were carrying bags and car was standing near temple outside the gali. After the car left you came back to the premises and then left the premises after some time. What you have to say?

Ans. **It is wrong.**

Q. It is in evidence against you that PW 34 identified the photographs of one of the terrorist Ext. PW 1/20 as one who had lived with you for few days in this premises. He identified the articles seized from the room as P 60 to P 79. What you have to say?

Ans. **It is wrong.**

Q. It is in evidence against you that Ext. PW 35/1 is the certificate issued by Capt. R.K. Guharay security Manager of AIRTEL. It gives the details of calls of mobile phone No. 98105 11085, 98106 93456, 98105 65284, 98105 10816, 98103 02438, 98104 46375. The computerised details are Ext. PW 35/2 to PW 35/7. He also gave computerised call details of cell No. 98100 81228 of SAR Gelani in nine pages as Ext. PW 35/A. What you have to say?

Ans. **I don't want to say anything.**

Q. It is further in evidence against you that call details in respect of cell No. 98115 73506 from 1.12.01 to 13.12.01 are Ext. PW 36/1 and from 1.12.01 to 18.12.01 are Ext. PW 36/2, call details of mobile No. 9198114 89429 from 1.11.01 to 18.12.01 are Ext. PW 36/3, of mobile No.98115 44860 are Ext. PW 36/4 and of cell No. 9198114 89429 are Ext. PW 36/5, as produced in evidence by Major A.R. Satish, Executive of Sterling Cellular Ltd. and supplied to him by Lt. Col. Rajiv Pandey, Genl. Manager of this Co. vide his letters Ext. PW 36/6 to Ext. Pw 36/8. What have you to say?

Ans. **I don't want to say anything.**

Q. It is further in evidence that on 6.11.01, you alongwith accused Shaukat Hussain Guru had approached PW 37 Sh. Prem Chand, through Rajneesh STD Booth for letting-out a room to you in his hostel, which he was running in the name of Yamuna Hostel at B-41, Christian Colony having 32 rooms therein. What have you to say?

Ans. **It is wrong.**

Q. It is further in evidence against you that PW 37 Prem Chand let-out room No.5 in Yamuna Hostel, on the ground floor to both of you at a monthly rent of Rs.1500/- and both of you came to that room on 7th or 8th November 01 and after putting your luggage there, you both went away. What have you to say?

Ans. **It is wrong.**

Q. It is further in evidence that on 26.11.01, PW 37 Prem Chand went to said hostel for checking the rooms and in room no.5, which was let-out to you, he found one Kashmiri boy, who told him his name was Rohail Ali Shah and further told him that he was doing diploma in computer from Aptech, Kamla Nagar and he also showed his identity card Ext. PW 4/4. What have you to say?

Ans. **I don't know.**

Q. It is further in evidence that on 6th or 8th December 01, PW 37 Prem Chand saw Rohail Ali Shah going out of abovesaid room and when Prem Chand asked for his particulars for the purpose of police verification, he told Prem Chand that he would give him the same after coming back but on 8.12.01, when Prem Chand again went to room no.5, he found the room lying vacant. What have you to say?

Ans. **I don't know.**

Q. It is further in evidence that on 19.12.01 PW Prem Chand was called at the Special Cell through a constable, where you, Shaukat and 4-5 other persons were present and PW Prem Chand identified you and Shaukat as the persons, who had come to him for hiring a room and then he came to know about your involvement in terrorist activities and PW 37 also identified the photograph Ext. PW 29/5 as that of Rohail Ali Shah in court. What have you to say?

Ans. **It is wrong.**

Q. It is further in evidence that PW 38 Rajneesh Kumar was approached by you and Shaukat for the purpose of hiring a room and he had taken both of you to the house of PW 37 Prem Chand at B-41. What have you to say?

Ans. **It is wrong.**

Q. It is further in evidence against you that your co-accused SAR Gilani used to live with his family in the rented house belonging to PW 39 Naresh Gulati, bearing No. 535, Mukherji Nagar, Delhi, on its second floor and you and co-accused Shaukat used to visit SAR Gilani and PW 39 had been seeing both of you going up and down the stairs of that house. What have you to say?

Ans. **It is wrong. I had never gone to his house. I knew that he was living at above address.**

Q. It is further in evidence against you that on 6-12-01, you had gone to the shop of PW40 Anil Kumar at 990, Gali Telian, Tilak Bazar, Delhi and placed an order for 50 kgs. of amonia nitrate and paid him Rs.800/- in advance and told him that delivery would be taken by you the next day. What have you to say?

Ans. **It is wrong.**

Q. It is further in evidence that on the next day, i.e., 7-12-01, you alongwith one more person, who has been identified as the slain terrorist vide photograph Ex. PW.40/2 by PW.40, went to his shop at 3.00 p.m. and by paying balance amount of Rs. 4000/- took delivery of amonia nitrate, which was in the packing of 500 gms. in powdry material, in plastic jars, which have been identified by this witness as Ex.P.54/1 to 24 and the memo prepared, for pointing-out you by this witness is Ex.PW.40/1. What have you to say?

Ans. **It is wrong.**

Q. It is further in evidence against you that on 11.12.01, you had purchased 15 kgs. of silver powder for Rs.240/- per kg. from PW.42 Ramesh Advani at his shop M/s. Tola Ram & Sons,

141, Tilak Bazar, Delhi and on 17.12.01, police had taken you to the said shop and PW.42 identified you as the person having purchased the silver powder Ex.P.51 from his shop. What have you to say?

Ans. **It is wrong.**

Q. It is further in evidence against you that PW.44 vide pointing-out memo Ex.PW.44/1 verified to police about your having purchased one mobile phone J.70 model Sony and cash card of Rs.500 from his shop at 26, Gaffar Mkt. and said mobile phone is Ex.P.37. What have you to say?

Ans. **It is wrong.**

Q. It is further in evidence against you that at the time you were apprehended by J&K police alongwith your co-accused Shaukat Hussain Guru in truck No. HR-38E 6733, the amount of Rs. 10 lacs was recovered in 23 bundles and other articles recovered including laptop, audio video camera, CDs adaptor, digital audio and video recorder, memory stick etc. were seized by Jammu and Kashmir police there vide memos Ex.PW 61/4. The laptop alongwith all accessories etc. as Ex.P-83 and the cash of Rs. 10 lacs is Rx.P-85. What you have to say?

Ans. **It is wrong. I alone was arrested from Sri Nagar, Batmalu bus stop. Nothing was recovered from me.**

Q. It is in evidence against you that your personal search memo were prepared at the place of your apprehension in J&K by Jammu and Kashmir police and the same is Ex. PW 61/1. What you have to say?

Ans. **It is correct.**

Q. It is further in evidence against you that the truck on which you and Shaukat had travelled from Delhi to Jammu & Kashmir after the attack on Parliament House was seized by J&K police and was handed over to SI Hriday Bhusan. The truck was brought to Delhi by SI Sharad Kohli and was deposited in Malkhana vide memo Ex. PW.65/1. What you have to say?

Ans. **It is wrong.**

Q. It is further in evidence against you that you made a disclosure statement to J&K police which was recorded and is Ex. PW 61/3. What you have to say?

Ans. **It is wrong.**

Q. It is further in evidence against you that one mobile phone apart from cash of Rs. 10 lacs and computer was also recovered from you in J&K by Jammu and Kashmir police. What you have to say?

Ans. **It is wrong.**

Q. It is further in evidence against you that you were produced before the court of Sh. V. K. Maheswari, ACMM, Patiala House Courts, New Delhi on 22.12.2001 for the confirmation from you about your confessional statement recorded by DCP Ashok Chand. What you have to say?

Ans. **I was not produced, but was kept outside in police van in Patiala House Court.**

Q. It is further in evidence against you that ACMM Sh. V. K. Maheswari drew proceedings about your production before him for confirmation and the same are Ex. PW. 63/2. What you have to say?

Ans. **The proceedings are false.**

Q. It is further in evidence against you that you were called in the chamber of ACMM and all others were sent outside and the chamber was closed and only you, peon of the judge and ACMM Sh. V. K. Maheshwari were in the chamber when you were explained that you were not bound to make any confessional statement before him. You were also explained that in case you make any confessional statement, the same can be used in evidence against you. What you have to say?

Ans. **It is wrong.**

Q. It is further in evidence against you that the ACMM inquired from you about the making of confessional statement before DCP Ashok Chand and you stated to the ACMM that you had made the statement voluntarily before DCP. You made no complaint against police personnel. You also told that you were not tortured for making this statement. Your this statement was recorded by ACMM and read over to you and explained to you. Your statement made before ACMM is Ex. PW 63/5. The statement in your own hand about the outstanding of statement is Ex. PW. 63/6. What you have to say?

Ans. **It is wrong.**

Q. It is further in evidence against you that the laptop which was in use of the slain terrorist and which was recovered from you and accused Shaukat Hussain was sent for expert examination and the report of expert is Ex. PW. 73/1. The annexure to this report are Ex. PW 73/2, Ex. PW 73/3, Ex. PW 73/4, Ex. PW 73/5, Ex. PW 73/6, Ex. PW 73/7. What you have to say?

Ans. **I was not having laptop. So I don't want to say anything.**

Q. It is further in evidence against you that the report of the expert shows that the files contained in the laptop contain the scanned image of Indian Army stickers, image of Ministry of Home Affairs stickers, the images of fake I-Cards which were recovered from deceased terrorist. What you have to say?

Ans. **I don't know.**

Q. It is further in evidence against you that your specimen signatures and writings were obtained by the police for comparison with the documents recovered from the witnesses. Your specimen signatures are Ex. S-1 to Ex. S-19 and your specimen handwriting of alphabets is Ex. S-20 and S-21. What you have to say?

Ans. **Police had obtained my specimen signatures on several sheets. On the sheets where 'Mohamad' is written I have doubt as I spell 'Mohammad' in this manner.**

Q. It is further in evidence against you that after the terrorist attack on Parliament House, after watching the T.V. news, PW Harpal Singh came to the SHO G.L. Meena and produced some documents relating to car to him. He stated that he had delivered this car in favour of Ashiq Hussain Khan. The delivery receipt produced by him is Ex. PW 1/6. What you have to say?

Ans. **I don't know.**

Q. It is further in evidence against you that Harpal Singh appeared as PW 20 and identified you as the person who has come along with so-called Ashiq Hussain for purchase of the car. What you have to say?

Ans. **I had not accompanied Ashiq Hussain. A sardarji had come to Spl. Cell & identified me then he & police persons beat me.**

Q. It is further in evidence against you that on 11.12.01, you alongwith one more person had gone to the shop of Mr. S.K. Mehta, namely Sawan Dry Fruits and Kiryana shop at Fateh Puri and had purchased dry fruit from that shop from its salesman Ajay Kumar. Ex. PW 41/2 to 4 are some of the boxes of dry fruit purchased by you and your associate and Ex. PW 45/1 is the photograph of your that associate who had gone with you. What have you to say?

Ans. **It is wrong.**

Q. It is further in evidence against you that sample voice cassettes of your co-accused persons were examined by PW 48, who gave his report in this regard as Ex. PW 48/1. What have you to say?

Ans. **I don't know.**

Q. It is in evidence against you that just before the attack on Parliament call was made by deceased terrorist Mohammad on your telephone. What you have to say?

Ans. **It is false.**

Q. It is in evidence against you that just before the attack on Parliament you had given telephone call on cell phone of Shaukat, as per the record of the cell phone. What you have to say?

Ans. **It is wrong.**

Q. It is in evidence against you that the cell phone record shows that on 13th Dec. 2001 and around that time your telephone instrument was used by the terrorist by using a different Sim card. What you have to say?

Ans. **It is wrong.**

Q. It is in evidence against you that on 13-12-2001 and around that you, accused Shaukat accused S.A.R. Geelani had been contacting each other on cell phone. What you have to say?

Ans. **It is wrong.**

Q. What else you have to say?

Ans. *I live in Sopre J&K and in the year 2000 when I was there Army used to harrass me almost daily, then said once in a week. One Raj Mohan Rai used to tell me that I should give information to him about militants. I was a surrendered militant and all militants have to mark attendance at Army camp every Sunday. I was not being physically tortured by me. He only used to just threatened me. I use to give him small information which I used to gather from newspaper, in order to save myself. In June/July 2000 I migrated from my village and went to town Baramullah. I was having a shop of distribution of Surgical instruments which I was running on commission basis. One day when I was going on my scooter S.T.F. (State Task Force) people came and picked me up and they continuously tortured me for five days. Some body had given information to S.T.F. that I was again indulging in militant activities. That person was confronted with me and was re-*

leased in my presence. Then I was kept by them in custody for about 25 days and I got myself released by paying Rs. 1 lakh. Special Cell people had confirmed this incident. Thereafter I was given a certificate by S.T.F. and they made me a Special Police Officer for six months. They were knowing that I will not work for them. Tariq had met me in Palhalan S.T.F. camp where I was in custody of S.T.F. Tariq met me later on in Sri Nagar and told me he was basically working for S.T.F. I also told him that I was also working for S.T.F. Mohammad who was killed in attack on Parliament was alongwith Tariq. Tariq told me that he was from Keran sector of Kashmir and he told me that I should take Mohammad to Delhi as Mohammad has to go out of country after some time from Delhi. I do not know why I was caught by the police of Sri Nagar on 15-12-2001. I was boarding bus at Sri Nagar bus stop, for going to my home when police caught me. Witness Akbar who had deposed in the court that he had apprehended Shaukat and me in Sri Nagar had conducted a raid at my shop about a year prior to Dec. 2001, and told me that I was selling fake surgical instruments and he took Rs. 5000/- from me. I was tortured at Special Cell and one Bhoop Singh had even compelled me to take urine and I saw family of S.A.R. Geelani also there, Geelani was in miserable condition. He was not in a position to stand. We were taken to Doctor for examination but instructions used to be issued that we have to tell Doctor that every thing was alright with a threat that if we do not do so we be again tortured.

Q. Why this case against you?

Ans. **It is a false case.**

Q. Why the witnesses have deposed against you?

Ans. **All the witnesses are false witnesses.**

Q. Will you lead defence evidence?

Ans. **No.**

Q. It is further in evidence against you that your co-accused Shaukat Hussain Guru in his confessional statement made before

DCP Ashok Chand (PW. 60) Ex. PW 60/5 that in the 1st week of November you and your associate militant Mohammad had come to Delhi and met Shaukat in his house No. 1021, Mukherji Nagar and told him that Mohammad was a Pak national and member of JeM and had come to Delhi for carrying out fidayeen attack in Delhi. What have you to say?

Ans. **It is wrong.**

Q. It is further in evidence that Shaukat had further disclosed that in the meanwhile, you went to Sri Nagar to deliver money collected in Delhi by you through hawala to Ghazi Baba of JeM in Kashmir and you brought from Kashmir to Delhi more Pak nationals and members of JeM namely Raja, Rana, Hyder @ Tufail and Hamza, alongwith arms & ammunitions and explosives etc. What have you to say?

Ans. **It is wrong.**

Q. It is further in evidence against you that accused Shaukat further discloses that he had been talking from his cell No. 98104-46375 to you and Ghazi Baba and militant Mohammad and you and Mohammad also used his Yamaha motorcycle to conduct recee of the targets to be attacked in Delhi. What have you to say?

Ans. **It is wrong.**

Q. It is further in evidence against you that it has come in Ex. PW 66/1 (discl. stt. of Shaukat) that as per the plan made in meetings, you and slain militant Mohammad bought a white Ambassadoor car No. DL 3C-J 1527 and prior to purchase of the car, you had taken another rented accomodation in Indira Vihar, whereon 12.12.01 night, you Shaukat and Gilani met Mohammad, who had then given you Rs. 10 lakhs and laptop directing that Rs. 10 lakhs were for you, Gilani and Shaukat and laptop was to be delivered to Ghazi Baba in Kashmir by you all. What have you to say?

Ans. **It is wrong.**

Q. It is further in evidence that Shaukat further disclosed in Ex. PW 66/1 that thereafter you, Shaukat and Gilani left Indira Vihar hideout at about 11.20 a.m. on 13.12.01. You called Shaukat from your cell No. 98114 89429 asking him to watch TV and confirm about latest position of VVIPs in Parliament. What have you to say?

Ans. **It is wrong.**

Q. It is further in evidence that immediately thereafter you again called Shaukat from your cell telling him that the mission was on and on the same day, you met Shaukat at Azadpur Mandi and you both went to Gilani's house for delivering him Rs. 2 lakhs as his share which he asked you to give at his house in Kashmir and then you and Shaukat left for Srinagar in the truck alongwith the laptop and Rs. 10 lakhs. What have you to say?

Ans. **It is wrong.**

Q. It is further in evidence against you that on 4.5.02 Lt. Governor of Delhi had granted sanction for prosecution of you and your co-accused persons u/s 50 POTA, which was communicated vide letter/order Ex. PW 11/1 of PW 11 Dy. Secretary (Home). What have you to say?

Ans. **I don't know.**

Q. It is further in evidence against you that L.G. also granted sanction on 4.5.02 u/s 196 Cr.P.C. for taking cognizance against you and your co-accused persons u/s 121/ 212-A/ 122/ 124 r/w Sec. 120B IPC and it was communicated vide his order Ex. PW 11/2. What have you to say?

Ans. **I don't know.**

Q. It is further in evidence against you that Commissioner of Police granted sanction u/s 7 of Explosives Substances Act for prosecuting you and your co-accused persons u/s 3.5 and 6 of Explosive Substances Act and it was accordingly communicated by PW-12 DCP HQs. vide his letter Ex. PW 12/1. What have you to say?

Ans. **I don't know.**

Statement of Accused Mohd. Afzal without oath under Section 313 Cr.P.C.

Accused Mohd. Afzal wants to say something more. His statement be recorded.

Mohammad, the slain terrorist of Parliament attack had come alongwith me from Kashmir. The person who handed him over to me is Tariq. Tariq is working with Security Force and S.T.F. JK Police. Tariq had told me that if I face any problem due to Mohammad he will help me as he knew security forces and STF very well. Tariq had also told me that Mohammad had stayed in Sri Nagar with STF people and had come from Keran in the security forces vehicle. Tariq had told me that I have just to drop Mohammad at Delhi and I have not to do anything else. And if I would not take Mohammad with me to Delhi then I would be implicated in some other case. I under these circumstances, brought Mohammad to Delhi under a compulsion without knowing that he was a terrorist.

Sd/-	Sd/-
RO&AC	Designated Judge
	New Delhi 21-09-02

Q. It is in evidence against you that the instrument of your cell No. 98114 89429 was very frequently used by terrorists Mohammad and others using different Sim cards.

Ans. **It is wrong.**

Q. It is further in evidence that terrorists had received call from GSM-cum-Satellite phone No. 882165115059 and they had also called at Dubai and Pakistan and calls were received by him from Satellite phone at your cell No. 98114-89429. What have you to say?

Ans. **It is wrong.**

Q. It is further in evidence that you and other terrorists had been frequently talking to each other for about one week prior to 13.12.01 on cell phones.

Ans. **It is wrong.**

Q. It is further in evidence against you that print-out of your mobile No. 98114 89429 is Ex. PW 36/3 and last call made to your this mobile was from mobile No. 9810693456 at 11.25 a.m., which was found on the person of a slain militant. What have you to say?

Ans. **It is wrong.**

Q. It is further in evidence that call details pertaining to calls made from your above-numbered cell, by the militants to Pakistan and Dubai were collected by PW 66 and same is Ex. PW 35/4. What have you to say?

Ans. **I don't know.**

Q. It is further in evidence that as per Ex. PW 35/4, Pakistan No. is at point P and that of Dubai is at point D and according to PW 35/4, cell No. 98114 89429 which belonged to you was found to have been in constant touch with the phones found on the persons of slain terrorists. What have you to say?

Ans. **I don't know.**

Q. It is further in evidence against you that explosives, arms and ammunitions recovered by police at your and your co-accused's pointing-out from different hideouts, were sent to CFSL for examination and analysis vide entry made in this regard as Ex. PW 9/1, 9/2, and 9/3. What have you to say?

Ans. **It is false.**

Q. It is further in evidence against you that reports of CFSL sent in this regard are Ex. PW 22/1 and 22/2 and 24/1 and 24/2. What have you to say?

Ans. **I don't know.**

ANNEXURE 6

Statement of Shaukat Hussain Guru Under Section 313

In the Court of Shri S. N. Dhingra, ASJ, N. Delhi
S/V Afzal Guru & Others
FIR 417/01

Statement of accused Shaukat Hussain Guru, s/o Abdul Sattar r/o Village Doabgar, Tehsil and P.S. Sopore, Dist. Baramullah J&K, under Section 313 Cr.P.C. without oath.

Q. It is in evidence against you that on 13th Dec. 2001 at about 11.40-11.45 a.m. a terrorist attack was done by the terrorist at Parliament House when Parliament was in session and Vice President of India, Ministers, M.Ps, V.I.Ps and V.V.I.Ps were in the Parliament. In this attack five Pakistani trained militants got killed at the hands of the security staff. 9 persons from security staff and other agencies also got killed. 15 persons were injured. In the attack explosive substances, hand grenades, AK 47 Rifles and pistol were used by the terrorist. What you have to say?

Ans. **I learnt about the attack from newspapers.**

Q. It is in evidence against you that on the checking of 5 slain terrorists, fake identity card of Websity Xansa Computer Education were recovered which are Ext. PW 4/2, PW 4/4, PW 3/3, PW 2/3, PW 2/4 and PW 2/5 and on these I.Cards photographs of the terrorist with fake name and phone No. 98114 89429 was found written. What you have to say?

Ans. **I don't know.**

Q. It is in evidence against you that on the persons of 5 (slain) terrorists 5 mobile phones and slips containing certain mobile phone numbers were recovered. Slips are Ext. PW 2/16, PW 4/6, PW 4/7. What you have to say?

Ans. **I learnt about it in the court.**

Q. It is in evidence against you that cell phone number 98114-89429 was cell number of Mohd. Afzal which was being used by Mohd. Afzal. What you have to say?

Ans. **I have no knowledge.**

Q. It is in evidence against you that you were arrested by the police at Srinagar, alongwith your co-accused Mohd. Afzal in truck No. HR 38E 6733 and in possesion of both of you one laptop alongwith accessories and cash amounting to Rs. 10 Lakhs was recovered. What you have to say?

Ans. **It is wrong. I was arrested on 14.12.01 from near my house in Mukherjee Ngr. in the evening. Time I don't remember.**

Q. It is in evidence against you that you were brought to Delhi by Delhi Police and arrested in this case and your disclosure statement Ext. PW 64/2 was recorded on 16-12-2001. What you have to say?

Ans. **It is wrong.**

Q. It is in evidence against you that you desired to make confessional statement before DCP voluntarily. What you have to say?

Ans. **It is wrong. I had expressed desire to make statement in the court.**

Q. It is in evidence against you that on 21.12.01 at about 10 a.m. you were produced before Shri Ashok Chand, DCP Spl. Cell by IO of this case ACP Rajbir Singh, for the purpose of recording your confessional statement and you were explained by DCP Ashok Chand that you were not bound to make any confessional statement but you expressed your willingness to do so by recording your willingness Ex. PW 60/5 in your own hand. What have you to say?

Ans. **It is false. I saw DCP Ashok Chand for the first time when he appeared in the court as a witness.**

Q. It is further in evidence that warning given to you by DCP Ashok Chand was drawn in proceedings and thereafter your disclosure statement Ex. PW 60/6 was recorded by the said DCP. What have you to say?

Ans. **It is wrong.**

Q. It is in evidence against you that you disclosed in your disclosure statement Ex. PW 60/6 that you had come to Delhi from Sopore, J&K in 1988 and completed your graduation in 1992 and during this period, you had come in contact with accused Abdul Rehman Gilani of Baramullah who was also doing graduation in Arabic language from Delhi University. What have you to say?

Ans. **I made no statement to DCP. Rest is correct. However, A.R. Gilani met me in 1992 in a Masjid.**

Q. It is further in evidence against you that after graduation, you also did some professional courses and also started doing work in private Cos. and of selling fruits after purchasing from Sopore and supplying at Delhi, Jammu & Calcutta and that you suffered a loss of Rs. 4-5 lakhs. What have you to say?

Ans. **It is correct.**

Q. It is further in evidence against you that in the meantime, you got married to Navjot Sandhu in March 2000 who was a Sikh lady and on marrying you, she converted to Islam and was renamed as Afshan Guru and she is also a co-accused in this case. What have you to say?

Ans. **It is correct.**

Q. It is further in evidence against you that with the help of your in-laws, who gave you Rs. 4 lakhs, you got financed a truck bearing No. HR 38E 6733 in the name of your wife Afshan Guru. What have you to say?

Ans. **It is correct.**

Q. It is further in evidence against you that you also disclosed in your statement Ex. PW 60/6 that co-accused Mohd. Afzal, who happened to be your real cousin, was a surrendered JKLF militant and he had also done his graduation from Delhi university in early 1990 and he also got acquainted with co-accused SAR Gilani during this period. What have you to say?

Ans. **It is correct except I cannot say whether he got acquainted with SAR Gilani or not.**

Q. It is further in evidence against you that accused Mohd. Afzal used to motivate you and SAR Gilani for joining Jehad in Kashmir and you were greatly influenced by Osama Bin Laden after attack on World Trade Centre of N. York on 11.9.01. What you have to say?

Ans. **It is wrong.**

Q. It is further in evidence against you that accused Mohd. Afzal called you from J&K asking you to arrange a rented house for him and one of his militant associate, who would look after the flow of funds to militants in J&K and accordingly, you arranged a room bearing No.5 in Boy's Hostel, Christian Colony, Delhi. What have you to say?

Ans. **It is wrong.**

Q. It is further in evidence against you that in the 1st week of November Afzal and his associate militant Mohammad (now deceased) had come to Delhi and met you at your house No. 1021, Mukherji Nagar and you were told by Afzal that Mohammad was a Pak national and belonged to JeM terrorist outfit and had come to carry out a fidayeen attack in Delhi. What have you to say?

Ans. **It is wrong.**

Q. It is further in evidence against you that you also discussed about Jehad with your co-accused SAR Gilani who agreed to work for Jehad and help in carrying out the fidayeen attack. What have you to say?

Ans. **It is wrong.**

Q. It is further in evidence that in the meanwhile, co-accused Mohd. Afzal went to Srinagar to deliver hawala money received in Delhi to Ghazi Baba @ Doctor, the so-called Supreme Cdr. of JeM in Kashmir and during this visit, Mohd. Afzal brought with him some Pak nationals and JeM militants namely Raja, Rana, Hyder @ Tufail and Hamza to Delhi. What have you to say?

Ans. **I don't know.**

Q. It is further in evidence that Mohd. Afzal arranged another accomodation at A-97 Gandhi Vihar, Timarpur and they all had brought alongwith them arms and ammunitions and explosives etc. and co-accused Afzal and militant Mohammad purchased new mobile phones, Sim cards and explosive material. What have you to say?

Ans. **I don't know.**

Q. It is further in evidence that during this period, you also changed your mobile number from 9810446375 to 9811573506 as a precaution as you had been talking to Ghazi Baba, Mohammad and Afzal from your previous mobile phone. What have you to say?

Ans. **It is wrong. I was not having any mobile phone.**

Q. It is further in evidence that you also provided your Yamaha motor cycle to Afzal and Mohammad for conducting recee of the targets.

Ans. **It is wrong.**

Q. It is further in evidence against you that meetings were also held at your house for discussing about execution of plans and your wife/ co-accused Afshan Guru used to be present and was having knowledge of your plans.

Ans. **It is false.**

Q. It is further in evidence against you that co-accused Mohd. Afzal took another rented accomodation in Indira Vihar, Mukharjee

Nagar and thereafter, as per the plan, Afzal and Mohammad (slain terrorist) purchased a second hand ambassador car having No. DL-3C-J1527. What have you to say?

Ans. **I don't know.**

Q. It is further in evidence against you that on the night of 12.12.2001 you along with co-accused Mohd. Afzal and SAR Geelani went to Gandhi Vihar hideout to meet said Mohammad and other Pak militants.

Ans. **It is wrong.**

Q. It is further in evidence that there, Mohammad gave laptop and Rs. 10 lakhs to accused Afzal directing to hand over the laptop to Ghazi Baba and the money was to be distributed amongst you, co-accused Mohd. Afzal and SAR Gilani.

Ans. **It is wrong.**

Q. It is further in evidence that terrorist Mohammad told on the next day i.e. 13.12.2001 they would carry out fidayeen attack on Parliament House and thereafter, you, Afzal and Gilani left that place. What have you to say?

Ans. **It is wrong.**

Q. It is further in evidence against you that on 13.12.2001 at about 11.20 A.M., accused Mohd. Afzal called you from his mobile number 98114-89429 asking you to watch TV and confirm about the latest position of the VVIPs in Parliament. What have you to say?

Ans. **It is wrong. I was not having Mobile phone.**

Q. It is further in evidence that you also disclosed in your discl. stt. Ex. PW 66 that by the time you switched on the TV you received another call from Mohd. Afzal that the 'mission' was on. What have you to say?

Ans. **It is wrong. On 13.12.01 I had gone to Hans Charitable Hospital with my wife around 11.30 a.m.**

Q. It is further in evidence that after the incident i.e. attack on Parliament, you met Mohd. Afzal at Azadpur Mandi, Delhi and you then both went to the house of SAR Gilani to deliver him Rs. 2 lakhs as his share. What have you to say?

Ans. **It is false.**

Q. It is further in evidence that SAR Gilani told you to take the money and give the same to his house in Kashmir and then you and Afzal left for Srinagar in your truck the same day. What have you to say?

Ans. **It is false.**

Q. It is further in evidence against you that on reaching Srinagar, you and Mohd. Afzal were apprehended on 15.12.01 and police recovered from you laptop with attachments and Rs. 10 lacs and you both were brought to Delhi. What have you to say?

Ans. **It is false.**

Q. It is further in evidence against you that after your arrest in Srinagar by police team headed by PW 61 Dy. SP SDPO Srinagar, your personal search was conducted vide memo Ex. PW 61/2 and that of Afzal vide memo Ex. PW 61/1. What have you to say?

Ans. **It is wrong.**

Q. It is further in evidence against you that disclosure statement of both of you i.e., you and Afzal recorded at Srinagar is Ex. PW 61/3 and Ex. PW 61/4 is the seizure memo of the articles seized at your instance from the truck No. HR 38E 6733. What have you to say?

Ans. **It is wrong.**

Q. It is further in evidence that the laptop recovered from you is Ex. P.83 with its attachments and the brief case, mobile phone recovered is Ex. P.84 and 23 bundles of currency notes of Rs.500, 1000 and 100 denomination, amounting to Rs.10 lakhs are Ex. P.85 collectively. What have you to say?

Ans. **It is false.**

Q. It is further in evidence against you that PW 61 informed Sr. Officers at Srinagar and got recorded DD entry Ex. PW 61/5 about your arrest and recoveries made from you and accused Afzal and Delhi police was informed, accordingly. What have you to say?

Ans. **It is wrong.**

Q. It is further in evidence against you that Delhi police officers namely SI Hriday Bhusan and SI Sharad Kohli reached there on the same day at about 2.15 p.m. and you alongwith the articles seized from you, seizure memos and other documents etc. were handed over to DP vide Ex. PW 61/6. What have you to say?

Ans. **It is false.**

Q. It is further in evidence against you that PW 64 SI Hriday Bhusan handed over you and accused Mohd. Afzal, documents, case property to PW 66 Insp. Mohan Chand Sharma, at Delhi, who interrogated you and recorded your discl. statement Ex. PW 64/2 and that of Mohd. Afzal Ex. PW 64/1. What have you to say?

Ans. **It is false.**

Q. It is further in evidence against you that call details of your cell No. 98104-46375 have been proved as Ex. PW 35/7 which run into three pages, which are computerized. What have you to say?

Ans. **I don't know.**

Q. It is further in evidence against you that your this cell No. was put on surveillance and on the evening of 14.12.01, your wife co-accused Afshan Guru @ Navjot Sandhu talked to you and the tape in this regard is Ex. PW 66/4. What have you to say?

Ans. **It is wrong. I was in Special Cell on 14.12.01 evening. Spl. Cell people did not allow me to talk to my wife.**

Q. It is further in evidence against you that your co-accused SAR Geelani after his arrest led police party to your house No.1021, first floor Mukherji Nagar, on 15.12.01, your wife Afshan Guru was present there, she was having cell phone N.9811573506, which is Ex. P.8 and it was seized vide memo Ex. PW 66/7. What have you to say?

Ans. **I have no knowledge as I was in the Special Cell at that time.**

Q. It is in evidence against you that in the registration document of your motor cycle No. DL 2S K 3122 your address given is House No. 70 SFS East of Kailash New Delhi. What you have to say?

Ans. **I was living at this address during those days.**

Q. It is in evidence against you that the address given in the registration of the truck No. HR 38E 6733 is 17/6 M. Road Faridabad. What you have to say?

Ans. **This address was given by Automobile Steering who were the agents of Tata Automobiles.**

Q. It is in evidence against you that address given in the insurance papers of your truck is House No. 32 Pocket 1 Sector 18 Rohini, New Delhi. What you have to say?

Ans. **I had lived at this address after marriage. Thereafter I shifted to Mukherjee Nagar.**

Q. Why is this case against you?

Ans. **As far as I think I have been involved in this case because of Mohd. Afzal who was my real cousin.**

Q. Why the witnesses have deposed against you?

Ans. **Witnesses are false witnesses. I was shown to the witness when I was in the lock up.**

Q. Do you want to say anything else?

Ans. *On 14-12-01 Insp. M.C. Sharma had apprehended me near my house. Then I was taken to Lodhi Colony Special Cell where I was beaten on that day, and then they undressed me and took my picture in odd position and they threatened me that they will make* *posture of picture and they used bad language against Islam and Allah, particularly when constable Tyagi had used that language. They stated that all Muslims and Sikhs are enemies of India. Police had made enquiries from me on 14th Dec. 2001 itself and thereafter I was tortured. On 15th Dec. 2001 I was beaten. On 15th Dec. evening myself, Afzal and Zeelani were put in one cell together. On 15th Dec. or 16th Dec. the date I do not remember correctly they told me that they had called my wife Afsan Guru. The family of SAR Zeelani was also called, again said that on the same night either 15th or 16th Dec. when we all three were together one officer came and told SAR Geelani that his wife, children and one more boy had been released. And I was told that my driver, Abdul Hamid and conductor Firdous Ahmed, and my worker Hilal Ahmed have also been released. On next day morning we were taken to some house where a Maidan was sitting inside the house alongwith A.C.P. Rajbir Singh, and other special cell officers were also there. She came out and saw that all of us were standing in line i.e. myself, Afsal, my wife and Geelani. After seeing us she went inside the room. Some officer was there who pointed out each of us to her telling our name. We were then taken back to special cell. My signatures were obtained on blank papers by some officer despite my protest. I had sent my truck after getting it loaded with banana from Kashmir Karnataka Roadways Azadpur at about 9 p.m. on 13th Dec. 2001 for J & K. and entry of the truck may be found at Lakhanpur Border or at other interstate border.*

Further Statement of Shaukat Hussain Guru without oath

On 14-12-2001 some officers apprehended from near my house. I do not remember if M. C. Sharma with them or not but he tortured me. Now I want to say I do not remember if I made a call to S.A.R. Zeelani on 13th Dec. 2001 or not. I had told my landlord after coming from Kashmir that my name of Shaukat Hussain Guru and my wife's name was Afsan Guru and I offered him copy of my passport for *verification but he refused and said that I have transaction with Muslims in Old Delhi so there was no need for verification. I was shown to the witnesses outside this court on stairs and not in the lock up. The truck is in the name of Navjot Sandhu but not in the name of Afsan Guru. I have no knowledge about computer.*

RO&AC

Sd/-
Designated Judge
New Delhi 20-9-02

Q. It is further in evidence against you that you were produced before the court of Sh. V.K. Maheswari, ACMM, Patiala House Courts, New Delhi on 22.12.2001 for the confirmation from you about your confessional statement recorded by DCP Ashok Chand (PW 60). What you have to say?

Ans. **I and other persons were made to stand outside courtroom, Rajbir Singh & ACMM were in the court. We were shown to ACMM outside the court, but calling our name and M.C. Sharma pointing out to us.**

Q. It is further in evidence against you that ACMM Sh. Maheswari (PW 63) drew proceedings regarding your production before him for confirmation of your discl./confessional stt. and the same are Ex. PW. 63/1. What you have to say?

Ans. **It is wrong.**

Q. It is further in evidence against you that you were called in the Chamber of ACMM and all others were sent outside and the chamber was closed and only you, peon of the judge and ACMM Sh. Maheshwari were in the chamber, when you were explained by the ACMM that you were not bound to make any confessional statement before him and further that in case you make any conf. stt., the same can be used in evidence against you. What you have to say?

Ans. **It is wrong. ACMM only asked "Kya yahi hai?"** (cited in Devnagari script).

Q. It is further in evidence against you that ACMM inquired from you about the making of confessional statement before DCP Ashok Chand and you stated to ACMM that you had made the stt. voluntarily before DCP. You made no complaint against police personnel and also told that you were not tortured for making the conf. statement. Your this stt. was recorded by ACMM and read over to you and explained to you. Your statement before ACMM is Ex. PW 63/ . The statement in your own hand about undertstanding of statement is Ex. PW. 63/ . What you have to say?

Ans. **It is wrong.**

Q. It is further in evidence against you that the laptop which was in use of the slain terrorists and which was recovered from you and co-accused Mohd. Afzal was sent for expert examination and the report of expert is Ex. PW. 73/1 and annexures thereto are Ex. PW 73/2 to 73/7. What you have to say?

Ans. **No laptop was recovered from me. I don't know the rest.**

Q. It is further in evidence against you that the report of the expert shows that the files contained in the laptop Ex. P-83 contained the scanned image of Indian Army stickers, images of fake I-Cards which were recovered from slain terrorists. What you have to say?

Ans. **I don't know.**

Q. It is further in evidence against you that police recovered from your house No. 1021, Mukherjee Nagar, photographs Ex. PW 66/8 and 66/9 of your wife Afshan Guru and seized the same vide memo Ex. PW 66/10, besides one another cell phone instrument and sim card recovered from there, which was seized vide memo Ex. PW 66/11 and said cell phone is Ex. P-89 and Sim card Ex. P-90. What have you to say?

Ans. **I admit recovery of photograph only. All other recoveries are denied.**

Q. It is further in evidence against you that on 4.5.02 Lt. Governor of Delhi had granted sanction for prosecution of you and your co-accused persons u/s 50 POTA, which was communicated vide letter/order Ex. PW 11/1 of PW 11 Dy. Secretary (Home). What have you to say?

Ans. **I don't know.**

Q. It is further in evidence against you that L.G. also granted sanction on 4.5.02 u/s 196 Cr.P.C. for taking cognizance against you and your co-accused persons u/s 121/ 121-A/ 122/ 124 r/w Sec. 120B IPC and it was communicated by PW-11 vide his order Ex. PW 11/2. What have you to say?

Ans. **I don't know.**

Q. It is further in evidence against you that Commissioner of Police granted sanction u/s 7 of Explosives Substances Act for prosecuting you and your co-accused persons u/s 3, 5 and 6 of Explosive Substances Act and it was accordingly communicated by PW-12 DCP HQs. vide his letter Ex. PW 12/1. What have you to say?

Ans. **I don't know.**

Q. It is further in evidence against you that on 13-12-2001 before and after attack on Parliament, you, co-accused Mohd. Afzal and S.A.R. Geelani had been contacting each other on cell phone. What you have to say?

Ans. **It is wrong. I made no phone call to Afzal or Gilani on 13.12.01.**

Q. It is further in evidence against you that your co-accused Mohd. Afzal in his confessional statement made before PW 60 DCP Ashok Chand, Ex. PW 60/7 stated that during his visits to Delhi he used to meet you and SAR Geelani and motivate you both for Jehad in Kashmir. What you have to say?

Ans. **It is wrong.**

Q. It is further in evidence against you that accused Mohd. Afzal had further disclosed that you had provided your motor cycle to him and the slain terrorists for making recee of the targets to be attacked by them. What have you to say?

Ans. **It is wrong.**

Q. It is further in evidence against you that as per Ex. PW 60/7, meetings of slain terrorists and accused Mohd. Afzal used to be held in your house for discussing the further course of action and you and co-accused SAR Geelani as also your wife Afsan Guru also used to be present in the meetings. What have you to say?

Ans. **It is wrong.**

Q. It is further in evidence against you that in these meetings, as has been stated by accused Mohd. Afzal in his confe. stt. Ex. PW 66/7, the targets for terrorist attacks discussed was Delhi assembly, UK & US embassies, Parliament and Airport. What have you to say?

Ans. **It is wrong.**

Q. It is further in evidence against you that final meeting was held at your house wherein you and your co-accused and militants were present and plan to attack on Parliament was finalized. What have you to say?

Ans. **It is wrong.**

Q. It is further in evidence against you that in pursuance of your disclosure statement Ex. PW 64/2 and that of your co-accused Mohd. Afzal Ex. PW 64/2 you both led the police party to a hideout of slain terrorists at A-97 Gandhi Vihar 2nd floor and got recovered from there three electronic detonators with yellow wire, two silver powder packs, ½ bucket of prepared explosive, two packs of sulphur for TCL, 2 cartons containing 20 sealed packs of amonia nitrate purified, one carton containing 20 empty packs of amonia nitrate and one empty pack of sulphur and all these articles are Ex. P.1 to P.2,3 and P.61 to 71 and same were seized vide seizure memo Ext. PW 34/1. What you have to say?

Ans. **It is wrong.**

Q. It is further in evidence that samples were taken out from the explosive substances and chemicals and separately sealed and seal of HSG was used, form C.F.S.L. was filled. What have you to say?

Ans. **It is wrong.**

Q. It is further in evidence that you and co-accused Mohd. Afzal led police party to premises No. A-97 Gandhi Vihar, P.S. Timarpur and from there, you both got recovered police uniform shirts in Khaki colour 3 in number, police uniform pant in Khaki colour four in number, police uniform, cards, police caps and some other house hold articles, which were seized vide memo Ex. PW 43/4. What have you to say?

Ans. **It is wrong.**

Q. It is further in evidence against you from the 'taand' of the premises, police recovered, six electronic time pieces, transistor, volta meter with leads of black colour one in number, 9 volt battery with wire one in number, battery cell (small) 12 in number, black starter one in number, battery caps with wire 3 in number, screw driver one in number, ear phone with leads two in number, wire pieces black 3 in number and one Sujata mixer grinder and seized the same also vide S.memo Ex. PW 34/4. What you have to say?

Ans. **It is wrong.**

Q. It is also in evidence against you that you and co-accused Afzal also got recovered from this premises A-97 Gandhi Vihar, one paper having specimen stamp of "Cyber Tech Computer Education Software Managing Director", one paper bearing map of Chanakya puri, one blank I.Card, two Airtel magic cards, some photographs and one map of Delhi and also some other papers which are collectively marked as Ext. P79 and same were seized vide Memo Ext. PW 34/3. What you have to say?

Ans. **It is wrong.**

Q. It is further in evidence against you that you alongwith accd. Mohd. Afzal also got recovered motor cycle Ex. P76 standing near the house No. A-97 abovesaid, which was seized by the police vide S. memo Ext. PW 34/2. What have you to say?

Ans. **It is wrong.**

Q. It is further in evidence that you and accd. Mohd. Afzal also led police to H.No.281, Indira Vihar, 2nd floor which was found locked and after breaking the lock, police entered in it and recovered 3 electronic detonators with yellow colour wire, six pressure detonators, 2 silver powder packets each of one kg., two boxes of sulphur for TCL, one carton of Ammonium Nitrate containing 25 packs and other house hold items, which are Ext. P 47 to P 57 and were seized vide S. memo Ext. PW 32/1 and articles. What have you to say?

Ans. **It is wrong.**

Q. It is further in evidence that you and your co-accused Afzal also got recovered one other motor cycle bearing number DL-1S K 3122 near the gate of H. No. 281 Indira Vihar Delhi. What have you to say?

Ans. **It is wrong. My M/c was at my house. I don't know wherefrom police seized it as I was in police custody.**

Q. It is also in evidence against you that you and accused Mohd. Afzal used to visit SAR Gilani at his rented house No. 535, Mukherji Nagar and owner of that house Naresh Gulati (PW 39) had been seeing both of you coming and going there. What have you to say?

Ans. **I had visited SAR Gilani's house one or two times. I don't know about Afzal.**

Q. It is further in evidence against you that motor cycle No. HR 51E 5769 (Ex. P.76) was purchased from PW 29 Sushil Kumar of Gupta Auto Deals, Karol Bagh, where you alongwith Mohd.

Afzal had gone for the deal and paid Rs.20000/- for it and alongwith you, your wife Afshan Guru had also gone, delivery receipt of the motor cycle is Ex. PW 29/2 and receipt of commission of the auto-sale agent is Ex. PW 29/3. What have you to say?

Ans. **It is wrong.**

Q. It is further in evidence against you that first floor portion of H.No.1021, Mukerji Nagar, Delhi was taken on rent by your wife Afshan Guru from PW 45 Tejpal Karbanda on 6.8.01 and she had told him her name as 'Jyoti' and had started living there alone from 8.8.01 saying that her husband i.e. you had gone to Kashmir in connection with business and join her soon. What have you to say?

Ans. **My wife had told her name as Navjot Sandhu, but wife of landlord told her that she would call her 'Jyoti'. I had gone to Kashmir when the house was taken on rent by my wife.**

Q. It is further in evidence against you that you joined her in that house only after about 1½ month and thereafter, your visitors started coming to you including accused Mohd. Afzal whom PW 42 identified before the Spl. Cell Police on 17.12.01 and also photographs of other persons, who used to visit you at your house as Ex. PW 40/2, 45/1, 41/5, 29/5 and 45/2, which are of the slain terrorists. What have you to say?

Ans. **It is correct that I came after one or 1½ month. Mohd. Afzal sometimes used to come to my house. Slain terrorists had never come to my house.**

Q. It is further in evidence against you that your voice samples marked C-2(a) C-2(b), S.1(a) and S.1(b) recorded in cassettes marked C.1 and S.1, belonging to you were got compared and analysed and detailed report of the Expert PW 48 in this regard is Ex. PW 48/1. What have you to say?

Ans. **Police might have taken my voice samples, but I don't remember.**

Q. It is further in evidence that registration record of motor cycle No. DL 1S A 3122 Yamaha in your name is Ex. PW 53/1. What have you to say?

Ans. **It is correct.**

Q. It is further in evidence against you that you alongwith accused Mohd. Afzal had purchased one mobile phone handset 'Motorola' with Sim card from shop No. B-10 Model Town-2 and pointing out memo in this regard is Ex. PW 49/1 and the bill book Ex. P.28 and receipt in this regard were seized by police vide memo Ex. PW 49/2. What have you to say?

Ans. **It is false.**

Q. It is in evidence against you that the laptop recovered from you and Afzal was got examined from Orion Convergence Ltd. by Spl. Cell Police and report in this regard is Ext. PW 72/1, as per which, the laptop was using Pakistan based ISP named micro-net-PK, internet and scanner was accessed on 5.12.01, laptop contained file showing Zee News T.V. channel news item of 3 alleged Pakistani terrorist killed in Lucknow and news clipping showing interview of Mr. George Fernandes in front of P. House, news clipping showing proceedings of Parliament as also clippings showing Arun Jaitly, Minister on the gate of Parliament House, Mulayam Singh Jadav entering the gate of Parliament house, Arun Jaitley addressing the press, some other ministers entering the gate of Parliament and some standing near the gate of Parliament, of the interview of Mr. V.K. Malhotra in front of Parliament house and of some people coming out of the gate and another news clipping showing the long-shot of blds., which look like Indian Parliament and Supreme Court. What have you to say?

Ans. **I don't know.**

Q. It is further in evidence against you that Ex. PW 35/1 is the certificate issued by PW 35 R.K. Guharay of AIRTEL which gives details of calls of mobile phone No. 98105 11085, 98106

93456, 98105 65284, 98105 10816, 98103 02438, 98104 46375 and computerised details thereof are Ext. PW 35/2 to PW 35/7. Ex. PW 35/7 is the call details (3 pages) of your cell No. 98104 46375. What have you to say?

Ans. **I don't know. I had no cell phone.**

Q. It is further in evidence against you that call details in respect of cell No. 98115 73506 which belonged to you, from 1.12.01 to 13.12.01 are Ext. PW 36/1 and from 1.12.01 to 18.12.01 are Ext. PW 36/2, of M. No. 9198114 89429 from 1.11.01 to 18.12.01 are Ext. PW 36/3, of 98115 44860 are Ext. PW 36/4 and of M. 9198114 89424 are Ext. PW 36/5, as produced by Maj. A.R. Satish, Executive of Sterling Cellulars and supplied to him by Genl. Manager of this Co. Lt. Col. Rajiv Pandey, vide his letters Ext. PW 36/6 to Ext. Pw 36/8. What have you to say?

Ans. **I don't know.**

Q. It is further in evidence that you had accompanied Mohd. Afzal on 6.11.01 to PW 37 Prem Chand through one Rajneesh (PW 38) of STD booth for hiring a room in his hostel at B-41, Christian Colony and said Prem Chand let-out room No.5 G.F. of Yamuna Hostel, on the ground floor to both of you at rent of Rs.1500/- p.m. and you both came to that room on 7th or 8th Nov. 01 and after putting your luggage, you both went away. What have you to say?

Ans. **It is wrong. Afzal had told me that he had to take a room but due to workload I was busy.**

Q. It is further in evidence that on 26.11.01, when PW 37 went to check the rooms, he found in said room no.5 one Kashmiri boy, who told his name as Rohail Ali Shah and that he was doing diploma in computer from Aptech, Kamla Nagar and showed his I. card Ext. PW 4/4. What have you to say?

Ans. **I don't know.**

Q. It is further in evidence that PW 37 saw said Rohail Ali Shah going out of that room on 6th or 8th December 01 and thereafter, said Ali Shah did not turn back and found lying vacant. What have you to say?

Ans. **I don't know.**

Q. It is further in evidence that on 19.12.01 PW Prem Chand identified you and Afzal at the Spl. Cell office, as persons, who had hired room no. 5 of his hostel and also identified photograph of Rohail Ali as Ex. PW 29/5. What have you to say?

Ans. **It is wrong.**

Q. It is further in evidence that prints of documents stored in laptop Ex. P.83 are PW 59/1 to 59/7 and PW 72/2 to 72/13. What have you to say?

Ans. **I don't know.**

Q. It is further in evidence that Ex. P83 the laptop was also examined by PW 73 for examining its media storage and his report in this regard is Ex. PW 73/1. What have you to say?

Ans. **I don't know.**

Q. It is further in evidence against you that case property was deposited in malkhana of PS vide memos Ex. PW 9/1 to 9/3. What have you to say?

Ans. **I don't know.**

Q. It is further in evidence against you that the chemicals, explosive substances recovered were got examined and report of CSL in this regard is Ex. PW 22/1 and 22/2. What have you to say?

Ans. **I don't know.**

Q. It is further in evidence that assault rifles, pistols, cartridges, fired bullet pcs, exploded H. grenades and other chemical matters, recovered in this case were also got analysed and PW 24 gave his detailed report as per Ex. PW 24/1 and 24/2.

Ans. **I don't know.**

Q. It is further in evidence that as per call details Ex. PW 35/4, Pakistan No. is at point P and that of Dubai is at point D and according to PW 35/4, cell phone of your co-accused Mohd. Afzal was found to have been in constant touch with the phones found on the persons of slain terrorists. What have you to say?

Ans. **I don't know.**

Q. It is further in evidence that instrument of your cell No.98104 46375 and Sim card, recovered from your house at the time of arrest of your wife/accused Navjot Sandhu @ Afsan Guru, were seized vide memo Ex. PW 66/1 and that cell phone is Ex. P.89. What have you to say?

Ans. **It is wrong.**

Q. It is further in evidence that explosives, arms and ammunitions recovered by police at your instance and that of co-accused Mohd. Afzal from different hideouts, were sent to CFSL for examination and analysis vide entries made in this regard as Ex. PW 9/1, 9/2, and 9/3. What have you to say?

Ans. **It is wrong.**

Q. It is further in evidence that reports of CFSL sent in this regard are Ex. PW 22/1 and 22/2 and 24/1 and 24/2. What have you to say?

Ans. **I don't know.**

Annexure 7

Extract from Deposition of Geelani's Wife October 11, 2002

Qurat-ul-am-Arifa wife of Shri S.A.R. Geelani aged about 30 yrs. r/o H. No. 568 Lane No.22 Zakir Nagar, New Delhi, House Wife

On S. A.

[From page2, para 2—]

On 14th Dec. 2001 my husband started from house at Mukherjee Nagar at about 1 p.m. for going to Mall Road Masjid for performing Jumma Namaj, and he told me that he would be coming back by 4 p.m. He was to send hearing-aid for his mother through my brother who was about to go to Kashmir and my brother was to meet him at J&K Bus Stand opposite Tis Hazari. My husband did not come back by 4 p.m. or 4.30 p.m., which was the time for opening Roza and brother of my husband also did not come by 4-4.30 p.m. My husband's brother was to take my brother to J&K Bus stop opp. Tis Hazari. When my husband did not come back by 4.30 p.m. on 14th Dec. I tried to talk to him on telephone. On dialing cell phone of my husband I was repeatedly getting message enter your phone number. I then stop dialing the phone. I thought that my husband's bus had come late or the bus which was to go to J&K got late, I therefore opened Roza myself.

At about 9.30 p.m. I and my two children were at home. 5-6 persons who were in civil dress entered my house. I started making noise. They caught hold of my two children and threatened me that I should shut up and keep silence otherwise they would kill my children. I kept mum out of fear that my children may not be killed. They told me that they were police person and they also told me that I could pack up some cloths of children and accompany them. I told them that my husband would be about to come from the college and I cannot accompany them but they told me that they know where my husband was, and told me that I would have to accompany them and they forcible took me with them and forced me and children to sit in the car. *[discontinued at page 3, para 2, line13]*

[Continued from page 4, line 22]

On 15th Dec. Police again came to my room and I was blind folded and we were made to sit in a car and removed some where else. In the lunch time when we were served food, on the food plate it was written B.S.F. Bhalaswa Camp we then learnt that we were in a B.S.F. camp and I got frightened. There again my husband was tortured by the police in my presence and had been threatened my husband that in case he did not say whatever they like they would kill him and the entire family and nobody even come to know about it. My husband kept on denying his involvement in the attack. There after my husband was taken into second other room. Then police came to my room, they were 5-6 persons. Then they told me that I should advise my husband to say whatever they like and if my husband did not agree then they would keep me for through out my life in the jail, in this case. Thereafter I went to the room of my husband and weepingly told him to agree to sign whatever the police people say as it was a question of life of children and our own life. Then I was brought back to my room. On the same day I do not know at what time we were brought back to Lodhi Colony blind folded. The police had been pressuring on the night of 15th Dec. also to say whatever police likes. I and my children got frightened. I remained at police station Lodhi Colony on 16th Dec. also in the same condition throughout the day. Police was coming on that day to us repeatedly at the instance of A.C.P. Rajbir and pressuring us even on that day for making statement. On the evening of 16th Dec. 2001 again my husband was brought to my room and 15-16 papers, which were blank, were placed before him and he was asked to sign those papers. My husband refused and then he was pressurised in my presence. We were again threatened and there after my husband under threat signed those blank papers. Thereafter police allowed me to go home along with children....

Note: The above extract is as it is recorded by the court.

ANNEXURE 8

Deposition of Aaj Tak Principal Correspondent

October 10, 2002

DW 4 Shams Tahir Khan, Principal Correspondent
Aaj Tak, T.V. Channel

On S.A.

I am working in Aaj Tak T.V. Channel for the last two years. I had interviewed accused Mohd. Afsal on 20th Dec. 2001, in the office of Special Cell, Lodhi Road. The interview was around 15 minutes. My question to accused Afsal was whether any literature concerning Osama-bin-laden recovered from S.A.R. Gellani. In the reply he stated that he was not aware about this much. (Counsel states that answer be clarification as to who was not aware of what). The witness has clarified as under.

Afsal did not directly reply the question asked by me about literature. I have brought the interview and the exact word used by Afsal can be seen from the interview. It was our own efforts to interview the accused persons caught in this case. We had tried with Delhi Police and three channel people were called with the permission of top officials of Delhi Police. We were allowed to interview only Afsal and not other accused persons. I have the video cassette of the interview. The cassette contained an unedited interview of accused Mohd. Afsal as well as our programme after 100 days of the attack which contained part of the interview. Cassette is Ext. DW 4/A.

The programme telecasted after 100 days of the attack is based upon the interview of the Afsal. (Counsel wants to ask the witness the answer given by Afsal to his query be stated as replied in the tape. I consider that since tape has been exhibited, there is no necessity for the witness to state from his memory or from his mouth what has been already documented and placed on record. This court shall consider the answer given in the document itself.)

By Sh. Aggarwal Addl. PP for the state.

I did not feel that the answer were being made by Afsal under any pressure. However, A.C.P. was present when the interview was being taken.

RO & AC Designated Judge;
New Delhi 10-10-02

DW 4 Sham Tahir Khan recalled for cross examination on behalf of accused Afsal.

On S.A.

By Mr. Afsal accused

It is correct that Zee T.V. and NDTV channel correspondent were also there when I was taking interview.

Q: I put it to you that after my interview by Aajtak some other T.V. channel had asked me a question about the role of SAR Geelani and I had told that SAR Gellani was innocent. On this ACP Rajbir got up and told me that he had already told me not to say SAR Geelani. This incident had happened in presence of DW 4.

Ans: It is correct that accused was told by ACP Rajbir Singh not to say anything about SAR Gellani by that time my interview had already been concluded and NDTV persons was interviewing. Rajbir had requested not to telecast the line stated by accused about Gellani. So when this interview was telecast on 20th Dec. 5 p.m. that line was removed but when this was rebroadcasted in our programme 100 days after attack this line has not been removed and is in the interview.

Ques: I put it to you that Rajbir had not simply told me but shouted at me not to say anything about Gellani?

Ans: It is correct.

RO & AC Designated Judge
New Delhi 10-10-02

Note: The above statement is as it is recorded by the court.

Annexure 9

Open Letter to Law Minister from the Amnesty International

8 July 2002

Dear Minister,

Amnesty International is concerned that, in the forthcoming trial of four persons who are charged with various crimes relating to the attack on the Indian parliament on 13 December 2001, international standards for fair trial which India is bound to observe as a state party to the International Covenant on Civil and Political Rights (ICCPR) may be disregarded. Pre-trial proceedings appear to have been flawed and the scheduling of hearings of the forthcoming trial, due to commence on 8 July 2002, indicates that the speed at which the trial is to be conducted may violate the defendants' right to present a full defence. Moreover the special legislation under which the accused are to be tried is flawed and likely to facilitate an unfair trial. Amnesty International is particularly concerned that the accused could be sentenced to death if found guilty of the crimes with which they are charged. Amnesty International opposes the death penalty in all cases as a violation of the right to life.

While acknowledging the obligation of states to uphold law and order and to protect their populations from violent criminal acts such as the attack on the Indian parliament on 13 December 2001, Amnesty International is concerned that in this context human rights protection is all too often relegated to second place. United Nations High Commissioner for Human Rights Mary

Robinson said on 20 March 2002: I am particularly concerned that counter-terrorism strategies pursued after September 11 [2001] have sometimes undermined efforts to enhance respect for human rights.

Amnesty International is concerned about the right to a fair trial of all four accused, Mohammad Afzal, Shaukat Hussain and his wife Navjot Sandhu and Abdul Rehman Geelani. Under international human rights law, as under the Constitution of India, the right to a fair trial applies to all accused persons; those accused of violent political acts must not be discriminated against and have the right to enjoy equality before law and equal protection of law.

Amnesty International in this letter concentrates on the case of Abdul Rehman Geelani whose case details are given in the appendix, to indicate its concerns about the forthcoming trial which may affect the rights of all the four accused to a fair trial; his case shows that those working in the criminal justice system appear willing to suspend even minimum safeguards available under special anti-terrorist legislation which is itself grossly defective. Amnesty International fears that the trial due to start on 8 July 2002, apparently one of the first in India under the Prevention of Terrorism Act 2002 (POTA), will have a signal effect for scores of other cases being brought under POTA in India and believes that it should therefore be subjected to very careful scrutiny. First indications in the present case are very negative as pre-trial procedures have already involved a range of abuses.

Amnesty International's concerns relate to:

1. Unfair pre-trial procedures

Amnesty International believes that POTA in several of its provisions violates international standards for fair trial and is particularly concerned that even the minimal safeguards contained in

POTA have not been implemented in the case of Abdul Rehman Geelani.

POTA provides in section 52 for the preparation of a custody memo to record relevant dates and times of custody. However, the official record of arrest of Abdul Rehman Geelani is faulty; it records the date of arrest as 15 December 2001 — he was arrested a day earlier and taken to an undeclared place of detention where police allegedly subjected him to torture including beating and hanging upside down and verbal abuse. Amnesty International fears that Geelani's right not to be subjected to torture was violated, and this was facilitated by his being held in incommunicado detention in an unauthorized place of detention. The safeguard of a custody record to ensure proper treatment of prisoners provided by POTA was violated.

Section 32(4) of POTA provides that a detainee is to be brought before a magistrate within 48 hours of the confession having been made. Under section 32(5) the detainee can report to the magistrate if he or she has been subjected to torture during interrogation in police custody. This is important as section 32 of POTA allows confessions to be admitted as evidence in court.

This important safeguard was disregarded in the pre-trial process. Abdul Rehman Geelani stated that he, along with the three other accused, was brought before the Additional Chief Metropolitan Magistrate (ACMM) on 22 December 2001 who asked the police inspector present if the statement of the accused had been recorded. He did not give an opportunity to the accused to report if they had been tortured. The presence of police would in itself been sufficiently intimidating to make the accused hesitate to report any ill-treatment they may have been subjected to. The charge sheet incorrectly reports this significant omission when it states that Geelani was brought alone, in the absence of any police officer, before the ACMM and stated before the ACMM that he had not been tortured when his statement was recorded by police (see case details below).

Abdul Rehman Geelani filed an application to the Additional Sessions Judge on 31 May 2002 requesting that the discrepancies contained in the charge sheet be clarified before charges were framed. This application was placed on record but was not taken into account before charges were framed on 4 June 2002.

There is little apparently evidence to link Abdul Rehman Geelani to the offence; the charge sheet merely states that his phone number was found on the mobile phone of the main accused and that in a telephone conversation recorded on 14 December 2001, Abdul Rehman Geelani was heard to comment positively on the attack on the Indian parliament. These are not recognizable criminal offences under Indian law. One of the other accused, Mohammad Afzal, stated at a press conference that Abdul Rehman Geelani had not been involved in the offences. Human rights activists in India have publicly expressed their concern that the available evidence does not warrant the serious criminal charges brought against Geelani and a trial under anti-terrorist legislation.

Amnesty International is concerned that media coverage of the arrests and concerning the person of Abdul Rehman Geelani during the pre-trial period has been extremely prejudicial to his case and that the Government of India has not taken any steps to halt this. The media coverage which largely presented Geelani as guilty before the trial had even begun, must be presumed to impact negatively on Abdul Rehman Geelani's right to be presumed innocent as required by Article 14(2) of the ICCPR and on the impartiality of the POTA court which is to hear the case from 8 July 2002. Reports have alleged that Abdul Rehman Geelani had bought a house in New Delhi with unaccounted for money (*Hindustan Times*, 17 December 2001), indoctrinated students in terrorism (*Hindustan Times*, *The Hindu*, both 17 December 2001) and participated in activities of the now banned Students Islamic Movement of India (*Times of India*, 20 December 2001); human rights activists in India have pointed out that these allegations are untrue. Moreover reports appeared in the media quoting from Geelani's confessional statement which imply his guilt despite the fact that he did not make a confessional statement (*Hindustan Times*, 21 December, *Sunday Times*, 23 December 2001).

On 21 December 2001, police paraded the four accused before the press. Subsequently the press conference was broadcast on national television; during the press conference only accused Mohammad Afzal was allowed to speak; he reportedly admitted to the attack on the parliament. The other accused were not allowed to speak nor was the press permitted to question any of the accused. Mohammad Afzal during the press conference reportedly declared that Abdul Rehman Geelani had not been involved in the attack. On 2 July 2002, Mohammad Afzal filed a statement in court withdrawing his confessional statement which he declared had been written by the Deputy Commissioner of Police.

Amnesty International believes that parading accused before national media during which they are made to incriminate themselves violates their right to be presumed innocent until convicted according to law in the course of fair proceedings and their right not to be compelled to testify against themselves or to confess guilt. These rights are provided in Articles 14(2) and 14 (3) (g) of the ICCPR respectively.

2. Restriction of the right to present a full defence

Amnesty International fears that the hearings will be conducted in great haste. There are some 180 witnesses to be examined and the schedule presented to the lawyers of the defendants lists 10 witnesses to be heard on 8 July 2002, 11 witnesses on the next day and so on, with all witnesses to be heard on consecutive days within two weeks. Such speed is unprecedented in judicial proceedings in India and may seriously violate the right of the defendants to present a full defence and adequately and fully cross examine prosecution witnesses, as required by Article 14(3)(e) of the ICCPR to which India is a state party.

3. Conditions of detention

At least since the beginning of January, Abdul Rehman Geelani was held in solitary confinement in Tihar Jail, New Delhi; he has not been allowed to leave his cell to walk in the open air and has been denied other facilities that other detainees are permitted to enjoy. An application to the POTA judge was filed in early February and eventually most of these restrictions were withdrawn.

Moreover, Abdul Rehman Geelani had expressed fears in the early weeks of his detention that he may be attacked or killed in jail with the connivance of prison authorities; while in Tihar Jail he had observed other Muslim prisoners being ill-treated solely on account of their religious background. Apparently, these fears have now reduced since Geelani has ceased to be held in solitary confinement.

4. Application of POTA

Human rights groups in India and international human rights bodies, including Amnesty International, have on a number of occasions raised concern about defects of POTA[1]; several petitions challenging POTA are pending in the Indian Supreme Court. It has been shown to violate many of the human rights guarantees relating to the rights to liberty and security of the person, to freedom from torture, to a fair trial and to statement, association and redress contained in the Constitution of India, Indian statutory law and international human rights commitments undertaken by India, for instance its ratification of the ICCPR.

Amnesty International is particularly concerned that several provisions of POTA undermine the principle of presumption of innocence: Section 4, under which Geelani is charged, raises an irrebuttable presumption that if a person is found in unauthorised possession of explosive substances, such possession is automatically connected with "terrorist acts" and the offence, normally punishable under the Explosive Substances Act, becomes triable under the POTA's special provisions, where few legal safeguards and heavier sentences upon conviction apply. However, the organization believes that the possession of a weapon or of an explosive substance cannot imply the involvement of its owner in an offence unless this is proved by the prosecution. Similarly, section 49(6) and (7) of the Act provides that no person accused of an offence should be released on bail unless the public prosecutor has been given an opportunity to oppose the application for such release and that where the public prosecutor opposes bail, it should not be granted unless "the court is satisfied that there are grounds for believing that the accused is not guilty of committing such offence". The granting of bail thus becomes effectively dependant on a *prima facie* assessment of guilt or innocence by the court and the failure of a court to grant bail can be considered as an assumption of guilt. This happens at a stage in the proceedings when the prosecution are not obliged to disclose evidence against the accused. Amnesty International believes that all courts must conduct trials without previously having formed an opinion on the guilt or innocence of the accused.

Amnesty International is concerned that in POTA the act of inviting support for a terrorist organization is made an offence, without a definition of what this act may include. The organization notes that inviting support may not involve any encouragement to commit violent and criminal acts. On the contrary it might include the peaceful, private discussion of political ideas. The Act therefore is potentially leading to violations of the rights of freedom of statement established in article 19 of the ICCPR. Amnesty International believes that, in the interest of legal certainty, prohibited acts must be recognizably criminal offences — so that everyone can modify their behaviour or know whether this behaviour is lawful or not — and avoid the application of criminal laws from being extended by analogy.

Amnesty International believes that section 32 of POTA, providing for confessions made to a police officer to be admissible in trial, subverts standards for assessing evidence set by Indian statutory law and upheld in the Indian Evidence Act, which clearly excludes such confessions from evidence at trial. Expressing its view on an identical section contained in the Prevention of Terrorism Bill, 2000, the NHRC stated that:

> *this would increase the possibility of coercion and torture in securing confessions and thus be inconsistent with Article 14(3) (f) of the ICCPR which requires that everyone shall be entitled to the guarantee of not being compelled to testify against himself or to confess guilt.*

Other sections of POTA legislate the interference of the executive in judicial matters: Section 23(3) of the Act, for example, provides that determination of issues relating to the jurisdiction of Special Courts is decided by the executive and not by law or the judiciary. The provision for "Review Committees" contained in Section 60 does not ensure sufficient independent supervision of the procedures established by the Act as envisaged in international standards. The Review Committees, in fact, make decisions about the de-notification of terrorist organizations and the interception of communications, which have a bearing on assessments of guilt or innocence and the admissibility of evidence and thus should be subject to all the guarantees of independence applicable to the judiciary. Section 60 does not contain detailed guidelines concerning the operation of these committees. It appears that they are made up of personnel appointed by the executive and that there is no mention of the right of the detainee to make a representation before a Review Committee. In addition, there are no provisions setting out the powers of such Committees, including for instance whether or not they would have the power to review whether the application of the Act is justified in terms of the objectives or lawful in terms of procedure. No periodicity is established for their reviews and it is not clear whether they would have the powers to discontinue a case if they consider it necessary.

Principle 3 of the Basic Principles on the Independence of the Judiciary states that "The judiciary shall have jurisdiction over all issues of a judicial nature and shall have exclusive authority to decide whether an issue submitted for its decision is within its competence as defined by law."

Amnesty International believes that anti-terrorist legislation such as POTA has undermined the safeguards which India, as a state party to the ICCPR, is obliged to uphold, thus encouraging law enforcement officials and those working in the criminal justice system to assume that legal safeguards and norms of judicial procedures may be suspended in the pursuit of anti-terrorism. Amnesty International calls on the Government of India to strictly adhere to its own constitutional human rights safeguards and international human rights law and standards. They require that all people against whom there is a suspicion of involvement in criminal activities be treated strictly in accordance with law. To discriminate against those suspected of terrorist offences by subjecting them to custodial violence and denying them their right to a fair trial, violates the principle of equality of law and equal protection of law which are fundamental rights recognized in the Constitution of India.

Amnesty International urges the Government of India to take all possible care to ensure a fair trial to the accused in the present case and to investigate, promptly, effectively, independently and impartially, the violations of rights of these four accused which appear to have taken place in the pre-trial period, and particularly the allegation that Abdul Rehman Geelani was tortured in police custody. Amnesty International also urges once again that the Government of India consider bringing POTA into conformity with international standards for fair trial.

I look forward to receiving your response to the issues raised in this letter. We intend to make this letter publicly available.

Yours sincerely,
Irene Khan
Secretary General

Cc: L.K. Advani, Home Minister
Cc: Justice Verma, Chairman, National Human Rights Commission

Appendix: Case Details

Abdul Rehman Geelani, a 32-year-old Kashmiri from Baramulla in Jammu and Kashmir and a lecturer of Arabic at a New Delhi college since 1997, was arrested on 14 December 2001 at around 1.15 p.m. at a bus stop in New Delhi, one day after the bomb attack on the Indian parliament which killed several people. Police in plain clothes took Geelani away in a van in which they allegedly abused and threatened him with dire consequences if he did not confess to his involvement in the bomb attack. He was then taken to a farm house where he was allegedly beaten and hung upside down in the presence of some named senior police officers to force him to confess to the crime. Geelani insisted throughout that he had no connection with the bomb blast. He was, however, forced to sign some blank pages.

Geelani was held in the farm house up to the morning of 16 December 2001 when police brought him before a judge at her residence where police obtained remand of Geelani. He was then taken to the Lodhi Road police station where his wife, two children (10 and 5 years old) and younger brother continued to be held without charges for three days.

At the end of the police remand period, Geelani was transferred to jail custody. In Tihar Jail, New Delhi, he was initially held in a cell which he shared with other accused in Ward No. 8 but after some three weeks he was transferred to a cell in another ward where he was held in solitary confinement; in late January he was returned to ward No. 8 but continued to be held in solitary confinement in a cell measuring about 10 feet by 7 feet. He was not allowed to leave his cell and come into the open air as other detainees are allowed to do, could not make use of the canteen facility, was not given fruits that his family brought to the prison and could not use the prison library. An application filed with the POTA court in early February led to his being transferred to a regular cell and other restrictions were withdrawn as well.

Geelani was implicated in First Information Report (FIR) No. 417 of 13 December 2001 which lists offences under sections 121, 121A, 122, 124, 120B, 186, 353, 332, 333, 302, 307 of the Indian Penal Code (IPC), sections 25 and 27 of the Arms Act and sections 3, 4, 5 and 6 of the Explosive Substances Act for allegedly conspiring to attack the Indian parliament. The FIR did not mention any names of suspects. The other accused arrested are Mohammad Afzal, Shaukat Hussain and his wife Navjot Sandhu who at the time of arrest was seven or eight months pregnant and gave birth in jail after being denied bail. She appears to have been charged with the range of offences solely because she is the wife of another accused. All the four accused come originally from Jammu and Kashmir.

According to the details contained in the charge sheet, on 19 December 2001, police added charges of terrorism under sections 3 [commission of terrorist act], 4 [possession of arms], 5 [enhanced penalty], 20 [membership in a terrorist organization], 21 [support for a terrorist organization], 22 [fundraising for a terrorist organization] of the Prevention of Terrorism Ordinance, 2001 (POTO, now POTA).

On 14 May 2002, police submitted the charge sheet. The only evidence against Geelani mentioned in the charge sheet is that of his telephone number was found on the mobile phone of the main accused and in a recorded phone conversation on 14 December, before his arrest, Geelani is reported to have commented positively on the attack on parliament.

Geelani's lawyer showed the charge sheet to his client on 20 May 2002; Geelani then pointed out several inaccuracies which were summarized in an application submitted to the Additional Sessions Judge, Delhi, on 31 May 2002 with the request to clarify the discrepancies in the charge sheet before framing charges. Its main points are:

— the charge sheet states that Geelani did not make any statement before the Deputy Commissioner of Police on 21 December 2001 and signed a paper to that effect on the same date; that Geelani was brought before the Additional Chief Metropolitan Magistrate (ACMM) on 22 December 2001 alone, without police personnel being present and that he stated before the ACMM that he had not been tortured to make his statement before police and had no complaint against the police officer. Geelani pointed out that in fact, all the four accused were brought early in the morning of 22 December 2001 to the ACMM court; while still in police custody in a police van outside the court, a named inspector forced Geelani to write and sign the statement as per the dictation of police. The four accused were then taken together to the ACMM who asked the police inspector present if their statements had been recorded; none of the accused persons who were brought in handcuffs before the magistrate, were given an opportunity to make any statement nor were they asked if they had been tortured.

— one of the other accused, Mohammad Afzal, stated at the press conference that Geelani had not been involved in the commission of the offences for which the four persons are being held. This statement was arbitrarily not recorded in the charge sheet.

— the date of arrest was recorded in the charge sheet as 15 December 2001 whereas Geelani was taken into custody and held in an undeclared place of detention on 14 December 2001.

This application was placed on record. On 4 June 2002 the charges were framed; some further charges were added; these include charges under section 123 IPC against Najot Sandhu which makes it an offence for a person who has knowledge of a planned criminal offence not to inform relevant authorities.

1. See: *India: The Prevention of Terrorism Bill 2000: Past abuses revisited?* AI Index: ASA 20/22/00, June 2000. Following the lapse of the Terrorist and Disruptive Activities (Prevention) Act, 1987 (TADA) in 1995, the Government of India in 1999 requested the Law Commission to undertake a fresh examination of the issue of a suitable legislation for combatting terrorism and other anti-national activities in response to which the Law Commission in April 2000 presented a draft legislation, the Preven-

tion of Terrorism Bill 2000. Civil liberty groups criticised the bill as facilitating violations of numerous human rights which the Government of India is obligated to safeguard. In the wake of the attacks in Washington and New York on 11 September 2001, and a US-led war on terrorism, the Indian Union cabinet on 15 October 2001 approved a new Ordinance, the Prevention of Terrorism Ordinance (POTO) which gives substantial powers to police and executive officials in the fight against terrorism. POTO was signed by the President of India on 24 October 2001 and came into force at once. (See: *India: Briefing on the Prevention of Terrorism Ordinance,* AI Index: ASA 20/049/2001, November 2001) Civil society at large and human rights and civil liberties organizations, minority groups and political parties had not been consulted before the promulgation of the Ordinance but expressed their opposition to it. The National Human Rights Commission, too, criticised the Ordinance and said that existing legislation, if properly implemented, was sufficient to combat all kinds of terrorist activities and that there was no need for an additional law. On 30 December 2001, the Ordinance was re-promulgated and on 26 March 2002, the Indian parliament passed the corresponding bill, which contained only minor changes, which came into effect at once. Scores of cases have since then been brought under the Prevention of Terrorism Act, 2002 (POTA), the majority against Kashmiris.

ANNEXURE 10

Open Letter to Chief Justice by University Teachers

The Hon'ble Chief Justice,
The Supreme Court of India,
New Delhi 11001

Dear Mr. Chief Justice,

We are concerned citizens who have been following the trial of the four accused in the Parliament attack case. We fully realize the gravity of the charge against the four accused and the implications of an attack on the prime institution of our democracy. However, we are equally concerned about the growing trend of human rights standards being violated by the executive with impunity. Unfortunately, the legislature encourages this trend by promulgating extraordinary laws which undermine the rights enshrined in our constitution.

We focus on how Mr. Syed Abdur Rehman Geelani, a lecturer teaching at Zakir Hussain College of Delhi University, has been denied his rights under the ordinary criminal law, his constitutional protections and even the safeguards under the Prevention of Terrorism Act.

We cite the following glaring examples:

Pre-Trial Safeguards

1. Geelani was arrested on December 14, 2001. On the same night his young wife and two small children were also arrested and detained for two days. The police showed the arrest of

Geelani on December 15, 2001 and there is no record of the arrest and detention of his family.

2. Geelani was brutally tortured by the police in an attempt to elicit a false confession. This is in violation of the sections 330, 331 of the IPC read with the provisions of the UN Convention against Torture to which India is a party.
3. After his arrest the police paraded Geelani and the other co-accused before the media so that they would incriminate themselves. However, all this while, Geelani was not allowed to speak.
4. Unfortunately, even the media did not behave responsibly and indulged in slanderous reporting almost amounting to a trial by media thus vitiating and prejudicing the opinion of the public against the accused even before the trial. This resulted in putting the various agencies involved in the trial under extreme pressure which further reduced the possibility of a fair trial.
5. Geelani was produced before Addl. Chief Magistrate who did not ask Geelani whether he had been tortured.
6. The Police imposed POTA on Geelani five days after his arrest even though there was no evidence against him. The imposition of POTA would deny him his right to bail. Amnesty International has also expressed its concerns about the possibility of a person charged under POTA getting a fair trial.
7. Geelani is denied access to books and other basic amenities.
8. Geelani's lawyers have brought all these facts to the attention of the relevant courts but the courts do not seem to respond.
9. The investigating officer, Rajbir Singh, has a record of being involved in fabricating evidence and false encounters.

The Trial

1. The Special Judge has decided to have a day to day trial and the prosecution has produced 80 witnesses. There is no way

Geelani or the other accused can adequately prepare their cross examination.

2. The Special Judge has even disallowed the Defence Counsel one day's time to prepare for the cross examination of an expert witness while allowing several adjournments to the prosecution.
3. Many of us, students and teachers, have attended the court and have been shocked by the open hostility and prejudice in the court.
4. Geelani has been physically assaulted inside the jail although the jail authorities have denied it. The Defence Committee has filed a complaint before the National Human Rights Commission.
5. Without any provocation, reason or ground the court allowed the police's petition to handcuff Geelani and the other accused while in court.
6. Geelani has challenged the order of handcuffing. However, the High Court has reserved the decision so far.
7. The only piece of evidence against Geelani is an intercepted telephone conversation. The Defence Counsel has been asking the court to play the cassette in court but the court has not permitted this so far. Furthermore, the Defence Counsel has argued that the so called evidence has been obtained in violation of the law on phone tapping but the High Court has chosen to remain silent. The police has not even bothered to prepare a transcript of the intercept. The translation of the conversation in Kashmiri submitted by the police has been challenged by the Defence Counsel as incorrect.

We, the undersigned, do not wish to interfere, in any way, with the judicial process but we are deeply concerned that the principles of natural justice and fair trial are apparently being ignored. We wish to raise our voice not only in defence of a well loved and respected teacher but also because the ideals and values on which our country's democracy is founded are being eroded by the politics of prejudice and hatred. It is this concern that compelled some of India's most prominent citizens known for their integrity and patriotism to recently form an All India Defense Committee for Syed Abdul Rehman Geelani.

We, urge you, the guardian of our constitution, to protect the principles of life and liberty and thus uphold the honour of our deep rooted democratic traditions and the future of Indian secularism.

Yours faithfully,

Note: This Open Letter has been posted to the Chief Justice on Sept. 17, 2002 with nearly 200 signatures, including senior faculty members and Heads of Departments from Delhi University and JNU. The signature campaign however continues.

Annexure 11

Sessions Court Judgment of December 16, 2002

Sessions Case No. 53/2002

(Cited paragraphs only in numerical order)

5. But for the swift action and alertness shown by the security staff present at the Parliament House, this country would have paid a heavy price on December 13, 2001 when the terrorists planned to capture the Parliament of India. The terrorists' intention was absolutely clear. The writing on the fake Home Ministry pass, pasted by terrorists on the car bomb brought by them to Parliament House read as under:-

"INDIA IS A VERY BAD COUNTRY AND WE HATE INDIA WE WANT TO DESTROY INDIA AND WITH THE GRACE OF GOD WE WILL DO IT GOD IS WITH US AND WE WILL TRY OUR BEST. THIS EDIET WAJPAEE AND ADVANI WE WILL KILL THEM. THEY HAVE KILLED MANY INNOCENT PEOPLE AND THEY ARE VERY BAD PERSONS THERE BROTHER BUSH HE IS ALSO A VERY BAD PERSON HE WILL BE NEXT TARGET HE IS ALSO THE KILLER OF INNOCENT PEOPLE HE HAVE TO DIE AND WE WILL DO IT................"

28. Five deceased terrorists were identified by Mohd.Afzal as Mohammad, Hamza, Raja, Rana and Haider. Fake I.cards were prepared for terrorist Mohammad—in the name of Rohel Sharma and Ashiq Hussain; for terrorist Hamza—in the name of Anil Kumar; for terrorist Raja—in the name of Raju Lal; for terrorist Rana—in the name of Sunil Verma and for terrorist Haider—in the name of Sanjay Kaul. I.cards were prepared with the help of laptop, which was with the terrorists. Fake I.cards showed them as students/teachers of Xansa Webcity, a computer education Institute functioning at 37, Bunglow Road, Kamla Nagar, Delhi. The terrorists and accused persons, who were co-operating them and helping them in this operation, prepared a car bomb. The chemicals, which had been procured from Tilak Bazar included Amonium Nitrate, Sulphur, Aluminium Powder, the combination of which forms explosive material of high quality. Appx. 8 kgs. of dry fruits were purchased from Khari Baoli, Delhi. Mobile phones and Sim cards were also purchased. Chemicals were procured in huge quantity. The terrorists also procured containers. One big steel drum and few small steel containers were procured. One Sujata mixer was also purchased and the chemicals were mixed in appropriate proportion. Appx. 31 kgs. of explosive substance was put in a steel container, most probably on the night of 12th and 13th Dec. 01 to convert ambassador into a car bomb. This steel container containing explosive substance was fitted with detonators, battery and wires, so that it could be exploded at the appropriate time. On 12/13.12.01 night, a crucial meeting between the terrorists and accused persons took place and it was decided that attack on Parliament would be made on the next day. On the morning of 13.12.01, deceased terrorists and accused Afzal left the hide-out at A.97, Gandhi Vihar at about 10 a.m.

42. (*Excerpts*) ... One handwritten letter was also recovered from the person of deceased terrorist Rana and same is Ex. PW.2/9. The language of the letter is reproduced hereunder only to show that the deceased terrorist's knowledge of English was very poor:

"DEAR SOMJ

I LOVE YOU VERY MUCH BUT YOU NOT GAVE ME A LIFT ARE YOU NOT ME LOVE SO IT YOU. BUT YOU NOT LOOKME SLOW DAY AND NIGHT COM …SOON MUCH DO YOU MUCH DO YOU MY DEAR SLOW MUCH DO YOU THING NOTHING AND MOVE SLOW INTENT AND MORE – BEEN THOSE AND …… LOOK. THIS IS NOT COMING SLOW WANTED MUCH AND LOOKING SCHOOL AND ….. SLOW WHAT – GOOD AND ME.

53. Mr. K.G. Kannabiran Advocate and other advocates on behalf of accused persons, during cross examination of this witness, wanted to ask him questions about what was written on the I.card and other documents. Since the I.card and document were exhibited and placed on record, this court disallowed the questions about the contents of the documents seized by the witness and also about the seizure of content memos that were proved. During arguments, counsel have raised issue that not allowing the questions about the contents of seized documents, had prejudiced the accused and this showed over-zealousness of the Judge conducting the trail. I consider that this is a baseless argument & must be rejected outrightly. The witness was not the author of the I.cards or the slips recovered from the deceased terrorists. He had placed on record, whatever was recovered. Neither the witness said that he had any personal knowledge of the contents, so no questions could have been allowed by the court to be asked about contents of these documents, which were already on record. The Judge is not an umpire sitting on the dias, who had only to blow a whistle. He has an active role during trial and has to see that irrelevant questions and the questions, which are asked only to waste time of the court or to harass the witnesses, are not allowed. This court, whenever had disallowed questions, had given liberty to accused's counsels to place in writing all disallowed questions on record and a perusal of these questions would show that these had nothing to do with the defence of the accused but were being asked only to harass the witnesses or to waste time of the court. It has not been shown, in what manner, the accused has been prejudiced by not asking these questions.

78. (*Excerpts*) The information about Shaukat and Afzal was sent to J&K police on the morning of 15.12.01 around 6 am. It is obvious that this information could not have been communicated to J&K police by the investigating agency at Delhi unless this information had been given to them by some source... Through SAR Gilani, they learnt the address and house of Shaukat and Afsan. Gilani took them to Shaukat's house and from there, his wife Afsan Guru must have been arrested on the night intervening 14th and 15th Dec. 01. After their interrogation alone during that night, police must have come to know the truck number on which two accused persons Shaukat and Afzal had run away from Delhi and could have sent this information to J&K police.

79. The plea of accused SAR Gilani that he was arrested between 1.15 and 1.30 p.m. on 14-12-2001 near Khalsa College from a bus is unbelievable. A perusal of the conversation between his half brother and him, which took place around 12.23 p.m. on 14.12.01, shows that at the time he received call, Gilani was in the bus and going to his home. He has not stated in the conversation as to at which bus stop his bus was at the time of conversation. He has not denied the conversation between himself and his half brother, nor he has stated that this part of conversation was interpolated or tampered, so his plea that he was around 1.15 p.m. going towards a Masjid on Mall Road is belied by this admitted conversation. It is true that there is no call made on cell

phone after 1.03 p.m. on 14.12.01 but it is not uncommon for a person not to use his cell phone for few hours. Moreover, police was keeping surveillance at his house, as has been stated by the witness and it is quite possible that the accused had smelled about the surveillance and taken care not to make any call.

84. In Tarun Bose vs. State of Assam, 2002 VII AD (SC) 41, Hon'ble Supreme Court observed as under:-

> "It is quite but natural that in a prevalent situation, obtaining in the area surcharged with the insurgency activities, striking a terror and fear psychosis in the mind of the people, the IO would definitely find difficulties to collect sufficient corroborative evidence. Witnesses will be reluctant to come to the court to depose or appear before the IO to give statement for fear of reprisals. Rarely, one comes across any corroborative evidence in such type of offence. This would be no ground to throw away otherwise trust-worthy evidence of prosecution witnesses."

85. Law Commission about the situation prevalent in J&K State has quoted as under: (Law Commission report on POTA)

> "Our experience of TADA in J&K has not been good. There has not been a single case, which has been decided by the court of Law. The difficulties encountered have been with regard to the non availability of witnesses to testify in the Courts of Law on account of fear of reprisal. There is another difficulty and that is the collection of evidence in cases, where the search, seizure and arrest in area, where there is no habitation and many a times these have been by security forces. In such a case, the arrested person's confession to the security forces leading to the recovery of arms and ammunition and explosives is the only thing which can be brought on record. Even the

security force personnel do not come forward for tendering evidence because they keep on moving from place to place for performance of their duties not only within J&K but even outside J&K and sometimes outside India. The security force personnel are reluctant to depose in any case as they feel that they are not attuned for this kind of exercise. In the last 15 years of militancy in J&K, thousands of people have been arrested, lakhs of weapons seized and millions of rounds collected and quintals of explosive material seized. These figures are real eye openers and the fact that not a single case has ended in conviction, nor has there been any recording of evidence and even this itself is very disturbing. TADA had a provision that no arrested person could be released on bail without giving an opportunity to the State to present its view points. In thousands of cases, bails were granted in situations far from satisfactory and full of suspicion. The State High Court did not interfere in the matter on the ground that the Appellate jurisdiction rested with Supreme Court. The Supreme Court did not interfere in the matter, nor did they take cognizance on the ground that no one has filed a petition before it in this matter. The High Court Bar Association has passed a resolution that no member of the Bar should appear for the State and they wanted judiciary to pass orders ex parte. Above facts are only indicative of the malady, which has been prevailing in J&K on account of terrorism ...... Expression of honest opinion have become difficult on account of damocles sword of contempt of court hanging on the heads of people ......"

86. I consider that keeping in view the prevalent situation in country, where terrorists are striking at will, blame cannot be put on the police persons as to why they did not procure public witnesses. None shall be ready. It is also noteworthy that attack on

Parliament was made when Parliament was in session. There is not a single witness either from MPs or other VVIPs who had deposed in court about attack on Parliament, although a large number of persons must have seen this attack, which included TV cameramen, their news reporters etc. The fear of terrorists is real fear. One of the witnesses, who was cited by prosecution, refused to depose in court in this case. She appeared as PW.46 but stated that on the previous night, a threat on telephone was given and she was scared and more concerned about her children and she refused to depose in court. The fear in the mind of J&K police was so much that they did not dare arrest Afzal and Shaukat when they were in fruit Mandi and waited for them to move out.

100. Counsel for accused persons have objected to the identification of deceased terrorists through photographs. It is argued that such an identification is no identification. In AIR 1963 SC 1974 Ram Lochan vs. State, it was held that photograph of deceased compared with the skeleton of human body (skull) recovered from a person is admissible to prove that skull was that of deceased. In AIR 1963 AP 314, Sharaf Shah vs. State, Hon'ble High Court held that there was no objection to the police showing the series of photographs to some of the witnesses in order to seek information as to the person or persons, who may have committed a crime. Where photographs have been shown, the value of any subsequent TIP by witnesses will be impaired. Showing of photograph for identification by itself is not illegal.

102. PW.40 is Anil Kumar, who was having a shop at Gali Taliyan, Tilak Bazar, Delhi and doing chemical business. He deposed that his shop was at 990, Gali Taliyan, Tilak Bazar. On 17.12.01, accused Mohd. Afzal had come to his shop alongwith police. He identified Mohd. Afzal. He stated that the same accused Mohd. Afzal had come to his shop on 6.12.01 to purchase amonium nitrate. He placed an order for 50 kgs. of amonium nitrate and paid an advance of Rs.800/- and told that he would take delivery on the next date. On 7.12.01 at about 3 p.m. he came with one more person and paid him the balance amount of Rs.4000/- and took delivery of 50 kg. of amonium nitrate. Amonium nitrate supplied by him was in the packing of 500 gm each, in plastic jars. It was a powdry material. He proved memo Ex.PW.40/1, which shows that accused Mohd. Afzal pointed at his shop and him as the person, from whom he had purchased amonium nitrate in the company of one of the deceased terrorists. The witness identified amonium nitrate which was recovered from the hide outs as the same which was purchased from his shop. He stated that he had supplied 100 jars, each of 500 gm. Jars supplied by him were same Ex.PW.54/1 to 24. He further testified that police had shown him photographs of terrorists, who were killed in the Parliament attack and he identified photograph PW.40/2 (Hamza) as that of the person, who had accompanied Mohd. Afzal. During cross examination, witness stated that amonium nitrate can be sold by any shop keeper keeping the chemicals. No legal formalities were required to be completed by the purchaser of the amonium nitrate. It will be worthwhile to mention here that amonium nitrate is also used as a chemical manure in the fields and is easily available on the shops. It is a chemical which can be put to several uses, including the use of preparing explosives. The witness stated that no receipt etc. was issued by him and the packing of amonium nitrate shown to him is available on other shops also. There was no stamp or label of his shop on these packs.

106. PW.42 is Ramesh Adwani, who was having shop in Tilak Bazar, Delhi dealing with silver powder and other colour material. He testified that his shop No. was 141, Tilak Bazar, in the name of M/s Tola & Sons. Accused alongwith police had come to the shop on 17.12.01, accused had purchased 15 kg silver powder from his shop on 11.12.01 at the rate of Rs.210 per kg. Pointing out memo Ex.PW.42/1 was signed by him and accused Mohd. Afzal. Silver powder was sold in polythene packing bearing name of his shop. He identified silver powder recovered from one of the hide outs as the same, which was purchased from his shop. Silver powder in packing is Ex.P.51. During cross examination, he stated that this powder is called silver powder because it is of silvery colour, but its trade name is aluminium powder and it is used in Holi festival for giving silver colour. It is also used in paints and no licence is required for its sale. No formalities are done before sale of the powder. It is a tax paid item, so no receipts etc. are issued. He was able to identify accused Mohd. Afzal because the quantity purchased by him was large quantity and he remembered his coming to the shop on 11.12.01. Police brought him again on 17.12.01 around 12 noon. Testimony of this witness regarding pointing out of his shop, similarly is not admissible. However, identification by this witness of accused as the purchaser of silver powder is admissible.

109. PW.44 is Sandeep Chaudhary, he had a shop of selling mobile phones, Sim cards etc. He testified that he had shop No. 26, in Gaffar Market, Karol Bagh, Delhi and was doing the business of selling mobile phones, cash cards, Sim cards etc. Accused Afzal had come to his shop on 7/8.12.01 and purchased one mobile phone model J.70 make Sony and cash card of Rs.500/-. He identified the mobile phone set sold by him as Ex. P.37 and proved the pointing out memo as Ex.PW.44/1. He identified accused Mohd. Afzal in court as well. In cross examination, he stated that he had told police that accused had taken mobile phone from his shop 4-5 days prior to 13.12.01. In his statement Ex.PW.44/DA, date of 13.12.01 was not mentioned but it was mentioned that 4-5 days prior to the incident. He stated that he did not maintain permanent record as to how many mobile phone sets were sold by him daily. He stated that Gaffar Market is a grey market, no bills etc. were used, only rough notes are prepared, which are destroyed every evening. Police had brought Afzal to his shop on 18.12.01 around 12.30/1 p.m. After 13.12.01 he had seen Afzal in court on the day of his testimony.

112. Counsel for accused persons have argued that testimony of the witnesses namely these shop keepers, from whom accused Afzal allegedly purchased cell phones, chemicals etc., cannot be believed as they are all procured witnesses. In any case, the names of shops were given on polythene bags and there is no resason why accused Afzal should be considered to have accompanied the deceased terrorist to purchase chemicals. It is also stated that identification by these witnesses of the accused Mohd. Afzal or Shaukat in court after such a long time is no identification. No test identification was held of accused Shaukat and Afzal. About PW49 it is argued that he allegedly sold SIM card to Afzal on 4-12-2002 but phone No. 9811489429 of Afzal is in operation since 6-11-2001 as per record of telephone company, so either this SIM card was cloned or PW49 was a false witness. The receipt book Ex.P82 and receipt Ex.P83 produced in the court show that these were documents maintained in normal course of business. The SIM card of phone No. 9811489429 was sold to PW49 on September 21, 2001. This card was sold by him to user Afzal. Call record shows that calls were made from it to Gilani and Shaukat right from 8-11-2001. Therefore, there was no possibility of its cloning. Deceased terrorists were having six SIM cards. Out of them only two had come into operation in November, 2001, two were used on 10th and 12th December, 2001 respectively and two were not brought in operation and were in reserve. These SIM cards and phone instrument were procured for terrorists by accused Afzal and Shaukat. Purchase of cell phone and one SIM card on 4-12-2001 to Afzal and Shaukat does not mean that SIM card with cell No. 9811489429 was sold on 4-12-2001. Witness has not stated that he sold SIM card of this number to Afzal.

113. In AIR 1953 SC 3364, it was held that a witness is normally to be considered independent, unless he or she swings from source, which are likely to be tainted and that usually means, unless the witness has cause such as an enmity against the accused, to implicate him falsely, the witness has to be considered as truthful. No such suggestion has been given to any witness in this case. Also the question of test identification did not arise because it was the accused, who led police to various places, where from he had purchased chemicals, mobile phones etc., police was not aware of the shops of mobile phones and chemicals except the shop of dry fruits and aluminium powder, the names of which were written on the poly bags. All other shop keepers from where mixer-grinder, cell phones etc. were purchased, were not known to police and it is accused Afzal, who led police to these shops. Testimony of these shop keepers, therefore, cannot be doubted. It has not been shown that any of the shop keeper had any kind of enmity against the accused and wanted to implicate him in false case.

118. The fact that PW.45 was landlord of Shaukat and Afsan is not disputed. It has not been disputed that Afzal used to visit Shaukat. Only dispute has been raised about visit of Gilani to house of Shaukat. I think it is immaterial. It is not the prosecution case that witness saw Gilani visiting Shaukat's house on 2-3 days prior to 13-12-2001. Witness has not stated that Gilani was visiting Shaukat.

133. The telephones of which records have been produced, have been used by accused persons. Accused SAR Gilani has not pointed out a single entry, which was not of a call made by him but has been shown by the computer. Neither accused Shaukat or Afzal have pointed out any such entries, which were incorrect. In call records some entries have been pointed out at points X1Y1 to X5Y5, which show the same calling numbers, the same called

Nos., the same calling time but different cell ID and different IMEI Nos. Computer experts were examined by accused persons, but no questions were asked to Computer experts about these entries. Prosecution also examined Sh. Majul Kapoor from Siemens, who was well acquainted with the telephone computers, but he was not asked a single question about these entries. Entry at points X1Y1 to X5Y5 show one phenomena that the same cell has been shown twice once by giving telephone No. of ten digit and second time, this No. has been given by adding 91 before it. Same has been done in respect of called number. The call ID and IMEI No. differ. These entries show that computer in case of X1Y1 to X5Y5 has given the entry of same call made at the same time twice; once by giving cell ID and IMEI Nos. of the Caller and second time by giving the cell ID and IMEI No. of Receiver. It is evident by comparing the cell records Ex.PW.36/3 and 36/2 of the call made on 13.12.01 at 11.19 a.m. This double entry is therefore appearing in both charts, i.e., in chart of cell phone No.9811489429 Ex.PW.36/3, cell ID of Shaukat's phone is reflected at the 2nd entry and in call record of phone No. 9811573506, cell ID of Afzal's phone is reflected in the second entry. Thus it is clear that the computer of Essar cell phone of Sterling Cellular Ltd. at some place has generated double entries of the same call, in the first entry, giving the cell ID and IMEI No. of the caller and the second entry, cell ID and IMEI of the receiver. This double entry does not affect authenticity of the chart, rather reflects that there is no manual intervention in the preparation of these charts. No attempt has been made to remove double entry generated by computer in respect of five calls and that proves the authenticity of these charts.

161. In view of the above discussion, I came to conclusion that the confessional statement of accused Shaukat Hussain and Mohd. Afzal were recorded in accordance with provisions of POTA, in an atmosphere free from threat and coercion and they were voluntary and admissible under law.

172. It is argued that Laptop computer was sealed after its examination by PW72 and sent to 'Malkhana' where it was lying sealed. However, the testimony of PW73 and PW79 shows that computer was accessed on 21-1-2002 which means computer was not lying sealed and was operated on 21-1-2002. True, the report of PW73 and PW79 shows computer was accessed on 21-1-2002, but their testimony also shows, the file accessed was an immaterial file which did not contain any relevant information. This further shows that investigating agency had no knowledge how to access a file on computer without leaving a trace otherwise it would have deleted the history using some software as deposed by DW8.

179. (*Excerpts*) I consider that this is usual practice nowadays to flog the investigating agencies without realizing in what conditions and circumstances they were working under the given situation. There is no reason to disbelieve the testimony of any of the police officers as none of the police officers were having any kind of enmity against any of the accused persons. It is not the case of any of the accused persons that any of the police officers was knowing them before and has involved them falsely due to enmity. The testimony of police officers carries the same weight as the testimony of any other witness and it has to be given the same value as the testimony of any other witness. The Hon'ble Supreme Court in State, Govt. of NCT of Delhi v. Sunil Kumar & another (2001) 1 Supreme Court Cases 652 observed as under: (see Annexure 16, para 259 for the citation).

188. The provisions of POTA, as laid down in Chap.V for interception of conversation are contained in Sections 36 to 48. These provide how and in what manner, the interception has to be done, who has to authorize interception, how the interception order is to be reviewed by Review Committee, how the intercepted conversation has to be protected and how it has to be taken into account by the court as evidence. It is also true that in this case, prosecution has not followed the detailed procedure, before intercepting the calls on phone nos. However, the fact is that in this case, after the Parliament was attacked on 13.12.01 around 12 noon, terrorists had killed 9 persons and injured 16 persons before getting killed at the hands of the security forces. There was doubt in the mind of security agencies that the terrorists may be having bomb belts around their bodies, which may explode, so the entire area was cordoned off. It was around 5 p.m. only that SHO PS P. Street could record the statement of first eye witness for registration of FIR. It must have been found that time only when Insp. MC Sharma collected from the spot few mobile phone Nos. which were found on the person of deceased terrorists. At that time, nobody was aware of the sections, under which the case was to be regd. Permission for interception was sought under Indian Telegraph Act immediately from Dy. Director IB for intercepting the relevant phones and phones were put under interception. Interception was terminated on the evening of next day. The prime concern of all investigating agencies was that apart from the deceased terrorists, if other terrorists were involved in the crime and if they were hiding in Delhi, those should be caught immediately. It was a case of true emergency and the doubt of the investigating agency about involvement of others was not without any basis. I consider that at that time, it was not the concern to see whether the case was to be registered under POTA or not but the concern was to catch hold of other terrorists. Moreover, POTA was in force, no doubt by way of an ordinance but it had not been invoked so far by the State.

195. (*Excerpts*) I consider that merely because prosecution had not followed the procedure laid down in tapping the conversation looking into the emergent requirement and interest of Nation, the evidence collected by prosecution in the form of taped conversation cannot be thrown out. However, irrespective of the fact whether the prosecution has followed the procedure or not, in tapping any conversation, the fact remains that this conversation 'word by word' has been admitted by the accused. The only difference is on one line, where prosecution witness PW71 states that accused SAR Gilani uttered the words "Ei chhey zaroori", the case of accused is that he had not uttered these words, rest of the conversation is undisputed. …

202. Prosecution has relied upon the last part of the conversation, which starts with the caller asking Receiver (Gilani) – 'yeh kya koroo'. This querry cannot relate to quarrel between husband and wife, as already explained above. This querry only relates to the incident in Delhi. DW.1 Sampat Prakash, who has appeared on behalf of accused SAR Gilani has stated that in Kashmiri language, 'yeh kya koroo' means 'what has happened' and this querry is made in general whenever anything happens anywhere. Same is the testimony of DW-2 Sanjay Kak, but it is not true. This court had no knowledge of Kashmiri language and had to take some lessons in Kashmiri language. It transpires that 'yeh kya koroo' in Kashmiri is also used for what you had done. Both witnesses are interested witnesses. Dr. Sampat Prakash is a Union Leader. He has stated that he was Kashmiri Pandit and known to one Mr. Balraj Puri, a convenor of PUCL and Balraj Puri told him that All India Defence Committee for fair trial of SAR Gilani was constituted and Rajni Kothari was the President of this committee. He gave him a tape and told him to hear the cassette and transcribe into Kashmiri, then into English and then into Hindusthani. He transcribed it after hearing the conversation and his transcription was Ex.DW.1/A (text above produced).

203. DW.2 is Sanjay Kak, who is member of this All India Committee. As per the documents filed in the court, the Committee has been writing articles and giving interviews in the newspapers proclaiming innocence of accused. Witnesses who are members of committee or related with the committee, who had already decided about the innocence of accused persons, cannot but be interested persons. Both these witnesses tried to give general meaning to the conversation. They also deliberately did not write the answer given by accused to the query. A careful hearing of the tape reveals that accused has answered his brother 'Ei Chhu Jaruri' 'Aasaan Manj Manj', meaning – This is necessary in between. The subsequent advice given by his brother also means he should keep quiet and not he should relax or take it easy. The question-answer and the advice given by half brother to Gilani prove that the question was not about quarrel between husband and wife but was about attack in Parliament.

204. Defence has criticized prosecution for calling PW71 who was only 5th/6th Standard pass for translating Kashmiri conversation to Hindi. Language is not monopoly of educated and elite class. A child starts learning mother tongue while sucking milk of her mother. A person educated upto 5th or 6th Standard may be knowing his mother tongue much better than a graduate or a post-graduate, who after acquiring knowledge of English starts forgetting his mother tongue and can speak only in Hinglish, Chinglish or Kashinglish. Tulsidas, Kabir and several other contemporary personalities had no or little formal education but had command over language and produced great works. Being a fruit seller is no sin. Today we do not understand the dignity of labour and look upon persons earning livelihood by labour as low class. If India is 10th among the most corrupt countries, it is not because of these poor people but because some other class of people. The witness could not understand English words in the conversation because of lack of knowledge of English language but he understood Kashmiri and Hindi well and translated the conversation to Hindi properly.

212. (*Excerpts*) ... <u>EVIDENCE AGAINST ACCUSED SAR GILANI</u>

1. Acquaintance of accused Gilani with accused Afzal and Shaukat is an admitted fact. Frequent calls made by accused Shaukat and Afzal to accused SAR Gilani before 13th December, 2001 on his cell phone No. 9810081228 from their cell phones.
2. Testimony of PW39 that accused Afzal and Shaukat used to visit house of SAR Gilani.
3. Making call by SAR Gilani to Shaukat post mid night of 12th and 13th December, 2001 around 0.40 a.m. when the preparations for attack on Parliament was at final stage, as shown in Ex.PW36/2 and PW35/8.
4. Recovery of mobile phone No. 9810081228 from accused.
5. Disclosure of accused that phone No. 9811573506 belongs to Shaukat and No. 981189429 belongs to accused Afzal and subsequent confirmation of these facts.
6. Disclosure made by accused Gilani leading police to house of Shaukat wherefrom co-accused Afsan Guru was arrested.
7. Call made by accused Shaukat at 12.13 p.m. on 13th December, 2001 when the attack on Parliament was still going on and the security forces had almost killed the terrorists.
8. Call by Gilani made to Shaukat at 12.23 p.m. when the attack on Parliament was just over.
9. Admitted conversations between Gilani and his half brother which gave indication about involvement of Gilani.
10. Confessional statement made by co-accused Afzal and co-accused Shaukat under section 32 of POTA involving accused Gilani in the planning and conspiracy, which has corroborative value.

220. All the five deceased terrorists were identified as Pakistanis by one of the co-accused. The bodies were kept in mortuary for several days. No person in India claimed their bodies that showed that they were not Indians. No valid documents of their coming to India were found on their person. These five deceased terrorists belonged to Punjab state of Pakistan. They were smuggled into India through J&K border. They must have achieved this with help of some person. Thereafter from J&K they were brought to Delhi along with huge arm and ammunition by one of the accused Mohd. Afzal. The evidence shows that Mohd. Afzal was a surrendered terrorist who was again motivated to work for '*Jehad*' by Ghazi Baba and Tariq. He brought these terrorists to Delhi at their instance. The evidence also shows that for them hideouts were prepared in Delhi, car was purchased to convert it into a car bomb and to transport these terrorists to Parliament House, motorcycle was purchased, chemicals were purchased, recee of Parliament House and other places were done. Entire topography of Parliament House was noted and recorded. All the five deceased terrorists were Pakistanis and were not familiar with New Delhi. They could not have accomplished the necessary paraphernalia in Delhi like hideouts, procuring chemicals and other materials for preparing IEDs, doing recee, purchasing police uniforms etc. without the help of the others. All acts starting from planning and ending with attack in Delhi on Parliament involved several more accused persons i.e. those who brought terrorists from Sri Nagar to Delhi, then arranged their stay at Delhi, prepared IEDs did recee etc. A chain of events that took place show that there was a deep planning and conspiracy done by the accused persons including deceased terrorists and Proclaimed Offenders for attacking the Parliament House. There is no doubt in my mind that this act of attack on the Parliament was not the act only of five deceased terrorists who died at the Parliament House.

224. It is argued that accused Afzal has been made as escape goat, he did bring Mohammad to Delhi but without knowing that he was a terrorist. He was told that Mohammad only wanted to stay in Delhi for few days and then go away. It is further argued that the confession was extracted from Mohd.Afzal by torture and no recovery of Laptop and Rs. 10 lacs was made. All these are planted. He was not arrested from truck with Shaukat but he was arrested from a bus stop in Srinagar and PW6 knew him from before. There is no reason to believe this version of accused Afzal when prosecution has proved each and every circumstance enumerated above. Although the confession made by accused Afzal was retracted later on after about 4 months but this retraction is of no value. The involvement of accused Afzal in the conspiracy is writ large on the wall. I, therefore, hold accused Afzal guilty of section 120B IPC for hatching up a conspiracy alongwith other accused persons for attacking the Parliament and making MPs and political executive of the country a hostage, a criminal act punishable under various provisions of IPC and other penal provisions of different acts.

227. The first circumstance, which has been proved against the accused SAR Gilani is his close links with accused Afzal and Shaukat. It is argued by counsel for accused that accused was merely acquainted with Shaukat and Afzal and he was not having close links. As already discussed, Shaukat immediately after acquiring cell phone or changing made telephone call to Gilani on both occasions. If Shaukat had been merely acquainted with Gilani, the conduct of Shaukat would not have been this. The testimony of landlord of Gilani that Shaukat and Afzal used to visit him also shows that they were not merely acquainted but were close friends. It is argued that landlord of Gilani had seen Shaukat and Afzal only twice or thrice visiting Gilani and that does not show closeness. The landlord has stated that he saw Afzal and Shaukat twice

or thrice going into the house of accused and coming down, but he was the landlord and not a chokidar of the house, who would have all the time stood out to note as to who was going up and coming down. It is a matter of chance that two or three times he saw Afzal and Shaukat going to the house of Gilani. There might have been other various times, when he did not see them. The fact that it was Gilani, who led police to the house of Shaukat has also been proved. Gilani would not have known the house of Shaukat, unless he had been visiting his house.

229. The most crucial link in this chain is making call by SAR Gilani to Shaukat on the night intervening 12th and 13th Dec. 01 around 0.40 a.m. This is the time, when terrorists were making final preparation for attacking the Parliament.

230. It has come in the confessional statement of accused Afzal and Shaukat that meetings had taken place between the terrorists, them and Gilani. This confession statement is not a piece of evidence against Gilani but u/s 30 of Evidence Act, the court can look into this confessional statement to lend assurance to other circumstantial evidence. Gilani attended the meeting or not cannot be inferred by the court from the confessional statement of accused Shaukat and Afzal but Gilani was very much alive to the preparations going on for attack on Parliament by terrorists and so he made this call on the night intervening 12th and 13th Dec. 01. This call might have been made either before the meeting had concluded or during continuation of meeting if he had not participated in the meetings to know the final result of the meeting as to whether the next date is the target date or not or after the meeting for seeking clarification. This call has not been explained by accused Gilani. Infact, SAR Gilani during his statement u/s 313 Cr.P.C. has taken the stand that he was not aware as to who were the holders of phone nos. 9811573506 and 9811489429. Infact, this stand of SAR Gilani, which is obviously a false stand, itself can be considered a circumstance in the chain. The call record of Gilani's phone shows that Gilani has been receiving phones from these two phone nos. and had been making calls to these phone nos. His disclosure statement to police, which has been proved, also shows that it is he who disclosed to police about holders of these phone numbers. His stand that he was not aware of the holders of these phone nos. is a false stand.

236. There is one more important fact. Wife of accused Gilani has also appeared as DW.5. She in her deposition stated that accused had cancelled his programme of going to J&K on the occasion of Id on the ground that there was only one holiday before the holiday of Id. Eid was falling on 17.12.01. Sunday was on 16.12.01 and 15.12.01 was Saturday which is a non-working day for Delhi University. It seems that the programme of going to Eid was cancelled by accused Gilani not because of paucity of holidays but because he was hopeful that the five terrorists would succeed in capturing Parliament and he had envisaged a role for himself thereafter.

237. (*Excerpts*) The next link in the chain, which has been proved by prosecution, is conversation between Gilani and his half brother. The entire conversation shows that there was no mention of any quarrel between the husband and wife, there was no querry made to accused about any quarrel. There was no mention of mother of Gilani, who told his half brother to make inquiries about the non-coming of accused on Eid. There is no querry, whether or not, accused was coming on Eid. The relevant querry, on which the prosecution is relying, is as to 'what has been done in Delhi' and accused Gilani in answer to the query, stated that 'this was necessary, with intervals.' It is unfortunate that two defence witnesses, who appeared in the court on behalf of accused, have translated and transcribed the tapped conversation, deliberately not mentioning the answer given by accused to the querry. A

careful listening of the tape would show that accused answered the querry saying in Kashmiri language "Eei chhey zaroori, Assan maj manj." This conversation confirmed the involvement of accused in the conspiracy and he considered that such kind of attacks were necessary from time to time. Wife of accused Gilani in order to show that her husband was with her throughout night of 12th/13th December stated that on the night between 12th and 13th Dec., she and her husband were reading Namaz alongwith brother of accused Bismillah and her brother Khan Sahib at their Mukherji Nagar house. This was a special Namaz called Sheb-e-Qadar. It is to be prayed through out night. She and all others were tired on the morning of 13th Dec. 01 as they had offered Namaz through out night and all slept thereafter and she got up around noon and after getting up, they all performed noon Namaz and it was at that time (4 p.m.) that her husband wanted to start for college. She stated that Namaz started at 9.30 pm on 12.12.01 and it closed on 13.12.01 at 7 a.m. and thereafter, all of them slept. Nobody went out of the room during Namaz nor anybody talked to each other, neither her husband made any phone call to anybody, cell phone was put off and kept aside. Her entire version is belied by the telephone record of the cell phone of Gilani, which shows that call was made post midnight between 12/13.12.01. Her testimony about her husband sleeping in the house on the morning of 13.12.01 is also belied by the calls made by her husband from his cell phone. She stated that her husband and she slept upto 1 p.m. on 13.12.01 but the call record shows that her husband was very much awake in the morning and he made/received calls at 9.53 a.m., then at 12.10 p.m., 12.15 p.m., 12.20 p.m. and 12.35 p.m. Her entire testimony about picking up of her husband and of herself and children, taking them to Special Cell or to a farm house and then to BSF camp, Bhalswa, is nothing but a concoction. She is not a trustworthy witness at all and her testimony cannot be relied. It is a self serving testimony....

238. It is also to be noted that all deceased terrorists were hardly educated, their knowledge of English was shown in the earlier paras. The note, which was found in possession of one of the deceased terrorist giving topography of Parliament, has been very neatly prepared, which shows that deceased terrorists were getting active help from the other accused persons. The most educated among them was SAR Gilani. It is argued that Gilani was a lecturer. He was well behaved to his landlord. He could not have agreed for such an act.

239. There is no presumption that a lecturer cannot enter into such activity. It is a matter of common knowledge that terrorists are able to hire and convince even best brains also for Jehad. I consider that prosecution has successfully proved that accused Gilani was part of conspiracy for attack on Parliament.

243. The meetings of minds in this case between accused SAR Gilani and other co-accused persons and deceased terrorists has been proved by prosecution beyond reasonable doubt. If there had been no agreement between accused SAR Gilani and other accused persons, on the very night of 12th and 13th December, 01, when the final meeting took place between all conspirators, phone call would not have been given by him. This phone call must have been given either to confirm something which remained unsettled or for the next programme about which some doubt remained in the mind of caller nor the call would have been given just after the terrorist attack so launched at the Parliament House. I have no doubt in my mind about the participation of accused in the conspiracy.

247. In view of the above judgment, confession made by accused u/s 32 POTA would have been sufficient to convict the accused even without corroboration but in this case, there is overwhelming corroboration of the confessional statement by the accused. The circumstances proved against the accused corroborate all the acts stated by the accused in his confessional statement. Accused accompanied Afzal to Christain Colony for arranging hide outs for terrorists. He provided his motor cycle No.... to the terrorists for use. His motor cycle was recovered from one of the hideouts of the terrorists. He as identified by landlord of the hideout at A-97, Gandhi Vihar, Delhi who stated that Shaukat visited Afzal at this hide out. PW.34 has also confirmed that Shaukat, Afzal and four more persons had left the hideout on 13th morning. It has been proved that accused used to visit one of the terrorist in room No.5, Yamuna Hostel, Christian Colony. It has also been corroborated that accused Shaukat had accompanied Afzal and others for purchase of motor cycle No. HR 59E 5766. It has also been proved that deceased terrorist visited house of Shaukat 2-3 days repeatedly prior to 13.12.01. It has been proved that he received phone calls from satellite phone of Ghazi Baba and he was in contact with Afzal constantly on mobile phone. I consider that statement of accused under 32 of POTA coupled with the evidence produced, proved it beyond reasonable doubt that Shaukat was a party to hatching up of conspiracy for attacking Parliament House alongwith deceased terrorists and other accused persons.

252. Section 57(11) of Indian Evidence Act provides that court shall take judicial notice of the commencement, continuance and termination of hostilities between the Govt. of India and any other state or body of persons. This court can therefore take judicial notice of proxy war and hostilities of Pakistan and the hostilities of terrorist groups being sponsored by it towards India.

257. Pakistan is providing financial and strategic assistance to these fundamentalist organizations. The arm and ammunition recovered from the terrorists in this case had Pakistani origin. The blood vessels of this monster of terrorism originate from Pakistan.

Pakistan helps these terrorists to cross border and enter into India. They are trained in camps held in Pakistan and the Pakistani army provides them money and arms for doing terrorist activities in India. All such terrorist attacks which are made in India and in which innocent persons are killed, or attempted to be killed are the acts of waging war against Indian Govt. and the people. To hold guilty a person for waging war, prosecution has to show

(i) That the accused arrayed himself in open defiance of sovereign in like manner as a foreign enemy,
(ii) There must be force accompanying the insurrection,
(iii) It must be for an object of general nature,
(iv) It must also be shown that the accused launched a planned operation and their intention was to overwhelm the state forces and to crush any opposition which they might meet until their movement succeeded.

262. The fourth accused Afsan Guru alias Navjot is wife of accused Shaukat Hussain Guru. The evidence produced in the court shows that all the meetings for hatching of conspiracy were within her knowledge. Some of the meetings had taken place in her presence at 1021 Mukherjee Nagar where she was living with her husband Shaukat. Terrorists used to visit this house two-three days prior to the attack. The conversation between her and her husband on the evening of 14th December 01 intercepted by the investigating agency, also shows that she was aware of entire conspiracy hatched up for waging war against India by attacking the Parliament. It was her constitutional obligation to uphold the sovereignty of India. She was duty bound to inform the state about the impending attack on Parliament. Section 123 IPC makes concealment of existence of design to wage war against India as an offence. She is not protected from this offence merely because of

her being wife of Shaukat. Her matrimonial duties towards her husband could not have stood in the way of her constitutional obligation and her duty towards the state. Section 39 of Cr.P.C. provides that every person aware of the commission of, or of the intention of any other person to commit any offence punishable under specified Sections of Indian Penal Code, including Section 121 to 126 IPC, shall in absence of any reasonable cause, forthwith give information to nearest magistrate or police officer of such commission or intention. The burden of proving the reasonable excuse is on the person who is aware of the commission of offence or intention of committing offence but fails to inform.

267. It is the case of counsel for accused persons that the attack on Parliament was a terrorist attack. They have attacked the FIR on the ground why provisions of POTA were not mentioned in FIR in the very beginning when it was obvious to every body that it was a terrorist Act and the Government had also taken the stand that it was a terrorist attack. But what is obvious is not necessarily the law and what is law is not necessarily obvious. Law in this country remains in a state of constant flux. Though POTA is a central legislation, passed by the Parliament, after consultation with Law Commission of India, but many of the state Governments have publicly announced that they would not invoke POTA. When debate was going in Parliament, Maharashtra Govt. made application for withdrawal of POTA charges from an accused so that its party can oppose POTA law in Parliament. Tomorrow if state assemblies in J&K, Maharashtra, MP etc. are made target by terrorists, policemen will dare not register a case under POTA, although it may be obvious to the entire world that it is terrorist attack. The response of the people in this country varies in accordance with their self-interest. There seems to be no national consensus in respect to response to terrorism and terrorists and the people of their clan. Some states believe in bartering with people like Veerapan, instead of discharging their duty of protecting lives of the people from criminals and terrorists which is the prime duty of a state. Some believe in dealing with them and some in taking benefits from the troubled waters. Can under such circumstances an ordinary Inspector of police be blamed that he did not include the provisions of ordinance POTO when he sent case for registration of FIR? Is it not the executive fiat whether a case will be registered under POTA or not?

281. The evidence brought on record shows that five deceased terrorists were members of terrorist organization Jesh-e-Mohammad. Accused Afzal, Shaukat and Gilani were roped in by this organization for a specific act of attack on the Parliament. No evidence has come on record that any of these three accused persons belonged to or professed to belong to terrorist organizations Jesh-e-Mohammad or Lasker-e-toiba. I, therefore, consider that section 20 of POTA is not made out against them.

Annexure 12

Trial of Errors : A critique of the POTA Court Judgement on the 13 December Case

Peoples Union for Democratic Rights, Delhi, February 2003

> In a world that prefers security to justice, there is loud applause whenever justice is sacrificed on the altar of security. The rite takes place on the streets. Every time a criminal falls in a hail of bullets, society feels some relief from the disease that makes it tremble. The death of each lowlife has a pharmaceutical effect on those living the high life. The word "pharmacy" comes from *pharmakos*, the Greek name for humans sacrificed to the gods in times of crises.
>
> — Eduardo Galeano
>
> *The Teaching of Fear* (*The World Upside Down*)

For years now, ever since India became a republic, India's circular parliament building has been a symbol of its independence and sovereignty. Regardless of what takes place inside, and however anti-people certain legislations may be, its very existence is a source of legitimate pride for Indians. No wonder then, when the parliament was attacked on 13 December 2001, it was widely portrayed, especially by politicians and the press, as an attack on Indian democracy. The focus in this report, however, is on the aftermath of this episode — the entire sequence of political and legal proceedings that followed the attack, including the arrests of four persons and their trial in a Special Court. The ramifications of this trial, we believe, are as dangerous for democracy in India as the attack itself. Parliament, after all, is too deep seated an institution to be overthrown by a few gunmen. But the rule of law is infinitely more fragile. It is our experience that laws like the now defunct MISA and TADA, the Armed Forces Special Powers Act or the new Prevention of Terrorism Act (POTA) set in motion a process whereby it is easy to subvert the procedural norms and civil liberties that are an essential part of democracy. When the rule of law is short-circuited, or dispensed with for the sake of political expediency, then citizens have serious cause to worry.

PUDR followed the trial closely for two reasons: (a) The manner in which the arrests were made by the Delhi Police Special Cell, and the accused triumphantly displayed in handcuffs before the media as *the persons* who had conspired to kill the nation's leadership, gave rise to the apprehension that the four accused had been incriminated even before they had been tried in a court of law. Given this context we wished to ensure that even within the limits of POTA, it would be a fair trial, i.e., the accused would be heard, they would be adequately represented in court in an atmosphere free from intimidation and prejudice, and the judgement would be based on clear and unambiguous evidence. (b) The trial was the first to be held under POTA. One of the major problems with laws like TADA and POTA is their power to label people. If a person has been detained under POTA, then chances are that people will believe that he/she is guilty of being a 'dangerous terrorist'. Worse, both in their conception and implementation, TADA and POTA rest on the erroneous perception that people who belong to minority communities are more likely to be 'terrorists' and 'anti-nationals' than others. In the present political and ideological atmosphere, where the very act of applying POTA prejudges the action, the rights of the accused are treated as an especially dispensable commodity.

Before we share our findings and analyses with the readers we would like to thank the trial judge for not conducting the trial in camera and keeping it open to the public. The court officials were cooperative and the defense and prosecution ever willing to clarify the points that we were confused over, or whose importance we did not understand. We alone are responsible for any error or fault in our analysis.

CONTENTS

I. Introduction
II. Trial under POTA
III. Prosecution case against the accused
IV. The defence
V. Trial and judgement
VI. The Unsustainable case against the accused
VII. Conviction
VIII. Conclusion

I. INTRODUCTION

On December 13, 2001, sometime between 11.40-11.45 a.m., five men in a white ambassador fitted with a red light and home ministry sticker drove into Parliament. When challenged they opened fire, killing nine security personnel, including the Parliament watch and ward staff, and injuring sixteen. In the shootout all five attackers were killed. The incident was widely condemned, both within the country and outside. The first suspicion fell on the Laskhar-e-Taiyabba and then on Jaishe-Mohammad and in both cases the Pakistani government was said to be at fault. Prime Minister Atal Bihari Vajpayee said in Parliament that war was not ruled out as a response. Nearly 700,000 Indian troops were put on high alert at the border and all army officials on leave were recalled in anticipation of a possible war. It was only towards the end of 2002 that the troops were finally called back. Pakistan too massed 300,000 of its troops along the border. While Iran offered to mediate between India and Pakistan, the US, Russia and United

Nations Secretary General Kofi Annan urged India to show restraint. Both the UN's request to be involved in the probe and Pakistan's offer to hold a joint probe into the attack were rejected. The situation was tense and belligerent on both sides, with ministers in the NDA government asserting that they were ready to take: "Two eyes for an eye, a jaw for a tooth". On December 21, India recalled its High Commissioner to Pakistan, banned Pakistani overflights over Indian territory and stopped rail and bus communications between the two countries. The NDA government had already issued the Prevention of Terrorism Ordinance before the attack. On 31st December 2001, a second ordinance was promulgated to extend the first. The NDA Government then used the attack on Parliament to justify the need for POTA (Prevention of Terrorism Act), despite the evidence that laws like TADA or POTA have little *preventive* value. Eventually, despite opposition protest, POTA was pushed through in a joint session of Parliament on 26 March 2002.

The investigations into the attack were handed over to the Special Cell of the Delhi Police the day the attack took place. As is well known, the Delhi Police operates directly under the Union Home Ministry. Within days of the attack the Delhi police implicated four persons on the charge of conspiracy: Mohammad Afzal, a former JKLF militant who had surrendered in 1994, his cousin Shaukat Husain Guru, Shaukat's wife Afsan Guru (Navjot Sandhu before marriage) and S.A.R. Gilani, a lecturer of Arabic at Delhi University. In addition to the four accused, three others were charged in the case, including Jaish-e-Mohammed chief Maulana Masood Azhar, who had been released by the NDA government in 1999 in response to the hijacking of IC 814; Azhar's aides, Ghazi Baba and Tariq Ahmed. These men could not be caught and were declared proclaimed offenders. They were not part of the trial.

Curiously, in this case, the provisions of POTO were added to the original charges only on 19 December 2001. The FIR lodged by the police on 13 December records an armed attack by terrorists but only mentions sections of the IPC. The accused were tried under Sections 121 (waging war), 121 A (conspiracy), 122 (collecting arms etc. to wage war), 123 (concealing with intent to facilitate design to wage war), 302 (murder), 307 (attempt to murder) read with 120-B (death sentence for waging war). The charges under POTO added later pertained to Sections 3 (punishment for terrorist acts), 4 (possession of certain unauthorized arms), 5 (enhanced penalties for contravening provisions or rules made under the Explosives Act, 1884, Explosive Substances Act, 1908, Inflammable Substances Act 1952, or the Arms Act 1959), 6 (confiscation of proceeds of terrorism), 20 (offences dealing with membership of a terrorist organisation). On 22 December 2001, the case was brought before a Special Court under Justice S.N. Dhingra. The trial started on 8 July and was conducted on a daily basis and the arguments concluded on 18 November 2002. The accused were convicted on 16 December 2002, and two days later, on 18 December, three of them were sentenced to death and the fourth given five years rigorous imprisonment.

II. TRIAL UNDER POTA

It must be stated at the outset that laws like POTA work on the principle that crimes of terror cannot be proved in the normal course and they require therefore, extra-ordinary measures including admission of evidence which cannot otherwise be admitted under ordinary law. Thus *confessions* made to a police officer and *telephone interceptions* are considered valid and reliable evidence under the Act. Under the Evidence Act ordinarily applicable, it is a central tenet that confessions to the police are not admissible as evidence because they can be easily extracted by torture. Similarly under the ordinary legal procedure, telephone interception may not be produced as primary evidence against an accused.

Moreover, several clauses under POTA *do* away with the personal safeguards that are available to an accused under normal law. Once a person is charged under any section of POTA, he/she is denied bail for a minimum of six months. Moreover, bail cannot be given if the prosecution opposes it and unless the Court is satisfied that there are grounds for believing that the accused is not guilty of committing such offence. This combined with the fact that confessions before a police officer are admissible as evidence, even if they are later retracted or denied, generates immense possibility of torture and abuse.

It is important to note, however, that POTA also provides for certain safeguards in the forms of procedures that must be adopted for intercepting communications. Thus for an interception to be accepted as valid evidence by the Court, the investigating agencies should have followed the norms laid out in POTA itself in terms of requisite authorization by a competent authority, and the protection of the information collected in this manner (Chapter V of POTA). Our experience of the trial showed that while the accused suffered all the disabilities of POTA, the mitigating safeguards were violated and the Court failed to take this violation into account in its judgement.

The tilt in favour of the prosecution especially disadvantages the accused by lowering the threshold for proving guilt. Besides, certain provisions in POTA place the burden for proving innocence onto the accused, further lowering this threshold. This encourages shoddy investigation, which was more than evident as the trial unfolded over the eight months. The loser in the entire episode is the public which has the right to know the truth, and justice and the rule of law, the cornerstones of democracy.

III. PROSECUTION CASE AGAINST THE ACCUSED

None of the four accused, Mohammad Afzal, Shaukat Husain Guru, Afsan Guru and S.A.R. Gilani, were present at the site of attack. The prosecution case is that the telephone numbers recovered from the dead militants provided the link to these four. The prosecution says that it recovered three mobile telephone instruments and six SIM cards from the spot, as well as fake I-cards of a computer institute, all mentioning 981148429 as a contact number. The mobile phone found on the body of dead militant Mohammad is also shown to have called 9811489429. This number allegedly belonged to Afzal. This phone in turn is shown by call records to have been in touch last on December 9, with 9810081228 (belonging to accused Gilani) and to have received two calls on December 13 from 9811573506 (belonging to accused Shaukat, which, however, he denies possessing). This alleged mobile telephone contact between the dead men and the accused is the lynchpin of the prosecution's conspiracy theory.

The prosecution claims that as Gilani's phone number was 'a regular telephone number' registered in his name with his address, he was the first person to have come into their surveillance net. It was, they claim, after having traced Gilani's address from his mobile phone that they mounted surveillance on his house on the 13th night. In the meantime all mobile telephone numbers including the international numbers were intercepted. On 14 December an incoming call from Srinagar was intercepted on Gilani's phone number and during the conversation that took place in Kashmiri the accused allegedly 'supported the attack on Parliament'. A transcript of the said conversation was prepared in Hindi. On the same day an incoming call from Srinagar was intercepted on another mobile number (allegedly belonging to Shaukat). In the conversation that ensued, the prosecution claim 'a lady (later found to be accused Afsan Guru) was talking to Shaukat Hussain Guru'. The prosecution claims that having heard and recorded conversations on the two phones that showed knowledge of the attack and complicity, they arrested Gilani on the 15th morning around 10 am from near his house. On being confronted with the two mobile phone numbers during his interrogation, Gilani allegedly said that 'he had knowledge of the attack' and that the two numbers were 'being used' by Shaukat and Afzal. Gilani is said to have led them to Afsan Guru's house in Mukherjee Nagar. Afsan Guru was found in her house with mobile phone 9811573506, and was arrested. She in turn told the police that Shaukat and Afzal had gone to Srinagar. The Delhi police informed the J&K police who located Shaukat and Afzal in a truck in the fruit mandi of Parampura 'on the morning of 15-12-01', allegedly together, and carrying a laptop and Rs.10 lakhs, and brought them back to Delhi the same day. The laptop allegedly had files carrying news clippings of the Parliament House and a programme that had been used by the attackers to prepare fake I-D cards. According to the prosecution, Afzal took the police to three hideouts where the attackers had stayed – a hostel in Christian Colony, and two houses in Gandhi Vihar and Indra Vihar respectively. All these places had been taken on rent by Afzal to accommodate the militants. The militants stayed in these premises at different times, and say the prosecution, left for Parliament on the morning of 13 December from Gandhi Vihar. The police also say that Afzal took them to the different shops where he had accompanied the militants to purchase the car used in the attack, a motorcycle, chemicals and a mixer that was used to make explosives. Shaukat and Afzal are also said to have volunteered confessions in which they said that Afzal had motivated Shaukat for *jehad*, who in turn incited Gilani.

Nevertheless, it is important to recall that it is not the prosecution's case that any of the four accused were present along with the five dead militants at the Parliament. These four are supposed to be part of the conspiracy in so far as they knew what was being planned, that they helped the five in acquiring 'hideouts', and purchasing various material used in the attack or preparation of the attack.

IV. THE DEFENCE

The arguments put forward by the defense can broadly be placed in two groups — (a) showing gross procedural lapses in the investigation and (b) *questioning the veracity* and credibility of the evidence presented by the prosecution to bolster its case of conspiracy against the accused. As far as the procedural lapses are concerned, the defence has raised the question whether a *sanction for the* trial to proceed under POTA and the *Explosive Substances Act* had been obtained in accordance with the procedure laid down under the Acts. The prosecution, the defence argued, had failed to produce witnesses or documentary evidence to show that the procedure had been followed, opening themselves to charges of arbitrariness and violation of the fundamental principle of protection laid down by the Supreme Court (Bisham Kumar vs. State *1999*). This violation, moreover, cast doubt over the Special Court's jurisdiction over the matter. The defence has also raised doubts on the admissibility of telephonic interceptions as evidence under POTA. It is to be noted that while telephonic interceptions can be made under the provisions of the Indian Telegraph Act, they can be presented as evidence proving guilt only under POTA. In order for the interceptions to be presented as valid evidence, POTA lays down certain procedural safeguards in Chapter V (Sections 36-48). The defence has argued that the investigating authorities have failed to bring before the court any documentary evidence showing that the procedure had been followed, i.e., an application for allowing interception had been made and order allowing the same had come from a competent authority (Sec. 38 POTA); and that each accused had been furnished with a copy of the said order as well as the application under which the order authorizing the interception was made, not less than ten days before trial, hearing or proceedings (Sec. 45). Moreover, while charges under POTA were added only on 19 December, the interception, by the prosecution's own account had begun on 13 December itself. It is significant that during the course of the trial the defence had in fact appealed to the High Court which had decided that in the absence of procedural safeguards, telephonic interceptions may not be considered by the Special Court to consider charges made under POTA.

Apart from procedural lapses, the defence has also questioned the prosecution's account of the date, time and place of arrest of each of the four accused. They have also questioned the genuineness of the confession allegedly made by Afzal and Shaukat before DCP Ashok Chand. Moreover, the defence has pointed out, that most of the material evidence presented by the prosecution, including the mobile phones and the laptop computer, have shown clear signs of tampering precisely during the period of their supposed 'safe custody' with the investigating authorities. Thus, by raising issues pertaining to procedural lapses, and questioning the genuineness of evidence against the accused, the defence has attempted to puncture the authenticity of the prosecution's case of conspiracy against the accused. They have asserted that the case against the accused is purely circumstantial, that the sequence of events presented by the prosecution as constituting evidence of conspiracy is inconsistent and contradictory, based on flimsy evidence obtained either without authority, and as the defence tried to show in the court through its witnesses, fabricated or tampered with.

V. TRIAL AND JUDGEMENT

In the judgement running into 296 pages, the judge accepts almost the entire prosecution case against the accused and covers the contradictions in the prosecution case by providing what appears to be a reasonable explanation. In other places he arrives at conclusions without giving an idea of the evidence that led him to it. For instance, given the contradictions in the prosecution account of the time of S.A.R.Gilani's arrest (15th December at 10 am according to police and the afternoon of 14th December according to defence), the judge concludes that he was arrested on the night of the 14th/15th. In the present case there was no direct evidence to link the four accused to the scene of the crime, and most of the evidence was intended to establish the links of the accused with the five deceased militants through circumstantial evidence to prove a conspiracy and their involvement in the conspiracy. Yet, if one were to read only the concluding part of the judgement (pages 247-293 which lay down the case against all the four accused individually), one would come away with the idea that the evidence presented, was in fact enough for most of the charges to be 'proved', 'established' or 'confirmed'. In other words, the judgement claims a degree of certainty in its conclusions, which does not in fact exist.

Our reading of the judgement and the trial that preceded it shows that not only was the evidence inadequate, in most cases it was not beyond doubt. In any criminal trial identification of the accused, their presence at key points of the preparations for crime, arrest and recovery in the presence of independent public witnesses, recording of confession without threat or fear, sanctity of physical evidence presented by the prosecution, etc. are all important to establish the guilt of the persons charged and tried. However, a study of the judgement and the case file (which includes disclosure statements and confessionals by the accused, statements by the witnesses u/s 161 Cr.P.C. which is the first statement by a witness to the police in which he or she is bound to tell the truth and which the police is bound to record truthfully, depositions of the prosecution and defence witnesses, statements of the accused in court u/s 313 Cr.P.C when the accused get the final chance to reply to questions put by the court, prosecution exhibits) brings out several anomalies, discrepancies, inconsistencies and misconstructions in vital areas of evidence which undermine the conclusions arrived at in the judgement.

A. Identification of Accused

In order to establish that those accused were actually associated with those involved in the crime, it is important that they must be identified by witnesses through a process that is not only fair but also ensures accuracy and guards against any prior prejudicing of the witnesses. Section 9 of the Indian Evidence Act provides for a Test Identification Parade (TIP) in order to establish the identity of the accused. The procedure involves the witness identifying an accused from a set of people who are brought before them. Even where the accused are dead, the witnesses should be able to pick out their photos from among a set of photos. In other words, the procedure should be similar to a TIP.

In at least two cases (Laxmipat Choraria v. State, 1967 and Appu v State, 1990), the Supreme Court while explaining how the evidence of identification is to be used, has held that the witnesses' ability to identify must be assured without showing him the suspect or his photograph, or furnishing him the data for identification. Showing a photograph prior to identification makes the identification worthless. This is especially important if the case is relying on the identification of the accused by the witness. Further, the identification parade should be held soon, in order to have the witness identify while memory is still fresh. Thus, the Supreme Court rejected as unreliable an identification parade that was held four months after the incident when Justice Venkatachaliah held that 'error is more frequent when recognition comes some time after seeing' (Hari Nath v State of UP, 1988).

In the present case, the identification of the deceased was done on the basis of photographs without adhering to the norms of a TIP. No TIP was held for any of the four accused even though they were taken into police custody within two days after the attack and the trial only began seven months later. The 15 witnesses who identified the accused were provided prior knowledge of the identity of the accused as those involved in the attack on the Parliament. As the following instances make clear, the absence of a Test Identification Parade raises doubts about the credibility of the witnesses as well as the conclusive identification provided by them.

(a) Photos of the dead militants (with mutilated faces) were shown to 2 witnesses (PW 34, Subhash Chand Malhotra, landlord of the Gandhi Vihar house and PW 45, Tejpal Kharbanda, Shaukat and Afsan's landlord in Mukherjee Nagar). While showing of photographs of the dead is legitimate, the point is that in order to lend authenticity to the identification the witnesses must select the photographs from a pack and the prints must be clear showing the face. There was, however, no attempt at identification here since only photographs of the deceased were shown to the witnesses. Thus only affirmation was demanded of the witnesses. But what is even more unusual is that the witnesses were then asked whether the persons found in the photos were seen in the company of the accused. When Tejpal Kharbanda (PW 45), Shaukat's landlord, was first shown photos of the dead men on the 17th, he 'recognises' them but makes no mention of seeing them at Shaukat's house *two-three days prior* to the Parliament attack. Yet nine months later, his memory seems to have improved to the extent that he recalls them as having accompanied Afzal to Shaukat's house during those critical days before the attack.

(b) In his first statement to the police on the 16th of December under 161 Cr.P.C (the first statement by a witness to the police in which he or she is bound to tell the truth and which the police is bound to record truthfully), Mr. Malhotra (landlord at Gandhi Vihar) claimed simply that on 13th morning he saw five boys (not named) getting into a white ambassador and driving off. Seven months later in court, he claimed 'On 13.12.01, Mohammad Afzal, Shaukat and four more persons had left the premises around 10 am'. The judge uses this second statement as one of the evidences against Shaukat. The addition of Shaukat on the basis of this later claim is significant since earlier in the judgement (p.33/para 28), the judge does not mention Shaukat when he notes that Afzal and the dead militants had left the house in the morning.

(c) The Special Cell took Afzal to the shops where he is alleged to have purchased vehicles, food items, cell phones, chemicals and clothes along with the militants, as well as to the various 'hideouts'. The police claim is that Afzal took them to these shops and premises. However, the depositions of the vendors make it clear that Afzal was brought to them for identification, and introduced as someone connected with the attack on Parliament. In other words, they were not called in to the

Special Cell and asked to identify him on their own, which would have made the identification foolproof.

(d) Motorcycle salesman, Sushil Kumar (PW 29) identified Shaukat on 18.12.01. In his statement under Cr.P.C 161 that day, Sushil Kumar said that on the day Afzal and others came to the shop to purchase the motorcycle, Shaukat was standing at a distance. Eight months later, during his court deposition on 16.7.02, he identified Shaukat unambiguously as one of the three men who came to purchase the motorcycle. During the court deposition he also said 'When I identified the accused Mohammad Afzal and Shaukat Hussein with the police, I did not know how many other persons were with the police. I was not shown other persons for identification.'

(e) Sushil Kumar's identification of Afsan Guru in the Special Cell as one of the four persons who came to his shop to purchase the motorcycle does not hold ground since TIP procedure was not followed. Moreover, later in the court Sushil Kumar expressed inability in identifying Afsan as the woman among the four, stating that the woman was standing at some distance.

(f) In his deposition before the court Mr. Kharbanda, Shaukat's landlord, states that he was called to the Special Cell on 17 December 2001, where he saw Jyoti (Navjot/Afsan), Shaukat and Afzal. He added that there was one more person sitting there but did not name or identify him. At this point in the deposition the prosecution asked for and was allowed the opportunity to ask a leading question about the fourth person's identity, and SAR Gilani present in the court was pointed out to the witness. The witness responds, 'I have seen accused pointed out to me, he is accused SAR Gilani also sitting in the Special Cell [sic]. It is correct that I had told police that he also used to visit house of Shaukat'. It is significant that the witness had not identified Gilani in the Special Cell and this reflects on the reliability of the witness. Kharbanda's statements on whether SAR Gilani visited Shaukat, made during his court deposition were also confused and unreliable, a fact which the judge himself accepts (Judgement, p. 128). However, this does not lead the Judge to doubt the reliability of Kharbanda as a witness per se.

(g) SAR Gilani's landlord PW 39 Naresh Gulati again identifies Afzal and Shaukat in court as persons who 'used to visit the house of SAR Gilani'. It is significant that this witness goes on to say that several other people including lecturers and students visited Gilani and that he 'might have seen Afzal and Shaukat visiting Jalani [sic] 2-3 times during the period he stayed in my house' (i.e. almost eleven months).

The process of identification of the accused therefore shows the norms were not adhered to, raising doubts about their accuracy and credibility. Thus the case of conspiracy based on this identification, whereby the four accused could be shown as involved, in concert with each other, in plotting and implementing a plan of action, cannot be established.

Rather than demanding to know why the TIP was not done, the judge condoned several infirmities in the identification. On p.111 (para 100) he proffers the position that showing photographs for identification is not illegal, without commenting on the fact that the identification was not done in a way that replicated a test identification parade, making the identification a mere affirmation. Moreover, as far as the identification of the four accused is concerned he is quiet about the absence of TIPs. In cases of inconsistencies in the accounts by witnesses the judge simply weeds out the inconsistent statement and accepts the rest of the account, without reflecting on the credibility of the witness. Thus in the case of the discrepancy in the deposition by Mr. Kharbanda, Shaukat's landlord pertaining to Gilani, the judge edges out the 'dispute' as 'immaterial' to the prosecution's case (p.127-128/ para 118). Similarly, Afzal's 'identification' by the shop keepers is accepted by the judge on the ground that it was Afzal who led the police to these shops, which is to say that the police would not been able to locate these shops without Afzal pointing them out. In doing so the judge overlooks the fact that the police had knowledge of the shops since these addresses were printed on the packets recovered from the Gandhi Vihar house. The judge further accepts these witnesses as reliable as the shopkeepers would have no personal grudge against the accused.

B. Public Witnesses

Having independent public witnesses is important during arrest/search and seizure to ensure the authenticity of the investigation and that investigating agencies do not commit any excesses or illegalities. Further, the Supreme Court in a 1997 judgment has mandated that the 'police officer carrying out the arrest of the arrestee shall prepare a memo of arrests at the time of arrest and such memo shall be attested by at least one witness, who may either be a member of the arrestee family or a respectable person of the locality from which the arrest is made. It shall also be countersigned by the arrestee and shall contain the time and date of arrest.' However, as the testimony of Sub Inspector Badrish Dutt (PW 67) shows, the police asked no such public witness to join in the arrest of any of the four accused or during the search of the so called 'hideouts'. The same is amply clear from the instances given below:

(a) In the case of Afzal and Shaukat's arrest in Srinagar, it is indeed curious that the J&K police chose not to arrest them at the Parampura fruit mandi, where they were first located by the police, and where plenty of witnesses would be available. They were arrested later from an area where there were no public witnesses.

(b) In other cases viz. Gilani and Afsan, it is also quite surprising that the police did not find witnesses, even when the locality where the two lived is densely populated and the houses were inhabited by other tenants as well.

(c) Curiously, neither of the two sub-inspectors who live in the same building as Shaukat and Afsan were called during the arrests or search of premises or to identify anyone suspected to be part of the conspiracy. Moreover, Gilani's house was not even searched, which is odd, for someone suspected of participating in this kind of conspiracy.

(d) The seizure of the mobile phone (No. 9811573506) from Afsan's house happened in the absence of witnesses and Afsan denied the police claim that they recovered the phone from her residence.

(e) The absence of witnesses also raises questions about the alleged seizure of chemicals and detonators made from the Gandhi Vihar flat.

The judgment (pgs. 92-96/ paras 84-6), however, condones the absence of public witnesses at the time of arrest and discovery by citing the Supreme Court in Tarun Bose versus State of Assam (2002) and the Law Commission Report on POTA regarding the difficulty of obtaining witnesses in Jammu and Kashmir for TADA cases. The judge also used the fact that Shaukat's landlords, Mr. and Mrs. Kharbanda claimed to have received a phone threat the day before they were to depose in court (19.7.02) to support his contention that conditions of 'terror' obtain in Delhi and that people would be afraid to come forward as public witnesses. However, the situation in Delhi is a far cry from that in Assam or Kashmir and getting corroborative evidence is not difficult. Moreover, if Shaukat's landlord was in fact threatened (a matter serious enough for the judge to use it as a point of evidence against Shaukat) surely here was a fresh lead available even as the trial was on, to show that someone connected with the conspiracy was at large. Since the threat was ostensibly made on the telephone between 6.30 and 6.45 a.m. on 18.7.02, and reported to the police, call records to which the police has so zealously resorted in the entire case, would have helped trace the origin of the call. Yet no such attempt was made by the police. It is indeed amazing that instead of censuring the investigating agencies for lapses, the judge accepts the police version and praises them for their commendable performance in adverse conditions. While denouncing the 'usual practice nowadays to flog the investigating agencies', the judge cites a Supreme Court judgement which cautions against harbouring the 'archaic notion that actions of the police officer should be approached with initial distrust'. What escapes the attention of the judge is that in this case there are just too many absences and lapses, so much so that the entire prosecution case seems to be resting and even thriving on them. The absence of public witnesses has had significant implications for the manner in which the trial has unfolded. It has made the disputes over the times, dates, and places of arrest of all four accused, irreconciliable.

C. Arrests

There is a discrepancy between the accounts given by the prosecution and the accused regarding the date, time and place of each arrest. A careful examination of the prosecution account of the sequence of events shows, that the sequence of arrests provided by them is internally inconsistent and self-contradictory, so much so that it becomes difficult to accept it as a true account. The judge too finds it difficult to accept the prosecution account and makes his own modifications to it.

Time and Place of Arrests: According to the prosecution, the first person to be arrested was SAR Gilani, at 10 am on 15th December, in front of his house. Gilani then allegedly led the police to Afsan Guru's house at 10.45 am. Afsan in turn is reported to have told the police that Shaukat and Afzal had gone to Srinagar on a truck. The Special Cell police informed the J&K police who then located and arrested the two. If this story is to be believed then the J&K police would have received the information only after 10.45 am. But Abdul Haq Butt DSP, Srinagar (PW 61) and Mohammed Akbar, Head Constable J&K Police (PW 62), claim that they received information from the Delhi Police at about 5.45 am on 15.12.01, around 8 am the truck was traced in the fruit mandi and that Afzal and Shaukat were arrested around 11 am.

The defence version of arrests is entirely different. Gilani claims that he was arrested on 14.12.01 around 1.15 pm outside Khalsa College, and made to sit in a car driven by Inspector MC Sharma. ACP Rajbir Singh was sitting in the front seat. Gilani says that he was taken blindfolded to a farmhouse (the sugar sachets had 'Ashoka countryside' printed on them) where he was beaten, tortured and kept in illegal confinement. Gilani's disclosure memo — the first statement given by an accused when arrested — also makes no mention of any mobile phones let alone the identification of their owners. He reiterated the same in his statement under 313 Cr.P.C (the accused's response to questions put by the court). Gilani also denied having led the police to Shaukat's house, he has also rejected the prosecution's claims that when confronted by the evidence of certain calls on his cell phone, he told the police that 9811489429 belonged to Afzal and 9811573506 belonged to

Shaukat. Significantly, the disclosure statement bears out the above since there is no reference to any mobile phone or their alleged owners.

Afsan says that she was picked up from her house on 14.12.01 after 6 pm, not on 15 December, as claimed by the prosecution. She does not mention Gilani's presence at her arrest. Qurratulain Arifa Gilani, Gilani's wife, corroborates Afsan's statement. Arifa says that she and her children were picked up by the police on the 14th night. She claims to have seen Afsan sitting in the van in which the police had come to take her for questioning. She also testifies that the teacups and plates had Border Security Force, Bhalaswa printed on them, and assumed that that is where they were taken. The prosecution claim that they intercepted a call between a then unidentified woman (Afsan) and Shaukat is contradicted by this account. Afsan claims she was in police custody at that time.

The judge, however, dismisses the claims of the accused even though the investigator's version of arrests has clearly been shown to suffer from internal inconsistencies. In his judgement (p. 87-88/ para 78), the judge accepts that the prosecution version of arrests as wrong. However, the judge tries to reconcile the differences by arguing that Gilani as well as Afsan Guru were arrested before 6 am, sometime in the night of 14th/15th (p. 88/ para 78) but provides no evidence that can substantiate the hypothesis. As a result of this reconciliation, the prosecution's story of the sequence of arrests is retained. In other words although the judge accepts that the time of arrests may have been different, he accepts that it was Gilani who was first arrested and through him Afsan and through her Shaukat and Afzal. This sequence is essential for the prosecution to establish the conspiracy theory, viz., that Gilani was in touch with Shaukat, knew his house, visited him sometimes, and knew therefore of the conspiracy to attack the Parliament.

While there is in the judgement a professed preference for the principle that the police account must, at least as an initial principle be taken as true, in the case of arrests the judge himself has had to correct the sequence of events to establish the truth of the account. He does this by rejecting all accounts to the contrary by the defence witnesses and as mentioned earlier, comes up with an alternate account, without questioning the whys and hows of the discrepancies in the prosecution account.

D. Confessions

Confessions are normally considered a crucial piece of evidence and accorded great legal value. So great is this value that even a retracted confession is permitted. The assumption is that a confession is the outcome of remorse on the part of the accused. Consequently, great stress is laid to ensure that the confession is voluntary. Given the well-known fact of use of torture by the police to extract statements, provisions exist in normal law that specifically rule out acceptance of confessions made to the police.

POTA eliminates the checks that ensure voluntariness by making confessions to a senior police officer admissible and yet it retains the importance attached to the confessional statement. The only safeguard in POTA is that the police officer should be of a senior rank and that a magistrate must confirm that the confession is voluntary. The magistrate's intervention however is limited — only evidence of physical torture that can be confirmed by a medical examination, (thus excluding threats, inducements and mental torture) can make the confession invalid. The test therefore is not one of voluntary or forced confession — only whether marks of physical injury are visible on the body of the accused. The facts of the present case show how obtaining a certificate of voluntariness is made into a farce.

In a radical departure from normal practice, accused Mohammad Afzal was produced before the media where he was made to 'repeat' his confession, before he actually confessed. On 18 December, the DCP, Ashok Chand, told the media that Afzal had *confessed.* In his deposition before the court, however, DCP Ashok Chand 'forgot' that he had 'told media especially NDTV that Afzal had already confessed'. On 20 December, a press conference was held at the Special Cell where the accused were presented to the media. The ACP, Rajbir Singh claims that he took the permission of the DCP, Ashok Chand, to hold the press conference. In his court deposition, however, the DCP denied having been informed of such a press conference prior to it being held and even denied having any knowledge of such a conference having been held on 20 December or any other date when the accused Afzal was produced before the media. (During the press conference, Afzal spoke of Gilani's innocence, and was immediately warned by ACP Rajbir Singh not to talk about Gilani. Two media persons testified in court that they were asked by ACP Rajbir Singh to delete all references to this exchange, and the same was complied with.)

The official recording of confessions took place only on 21 December, before the DCP of the Special cell, Ashok Chand, where both Afzal and Shaukat 'incriminated' themselves and also 'implicated' Gilani in the conspiracy. Given that the accused were in police custody before the said confession and also knew that they would be going back into police custody immediately after, by no stretch of imagination can the confessions be considered 'free'. Apart from the fact that the confessions were officially recorded after a press conference, the confessions are remarkable for other reasons as well, and none of these lends it credibility. The DCP

phone records – are mutually contradictory. It also proves that only one of them, or neither can be true. That the telephone calls themselves are far from trustworthy can be seen in the next section. Since confessions under POTA are proof in itself and play a vital role in conviction of the accused, authenticity and voluntariness of the statement must be ensured. If there are doubts that pertain to actual recording of confessions, whether it was made free of threat and fear, when an accused is made to incriminate himself before the media prior to the recording of confession, and some portions are disbelieved by even the judge, then the confessions cease to be credible.

E. Other Evidence

(I) PHONE CALLS

A critical material evidence presented by the prosecution in this case pertains to the call records of the three mobile phones. The prosecution has used these call records to link the four accused to each other. It is the prosecution's case that the first lead they found was the mobile phone number 98-106-93456 found on the body of one of the deceased militants, Mohammed. This phone was allegedly in touch with 98-114-89429 (said to be Afzal's phone number) just before the attack on the Parliament which began around 11.40-45 a.m. of December 13th. On further inquiry they found that 89429 had been in contact with 98-115-73506 (Shaukat's phone number), which in turn had been in touch with 98-100-81228 (Gilani's phone number) within an hour or more before and after the attack. The only proofs of this link are the call records. All that the investigating agency needed to do was to ensure that certified copies of the call records in accordance with Section 65A and B of The Evidence Act were brought as evidence. And it is here that several discrepancies come to the fore and are once again explained away by the Judge.

The Call Records

Under section 65 A & B of the Evidence Act computer printouts can be used as evidence provided they fulfil certain conditions and are certified by someone responsible/in-charge of such operations. This was not done. The call records placed before the trial court are *uncertified* computer printouts. Moreover, the two *witnesses* presented before the court by the prosecution, a Security Manager from Airtel (PW35) and a retired Executive from Essar (PW 36) stated that they were *not technical persons*, knew nothing about the working of the switch i.e. the equipment that handles all the calls, or feeding data into computers. Moreover, the call records placed before the Court, as evidence, cannot be considered valid since they are not even copies of the primary document that could prove the telephonic contact. The purported call records, as the expert witness brought by the defence deposed, were mere outputs of the billing system, and were therefore part of the business support of the telephone network. The business support network is not the same as the actual operation of provision of services. In this case of the telephone network, it is the Operating System Support that handles the actual calls and the output from this system is in a technical ASNI format. The output from the billing system that the prosecution presented *as the call records*, does not represent therefore the actual calls, and is the familiar 'text format' that 'can be edited at any time'. Can such printouts which are susceptible to being doctored and are not certified be considered evidence? In the judgement, they are considered reliable evidence against the accused.

SIM Cards

Two calls in the entire history of 73506 (Shaukat's phone number) received from 89429 (Afzal's phone number) show that at both points, while called and calling numbers are identical, time and location are identical, the IMEI and cell ID are changing. This is in the records of both SIMs and pertains to Essar. Thus the Call Detail Record (CDR) shows that at 11.19.14 am on December 13, two calls were made simultaneously from the same calling number 89429 (Afzal's) to the same called number 73506 (Shaukat's) but were made on handsets with different IMEI numbers. The same phenomenon was repeated at 11.32.40 the same day. The IMEI number is a unique number each cellular handset has and which is transmitted each time the phone is operated. It is therefore impossible for this phenomenon to occur unless the Call Detail Records have been doctored. (see Box, P. 286-7)

In the judgment, however, the authenticity and admissibility of the call records is never doubted. Moreover, the judge does not read the above stated contradiction in the call records as a factor casting them in doubt. Rather he sees the contradiction as a factor strengthening the prosecution case. Without explaining how, the judge concludes: 'This double entry does not affect authenticity of the chart rather reflects that there is no manual intervention in the preparation of these charts. No attempt has been made to remove double entry generated by computer in respect of the calls and that proves the authenticity of these charts' (p.143/ para 133). It is significant that the switch operator (PW 78) brought in after this contradiction was pointed out by the defence, did not say anything about this matter. There does not seem to be any basis, therefore, for the explanation arrived at by the judge. The judge did not also ask the investigators why a clarification from the cell operator was not sought. Considering that the computer was generating double entries in some cases and not in others, especially in the calls purported to have been made between Shaukat and Gilani on the day of the attack on the parliament and that forms the crux of prosecution's case and based on which SAR Gilani was roped into the conspiracy, it was certainly a point which deserved concerted questioning.

In the entire prosecution story, as has been mentioned earlier, the links between Afzal, Shaukat and Gilani are established through mobile telephones. The crucial telephone number in this story is telephone number 9811489429 allegedly belonging to Afzal. It is through this telephone number that all three are linked to the case. This number was allegedly mentioned in the Identity Cards of the dead militants and the dial number list of the telephone number 9810693456 allegedly recovered from the site showed that it was in touch with 9811489429. What is indeed curious is that the SIM of this number was never recovered. Moreover, that the Identity Cards indeed showed this number can never be established beyond doubt. The reason being that whereas all such evidence has to be sealed after recovery in order to assure that they may not be tampered with, the Identity Cards were not sealed but pasted on a paper and remained in the custody of investigators. It is also to be noted that Head Constable Ashwini Kumar (PW 8) posted at the Parliament Street Police Station, who was among the first to reach the dead men and prepared the seizure memo listing the articles recovered from the site and the bodies, stated explicitly in the court that as far as he could remember, 'the telephone number was not written on the seizure'.

The story of this significant telephone number gets even more curious, if one looks at the testimony of Kamal Kishore (PW 49) who claims to have sold a Motorola phone and SIM of 9811489429 to Afzal on 4.12.01. He had no record of any kind relating to the sale receipt to show what he had sold, if anything, to Afzal. The call records for the number, however, show that the phone had been in use since 6 November 2001! Which is to say that the card was sold a month after it came in to use! Since this number is the key link that implicated Afzal and through him the others, the contradiction between the prosecution witness' claimed date of sale and, person it was sold to, and the date of activation raises a question about the credibility of this witness. That the same could happen due to cloning of SIM cards raises questions about Afzal's ownership of the said SIM (see Box). To link Afzal through the SIM card purchase drives a hole into the prosecution case. Confronted with this fatal flaw in the prosecution case the judge claims that witness 'has not stated that he sold SIM card of this number (98 114 89429) to Afzal' (p.121/ para 112). The entire claim of the prosecution is that on December 4, 2001, Kamal Kishore (PW 49) had sold a mobile phone and SIM of 98-114-89429. The shopkeeper purchased the SIM from a distributor and there is purchase bill dated 21 September 2001 which says so. Thus if this SIM was not sold to Afzal on December 4th, the only time the shopkeeper claims to have seen the accused, how does this incriminate Afzal let alone Shaukat?

The other witness, Sandeep Chaudhary (PW 44) claimed to have sold a Sony mobile phone and a cash card (details unknown) to Afzal on 7/8 December 2001. Once again there is no proof of sale. The judge accepts that 'Gaffar Market (Karol Bagh) is a grey market, no bills etc, were used, only rough notes are prepared, which are destroyed every evening' (p.117/ para 109). Moreover none of the other SIM cards or mobile phones allegedly used by the militants were traced. To use this patchy 'evidence' to conclude, as the judge does, that '(t)hese SIM cards and phone instruments were procured for terrorists by accused Afzal and Shaukat' is, to say the least, astonishing. Thus what is critical to the prosecution's theory in the form of call records and mobile tele-

What is Cloning and How it can be done?

Deposition of Defence Witness 10 (A Farhan, a Telecommunication-Electronics Engineer)

I have worked with Internet Engg.Task Force and standardized some protocol in telecommunications. Each sim card carries IMEI code which corresponds to its telephone number, these telephone numbers are assigned by telephone Companies to IMSI codes. They are unique, each code as one unique telephone number.

Q. If a sim card is completely sealed can a call be made from corresponding mobile number?

A. No.

Q. Can a sim be duplicated, re-programmed or cloned?

A. Simcard contains a chip, which is programmed. Mobile companies which distribute the sim, preprogramme the chip with IMSI number. Chip can always be re-programmed with other number using a sim programmer.

Q. If there is a sim card which is in a sealed condition issued by the company to the retailer and it appears fresh and unsold, is there a possibility of a call having been made prior to opening of seal?

A. It is possible to take the whole plastic card, in which the sim is lying affixed in a sealed condition and put it in a programmer, and to replicate it on another sim card, and the call may be made from duplicated sim card. Same is called cloning of sim card.

Q. Can IMEI number be duplicated?

A. IMEI number is programmed into every telephone instrument and it can easily be re-programmed by giving it suitable instructions through a datacable connected through a suitable computer. Over internet, some of the programmes are available, with the help of which one can change IMEI number. Some of them are free. IMEI has programme on a mobile instrument. It is a 14 digit number. The fifteenth digit is called a 'check digit'. The 15th digit is arrived at by applying a mathematical process over the 14th digit. The process of calculating the check digit is well documented in the GMS protocol.

Q. I show you Ex.PW.36/1. At point 19.14 hrs., there are two entries, pertaining to the same point and called number and same duration, call ID is different.

A. *On the face of it, it appears impossible* that at the same time, call would have been made by two IMEI numbers as IMEI number is unique. If the phone has to be switched, one will have to take out the sim card and put it in the other instrument and then make the call.

Q. What are the devices required for cloning/duplicating the sim card without breaking the seal and what is the process involved?

A. The device is called sim programmer, it can be used to read the contents of the same, as well as to re-write the contents.

Q. Can any layman re-write the contents of the sim card and clone it?

A. If a person is capable of understanding principles and concept of IMEI and is able to operate computer, then it is possible. No technical expertise is required for re-writing a sim card.

phones and is said to confirm the link between the accused in the conspiracy, is found to leave far too many questions unanswered to be treated as clinching evidence.

Interceptions

The prosecution claims to have intercepted and recorded the contents of two calls. The first was a call received by Gilani from his half brother at 12.22 p.m. on 14.12.2001. The content of this call forms the backbone of the charge against Gilani. The prosecution claims that during this phone call Gilani justified the attack on Parliament by saying '*yeh zaroori hota hai*' and laughing. The police version is based on a verbal translation done by Rashid, a fifth class pass Kashmiri fruit seller, which was then transcribed into Hindustani by a policeman. Significantly, Rashid insisted that there were no English words in the conversation. However, two defence witnesses – both graduate Kashmiri Pandits – refuted Rashid's translation and pointed out that the conversation was about a prospectus and syllabus for Delhi University and that these English words were clearly audible in the tape. As for the crucial line, both the defence witnesses find that Gilani only laughed and did not say those words. The judge, however, claimed that both the defence witnesses were 'interested persons' and defended Rashid's translation skills on the grounds that some of the greatest Indian poets like Tulsidas and Kabir were uneducated people! Whatever the case, a phone conversation whose translation is disputed is hardly sufficient evidence to hang a man on.

The second call was allegedly made by Shaukat to his wife Afsan on the evening of 14 December, in which she sounded frightened. This frightened tone is used by the prosecution as a substantiation of the charge that 'she was aware of the entire conspiracy'. The judge accepts this prosecution claim (p. 273/ para 262) and concludes that 'She was duty bound to inform the state about the impending attack on Parliament'. As the section on arrests shows, Afsan's whereabouts at this time are contested – the defence claims that she was in police custody at this time.

(II) LAPTOP COMPUTER

The glossing over of material facts extends to the laptop that was allegedly recovered from Shaukat and Afzal in Srinagar and was used by the five terrorists to prepare fake identity cards. As in the case of the Identity Cards, the investigators did not take the appropriate steps to preserve it as valid evidence for presentation before the court. The investigators did not make a copy of the hard disk before commencing their search of the contents in the laptop computer. This is an elementary step that any professional investigation ought to have undertaken in such an important case. Moreover, the Investigating Officer, ACP Rajbir Singh (PW80) claims that the laptop computer was sealed on 16 January 2002. Yet the computer shows that it was accessed on 21 January 2002. The material accessed related to files containing the identity cards and the home ministry sticker. This fact was established by the Union Home Ministry controlled GEQD Hyderabad. While the judge chose to ignore this, characterising the accessed files as being 'immaterial' (page 184/ para 172), the files are indeed important because they contained the Identity Cards from which the investigators claimed to have got the lead in shape of a mobile number. (Recall that Afzal's phone number was written on the back of the identity cards).

F. Restrictions on Cross-examination

A number of these discrepancies that had crept in the case could have been sorted out, had the court taken a judicious position on the right of cross-examination. A number of questions put in cross-examination were disallowed in the course of the trial. This was particularly striking with regards to cross-examination of ACP Rajbir Singh (PW 80) the Investigating Officer who supervised the investigations as well as of the DCP Ashok Chand (PW 60) who recorded the confession. In the case of the former the reason advanced was that matters that are part of record or pertain to judicial record 'may not be asked from the witness'. Since PW 80 supervised the investigations this ought to have been allowed especially because in a cross-examination, the sorting of contradictions and testing the credibility of the witness, etc. are usual. Similarly, questions put to PW 60 beyond confession were disallowed when it is a settled principle that questions regarding any briefing given to this witness by the IO (PW80) ought to have been allowed. Similarly the defence was denied even a daylong adjournment to prepare for cross-examining an expert witness called by the prosecution (PW 78) on the grounds that it amounted to asking 'irrelevant questions', 'harassing' the witness and 'wasting' time of the court (p 61-62/ para 53). An examination of this witness could have thrown significant light on the issue of cloning as well as CDR tampering, the possibilities of which had been raised by the defense.

VI. THE UNSUSTAINABLE CASE AGAINST THE ACCUSED

We have mentioned earlier that POTA by placing the burden of proof much lower, encourages shoddy investigation. While numerous such instances of carelessness have already been noted, there are some that need to be placed before the reader separately. Significantly, most of the questions pertaining to investigations, were routinely dismissed by the judge as inconsequential. A professional and scientific investigation, however, would have gone a long way in removing these glitches before the trial began, and would have lifted the doubts and suspicions that continue to linger, viz.,

(a) Three mobile phones were recovered from the five dead men on 13th December, one on Mohammad at Gate No.1 of the Parliament and two between Raja, Rana & Hamza at gate No. 9 and none with Haider at Gate No. 5. The police also recovered 6 SIM cards, identity cards, and slips of paper with 7 numbers. Now the body of Mohammad at Gate No.1 was searched by SI Yograj & HC Jaiveer. They deny presence of M.C. Sharma, Inspector in the Special Operations Cell, Lodhi Road (PW66). Yet M.C. Sharma claimed that he reached the Parliament House with ACP Rajbir Singh and during the course of the day he switched off the mobile and removed the SIM card and noted its number. He insists that he did not remove SIM No. 9810693456 (which was allegedly in contact with Afzal's number) but does not say which SIM was removed.

(b) There is no explanation as to why the order of Union Home Secretary dated 31 December 2001 and 19 January 2002 granting permission for interception, refers to user of 9811573506 as 'unknown' though by 15 December 2001 the accused were all in police custody?

(c) The question that also calls for explanation is why no investigation was done to trace the retailer and distributor of 9811573506 particularly when this card came into use after 7 December 2001 and was a relatively fresh lead.

(d) Why did the prosecution not call or was reluctant to call the personnel who are responsible for feeding data into computer which generated the call records or dealt with the upkeep or management of cell phone operator's computer? Why were the call records not presented in the Operating Systems format? If call data record is critical to establish the link between the accused why did the investigators not insist on certified copies based on the Operating Systems records when they had both the authority as well as the time to have done so?

(e) Another inexplicable aspect pertaining to the laptop is why Orion Convergence was engaged by the investigating agencies to garner the technical evidence contained in it. It is not clear as to why this company was used rather than computer experts available in the Special Cell or even the CFSL. Significantly questions seeking this clarification were not allowed to be put to the Investigating Officer, ACP Rajbir Singh (PW 80). This becomes all the more important if one looks at the discrepancy between the witness Vimalkant Arora's (an employee of Orion, PW 72) statement in court that he used to discuss the case with the IO ACP Rajbir Singh and the latter's denial of such discussions. Considering that the requisite norms for preserving the laptop as evidence were not taken, the IO's deliberate distancing from the technical expert becomes curious. There should have been no reason for the I.O to hide the fact that he was in touch with the expert. It would not have besmirched the evidence being collected. But the judge refused to address this discrepancy.

(f) Why did the investigators not lift fingerprints from any of the material recovered from the 'hideouts' searched by them? And why did they not try to match them with the fingerprints of Shaukat as well as Afzal to see whether they had handled any of the material?

The combined effect of all the above goes a long way in demolishing the prosecution's case against the accused. There is no evidence that links either SAR Gilani or Afsan Guru with any of the dead militants anywhere between the 'final preparations for attack on Parliament (which) started after 5th December, 2001' and 13th December (p 248). Indeed there is no evidence which unerringly implicates them or whose authenticity is beyond reproach, nor is it alleged that they were present at any of the 'hideouts' or 'shops'? The evidence cited against Shaukat too suffers from being of doubtful veracity and indeed there is no evidence that places him in the company of the militants between 5 and 13 December. The evidence showing his presence at Gandhi Vihar on the night of 12-13 December is suspect just as the alleged meetings held at his house '2-3 days prior to' 13th December. Identification of Afzal by shopkeepers (PW 40-44) and by PW 34 on 12th as well as PW 45 '2-3 days prior to 13.12.01' raise questions that cannot be dismissed as irrelevant.

VII. CONVICTION

At the end of this long litany of inconsistencies and contradictions, almost every reader will find themselves with more ques-

Case Against Shaukat Hussain Guru

Charge	Evidence	Implication drawn	Inconsistency
Conspiracy	Confession	Guilty	There are doubts about the voluntariness of the confession and its authenticity
Conspiracy	Landlord of the Gandhi Vihar 'hideout' claims (eight months after the incident) that Shaukat with Afzal and four more persons left the hideout in the morning of 13 December.	Was party to the conspiracy.	The landlord's testimony is not reliable since on 16 December when his memory is still fresh, he does not say anything about having seen Shaukat on the morning of 13th or around that date in the house.
Conspiracy	Accompanied Afzal to buy a motorcycle.	Was party to the conspiracy.	The identification of Shaukat by salesman Sushil Kumar is not valid as the police took Afzal and Shaukat to the shop and introduced them as persons involved in the attack. Also, Sushil Kumar admits that on the day the purchase took place, the person he identifies as Shaukat was standing at a distance.
Conspiracy	Shaukat's landlord claims that the militants visited his house repeatedly 2 to 3 days prior to 13 December.	Party to the conspiracy.	The identification of the deceased through photographs does not follow norms and is not valid. Moreover, the visits are not mentioned by him on 17 December when he makes his statement to the police. Yet after eight months he seems to have become convinced of the visit.
Conspiracy	He received phone calls from satellite phone from Gazi Baba (p276)	Party to the conspiracy on the directions of Gazi Baba	No evidence

Case Against Afsan Guru

Charge	Evidence	Implication drawn	Inconsistency
Conspiracy	Shaukat's confession	Knew of the conspiracy	The confession itself is doubtful. Under section 32 of POTA confession cannot be used against a co-accused.
Conspiracy	Her presence in the house	Knew of the conspiracy	Where else could she be if not in her home.
Conspiracy	Landlord's statement that the terrorists visited her house	That meetings were held in her house to plan the conspiracy and that she had all the information	The visits by the militants based on the landlord's testimony are doubtful (see table on Shaukat

Case Against S.A.R. Gilani

Charge	Evidence	Implication drawn	Inconsistency
Participated in the conspiracy to attack the Parliament along with Afzal and Shaukat.	Call made by Gilani to Shaukat on the night intervening 12 and 13 December, 2001 around 4 a.m.	This was the time when the final preparations for the attack were being made and shows Gilani's complicity.	This assumes that the call data record is authentic and had not been edited. (b) Shaukat and Afzal in their confessions have said that Gilani was present with them. The judgement resolves the inconsistency by saying that 'confession in not a piece of evidence against Gilani but u/s 30 of the Evidence Act, the court can look into this confessional statement to lend assurance to other circumstantial evidence'
Conspiracy	Knew Shaukat and his address	Gilani led the police team to Shaukat's house on 15 December	The manner of arrest and the dates are disputed. Both Gilani and Afsan claim to have been arrested earlier and Afsan denies that Gilani was with the police team which came to her house
Conspiracy	Intercepted telephone conversation between Gilani and his half brother	Gilani knew of the attack and supported it	The translation of the intercepted call is disputed. In the judgement the prosecution's translation is upheld even when there are obvious discrepancies

Case Against Mohammad Afzal

Charge	Evidence	Implication drawn	Inconsistency
Conspiracy	Confession	Party to the conspiracy	There are doubts about the voluntariness of the confession and its authenticity.
Conspiracy	Identification by various shopkeepers where Afzal allegedly bought chemicals and dry fruits in preparation for the attack.	Planned the conspiracy	Identification by the shopkeepers is not valid since Afzal was taken to all these shops and introduced as one of the persons involved in the attack.
Conspiracy	Gandhi Vihar 'hideout' landlord's deposition that Afzal left the 'hideout' in the company of the terrorists on the morning of 13th Dec.	Party to the conspiracy	In his first statement to the police under 161 CrPC, the landlord says nothing about Afzal's presence in the house either on the 12th or 13th of December.
Conspiracy	Recovery of mobile phone which had been in touch with deceased militants immediately before the attack.	Party to the conspiracy	Call records show phone was in use a month before Afzal's purchase of it on 4.12.01. This questions the claim that Afzal owned the said phone.
Conspiracy	Recovery of laptop (containing file of home ministry sticker) and cash when arrested	Party to the conspiracy	No public witness to attest the seizure. Given file on laptop tampered while in police custody. No evidence to make the connection with Ghazi Baba

tions than answers. Critical areas – identification by witnesses without TIP, absence of independent public witness at the time of arrest or during the search and seizure, discrepancies in time and place of arrest, doubts about authenticity of call records in the absence of certified statements, possibility of tampering of evidence related to mobile phones and the laptop computer, details provided in the confession that are doubted by the judge himself — all place a huge question mark on the quality of investigation undertaken by the Special Cell. Because Section 56 of POTA ousts all laws inconsistent with POTA in a POTA trial, it does not mean that all procedures laid down under the Evidence Act also stand ousted. It is the judiciary's task to hold the prosecution accountable for proper investigation — something the judge has declined to do here in the name of not wishing to 'flog the investigating agencies'.

The investigating agency in this case — the antiterrorist squad of the Delhi Police euphemistically called the Special Cell, is, however, already under suspicion. The Special Cell has been much in the news lately. They were responsible for filing the case against *Kashmir Times* journalist Iftekhar Geelani under the Official Secrets Act and for concocting evidence against him, a case which was so flimsy that the Government was forced to withdraw it. They were in the news in the Ansal Plaza shootout in which two eyewitnesses claimed they saw two unarmed persons shot by cops and where physical evidence in shape of bullet marks and empty cartridges belie the claim of an encounter. It is indeed surprising that in such an important case involving an attack on one of the country's highest institutions, and which nearly brought India and Pakistan to war, the investigations were not handed over to the premier investigating agency, the CBI, but to an agency whose capacities are so much in doubt.

The judgement convicted all the four accused. Of them Afzal and Shaukat were convicted on 12 counts, Gilani on 11 counts and Afsan on one count. (Details are provided in the Box on Charge and Punishment.) The flimsy and objectionable nature of arguments put forward by the judge to establish the conspiracy is revealed through a telling example:

A damning evidence put up against Gilani was the contents of an intercepted phone call between Gilani and his half-brother Shah Faizal. In order to explain the context of this phone call Gilani's wife, Arifa, had stated in court that the phone call was the outcome of a quarrel she had with her husband over the cancellation of their plan to visit Srinagar on the occasion of Id. The judgement records that Arifa's argument does not explain the phone conversation and rules that 'she is not a trustworthy witness at all and her testimony cannot be relied. It is a self serving testimony.' However, while arguing for the conviction of Gilani, the judgement resurrects the same discarded testimony to make a fanciful and baseless argument that Gilani had cancelled going to Srinagar on Id, in the hope that the 'five terrorists would be successful in capturing parliament and he had envisaged a role for himself thereafter.'

A cursory look at the sentences awarded reveal that Afzal and Shaukat have been given punishments that are either the maximum permissible (on 8 counts) or marginally lower (on 4 counts). In the case of Gilani the respective figures are 8 and 3. Given the flimsy and at many places internally inconsistent evidence such damning sentences seem more than a bit out of place. However, the defence plea that irreversible punishments such as the death sentence requires a 'higher degree of certainty', is rejected by the Judge by asserting that this sentence has a 'deterrent' value.

On the question that death penalty is awarded only in the rarest of rare cases, the judge argues in the "Order on Sentence" that death sentence is justified where either VIPs are killed or else a very large number of people are killed (as in the example of 35 people being killed by the MCC at Bara village, cited in the judgement). Towards that end, the sentencing order persistently alleges that the militant's design was to kill the prime minister and the home minister. But the facts that little or no evidence is available to substantiate this claim, and that the "VIPs" were not killed, are seemingly slighted when awarding the death penalty. A stream of adjectives "horrendous, revolting and dastardly" seem to make up for the lack of a criterion. These terms too find little justification. "Dastardly", for example, is used to convey that Indian citizens "inspired by Osama bin Laden and Masood Azhar" betray the country by helping foreign terrorists. Yet there is little by way of evidence to prove the same. It is neither reasonably established that the dead militants were foreigners, and on the question of identification with the terrorist organisation, Jaish-e-Mohammed, alleged to be behind the attack, the judgement acquits all the four being tried of the charge of S20 of POTA relating to membership of a banned organisation.

Arguments lacking a substantial basis is not the only weakness apparent in the sentencing order. There is also visibly a lack of application of mind. Two instances stand out starkly:

First, Afzal, Shaukat and Gilani are convicted under S4(b) of POTA and sentenced to life imprisonment. But even by the prosecution claim, it is neither alleged nor is any evidence brought forth to connect Gilani with unauthorised possession of explosives. In the case of Shaukat, the only connection with explosives/chemicals is made out in the retracted 'confessions'. In other words, they are to suffer life imprisonment for a charge which either does not exist or is flimsy enough to be discarded.

Second, the three accused are sentenced twice for the same offence. Having being held guilty of conspiracy to cause terrorist acts by the judgement, the sentencing order awards a punishment

Charges and Punishment

Charge	Description	Accused	Punishment
121 IPC	Waging or attempting to wage war or abetting waging war against Government of India	Afzal, Shaukat, Gilani	Life imprisonment + Rs. 25,000 or addl. 1 year RI
121-A IPC	Conspiracy for S. 121	Afzal, Shaukat, Gilani	10 years RI + Rs. 10,000 or addl. 6 months RI
122 IPC	Collecting arms etc. with intention on waging war against government of India	Afzal, Shaukat, Gilani	Life imprisonment + Rs. 25,000 each or addl. 1 year RI
123 IPC	Concealing with intent to facilitate design to wage war	Afsan Guru	5 years RI + Rs. 10,000 or addl. 6 months RI
302 read with 120-B, IPC	Conspiracy to murder	Afzal, Shaukat, Gilani	Death sentence + Rs. 5 lakhs
307 read with 120-B, IPC	Conspiracy to attempt murder	Afzal, Shaukat, Gilani	10 year RI + 1.75 lakh or addl. 1 year RI
3(2) POTA read with 120B	Terrorist act	Afzal, Shaukat, Gilani	Death sentence + Rs. 5 lakh
3(3) POTA	Conspiracy, attempt, abet etc. to terrorist act	Afzal, Shaukat, Gilani	Life imprisonment + Rs. 25,000 or addl. 1 year RI
3(4) POTA	Harbouring or concealing terrorist	Afzal, Shaukat	Life Imprisonment + Rs. 25,000 or addl. 1 year RI
3(5) POTA	Membership of terrorist gang	Afzal, Shaukat, Gilani	Life Imprisonment + Rs. 25,000 or addl. 1 year RI
4(B) POTA	Unauthorised possession of explosives etc.	Afzal, Shaukat, Gilani	Life Imprisonment + Rs. 25,000 or addl. 1 year RI
3 Explosive Substances Act	Causing explosion threatening life or property	Afzal, Shaukat, Gilani	Life imprisonment + Rs. 25,000 or addl. 1 year RI
4 Explosive Substances Act	Attempt to cause explosion	Afzal, Shaukat, Gilani	20 years RI + Rs. 25,000 or addl. 1 year RI

under S3(2) of POTA read with S120-B of IPC. They are sentenced to death and fine. However they are again sentenced for conspiracy to commit terrorist act under S3(3) of POTA, this time to life imprisonment! It should be noted that POTA contains the specific provision of S3(3) to deal with conspiracy to commit terrorist acts. In addition S54 of POTA stipulates that the provisions of POTA shall have overriding effect i.e. POTA provisions shall continue in case of any inconsistency with any other law. There should therefore be no confusion that S3(3) of POTA would apply. Since POTA specifies a maximum punishment of life imprisonment for conspiring to commit a terrorist act, and the same has been awarded, S3(2) read with S120-B does not come into the picture. The order of sentencing, however, does not even care to mention S120-B, IPC making it seem that the three accused are sentenced to death for personally committing a terrorist act, an allegation for which there is not even a scrap of evidence.

But then POTA creates a class of criminals called *terrorists* who are denied the usual procedures of democratic law. And the power that creates laws like POTA also creates the image of a terrorist—blood thirsty, unpatriotic and senseless—an object of revulsion. These procedures and images meet in the special court, each interacting and intensifying the other. It is not strange therefore that the gravest of punishments can being awarded in a most cavalier manner.

VIII. CONCLUSION

There can be no two views that the attack on parliament must be condemned and suitably punished. The kind of politics that such attacks manifest, is clearly undemocratic and counterproductive. At the same time, such events cannot and must not serve as an excuse for the state to weaken the civil liberties of its citizens through the operation of laws like POTA, or to 'sacrifice justice on the altar of security.'

Much as we would have liked our apprehensions regarding POTA and trial under this law to have been misplaced our experience of monitoring this trial shows otherwise. That POTA is anti-democratic became more than evident in the course of the trial. It is perhaps inherent in a trial under POTA that the accused is disabled to a point where rules of evidence become pliable and conjecure can take over and death sentences become easy to award. Any trial based on unreliable and self contradictory evidence with the support of an anti-democratic law and public pre-judging of the accused could arrive at the conclusion only by mistake. Verily an unjust law and unfair trial, in the name of fighting terrorism, has in all probability ended up committing a grievous error sentencing three men to death and a woman to five years of RI on dubious evidence and shoddy investigations.

What is therefore sought to be hidden from public gaze is the human agony and suffering, the spectre of a noose hanging over the head, of people who are condemned only because hanging is the need of the hour. The blame for this lies squarely on India's democracy and democratic institutions. And the manner in which they work under the infuence of a political directive and a political law. This report is an attempt to prevent a gross violation of justice. It therefore demands the repeal of POTA.

Published by: Secretary, Peoples Union for Democratic Rights

For Copies: Sharmila Purkayastha, Flat No. 5, Miranda House Teachers Quarters, Chhatra Marg, Delhi University, Delhi - 110007

Suggested Contribution: Rs. 10

Printed at: Nagari Printers, Naveen Shahdara, Delhi - 110032

Annexure 13

Eighteen months ago, the Indian parliament was attacked. Fourteen people were killed. But now, more lives are at stake: three Kashmiris accused of conspiring in the attack have been sentenced to death, one of them - university lecturer Syed Geelani – on the basis of two phone calls. Kashmiris and many others are convinced of his innocence. If his appeal, now under way, fails, uproar in the inflammable border state threatens.

Basharat Peer *reports*

Victims of December 13

The Guardian Weekend, Saturday July 5, 2003

The circular, colonnaded building of the Indian parliament, designed in 1921 by two British architects, Sir Edwin Lutyens and Sir Herbert Baker, is a majestic presence in the heart of New Delhi. On the morning of December 13 2001, legislators in the domed central hall of the parliament were arguing angrily about the involvement of the Indian defence minister in an arms scandal. White Ambassador cars – the preferred vehicle of Indian politicians and bureaucrats – were lining up on the concourse.

Around 11.30 am, policemen at the main parliament gate saw an official-looking white Ambassador, with five men inside, approaching. It appeared to have the necessary entry pass on the windshield; they stepped aside. The car accelerated as it moved past the red sandstone wall of the parliament. The next moment it had collided with one of the cars in the motorcade of the Indian vice-president, who was expected to emerge from the parliament any moment. As policemen ran towards the Ambassador, its doors opened. Five men with guns jumped out and started firing at the police. Before they could retaliate, the armed men scattered into the parliament's large grounds.

The speaker abruptly adjourned proceedings in the debating chamber. Emergency messages crackled across police radios: terrorists had attacked the parliament. More police and paramilitaries were urgently summoned. For half an hour, a fierce battle raged outside the building; inside, around 200 trapped and terrified politicians listened to gunfire and grenade explosions.

By noon, it was all over. The five armed men were killed. Eight policemen and a gardener were also dead. Within a few hours, television crews began to beam images of the bullet-ridden corpses of the terrorists, clean-shaven and dressed in fatigues, to millions of Indian homes.

That same morning, I was sitting with my grandfather, sipping tea in the drawing room of our house in a village in the Kashmir valley. Winter means a heavy snowfall, a slower pace of life and less blood spilled in conflict-ridden Kashmir. My grandfather, a retired teacher, was looking forward to the relative peace of the colder months, along with flu and frostbite. Suddenly, we heard news of the attack — the television channels were full of it. We immediately began to fear that a war might erupt between India and Pakistan. "This winter the snow will turn red," Grandpa sighed.

India and Pakistan have fought three wars over the Muslim-majority valley of Kashmir. The hostile neighbours each control a part of the old princely state and stake an aggressive claim upon the whole. Relative peace had prevailed in Kashmir after the Indo-Pak war in 1971. But in 1987, the government in the Indian-administered Kashmir valley rigged a local election. Kashmiris lost their faith in Indian democracy and began a secessionist armed uprising in 1990. By the mid-1990s, Pakistan-based Jehadi groups had taken control of the anti-India insurgency. In 13 years, more than 50,000 have died.

The Hindu nationalist government of India blamed terrorist groups based in, and supported by, Pakistan for the attack on the Indian parliament; these groups have been operating mostly in Kashmir. Hardliners inside and outside the Hindu nationalist Bharatiya Janata Party (Indian People's party, or BJP) claimed that December 13 was India's 9/11. They demanded that Indian soldiers cross the line of control – the temporary border between India and Pakistan – and attack the terrorist camps in the part of Kashmir held by Pakistan.

Leading the hardliners was the Indian home minister, LK Advani, who engineered the rise to power of the BJP in the 1990s. Born in Sindh, at present in Pakistan, Advani migrated to India in 1947 when the large, British-ruled entity of India was partitioned into the nation states of India and Pakistan. Widespread communal riots and mass migration of Hindus from what became Pakistan and of Muslims from India tainted the dawn of Indian freedom and the birth of Pakistan. It was one of those panic-stricken flights that brought Advani to India, where he rose to be federal home minister and the deputy prime minister in the Hindu nationalist-led government.

Strategic analysts discussing on television the possible use of nuclear weapons aroused widespread fears of a holocaust. It was only some hectic US and British shuttle diplomacy that forced Pakistan to act against terrorist groups "operating in Kashmir" and managed to restrain India from attacking Pakistan.

But the Hindu nationalists in India succeeded in stoking an ugly xenophobia. Soon after the attack on the parliament, I met a doctor from Kashmir who worked in a New Delhi hospital. A practising Muslim, he sported a long, flowing beard. To me, he seemed to embody a curious mixture of peaceful religiosity and scientific knowledge. But passersby on the streets of Delhi stared at him suspiciously. His colleagues at the hospital taunted him. He shaved off his beard.

A month after the attack, I returned to New Delhi, where I was working as a journalist for a news portal. I was looking for a place to stay. I tried the middle-class neighbourhoods of south Delhi, inhabited by business executives, lawyers, professors and doctors. Most of them had come to Delhi, like myself, to begin a professional career. They had to work for decades before owning an apartment or a house. Many landlords I met were willing to rent out a room. But then they would ask the dreaded question.

"Where are you from?"

"Kashmir."

"Oh! You are Kashmiri Muslim."

I kept looking for a house for months.

The Delhi police claimed to have recovered, within hours of the attack on the parliament, a mobile phone, three Sim cards and some telephone numbers from "Mohammed", an allegedly Pakistani terrorist killed by the police. Two days later, they arrested three Kashmiri men and a pregnant housewife, and charged them with "conspiring in the attack on the parliament". The police asserted that the telephone numbers found on Mohammed had led them to the arrested Kashmiris.

Syed Abdul Rahman Geelani, 32, a teacher of Arabic at Delhi University, was the first to be arrested on December 15. The police said they picked him up outside his rented house in north Delhi. The news of his arrest shocked me. I had met Geelani one evening in autumn 1999, at Delhi University, where I was an undergraduate law student. A mutual acquaintance from Kashmir had introduced us. A short, soft-spoken, handsome man, Geelani told me that he had left Kashmir before the insurgency began. He had studied in other parts of India before joining Delhi University in the early 1990s. He seemed happy to see me at the university and lamented the collapse of the educational system in Kashmir. "Delhi will teach you a lot and open your horizons," he said. "Here, the bigger world opens to you. Work hard."

Geelani talked a lot about his teaching job. I thought he spoke with the pride of a small-town boy who had worked his way to the faculty of a prestigious university. We walked to the hostel canteen and had a cup of sweet, milky tea. His easy-going manner contrasted with the nervousness that I had seen in many other young Kashmiris in Delhi. When we talked about Kashmir, he showed none of the raw passion or emotion that most Kashmiris do. He seemed to have accepted Delhi as his world. I saw Geelani occasionally on campus after that, but our acquaintance could not progress: I was busy in my own world, trying to be a journalist.

In Srinagar, the police arrested two other Kashmiri men: Mohammed Afzal, who joined a Kashmiri militant group in the early 1990s, then laid down his arms and apparently started a business, and Shaukat Guru, his businessman cousin. They lived in Delhi, but had left for the valley on the day of the attack. The police also arrested Afshan Guru, Shaukat's wife. All three arrested men were from Baramulla, a border district in north Kashmir; they stayed in the same locality in Delhi and knew each other.

They were booked under a draconian anti-terrorism ordinance, Prevention Of Terrorism Ordinance (Poto), introduced a month after the September 11 attacks by the Hindu nationalist government. In March 2002, three months after the attack on the Indian parliament, the ordinance became law – the Prevention Of Terrorism Act, 2002 (Pota). Indian opposition parties and civil rights groups such as Amnesty International opposed it, but the global war against terrorism took its toll on civil liberties in India as ruthlessly as elsewhere in the world.

The arrested men were interrogated. The police claimed that Afzal, the main accused, had confessed to his involvement. Rajbir Singh, the Assistant Commissioner in the anti-terrorism cell of the Delhi police, invited television crews to record Afzal's public confession, which was then broadcast across India. A tall, sturdy man with rugged features, Singh has risen from the lowly position of sub-inspector to his present prestigious position in just a few years. His record of eliminating terrorists is matched only by the allegations of human rights violations against him. His role in six separate killings of alleged terrorists and gangsters has been questioned by the Indian media, and his involvement in a shoot-out at a shopping mall by the National Human Rights Commission of India: last November, Singh and his men claimed to have killed two terrorists associated with a banned Pakistan-based terrorist outfit, Lashkar-e-Taiba, at a shopping mall in New Delhi, but a local Hindu doctor, Hari Krishna, told the media that he saw the police shoot in cold blood the two unarmed and apparently drugged men, who, Krishna said, could barely walk.

Singh was already under a cloud when the home ministry, under Advani, appointed him to head the investigation into the attack on the Indian parliament. It was under Singh's direction that the Kashmiri teacher, Geelani, was arrested.

Soon after Geelani's arrest in winter 2001, I travelled to his north Kashmir town, Baramulla, to interview his relatives. His mother, a widow, was inarticulate with grief. His father-in-law, Habibullah, a retired schoolteacher, could not believe that his son-in-law, a university lecturer and a father of two, could be involved in an act of terrorism. Despite his grief and shock, Habibullah had a dignified air about him. He told me that hundreds of townsfolk had gathered outside his house to express their support and their faith in Geelani's innocence. They wanted to demonstrate against the arrest. But he stopped them. He feared that demonstrations, as they typically did in Kashmir, would lead to anti-India sloganeering, which would anger the government and damage the chances of his son-in-law's release. Habibullah was worried about Geelani, who was then being interrogated by the police, and about his wife, two children and his younger brother, Bismillah, all of whom lived in a rented house in north Delhi.

Bismillah told me that he had visited his brother a week after his arrest, in a cage-like room at a Delhi police interrogation centre. Geelani was limping, had wounds on his ankles; nylon ropes tied around his wrists had left blue marks. Bismillah had brought him some food, but the police torture had left Geelani without the appetite or energy to eat.

The brothers met again a week later, this time in jail. Bismillah found out that Geelani was in solitary confinement and was denied access to books, paper or the jail library. Criminals in the jail looked upon him as a terrorist, an anti-national, and physically assaulted him a few times. Around that time, university officials suspended Geelani from his teaching job.

Nothing much happened for months. I didn't often think of Geelani; I was working on other stories. In May 2002, the police filed a charge sheet against Geelani. At the same time, his landlord evicted his wife and children, who had to find refuge in a Muslim ghetto in another part of the city. It was not until July that Geelani's trial could begin.

The trial proceeded not under the usual Indian law, but under the controversial Pota. Amnesty International questioned whether a free trial was possible under Pota, especially in the case of the accused teacher. The Indian law ministry appointed Shiv Narayan Dhingra as a special judge. The son of a labourer, Dhingra had worked as a newspaper boy, street vendor, radio mechanic and private tutor in his childhood and early youth in order to support his family and his education. After studying law at Delhi University, he found a teaching job there before joining the judiciary. By the 1990s, he was handling cases of terrorism and had earned the name The Hanging Judge.

I was assigned to report on the trial. Policemen with automatic rifles guarded the courtroom; they checked my identity card and frisked me before allowing me inside. I had expected a crowd of reporters at what seemed to me the most high-profile legal case in India, but was surprised to see very few there. Policemen, both uniformed and plain-clothed, occupied most of the chairs, along with the lawyers in black gowns. Geelani stood in the dock with the other accused.

I thought of our first meeting at Delhi University in 1999. He now stood before me, accused of conspiring in an attack on the Indian parliament that had almost triggered a nuclear war between India and Pakistan. I couldn't stop looking at Geelani, at his handcuffs and at the three armed policemen watching him. Over the next few months, I kept going back to the trial to cover the "important" hearings. Every time, Geelani stood in the dock with the same serene expression on his face. I often wondered why he appeared so unfazed.

Perhaps he was given hope by the Indian intellectuals who believed that he was innocent and had come together under the banner of the All India Defence Committee for Syed Abdul Rahman Geelani. Many teachers and journalists had written letters of protest to the chief justice. There was initially no criminal lawyer ready to defend him in court. Finally, Seema Gulati, a well-known, much sought-after criminal lawyer, agreed. Her high fees were paid by contributions from university teachers, lawyers and civil rights activists. Rajni Kothari, a veteran Indian social scientist, told me the committee to defend Geelani was formed "to defend the right of fair trial of a courageous man and to defend the values enshrined in our constitution by the founding fathers and mothers of the Indian state". The committee, formed last August, includes illustrious names such as two Magsaysay award-winning social workers, Aruna Roy and Sandeep Pandey, human rights activist and jurist Nandita Haksar and writer Arundhati Roy.

As the trial proceeded, the prosecution presented the evidence against Geelani. It said that he received a call on his mobile phone on December 14 2001, from Kashmir, and, while talking in Kashmiri, he supported the previous day's attack on the parliament. The two-and-a-half-minute telephone conversation with his younger brother was the main evidence against him. The police had it translated by a semiliterate Kashmiri youth, Rashid Ali, who worked as a fruit vendor in north Delhi. The "incriminating" evidence in the call, according to the police translation, is this: Caller: "What is this you have done in Delhi?" Receiver (the accused teacher, Geelani): "This was necessary."

The conversation, police said, revealed the role of the teacher in the conspiracy to attack the parliament. Geelani's lawyer, Seema Gulati, challenged this, producing Sampath Prakash, a veteran trade union leader from Srinagar, and Sanjay Kak, a respected filmmaker, as defence witnesses. Proficient in the Kashmiri language, the witnesses presented to the court transcripts of the intercepted call and its English translations. They maintained that the call was an innocent conversation between two brothers. Kak translated as follows the parts of the call that police claimed showed Geelani's culpability: Caller (accused teacher's brother): "What's happened?" Receiver (Geelani): "What? In Delhi?" Caller: "What's happened? In Delhi?" Receiver: (noise, laughter) "By God!"

Giving evidence in court, Kak said, "The Kashmiri equivalent of 'What's happened?' is 'Yeh Kya Korua'. It is a generic term used for a range of ordinary circumstances, such as when a child spills a glass of milk or when there is snowfall or a marital dispute." The younger brother of the accused teacher had called simply to get a syllabus and a prospectus. He translated that portion of the call as: Receiver (accused teacher): "Tell me what you want?" Caller (his brother): "Syllabus and prospectus."

During the cross-examination, Ali, the police translator, admitted that he could not understand English; he was also shaky in Hindi, the Indian language into which he had translated the call. Geelani's brother Bismillah and father-in-law Habibullah normally sat in the courtroom with gloomy faces. That day, I saw them smile.

Testimonies by independent witnesses seemed to tilt the balance in favour of Geelani's innocence. One day a fellow reporter, Shams Tahir Khan, who works for Aaj Tak, a popular Hindi-language Indian news channel, took the stand. He was one of the television reporters invited by Singh, the Delhi police officer, to record the confession of the main accused, Mohammed Afzal, after his arrest. The full version of the video-recorded interview was played in the courtroom. Afzal was seen saying that Geelani was a professor and that he, Afzal, "never shared any of this (terrorism-related) information with him". Khan told the court that assistant commissioner Singh had requested the media not to relay that part of the interview. Geelani, his relatives and lawyer seemed more relieved; their smiles were broader.

Another day revealed a serious contradiction in the prosecution case. Delhi police had claimed that the records of the phone numbers found on Mohammed – the slain terrorist – had led to Geelani's arrest on December 15 2001. The phone records obtained by police from Airtel, the cellular company, were part of the evidence against him. Geelani's lawyer pointed out that the phone records cited by the police were dated December 17 2001. It left many wondering how the police could arrest the accused teacher two days before it got the phone records that "led" them to him. The prosecution had no explanation to offer. Afterwards, I saw Geelani's friends and relatives talking outside the courtroom with a childlike excitement.

By November, the witnesses had testified, the accused had given their statements, and the final arguments in the case began. Delhi high court had ordered that Geelani's handcuffs be taken off. Armed policemen still filled the courtroom. Barring a few reporters, the media continued to ignore the trial.

The prosecution argued for Geelani's conviction for conspiring in the attack on the Indian parliament. The grounds were that he had supported the attack while talking on the phone; he knew the other accused; his phone number was found on their phones; he had received calls from a co-accused on the day of the attack. Geelani did not deny knowing the co-accused and speaking to them on the phone. Judge Dhingra dictated the proceedings to a clerk who produced the court records on an archaic typewriter.

I wondered why none of the 80 prosecution witnesses who gave evidence in court accused Geelani of being a member of a terrorist group or having possessed explosives or weapons. Was he innocent? I could not be sure. Maybe there was just not enough evidence against him. I lived with my doubts.

Geelani's father-in-law, Habibullah, had come from Kashmir to Delhi to follow the case. He sat in the courtroom lost in his thoughts. On December 16, when the judge was to deliver the verdict, Habibullah did not come to the court. Instead, led by Singh, personnel from the Delhi police's anti-terrorism wing, who had arrested Geelani and conducted the investigation, filled the courtroom. The policemen, who were usually unshaven and shabbily clothed, were dressed in expensive suits, with matching neckties. They would look good in the newspaper photographs tomorrow, I thought.

The courtroom was for once crowded with reporters. I stood close to the judge's table, hoping to hear every word of the verdict.

It was very humid. A reporter shouted at an attendant to switch on the air conditioner. It did not work. A reporter standing behind me placed his notebook on my back for support to take notes.

Judge Dhingra walked in. There was a long silence in the courtroom. Nobody moved while he pronounced the verdict. He held the accused teacher, Geelani, guilty of "conspiracy to attack the parliament, wage war against the government of India, murder and grievous hurt". The other two men were also found guilty.

Geelani made no sound. I kept looking at him. He seemed to see me but his eyes said nothing; his face seemed numb. My mind wandered off to another Kashmiri who was executed in Delhi in 1984 — Maqbool Bhat, the founder of the armed struggle in Kashmir. Even today, Bhat's execution fuels an anti-India rage in many Kashmiris. As an adolescent in Kashmir, I had seen posters remembering Bhat's "martyrdom" pasted on the wooden electricity poles that dot roadsides in the valley. Would Geelani end up as a commemorative poster on a wooden electricity pole? The thought scared me.

Two days after the verdict, Judge Dhingra announced his sentence. He opened the judgment with a long commentary on terrorism, how to tackle it, and the necessity of a centralised policy. He called the two defence witnesses, who testified that the accused teacher had not supported the parliament attack while talking on the phone, "interested witnesses". According to Dhingra, the key defence witness, film-maker Sanjay Kak, was a member of the committee formed for the fair trial of the accused teacher. Therefore his evidence was "unreliable". And the other witness, Sampath Prakash, the trade union leader, was equally partial and unreliable because he was introduced by Balraj Puri, a writer on Kashmir and a civil rights activist.

Dhingra sentenced Geelani to death, along with the co-accused Kashmiris, Mohammed Afzal and Shaukat Guru. Geelani was stoic and sought the judge's permission to speak to the journalists. Soon afterwards, policemen whisked the three convicted men towards prison lorries, as television crews jostled for close-ups. Geelani managed to say, "Without justice, there will be no democracy. It is Indian democracy that is under threat." His younger brother, Bismillah, watched him being taken away and burst into tears. The intellectuals who had worked against many odds for his fair trial were surprised and shocked. In Baramulla, hundreds of protesters burst out on to the streets as the news of Geelani's sentencing spread.

Activists of a militant Hindu fundamentalist outfit, Shiv Sena (Lord Shiva's Army), were the first to celebrate the death sentence. They burst crackers outside the court complex and broke into dances. The ruling Hindu nationalist BJP welcomed Dhingra's judgment and its spokesperson, VK Malhotra, claimed that the speed with which the accused in the parliament attack case had been tried and sentenced had established the efficiency of the Prevention Of Terrorism Ordinance. He also recommended punishment under the controversial anti-terror law Pota for those who had opposed the death sentence on the grounds that they were agents of Pakistan's spy agency, the Inter-Services Intelligence.

Malhotra's aggressiveness may stem from the fact that, days before the judgment, the BJP won elections in the western Indian state of Gujarat, despite being implicated in the massacre of around 2,000 Muslims in early 2002. This victory lengthened the shadow of Hindu religious violence and Islamic terror attacks that loomed over India throughout 2002. In Gujarat, the fear of Muslim-sponsored terrorism consolidated effectively the Hindu nationalist votes. Hindu nationalist leaders now talk of turning India into a "Hindu nation" in two years, probably making use of the same mix of militant rhetoric about Muslims and Pakistan that has served them well so far. With its drum-beating about national security and terrorism, the party has also made its critics vulnerable to the accusation that they are "anti-national". When endorsed by the police and the judiciary – both of which appear to have been infiltrated by Hindu nationalists – the accusation has a malevolent power.

In a public meeting before the judgment, Arundhati Roy said that, of late, even she felt insecure when she woke up in the morning. "The people who have framed Geelani are the real terrorists, who steal our freedom," she said. "For the sake of democracy, we have to fight, not just till Geelani is acquitted but till those who framed him are punished."

India's most respected lawyer and former Indian law minister, Ram Jethmalani agreed to defend Geelani in the higher courts without payment — prompting Shiv Sena activists to burn his effigy as a "traitor" and threaten him with "consequences" if he honoured his promise. Jethmalani stood his ground. He filed an appeal against Geelani's conviction in the Delhi high court. Its judges began their hearings on April 2; they are expected to take three or four months to reach their decision. Until then, Geelani will be held in the Delhi prison where he has been for more than a year.

If the high court does not acquit Geelani, his family will appeal to the supreme court of India. The court has in the past acquitted defendants whom lower courts had sentenced to death — notably the accused in the assassination of Rajeev Gandhi, the Indian prime minister, in the mid-1990s. If the Geelanis do have to appeal to the supreme court, it will mean at least another six months' wait for a decision.

An acquittal can take Geelani back to the classrooms of Delhi University; a reduction in the sentence would bring unknown years in the prison where he currently awaits his fate; if Dhingra's order is upheld, Geelani will be hanged.

ANNEXURE 14

A Presumptuous Judgment: A New Concept of Democracy?

A Critique on the Lower Court Judgment on Dec 13 Parliament Attack

Nandita Haksar
Human Rights Lawyer

> We have cause to regret that a legal concept of terrorism was ever inflicted upon us. The term is imprecise, it is ambiguous and above all, it serves no operative purpose.
>
> — Judge R. Baxter, US Supreme Court Judge

> (We) should all be clear that there is no trade-off between effective action against terrorism and the protection of human rights. On the contrary, I believe that in the long term we shall find that human rights, along with democracy and social justice, are one of the best prophylactics against terrorism.
>
> — UN Secretary-General, Kofi Annan, at the Security Council's Session on Counter Terrorism, January 2002

On December 16, 2002 Shri. S.N. Dhingra, Additional Sessions Judge, Designated Court at New Delhi delivered his 296-page judgement in the Parliament attack case. The judgement is one of the first by a designated court set up under the Prevention of Terrorism Act (POTA). It is also the first to explicitly take judicial note of India's war against terrorism.

Under section 57 of the Indian Evidence Act there are certain facts that a Court must take judicial notice of. These facts do not need to be proved. The section lists 13 kinds of facts which the court must take note of and clause 11 reads: "The commencement, continuance, and termination of hostilities between (the Government of India) and any other State or body of persons".

Thus the judge is well within his right under the law to take judicial notice of the current hostilities between India and Pakistan. Shri S.N. Dhingra thus takes "judicial notice of proxy war and hostilities of Pakistan and the hostilities of terrorist groups being sponsored by it towards India." (Annexure 11, Paragraph 252)

Having taken judicial note of the war against terrorism under section 57 of the Indian Evidence Act, Shri S.N. Dhingra then goes on to make a series of presumptions. Under section 114 of the Indian Evidence Act the court can make certain presumptions. The section reads: "The Court may presume the existence of any fact which it thinks likely to have happened, regard being made to the common course of natural events, human conduct and public and private business, in relation to the facts of a particular case."

However, the judgement does not make clear why the judge is taking note of terrorism and what bearing this has on the assessment of evidence against the accused. The question is whether the law allows the judge to make certain special presumptions if he is dealing with cases of terrorism. Shri S.N. Dhingra seems to think that once he has taken judicial note of the war against terrorism he has the authority to make certain presumptions, which are not ordinarily allowed under the law. The Prevention of Terrorism Act does allow the admission of evidence, which is not allowed under the ordinary criminal law though it does not allow the judge to make presumptions beyond those allowed under Section 114 of the Indian Evidence Act.

Reading the judgement by Shri S.N. Dhingra one is struck by the fact that he makes so many presumptions, all of them in favour of the investigating agencies and against the accused. For instance, while dealing with the fact that the police did not follow procedures and may have tampered with the evidence the judge devotes an entire Paragraph on his presumptions on police behaviour. Paragraph 179 begins with these words: "I consider that this is usual practice nowadays to flog the investigating agencies without realizing in what conditions and circumstances they were working under the given situation. There is no reason to disbelieve the testimony of any of the police officers as none of police officers were having any kind of enmity against any of the accused persons."

Anyone who has been following the case and read the testimonies of the police would not be easily persuaded by Shri Dhingra's views. Shri Dhingra seems totally oblivious of the fact that the ACP in charge of the investigation in the Parliament attack case, Rajbir Singh, has a particularly unsavoury reputation and many questions have been raised by the public on his role in encounter deaths. Besides, under the ordinary criminal law confessions to a policeman are not admissible evidence because it is presumed that they must have been extorted under torture. It is all the more difficult to believe in the credibility of the police when they short circuit procedures laid down under the law in order to make up for deficiencies in their investigation.

None of the presumptions made by Shri S.N. Dhingra in the course of his lengthy judgement are either sanctioned under the ordinary criminal law or even under the POTA. The judge justifies the violation of rules, regulations and procedures by the police by reference to the seriousness of the offence and denies the accused their rights under the law. Implicit in his reasoning is that the accused are enemies of the Government of India and therefore they have no right to the protections and safeguards provided under the law or under the Constitution.

Shri Dhingra states that all terrorist attacks, which are made in India, are acts of waging war against the Indian Government and the people and that waging war "means acting like an enemy" (Para 257). The Judge is coming close to the way US President Bush and his lawyers are trying to characterize "terrorists" as "unlawful combatants" who are not entitled to the protection of the Bill of Rights. This reasoning has been criticized on the ground that it defeats the entire concept of fair trial.

As one US writer points out: "A primary function of the trial process is to sort through conflicting evidence in order to find the truth. Anyone who assumes that a person who has merely been accused of being an unlawful combatant is, in fact, an unlawful combatant can understandably maintain that such a person is not entitled to the protection of our constitutional safeguards. The flaw, however, is that the argument begs the very question under consideration." (Timothy Lynch, "Breaking the vicious cycle, preserving our liberties while fighting terrorism", June 2002)

Fortunately, Shri S.N. Dhingra's legal acumen does not extend to propounding new legal doctrines but his prejudices and uninformed understanding of the law on terrorism brings him close to President Bush's circular reasoning.

It is interesting that the judge acknowledges that there is no agreed definition of terrorism. However, he thinks that this is a reflection of differences between the Center and the States rather than inherent problem in defining "terrorism". At Para 267 he expresses his regret that some States do not see the importance of POTA. He writes: "The response of the people of this country to the terrorism varies in accordance with their self-interest. There seems to be no national consensus in respect to response to terrorism and terrorists and the people of their clan. Some states believe in bartering with the people like Veerappan, instead of discharging their duty of protecting lives of people from criminals and terrorists which is the prime duty of a state."

The Judge seems to be totally unaware of the fact that the international community has been trying to arrive at a definition of "terrorism" since 1972 and the United Nations has been unable to arrive at any consensus. One study counted 109 definitions of "terrorism" and concluded that there is no agreed legal definition of the word because the problem is political and not legal. For Shri S.N. Dhingra the definition of terrorist is self-evident and so is the need for POTA. It is interesting that the provisions of POTA were not invoked in the first instant in the Parliament attack case even though it seemed to be a textbook case of terrorism. POTA was imposed on the accused almost a week later, mainly to circumvent the procedures laid down under the criminal law.

The judgement has proved beyond reasonable doubt the worst fears of the human rights community regarding the possibilities of abuse of power and erosion of civil liberties in the name of war against terrorism. It has proved that the POTA is only a device to undermine the principles of natural justice and human rights and it is virtually impossible for an innocent man to defend himself because it violates all norms of fair trial. Unfortunately the Indian human rights community has not responded to it adequately and not produced a comprehensive critique of the judgement.

There are 12 persons who are accused of being part of the conspiracy to attack the Parliament: three Pakistani nationals (about whom there are no details), five deceased terrorists who died in the attack (whose identity is still a mystery) and the four who were actually tried by Shri S.N. Dhingra. None of the four has been given a fair trial.

Here, I will examine the judgement only with reference to the evidence against one of the accused in the Parliament attack case: Syed Abdul Rehman Geelani, a lecturer in Delhi University. Geelani has from the beginning maintained that he is innocent and that the police is trying to frame him. He has been subjected to a trial by the media even before the charges were framed.

Geelani's arrest

The Parliament was attacked on December 13, 2001. In the attack nine security personnel were killed in trying to repel the attack by five heavily armed men who were also killed in the encounter. On the spot three mobile phones and eight mobile numbers were recovered. The call details revealed that one of the deceased attackers was in touch with one of the co-accused, Shaukat Hussain who was in turn in contact with S.A.R. Geelani.

The police discovered that Geelani was the only one who had a regular connection whereas the other mobile phones had cash cards and no details of holders of these cash cards were available.

The Judgement states that the police got permission to tap Geelani's phone from the Joint Director, IB, and on December 14th the police intercepted a conversation in the Kashmiri language between Geelani and someone in Srinagar. The police got someone to translate this conversation into Hindi and discovered that the conversation showed that Geelani had prior knowledge of the attack. Accordingly, the police arrested Geelani from his house in Mukherjee Nagar the next day, December 15th at around 10 am.

The mobile phone was seized from Geelani but the police did not recover anything else. No arms, ammunition or even a pamphlet.

Geelani has consistently said he was arrested on December 14, while he was going from his home to the mosque for Friday prayers in the afternoon. He said he was blindfolded and taken to a farmhouse where he was tortured. Later he was taken to the Lodi Road Police Station where the Special cell is located. There he saw his wife, two small children and brother-in-law were also present. The police threatened to eliminate his family if he did not make a false confession.

Geelani states that the fact that no calls were received on his mobile after 1.30 pm proves the truth of his statement that he was arrested on 14th. The Judge concedes that Geelani did not receive any calls after 1pm on December 14th but he refuses to believe Geelani's testimony by making a presumption that "the accused had smelled about the surveillance and taken care not to make any call." (Para 79)

The court records show that Geelani did not make any confession. They also show that he filed an application in court the moment he got an opportunity stating that he was picked up on December 14th. Geelani's wife's moving testimony in court as a defence witness also corroborates the fact that Geelani was arrested and tortured on December 14th. The Judge dismisses Geelani's wife's testimony as a concoction, he ignores Geelani's applications alleging that he was tortured and substitutes it with his own presumptions.

The Judge decided arbitrarily that Geelani was arrested on the night intervening 14th and 15th December. He does not give any reason why he rejects Geelani's story of his arrest. Also, Shri S. N. Dhingra does not disclose the reasoning by which he came to disbelieve the Prosecution, which claimed to have arrested him at ten in the morning of 15th December while asserting their basis of information on the ownership of the cellular phone and that the address and identity of the caller was revealed only when they received the information from Airtel on December 17th.

Then the judge goes on to the question of why there were no public witnesses at the time of Geelani's arrest, especially since Mukherjee Nagar is a crowded place and there would be any number of persons who could have been called to be public witnesses. The presence of public witnesses is a crucial safeguard against illegal arrests and abuse of power by the police. The Judge devotes five long Paragraphs to justify the police's failure to get a single public witness at the time of Geelani's arrest.

Quoting the Law Commission report on POTA the Judge says that in J&K no public witnesses can be found because of the fear of reprisal from terrorists. Shri S.N. Dhingra quotes the report at Para 85: "Our experience of TADA in J&K has not been good. There has not been a single case, which has been decided by the court of law. The difficulties encountered have been with regard to the non-availability of witnesses to testify in the courts of law on account of fear of reprisal."

The Judge goes on to further justify the police's neglect to get public witnesses by making this extraordinary observation: "It is noteworthy that attack on Parliament was made, when Parliament was in Session. There is not a single witness either from MPs or other VVIPs who had deposed in court about attack on parliament, although a large number of persons must have seen this attack, which included TV cameramen, their news reporters etc."

Shri S.N. Dhingra has gone to extraordinary lengths to protect the police. However, the facts speak for themselves. First of all Geelani was arrested in Delhi and not in Kashmir. The Judge should have taken judicial note of the fact that neither Delhi nor Mukherjee Nagar is insurgency-prone.

Secondly, the prosecution had no problem in finding witnesses in this case. In fact they produced 80 witnesses and the court had no difficulty in deciding the case in a record time of six months. Half a dozen shopkeepers testified in the court and each of them miraculously remembered the face of Mohd. Afzal co-accused buying various goods from their shops. When the defence lawyers suggested that these were all procured witnesses the judge asserted that each of these shopkeepers were credit worthy and were not procured by the prosecution since it "has not been shown that any of the shopkeeper had any kind of enmity against the accused and wanted to implicate him in false case." (Para 113).

Acquaintance between the co-accused

In contrast to Shri S.N. Dhingra's sympathetic presumptions about the police and shopkeepers are his presumptions against Syed Abdul Rehman Geelani. The Judge admits that there is no evidence against Geelani except some circumstantial evidence and there are many missing links in the Prosecution story. The Judge provides the missing links by making a series of presumptions which are well beyond the permissible limits of law.

The first evidence against Geelani, according to the prosecution, is that Geelani was acquainted with the other three accused. Geelani did not deny having an acquaintance with the co-accused. He said he knew Afzal and Shaukat since they were also from Baramullah Distirct of Kashmir. Besides Shaukat was also studying in Delhi University, where Geelani was registered for Phd. However, mere acquaintance with the co-accused does not allow a judge to infer anything against the accused in law. Once again the Judge has provided the missing links by making a series of presumptions.

Geelani's landlord, who testified as a prosecution witness, corroborated Geelani's claim that Afzal and Shaukat had visited the house only a few times in the course of his tenancy. The Judge supplies the missing links with the following presumption: "the landlord was not a chowkidar of the house, who would have all the time stood out to note as to who was going up and coming down. It is a matter of chance that two or three times he saw Afzal and Shaukat going to the house of Geelani. There might have been other various times, when he did not see them." (Paragraph 227)

Further, Geelani admitted to the court that he did call the co-accused but the telephone call had nothing to do with the Parliament attack case. Shri S.N. Dhingra decides on his own that this "phone call must have been given either to confirm something which remained unsettled or for the next programme about which some doubt remained in the mind of the caller nor the call would have been given just after the terrorists attack so launched at the Parliament House. I have no doubt in my mind about the participation of the accused in the conspiracy." (Para 243)

It did not occur to the Judge that no terrorist would ever use a mobile phone with a regular connection to discuss such secret matters. In fact Geelani is the only one who had a regular connection whereas all the others used cash cards.

Having made these presumptions, Shri S.N. Dhingra denied the right to benefit of doubt to Geelani, which was his right under the law and sentenced Syed Abdul Rehman Geelani to death.

The deceased terrorists

Shri S.N. Dhingra goes on further to make another presumption about why he thinks Geelani was involved in the conspiracy. Paragraph 238 reads: "It is also to be noted that all deceased terrorists were hardly educated, their knowledge of English has been shown in the earlier paras. The note, which was found in possession of one of the deceased terrorist giving topography of parliament, has been very neatly prepared which shows the deceased terrorists were getting active help from the other accused persons. The most educated among them was SAR Geelani. It argued that Geelani was a lecturer. He was well behaved to his landlord. He could not have agreed for such an act."

Para 239 continues: "There is no presumption that a lecturer cannot enter into such activity. It is a matter of common knowledge that terrorists are able to hire and convince even the best brains also for Jehad. I consider that prosecution has successfully proved that accused Geelani was part of conspiracy for attack on Parliament."

The Judge states that the terrorists who attacked the Parliament were not educated. There is no evidence to suggest this except for a love letter supposedly written by one of the deceased terrorists identified as Rana, and reproduced by the judge at Paragraph 42. This letter does not prove that all the deceased terrorists were as uneducated. The judge has produced another writing by the terrorists at Paragraph 5, which shows they knew English well.

In fact after reading the 296-page judgement we still do not know who the terrorists were. Shri S.N. Dhingra is not ever concerned about the identity of the five and states that all the "five deceased terrorists were identified as Pakistanis by one of the co-accused. The bodies were kept in mortuary for several days. No person in India claimed their bodies that showed that they were not Indians." (Paragraph 220) This is not a presumption sustainable under the law.

The Judge did not consider the evidence carefully because he was blinded by his own prejudices, which he passed off as permissible presumptions in law. He did not consider the fact that there was no evidence of Geelani ever having met any of the five deceased terrorists. There was no evidence whatsoever of Geelani having ever visited the hideouts where they lived prior to the attack, namely in Gandhi Vihar or Christian Colony. Further, even the Prosecution did not allege that he ever met the five terrorists. Of the 80 Prosecution witnesses the testimony of only 10 has any bearing on Geelani and none of them even alleged that he ever belonged or was sympathetic to any banned or illegal organization. The Prosecution could not prove that any of the four accused put on trial were members of any such organization. Shri S. N. Dhingra is forced to reluctantly concede in Para 281 that no evidence was brought on record to show that any of the accused belonged to any terrorist organization.

The intercepted telephone conversation

The only other evidence against Geelani is the two and half minute telephone conversation he had with his brother on 14th of December. Shri S.N. Dhingra has devoted nearly 30 pages of his judgement to evaluate this piece of evidence.

The first question raised by Geelani's lawyers was on the admissibility of the intercepted phone conversation since the interception was not carried out in accordance with the law. Shri S. N. Dhingra states that the police did not follow the procedure laid down under POTA but he provides the police a justification for not following any rules and procedures. Para 188 reads: "It was a case of true emergency and the doubt of the investigating agency about the involvement of others was not without any basis. I consider that at that time, it was not the concern to see whether the case was to be registered under POTA or not but the concern was to catch hold of other terrorists. Moreover, POTA was in force, no doubt by way of an ordinance but it had not been invoked so far by the State."

The import of the entire judgement is that procedures laid down under the law are mere technicalities, which can be brushed aside in times of emergency. But the central concern of human rights community is precisely this. Procedures prescribed by the law are the only safeguard against abuse of power by the executive and a check on misappropriation of power by the State. The central concern of human rights law is the enforcement of procedures, which alone can protect substantive rights.

However, Shri S.N. Dhingra understands the relevance of procedures differently. In the course of his discussion on the admissibility of the intercepted conversation he states: "I consider that merely because prosecution had not followed the procedure laid down in tapping the conversation looking into the emergent requirement and interest of the nation, the evidence collected by the prosecution in the form of the taped conversation cannot be thrown out." (Para 195) The logical conclusion of Shri S.N. Dhingra's reasoning would be that the hanging of an innocent citizen on the basis of spurious evidence might sometimes be in national interest.

The Judge goes on to examine the contents of the intercepted telephone conversation. The Prosecution did not put the transcript of the conversation on record. They produced a witness who is a fruit vendor and who stated that he translated the taped conversation after hearing the tape two to four times. He stated that there were no English words in the conversation. He also said that the caller asked Geelani: "What have you done in Delhi?" to which Geelani replied: "Ei chhey zaroori" (It is essential) and laughed. The prosecution relied on this part of the conversation as evidence of Geelani's guilt.

The Defence produced two witnesses who transcribed and translated the intercepted conversation. The first witness was Sampat Prakash, a trade union leader living and working in Kashmir. He is a Kashmiri Pandit and was requested to make a transcription and translate the conversation by Balraj Puri, the well-known member of the Peoples Union of Civil Liberties (PUCL) in Jammu. His transcript along with the translation is reproduced at the end of this article.[1]

The second defence witness was Sanjay Kak, a documentary filmmaker living in Delhi who has won many international awards. He is also a Kashmiri Pandit. He has special skills in transcribing and sound technology. Since the intercepted conversation took place while Geelani was traveling in a bus there was a lot of outside disturbance and the taped conversation was indistinct and difficult to decipher. Sanjay Kak also transcribed the conversation and translated it for the court.

There were three differences between the testimony of the prosecution witness and the defence witnesses. First, was on the existence of a phrase. Both the defence witnesses categorically stated that no point in the taped conversation could they hear the words "Ei Chhey zaroori" and they had heard the cassette 10 to 12 times and transcribed the tape word by word. This was in contrast to the Prosecution witness who had merely heard the taped conversation two to four times and orally translated the taped conversation while the police wrote it down.

Second, the prosecution witness stated that the caller asked Geelani: "Yeh kyah korva?" and this was with reference to the attack on Parliament. The defence witnesses said the query "Ye kyah korva?" (What has happenened?) could be a reference to anything, including a quarrel between Geelani and his wife over the cancellation of the trip to Srinagar for Id. The Judge goes on to refer to Geelani's wife's deposition in which she had said that Geelani and she were supposed to go to Srinagar for Id (which fell on the 17th of December) but Geelani had cancelled the programme because he did not have holidays. The Judge dismisses her testimony without giving any reasons and presumes that the reason for the cancellation of the programme of going to Srinagar was something to do with the conspiracy to attack the Parliament. He states: "It seems that the programme of going to Eid was cancelled by accused Geelani not because of paucity of holidays but because he was hopeful that the five terrorists would succeed in capturing parliament and he had envisaged a role for himself thereafter." (Paragraph 236)

The Judge does not care to state how he came to this conclusion and what was the evidence for his conclusion.

Both the defence witnesses said it was a common Kashmiri expression and the conversation had nothing to do with the attack on Parliament.

Third, the prosecution witness insisted that there were no English words in the conversation whereas the defence witnesses categorically stated that there were several English words in the conversation, including the words Syllabus and Prospectus.

The Prosecution did not play the tape in the court despite repeated requests from both Geelani and his lawyer. However, the judge finally agreed to play the tape in the court when the defence witnesses gave their testimony in the court. He took one of the defence witnesses into the chamber and made him play the tape to him, asking him to translate the conversation.

However, in his judgement, Shri S.N. Dhingra dismisses the two defence witnesses as "interested witnesses". He holds that they are interested witnesses because they both came to court on the request of the All India Defence Committee for Syed Abdul Rehman Geelani whose chairman is Prof. Rajni Kothari. At Para 203 of the judgement Shri S.N. Dhingra states that both the defence witnesses "tried to give a general meaning of the conversation. They also did not deliberately write the answer given by the accused to the query." Later on in the judgement the judge holds: "This conversation confirmed the involvement of accused in the conspiracy and he considered that such kind of attacks were necessary from time to time." (Para 237)

How does Shri S.N. Dhingra decide whom to believe? He decided to take lessons in Kashmiri language and became proficient enough to judge the meaning of phrases and nuances of the language. At Para 202 of the judgement Shri Dhingra writes: "Prosecution has relied upon the last part of the conversation, which starts with the caller asking Receiver (Geelani) — yeh kya koroo. This query cannot relate to quarrel between husband and wife as already explained above. This query only relates to the incident in Delhi. DW 1 Sampat Prakash, who has appeared on behalf of accused SAR Geelani has stated that in Kashmiri language, "yeh kaya koroo" means "what has happened" and this query is made in general whenever anything happens anywhere. Same is the testimony of DW2 Sanjay Kak, but it is not true. This court had no knowledge of Kashmiri language and had to take some lessons on Kashmiri language. It transpires that "yeh kya koroo" in Kashmiri is also used for what you had done. Both witnesses are interested witnesses."

It is true that both Sampat Prakash and Sanjay Kak deposed in the court on the request of the All India Defence Committee for Syed Abdul Rehman Geelani. The Chairman of the Committee is Prof. Rajni Kothari. This Committee was set up in August 2002 with the express intention of ensuring that Geelani gets a fair trial. The members of the Committee are men and women known for their integrity and patriotism: Surendra Mohan, Babu Mathew, Prabhash Joshi, Y P Chhibber, Aruna Roy, Sandeep Pandey (both Magsaysay award winners), Arundhati Roy, Sanjay Kak, Syeda Hameed, Nandita Haksar and Kr. Sanjay Singh.

None of these people are "interested" witnesses as ordinarily understood in criminal law. They have an impeccable reputation for integrity and patriotism. They are not related to the accused and most of them do not know him personally. In fact they are textbook disinterested witnesses. The definition of a disinterested witness is: Impartial, fair-minded, unbiased. A disinterested witness is one "who has no personal interest in the case being tried or the matter at issue and is legally competent to give testimony."

Although Sampat Prakash and Sanjay Kak came to the court as defence witnesses they were actually expert witnesses. The Indian Evidence Act provides for expert witnesses who may be summoned either as prosecution or defence witnesses under sections 45 and 46. A standard law dictionary defines an expert witness: "A person who, on the basis of training, work or experience in a particular science, trade, or art is qualified to speak authoritatively on the standard and scientific facts in that particular field."

Sampat Prakash told the court that he has been translating speeches from Kashmiri into English and Urdu on a regular basis in the course of his trade union work. Sanjay Kak testified that his work required special skills in sound technology and careful transcribing. Besides, both the men had knowledge of the language and its nuances.

However, Shri S.N. Dhingra decided to treat the uneducated fruit vendor from Azad market as the expert on Kashmiri language. At Para 204 the judge surpasses himself in making amazing presumptions. I reproduce the entire paragraph: "Defence has criticized prosecution for calling PW71 who was only 5th / 6th Standard pass for translating Kashmiri conversation to Hindi. Language is not monopoly of educated and elite class. A child starts learning mother tongue while sucking milk of her mother. A person educated up to 5th or 6th Standard may be knowing his mother tongue much better than a graduate or post-graduate, who after acquiring knowledge of English starts forgetting his mother tongue and can speak only in Hinglish, Chinglish or Kashinglish. Tulsidas, Kabir, and several other contemporary personalities had no or little formal education but had command over language and produced great 'works'. Being a fruit seller is no sin. Today we do not understand the dignity of labour and look upon persons earning livelihood by labour as low class. If India is 10th among the most corrupt countries, it is not because of these poor people but because of some other class of people. The witness could not understand English words in the conversation because of lack of knowledge of English language but he understood Kashmiri and Hindi well and translated the conversation to Hindi properly."

Shri S.N. Dhingra's 296-page judgement is chilling reading. He has condemned three men to death and a woman to five years imprisonment without giving them a fair trial. He has shown scant respect for the principles and ideals of human rights enshrined in our Constitution by the Founding Fathers. He has wiped out the gains of the human rights movement in the post-emergency period in one stroke and he has done all this in the name of the nation. If his judgement is upheld it would lay the foundation for a police state where every citizen would be a potential victim of institutionalized repression.

The international human rights community has warned of the consequences of the war against terrorism. On November 29, 2001 Mary Robinson, the then UN High Commissioner for Human Rights issued a joint statement with the Council of Europe and the Organization for Security and Co-operation in Europe (OSCE) which urged states "to ensure that any measures restricting human rights in response to terrorism strike a fair balance between legitimate national security concerns and fundamental freedoms that is fully consistent with their international law commitments."

The statement warned: "Anti-terrorism measures targeting specific ethnic or religious groups would also be contrary to human rights law and international commitments and would carry the risk of sparking a dangerous upsurge of discrimination and racism."

All those concerned with preserving the values of democracy and human rights need to take heed to those words and to ensure that Geelani is not sacrificed at the altar of national security and communal hatred.

1. The transcript has not been included here.

ANNEXURE 15

Statements from Delhi University Teachers and Noam Chomsky

Delhi University Teachers in Defence of S.A.R. Geelani

Press Conference, Press Club of India, New Delhi,
18 September 2003

Statement for the Press

The Delhi University Teachers in Defence of S.A.R. Geelani has been deeply concerned about the denial of justice to a fellow teacher, S.A.R. Geelani, an accused in the case concerning the attack on the Parliament on December 13, 2001. Shockingly, Geelani was convicted by the Special Court, designated under the Prevention of Terrorism Act (POTA), and given the death penalty only on the basis of a telephonic conversation in Kashmiri with his brother, lasting two minutes and sixteen seconds. However, the defence argued that both the procedure and the content of the translation from Kashmiri to English were seriously flawed.

No link between Geelani and the five persons who attacked the Parliament, or with any banned organization, was established or even alleged by any of the 80 prosecution witnesses. No arms or ammunition or incriminating document of any kind were recovered from his person or his house.

His only crime appears to have been a casual acquaintance with the co-accused, a fact that Geelani has never denied. Significantly, these individuals happened to be from the same district, Baramullah, in Kashmir; they were also students of Delhi University where Geelani met them. Thus, it was only natural that Geelani would be acquainted with them. The reasoning that a person is guilty just because he is acquainted with persons subsequently accused of a crime is both absurd and tragic.

Our apprehensions about this travesty of justice is further compounded by the fact that, in the High Court, the prosecution has now shifted emphasis from the said call to his brother to some unrecorded calls with the co-accused. It is to be noted that Geelani made a written application to the Court asking for an opportunity to explain these calls, but this basic legal right was denied to him.

We also feel that the lack of evidence and irregularity of procedures is sought to be substituted by a virulent campaign of disinformation about the facts of the case. We note with concern that the media, largely, has buckled under pressure, and has contributed to prejudicing public opinion against Geelani by condemning him even before the trial had begun.

In an amazing violation of journalistic ethics, one TV channel repeatedly telecast a "recreation" of the attack on the Parliament based only on the version of the prosecution in an attempt to prejudice public opinion. Unfortunately, the Supreme Court allowed the telecasting of a film that pronounced Geelani guilty even before judgement was delivered. It is a matter of great concern for us that the same film is being telecast again now when the judgement of the High Court is due.

To add to the trial by the media, several fundamentalist organizations have openly threatened violence against lawyers who have dared to defend Geelani. Not even a lawyer as eminent as Mr. Ram Jethmalani was spared when he decided to defend Geelani in the High Court. Jethmalani's office was vandalized in Mumbai by the Shiv Sena.

S.A.R. Geelani is personally known to many of us. He is a popular teacher and a serious scholar. Many of us remember his engaging discussions with students and friends. We also remember him as a person always willing to give time to help others.

Geelani's secular credentials are impeccable, and he has always condemned violence. Even when convicted by the Special Court and sentenced to death, he said,

> *I have always considered terrorism, be it unleashed by the state or by parties outside the state, as condemnable and have clearly criticised it. The killing of innocents, the rape of women, the murder of justice, these are all the worst forms of terrorism. Every effort needs to be made to end this terror.*

As citizens, we condemn the attack on the Parliament in unequivocal terms. We demand that the perpetrators of this atrocious crime be identified and brought to justice. But the cardinal principle of natural justice that every accused is deemed to be innocent until found guilty must not only prevail, it should be seen as prevailing.

In this sense, we believe that S.A.R. Geelani's case raises disturbing questions even larger than the fate of an individual citizen. It is a test case for the Indian legal system and its ability to deliver justice. In fact, Indian democracy itself is on trial.

Statement from Noam Chomsky

MASSACHUSETTS INSTITUTE OF TECHNOLOGY
E39-219
Department of Linguistics and Philosophy
Cambridge, Massachusetts 02139

September 23, 2003

To

Convenor, Delhi University Teachers In Defence of S.A.R. Geelani

I read with much concern the statement of the Delhi University Teachers in Defence of S.A.R. Geelani. What it describes is utterly outrageous, and surely should not be tolerated. The phrase "absurd and tragic" is fully warranted.

The atrocities of 9-11 were exploited in a vulgar way by governments all over the world, in some cases by escalating massive crimes on the pretext of "combating terrorism," in others by implementing repressive legislation to discipline their own citizens with no credible connection to preventing terrorist threats, in some cases by carrying out programs that had not the remotest connection to terrorism and might even enhance it and that were opposed by the majority of the population. Terrorism is a serious matter, and merits careful attention and scrupulous preventive measures and response. It is disgraceful for the authentic threat of terrorism to be exploited as a window of opportunity for intolerable actions.

I hope and trust that Indian democracy and its legal system will rise to the challenge, reverse this decision, and ensure that human and civil rights are properly protected.

Sincerely yours,
Sd/-
Noam Chomsky

Annexure 16

High Court Judgment of October 29, 2003

Murder Reference No. 1/2003

(Cited paragraphs only in numerical order)

62. PW-40 Anil Kumar deposed that on 6.12.2001 accused Mohd. Afzal accompanied by another person identified to be the same person whose photograph was Ex.PW-40/2 (Hamza) had visited his shop and placed an order for 50 kilograms of Ammonium Nitrate and paid an advance of Rs.800/-. On 7.12.2001 delivery was taken after paying the balance sum of Rs.4,000/-. Ammonium Nitrate which was supplied was packed in 500 grams jars. On 17.12.2001 Afzal had come with the police to the shop, pointing out memo was Ex.PW-40/1 which was signed by him. Some of the jars which were shown to him were identified as Ex.PW-54/1 to 24 as being supplied by him. On being cross-examined by Shri Neeraj Bansal, Amicus for accused Mohd. Afzal, he stated that Ammonium Nitrate could be sold by any person and no legal formalities was required for its sale. He had no documentary proof showing sale to accused Mohd. Afzal nor he had issued any receipt for the money received. The packaging of the Ammonium Nitrate was available at other shops and there is no stamp on it of his shop.

113. DW-4, Shams Tahir Khan, Principal correspondent Aajtak T.V. Channel deposed that he had interviewed Mohd. Afzal on 20th December, 2001 for 15 minutes. The audio visual tape prepared was Ex. DW-4A. (The witness was not allowed to be examined as the Court recorded that it's contents would be read in evidence, as it was an exhibited document.) In cross-examination, witness stated that he did not feel that answers were given under pressure. However, ACP was present when the interview was being taken. The witness was cross-examined by accused Mohd. Afzal wherein he admitted that Zee T.V. and NDTV correspondent was also present when the interview was taken. One of the interviewer had put a question to him about the role of S.A.R. Gilani, to which Mohd. Afzal stated that S.A.R. Gilani was innocent at which ACP Rajbir got up and said that he should not speak about S.A.R. Gilani. Rajbir Singh has requested not to telecast the lines stated by the accused about S.A.R. Gilani and, therefore, when the interview was telecast on 20th December, 2001 line was removed but when it was re-broadcasted in the program 100 days after the attack the line was not removed.

139. We may, however, lodge a caveat on this aspect of the matter. It has indeed become a disturbing feature as is being noticed by us repeatedly that the accused persons, after their remand by the Magistrate, are brazenly paraded before the press and interviews are being allowed. Accused persons are exposed to public glare through T.V. and in case where Test Identification Parade or the accused person being identified by witnesses (as in the present case) arise, the case of the prosecution is vulnerable to be attacked on the ground of exposure of the accused persons to public glare, weakening the impact of the identification. Further, what is more fundamentally disturbing to our mind is the fact that police custody is given by the Court to the investigating authorities on the premise that the accused is required for the purpose of investigation. This custody is not to be mis-used by allowing the media to interview the accused persons. The practice of allowing the media to interview the accused persons when they are in police custody under the orders of the Court, has therefore, to be deprecated.

216. The fire power was awesome. Enough to engage a battalion. Had the terrorists succeeded the entire building with all inside would have perished. The foundation of the country would have shaken. The act was clearly an act of waging war against the Government of India.

247. Accused S.A.R. Gilani did not dispute ownership and possession of mobile No.9810081228 and its recovery from him. He also admitted to having received a call on the number at 12.21 hours on 14.12.2002. Recovery is thus proved. However, he denied his arrest on 15.12.2001 at 10 A.M. from his house. He stated that he was arrested on 14.12.2001 at about 1.30 noon while he was travelling in a bus when it was near Khalsa College, University of Delhi. Mr. Ram Jethmalani, learned Senior Counsel for accused S.A.R. Gilani urged before us, that:

a) The call at 13.03 noon on 14.12.2001 was the last call made or received on Gilani's mobile phone and call record showed between 5 to 15 calls received or made on this number each day. Gilani was deprived use of the phone, suggesting his arrest.

b) Call records showed that on 13.12.2001 at 9.37 P.M. and 11.19 P.M. he had received incoming calls on this number. As per the cross-examination by the prosecution of his wife DW-5, these calls were admitted by the prosecution to be received in the house. This falsified the prosecution case that in the night of 13.12.2001 Gilani's house was kept under surveillance and no movement being noticed, the surveillance was withdrawn and again mounted on 14.12.2001 in the morning. Call record showed that at 8.53 A.M. Gilani had received a call on this number at his house.

c) Arrest memo of SAR Gilani was not produced. PW-39 Naresh Gulati, the landlord of S.A.R. Gilani did not depose that Gilani was arrested on his identification though PW-66 and PW-67 were categorical that it was on the identification of PW-39 that they arrested SAR Gilani. The prosecution was hiding facts. No relative was informed about the arrest.

d) DW-5, wife of S.A.R. Gilani, had deposed that Gilani left for offering the Jumma Namaj at the Mall Road Mosque at about 1 or 1.30 P.M. and from there was to meet her brother at J&K Bus Stop opposite Tis Hazari and was to come back at 4 P.M. When he did not return, she tried to contact him over his mobile phone which was not responding. This part of her testimony went unchallenged in the cross-examination. She had to be believed.

e) The most important piece of evidence come from the testimony of PW-61 and PW-62. Information to track down truck number HR-38E-6733 was available with the Srinagar Police in the morning of 15.12.2001 and the truck was tracked at 8 A.M. According to the prosecution, the police got the truck number when Afzan was arrested at 10.30 A.M. There was material contradiction. If the truck was tracked at 8 A.M., information would have been available with the Srinagar police in the early morning hours. This again belied the prosecution's time of arrest and was in tune with the defence that SAR Gilani was arrested on 14.12.2001 in the afternoon.

f) DW-5 had stated that at 10 P.M. on the night of 14.12.2001, she and her children were illegally picked up from the house and taken to Special Cell, Lodhi Colony where she saw her husband with injuries showing torture. Her brother-in-law Bismillah was also in illegal confinement. Her husband and Bismillah were forced to sign on blank papers. This testimony also went unchallenged.

248. Shri Gopal Subramaniam, learned Senior Counsel for the prosecution refuted as under:-

a) Accused Afzan Guru has stated in her statement under Section 313 Cr.P.C. that accused S.A.R. Gilani knew her house and he had shown the house to the police. This shows that S.A.R. Gilani was arrested prior to her arrest and he had taken the police to her house.

b) To PW-66 suggestion was put by Afzan Guru that she was arrested on 14.12.2001 but to PW-67 the suggestion put was that she was arrested at about 6 A.M. on 15.12.2001.

c) In her statement recorded under Section 313 Cr.P.C. she stated that she was arrested on 14.12.2001 between 6 P.M. and 7 P.M. A palpably false statement as she had a talk with accused Shaukat on 14.12.2001 at 8.15 P.M. which fact she admitted in her statement under Section 313 Cr.P.C. Question and answer being as under:

   Q. It is in evidence against you that your cell No.9811573506 was put on surveillance and on the evening of 14.12.2001 you had talked to your husband Shaukat Hussain on his cell No. and tape in this regard is Ex.PW-66/4. What have you to say?

   Ans. It is correct. I enquired as to what has been brought in truck. I talked to him in Police Station.

d) DW-5 being wife of accused S.A.R. Gilani was an interested person and her testimony stood falsified by her denial that accused SAR Gilani who was in the house in the night of 12th and 13th December had not used the phone, as call records showed that indeed calls had been received on this number. She had denied the calls received at the night of 13th December which again was false. Facts deposed by her about her illegal confinement, torture of SAR Gilani etc. were not put by her to PW-66 or PW-80 and were being stated for the first time in court.

e) From the evidence it emerged that SAR Gilani was arrested first and thereafter Afzan Guru at the instance of SAR Gilani and it was he who led the police to the house of Afzan Guru. On overall conspectus of the evidence it stood established that arrest took place on 15.12.2001.

f) PW-61 and PW-62 were overzealous in their testimony and it was natural human conduct to take credit. From the testimony of PW-66 it stood established that police at Srinagar was flashed a message on 14.12.2001 to look out for two persons, one named Shaukat, near fruit mandi as the police had got said information from the call intercepted at 8.15 P.M. on the phone of Afzan Guru. Information about the truck was flashed on 15.12.2001 after Afzan Guru gave disclosure. Possibility of PW-61 mixing up the two could not be ruled out.

g) PW-61 on being cross-examined, apart from being put a suggestion that he was deposing falsely (which he denied), was put a suggestion that he arrested Shaukat and Mohd. Afzal from different places, thereby admitting that PW-61 arrested them. PW-62, who was with PW-61 when Shaukat and Mohd. Afzal were arrested, was given the suggestion that Shaukat and Mohd. Afzal were first brought to the police station and truck was brought later, thus arrest was admitted.

250. We need not discuss and analyze the rival contentions on the time of arrest as per the rival contentions noted above. To our mind, a very disturbing feature pertaining to the accused persons has been noted by us. The Hon'ble Supreme Court in the judgment of D.K. Basu Vs. State of West Bengal, 1997 SC 610 has laid down guidelines to be followed by the police at the time of arrest of an accused, one of them being to notify the near relative of the accused of the arrest. The overzealous prosecution in its written submissions filed stated thus:

"Defence did not even lead evidence of Bismillah (brother of Gilani) or Khan Saheb (Brother-in-law of Gilani) which evidence would have been material in light of DW-5's testimony. Their evidence would have been important especially in light of the fact that Bismillah is the relative who has attested the arrest memo of Gilani, Afzal and Shaukat."

251. We have perused the case diaries. Indeed, the arrest memo of SAR Gilani, Mohd. Afzal and Shaukat bear the signatures of Bismillah as having attested the same. Mohd. Afzal's and Shaukat's arrest memos have been prepared at Delhi. The presence of Bismillah's signatures as having attested the arrest memos of the three accused probabilises the testimony of DW-5 that Bismillah was in illegal confinement and was forced to sign papers. In any case, the prosecution stands discredited qua the time of arrest of accused S.A.R. Gilani and accuseed Afzan Guru. But where does that lead us?

255. That a person was arrested, at a particular place, at a particular time, he was searched, resulting in a recovery are all distinct facts. Unreliability of the prosecution witnesses on one fact does not mean one has to discard the other facts deposed, if they are sufficiently proved and stand the test of credibility. Grain has to be separated from the chaff. We are concerned here with the recoveries. S.A.R. Gilani's case is no problem. He admits that the mobile phone number 9810081228 was recovered from him. He admits the call details thereof. The other three accused deny the recoveries effected from them. We proceed to consider the evidence of the prosecution with caution as time of arrest of accused persons has been seriously dented.

259. The facts aforesaid lend assurance to the testimony of PW-66 and PW-67. We accept their testimony qua the recoveries as truthful. The recoveries from the person and house of accused Afzan Guru thus stand proved. Counsel for the accused submitted that no independent witnesses were associated and, therefore, recoveries must fail. We do not agree. If the police witnesses are credible and their testimony not shaken, mere non-association of independent witness by itself is no ground to reject the recovery by disbelieving the police. In the judgment reported as 2000 (vii) A.D. (SC) 613, Government of NCT of Delhi Vs. Sunil, it was held:

"We feel that it is an archaic notion that actions of the police officer should be approached with initial distrust. We are aware that such a notion was lavishly entertained during British period and policemen also knew about it. Its hangover persisted during post-independent years but it is time now to start placing at least initial trust on the actions and the documents made by the police. At any rate, the court cannot start with the presumption that the police records are untrustworthy. As a proposition of law the presumption should be the other way around. That official acts of the police have been regularly performed is a wise principle of presumption and recognised even by the legislature. Hence, when a police officer gives evidence in Court that a certain article was recovered by him on the strength of the statement by the accused it is open to the Court to believe the version to be correct if it is not otherwise shown to be unreliable. It is for the accused, through cross-examination of witnesses or through any other materials, to show that the evidence of the police officer is either unreliable or at least unsafe to be acted upon in a particular case. If the Court has any good reason to suspect the truthfulness of such records of the police, the court could certainly take into account the fact that no other independent person was present at the time of recovery. But is not a legally approvable procedure to presume the police action as unreliable to start with, nor to jettison such action merely for the reason that police did not collect signatures of independent persons in the documents made contemporaneous with such actions."

295. The technical flaw whereby on four occasions double entries have been recorded are explainable, in that, they are double entries to the called and caller numbers. Even otherwise as held in Ana Marcolino (Supra) the malfunction is not sufficient to cast a doubt upon the capacity of the computer to process information correctly. It does not establish in any way that the capacity of the computer to process, store and retrieve information used to generate the statement, tendered in evidence, was effected.

340. In her statement recorded under Section 313 Cr.P.C., accused Afzan admitted having talked to her husband on the mobile phone 9811573506 but said that this conversation she had when she was in the police cell. The call in any case stands admitted by her and it also stands admitted that she had a talk with Shaukat. There is, however, one factor which leads us to the conclusion that this call has to be ignored. The call records of the mobile phone No. 9811573506 on which number this call was received shows that on 14.12.2001 at 20:09:07 hours a call from the calling No. 0194492619 was made which lasted for a duration of 49 seconds. The taped conversation which was sent to the experts, as noted above was of 2 minutes and 16 seconds as per the deposition of PW-48. This discrepancy was not explained by the prosecution even during oral arguments at the bar. The only explanation given was that this aspect was not confronted to PW-48. It was necessary to confront PW-48 with the entry in the mobile phone record pertaining to the number because it was not the previous statement or the document emanating from PW-48. PW-48 was put a specific cross-examination as to from where he had recorded the time of two minutes and sixteen seconds as the duration of the call in the disputed cassettes sent to him and he categorically replied that the time was noted by him after he played the cassette and so recorded. It was for the prosecution to have re-examined the witness and obtained verification or led independent evidence to reconcile the truth.

341. In any case, assuming it to be correct, the taped conversation is as under:-

14.12.2001

Time: 2013 Hrs. 9811573506

Caller: Hello I am! Was there any telephone call?

Receiver: Shaokat where are you?

Caller: I am in Srinagar.

Receiver: Reached there?

Caller: Yes.

Receiver: Some person had just come now.

Caller: From where?

Receiver: I don't know. Don't say anything.

Caller: O.K.

Receiver: I don't know they are with the lady of the ground floor. Some vehicle is still parked outside.

Caller: O.K.

Receiver: I don't know. I did not speak anything.

Caller: O.K. Alright.

Receiver: Tell more, don't speak anything now and tell me. I am much afraid.

Caller: No, No nothing dear. O.K.

Receiver: Are you fine?

Caller: Yes, Yes.

Receiver: Reached safely?

Caller: Yes, Yes.

Receiver: And Chotu?

Caller: Yes Yes.
Receiver: Do you know?
Caller: Yes Yes alright you may make a call.
Receiver: When?
Caller: In the night. Right now, I am calling from out side.
Receiver: Alright I will call up tomorrow (while weeping)
Caller: O.K.

Conversation between accused Shaukat Hussain Guru (Caller) and Navjot Sidhu alias Afshan Guru (Receiver).

342. Prosecution relied on two parts of the conversation (underlined by us) namely when Afzan tells Shaukat not to speak over the phone and the part of the conversation where in response to the query "whether anyone had come?", she had responded that a car was standing downstairs to infer that it showed that Afzan knew that she and her husband were under some kind of a surveillance by the police being involved in the attack on Parliament House, which is an incriminating circumstance. If it is correct transcript of the talk, there can be no doubt that Shaukat and Afzan were talking between the lines. Afzan was scared. Certainly, an inference may be drawn she was concerned about the safety of Shaukat. But does it probabilise her involvement in the conspiracy or attributes knowledge of the conspiracy to her? In the context of law of conspiracy and proof required, we shall deal with it a little later.

346. During the hearing of the appeal, we had called for the tape from Malkhana and in the presence of the parties played the same. Indeed the voice was so inaudible that we could not make head or tail of the conversation. We tried our best to pick up the phonetical sounds where there was a dispute as to what words were used, but were unable to do so. Testimony of PW-48 reveals that he could not analyse the talk as it was highly inaudible. PW-48 is a phonetic expert. If he could not comprehend the conversation in a clearly audible tone, the probability of ordinary layman picking up the phonetic sounds differently cannot be ruled out. The prosecution witness, PW-71, Rashid, who prepared a transcript of the tape is fifth class pass and it was not his profession to prepare a transcript of taped conversation. The possibility of his being in error cannot be ruled out. Benefit of doubt must go to the defence.

347. To the query of his brother "Yeh Kya Karoo" to which the response was "Eh Chhe Zururi", the prosecution alleges that the conversation showed that Gilani was involved in the conspiracy in the attack on Parliament House. Prosecution alleges that when his brother asked him what had been done in Delhi, he replied this was necessary. This inference as drawn by the prosecution, to our mind, does not hold good. Firstly, if it was so, the natural corollary would be that the person querying would have to be imputed with the knowledge that he was aware that accuseed S.A.R. Gilani was involved in the attack on Parliament House and this would make the said person as an accused. Admittedly, brother of accused S.A.R. Gilani was not charged as being part of the conspiracy. Secondly, the defence has given a plausible acceptable version of the talk. As noticed in the deposition of Shah Faizal, brother of accused S.A.R. Gilani, who deposed as DW-6, had spoken to his brother on 13.12.2001 at 1./1.30 P.M. which fact is proved from the call records of the phone number of accused S.A.R. Gilani which shows that on 13.12.2001, he had received a call at 13:21:01 from the number 0194458131 which was a call from Srinagar. DW-6 had stated that he had wanted his brother to bring syllabus and prospectus as he wanted to appear in the medical entrance examination and the testimony of DW-6 went unchallenged by the prosecution. This witness has deposed that his mother had

told him that his brother's wife had told her that they were not coming for Id to Srinagar and his Bhabi sounded annoyed and it was in this context that asked the question "Yeh Kya Karoo" to which Gilani counter querried "Kya Dilah" to which he responded "Delhi Kya Karoo", and his brother laughed. This part of the talk is undoubtedly in colloquial style. The conclusion drawn by the prosecution can hardly be contended, much less accepted. The witness explained, which was corroborated by DW-1 and DW-2, that in Kashmir such type of exclamatory querying was usual when unexpected things happen and in the context of the testimony of DW-6 that what he meant by the question was the fight between Gilani and his wife, we find that assuming the talk to be the one as per the transcription of the prosecution, nothing incriminating emerges and no fact apart from the fact of the talk stands established.

368. If we look to the two confessional statements, they are substantially the same. Both referred to Afzal's past as a surrendered militant. Relationship between Afzal and Shaukat as being cousins. Their past history of schooling in Sopore and graduation in Delhi. Their coming into contact with accused SAR Gilani who was a professor. Afzal's motivation for Jehad and struggle for liberation of Jammu and Kashmir and his in turn motivating Shaukat. Afzal's coming into company with Tariq and Ghazi Baba. Afzal's motivation to help in carrying out a fidayeen attack in Delhi. Afzal's seeking help from Shaukat in providing hideouts and Shaukat helping in procuring hideouts. Afzal's bringing the five terrorists to Delhi and procuring chemicals and bringing arms with the terrorists, are all common features of both the confessional statements. The discussion of the plans to carry out a fidayeen attack in Delhi, Shaukat providing his motor cycle for recee, phone numbers used by Shaukat and Afzal and procuring the Ambassador car are further common features of the two confessional statements. Minor contradictions here and there as to whether Shaukat procured the hideout at Christian Colony or both of them procured the hide-out are minor variations. The broad contours of the conspiracy are the broad contours of the confessional statements.

376. The Legislature had, therefore, consciously made the confession of a co-accused admissible in evidence against a accused when TADA was enacted. Since there was criticism of TADA, one of which being the presumption against the accused on a mere confession of a co-accused who obviously could not be cross-examined at the trial, the Legislature amended TADA by Act No.3 of 1993 and deleted sub-clause (c) of Section 21 (1) of TADA. However, intending only to remove the legislation pertaining to the statutory presumption which was created against an accused, based on the confessional statement of a co-accused, the Legislature by the same Act made a corresponding amendment in Section 15 of TADA. The amended Section reads as under:-

> "15. Certain confessions made to Police Officers to be taken into consideration. – Notwithstanding anything in the Code or in the Indian Evidence Act, 1872 (1 of 1872), but subject to the provisions of this section, a confession made by a person before a police officer not lower in rank than a Superintendent of Police and recorded by such police officer in writing or on any mechanical device like cassettes, tapes or sound tracks from out of which sounds of images can be reproduced, shall be admissible in the trial of such person or co-accused, abettor or conspirator for an offence under this Act or rules made thereunder:
>
> Provided that co-accused, abettor or conspirator is charged and tried in the same case together with the accused."

377. The absence of a provision corresponding to sub Clause (c) of sub-Section 1 of Section 21 and the clear amendment incorporated in sub-Section 1 of Section 15 of TADA when sub-clause (c) of sub-Section 1 of Section 21 of TADA was amended when compared with the language of sub-Section (1) of Section 32 makes the legislative intent quite clear. The confession of a co-accused recorded before a police officer under POTA would not be admissible in evidence against the accused.

400. From the facts and circumstances, it therefore, stands established that accused Mohd. Afzal was a part to the conspiracy to attack Parliament when it was in Session. He procured hideouts for the terrorists, was instrumental in the smuggling of arms and ammunitions used by the terrorists. Had actively purchased the chemicals used for making the explosives. Had been involved in the purchase of a motor cycle used for recee by the terrorists and had been involved in the purchase of the white Ambassador Car used by the terrorists.

401. Shaukat's role in the conspiracy was clearly that of an active participant. Evidence on record does not show that he has been brought within the sweep of the dragnet of conspiracy by merely being seen associated with Afzal. There is more than mere knowledge, acquiscence, carelessness, indifference or lack of concern. There is clear and cogent evidence of informed and interested co-operation, simulation and instigation against accused Shaukat. Evidence qua Shaukat clearly establishes the steps from knowledge to intent and finally agreement.

405. We have pondered over this evidence, it is a relevant circumstance but by itself without anything more on record is not sufficient to draw an inference against S.A.R. Gilani that he was involved in the conspiracy. After all S.A.R. Gilani was known to Shaukat and Afzal. When one acquires a mobile phone, it is but natural that one would test it for use. What other number would one connect other than that of a known person. By itself, with nothing more, we are afraid that conviction cannot be sustained on this basis.

408. Prosecution had relied upon the conversation between Gilani and his brother in the afternoon of 14th December, 2001 and had contended that the talk was incriminating, in that, it showed Gilani's participation in the attack on Parliament House. We had, while discussing the taped conversation, even assuming the prosecution version to be correct, come to the conclusion that there was nothing which could incriminate Gilani as far as the conversation is concerned.

411. We have already held that under POTA a confession of an accused is not admissible in evidence against the co-accused.

412. We are, therefore, left with only one piece of evidence against accused S.A.R. Gilani being the record of telephone calls between him and accused Mohd. Afzal & Shaukat. This circumstance, in our opinion, do not even remotely, far less definitely and unerringly point towards the guilt of accused S.A.R. Gilani. We, therefore, conclude that the prosecution has failed to bring on record evidence which cumulatively forms a chain, so complete that there is no escape from the conclusion that in all human probabilities accused S.A.R. Gilani was involved in the conspiracy.

419. The only other piece of evidence against her is the telephone call she had with Shaukat in the night of 18.12.2001 which was taped. The evidence is border line. Firstly, the call records show that it was of 49 seconds duration but the expert PW-48 Dr. Rajinder Singh who conducted the auditory and voice spectograph analysis of the taped conversation was categorical that the tape sent to him was of 2 minutes and 19 seconds duration. Secondly, assuming the conversation to be correct, it is certainly indicative of something suspicious. The cause could be, as stated by the prosecution that she was aware of her husband's activities and was therefore concerned. But it could well be that she was aware of the fact that Afzal was a surrendered militant and post attack on Parliament, her husband and Afzal leaving for Srinagar had roused her suspicion. S.A.R. Gilani's address was known to the police on 13.12.2001. Police was on the look out for Gilani. Afzan resided in Mukherji Nagar, so did S.A.R. Gilani. She may have seen police conducting surveillance in the area. Many probable causes may have induced the fear. Had there been any more evidence, position would have been different. Again, we may note that no role whatsoever has been assigned to accused Afzan as a participative member in the conspiracy. She provided no logistics; she procured no hide outs; she procured no arms and ammunitions; she was not even a motivator.

448. The attack was on Parliament, when in session. The sovereignty of the country was attacked. To borrow the words of the Apex Court in the judgment reported as 2002 (Vol. IV) A.D. (S.C.) 445 (Para 87), Krishna Mochi v. State of Bihar, the gravity of the offence is of a magnitude that the collective conscious of the community is so shocked that it will expect the holders of the judicial power centre, to inflict death penalty irrespective of their personal opinion as regards desirability or otherwise of retaining the death penalty. Indeed, after the unfortunate incident, this country had to station its troops at the border and large scale mobilisation of the armed forces took place. The clouds of war with our neighbour loomed large for a long period of time. The nation suffered not only an economic strain but even the trauma of an imminent war. We agree with the submissions made by the prosecution that for the offence of waging war, accused Mohd. Afzal and accused Shaukat Hussain Guru deserve the higher penalty. We accordingly modify the sentence imposed on the said two accused persons under Section 121 IPC by awarding death sentence to these two accused. The rest of the sentences imposed by the learned Special Judge stand affirmed.

Annexure 17

Balancing Act
High Court Judgement on the 13th December 2001 Case

(A Sequel to *Trial of Errors,* Annexure 12)

Peoples Union for Democratic Rights, Delhi, 2004

After the conviction by the Special Court, the accused went on appeal to the High Court. The High Court gave its verdict on October 29, 2003. The High Court upheld the death sentence on Mohammad Afzal and Shaukat Hussain and indeed enhanced a sentence of life imprisonment under Section 121 of IPC to the death penalty. It exonerated S.A.R Gilani and Afsan Guru.

Predictably, there was intense and adverse reaction to the exoneration of S.A.R.Gilani and Afsan Guru. While some newspaper editorials welcomed it, other sections of the media, particularly television, portrayed it as a 'setback to India's war on terror'. The political elite, as much as the police, needed a summary punishment in the case to demonstrate their efficiency and resolve in the face of terrorism. The pressure to convict, that may have operated, even if unconsciously, on the Sessions Court, must have been equally enormous in the case of the High Court. Considering the context, the reversal of the Sessions Court's judgement in the two acquittals was a demonstration of the independence of the judiciary. The verdict may also be seen as a fruition of the concerted and collective efforts to defend individual rights, by a few committed lawyers, democratic right groups, and the Gilani Defence Committee.

While the exoneration of two of the accused was indeed a moment for redeeming one's faith in the judicial process, our reading of the judgement reveals that in the case of Shaukat Hussain Guru and Mohammad Afzal many of the concerns expressed in our report continue to hold. Wherever possible, and despite occasional glaring discrepancies in its account, the prosecution has been given the benefit of the doubt, leading us to the unfortunate conclusion that the judges have performed a balancing act. The obvious innocence of S.A.R. Gilani and Afsan Guru appears to have necessitated the conviction of Mohammad Afzal and Shaukat Hussain.

Since this case sets a precedent, not just for the conduct of POTA cases (a law which deserves to be abolished), but for the treatment of computer generated evidence and phone interceptions, we think it is important to record our concerns regarding the right to a fair trial. We will also comment on the assumptions and political context surrounding the case.

OUTLINE OF THE JUDGMENT

The High Court Judgment begins by framing eleven broad issues which need to be addressed: whether there were breaches of statutory safeguards during investigation, and if so, the consequences of this; the status of investigation till 18.12.2001 the ostensible day before POTA was applied; whether there were valid sanctions for trial under Explosive Substances Act, and POTA; whether any charges could be framed against the accused under IPC; whether imperfect framing of charges had caused prejudice to the accused; whether there was a denial of justice to Afzal by denying him adequate legal aid; whether the trial stands vitiated by admission of inadmissible evidence; whether the Designated Judge had applied correct legal principles pertaining to conduct, disclosure, recovery and confessions; whether the evidence before the Designated Judge was proved and admissible; whether Sec 313 CrPC had been complied with and whether the judgment of the Designated Judge was sustainable. The first 140 pages or so give the sequence of events based on the evidence from the Special Court proceedings, covering the parliament attack and leading up to the arrest of the accused, their trial and their conviction. The Judgment then goes on to analyse the evidence, finally coming to its conclusions from page 362 onwards.

I Trial by Media and Implications for the Rights of the Accused

One of the issues raised by the defense was the prejudice caused by the media. The media was allowed to interview Mohammad Afzal on 20 December 2001, and this was repeatedly broadcast for two days (20, 21 December) and then a hundred days after the attack. A Zee TV film, which dramatised the parliament attack, based its version of events entirely on the prosecution account. The Supreme Court refused to stay the film, despite the clear defamation of the accused, even before they were convicted. The learned High Court Judges reiterated the SC stand, holding that even if the media influenced a jury, judges were beyond its reach. 'Judges do not get influenced by propaganda or adverse publicity. We may only add that Judges are trained, skilled and have sufficient experience to shut their minds receiving hearsay evidence or being influenced by the media.' There are, however, several judgements of the European Court of Human Rights, and indeed the existence of the phrase 'trial by Media' itself suggests that it is a common phenomenon, and not just in the case of jury trials.

The Judges did pass negative remarks against police conduct in allowing media interviews, in the first case because it weakened the independence of the test identification parade. Going beyond the procedural ramifications of the lapse, the judges also reflected on its implications for the rights of the accused, reminding the police/investigating authorities of their custodial responsibilities: 'what is more fundamentally disturbing to our mind is the fact that police custody is given by the court to the investigation authorities on the premise that the accused is required for the purpose of investigation. This custody is not to be misused by allowing the media to interview the accused persons.'

In this case the misuse was aggravated by the selective and premeditated use that the police made of the media – for instance Afzal's 'confession' was telecast but evidence given by one of the reporters in court revealed that the police did not allow the reporter to telecast Afzal's statement regarding Gilani's innocence. That the public has a right to know about cases, and the media the right to tell/comment on them, cannot be disputed. When, however, the media obliterates vital aspects of information or disseminates it selectively, the people's right to know is seriously violated. An independent and mature media should have been aware and taken care to note that the public statement of a person in custody can never be entirely 'free' or 'uncoerced'.

Moreover, in a political context where particular communities get systematically targeted for having a different religion, such selective media coverage becomes complicit in creating the specter of 'suspect communities'. In India, minorities and certain nationalities like Kashmiris are particularly vulnerable to being labeled terrorists. Such labeling has significant social implications for the accused and his/ her family. Once booked under POTA, a person becomes a marked figure in the public eye. Simple things – finding a place to live, a school to send one's children to, a job – all become difficult. Here, any irresponsible and prejudicial coverage by the media becomes a major problem for the accused.

While the trial by media took away the right of the accused to be considered innocent till proven guilty, at a deeper level, the entire sequence of events, manifests how processes of exclusion unfold in society. The press was convened by the police to witness Afzal's confession to having committed a crime of terror. Ultimately, the initiative to convene a press conference lay with the police, and the power to present it to the public lay with the media. Can the accused ever claim the right to speak and be heard? The answer is a resounding No! The accused, it appears, can only speak to condemn him/herself, never to put his/her own point across. S.A.R. Gilani wanted to speak after the trial court had handed down a death sentence to him and the other accused but was promptly shut up.

II. Violation of Safeguards

The defence had argued that since POTA charges were included only on 19 December 2001 and because POTA has certain safeguards, all evidence collected prior to 19.12.01 had to be ignored in relation to the POTA offences. In fact there is possibly reason to believe that the accused were charged under POTA from the beginning, but all its safeguards were violated during the investigation. In order to get around this, the prosecution claimed to have added it only later on. One piece of evidence for this comes from Air Tel.

A letter from Air Tel dated 17 December 2001, responding to a police request for the call records, refers to Section 3/4/5/21/ 22 POTO. It is inconceivable that AirTel would make up these sections on their own. However, according to the prosecution these charges were added only on 19 December. When the Defence raised this discrepancy in the High Court, the Judges gave the prosecution the benefit of the doubt. (a) The Court ruled that this point could not be admitted as it was not raised in the Special Court and did not therefore give the prosecution a right of reply. (b) More problematically, the Court accepted the prosecution plea that the date of 17.12. 2001 on the Air Tel letter was a typographical error.

The Judges ruled that since Sec. 43 of POTA dealing with interception in case of emergency situation and rule 419 of the Indian Telegraph Act Rules 1951 are virtually the same, it made little difference to the case whether the police used the former or the latter. However, the police both violated the Telegraph Act and avoided the safeguards provided under POTA:

Violation of Telegraph Rules: Under Rule 419A of the Indian Telegraph Rules 1951, in case of emergency, permission to intercept phones has to be taken from the Joint Secretary who is authorised to do so, subject to confirmation by the Secretary. In this case, permission was taken from the Joint Director, Information and Broadcasting on 13. 12. 2001 (who is an officer junior to the rank specified).

Avoiding POTA safeguards: (a) Sec 45 of POTA states that the contents of any wire, electronic or oral interception shall be admissible as evidence only if each accused has been furnished with a copy of the order of the Competent Authority, and accompanying application, under which the interception was authorized or approved not less than ten days before trial, hearing or proceeding.' This was avoided, and the sanction granted under the Telegraph Rules and confirmation obtained were not filed with the charge sheet 'on the ground that for security reasons the name of the two officers could not be disclosed.' Instead the main body of the letter was simply read out to the accused in court.

(b) Section 51 of POTA mandates that the investigation cannot be conducted by an officer less than the rank of a Deputy Superintendent of Police (DySP). This safeguard was violated even though the possibility of abuse by higher officials is equally likely, but even this minor safeguard was violated. This investigation was conducted by an ACP. The Court refused to recognise this as a problem, citing an earlier SC judgement, that an illegality or defect in the investigation did not affect the jurisdiction of the Court to take cognisance.

III. Police is let off despite glaring problems in the investigation

Throughout the judgment, the Judges have placed the utmost faith in the police, despite conceding instances of police violation of rules, for instance in the illegality of arrests (see below). Further, despite exonerating Gilani and Afsan Guru, the Judges have not questioned the police role in framing two innocent people.

1. *Identification of accused*: We have already pointed out in our report that no test identification parade had been conducted and that the accused were introduced to the witnesses as those involved in the Parliament attack. The Judges, however, discount this, arguing that the witnesses were members of the public who could have no motive for falsely implicating the accused. They also argue that the shopkeepers who sold the motorbike and the Sujata mixer grinder (in which the explosives were made), or the landlord of Christian colony (which Afzal had rented and where the attackers stayed) had sufficient time to interact with Afzal and Shaukat and identify them. We do not dispute the courts' observation that the motive of witnesses who were members of the public should not be suspected. We wish, however, to state emphatically that the entire gamut of procedural norms surrounding iden-

tification of accused by public witnesses exists precisely to ensure that while the public discharges its duties in an appropriate manner, the rights of the accused are also protected. While theoretically the witnesses should have no reason for falsely implicating the accused, no one can deny that the police in India wield tremendous power and the public – especially shopkeepers – would feel it unwise to go against the police. Secondly, given the prevalent stereotypes about Islamic, especially Kashmiri terrorism, witnesses are very likely to be biased. Thirdly, even without this bias, when people have been described by the police as implicated, the natural psychological tendency is to then 'recognise' them as involved.

2. *Illegal Arrests:* As we noted in the report, there were serious discrepancies in police accounts of the time and place of arrests of the four accused. The judgement accepts the illegality of arrests: 'a very disturbing feature pertaining to the arrest of the accused persons has been noted by us ... the prosecution stands discredited qua the time of arrest of accused S.A.R. Gilani and accused Afsan Guru.' (Judgement Pp.236-37/ para 250, 251) The judges also noted that 'Bismillah (Gilani's brother) was in illegal confinement and was forced to sign papers.' The High Court judges should have asked then for an enquiry into the blatant misuse of power by the police: the police were guilty of wrongful confinement (Sec 340 IPC) and attempt to fabricate and use false evidence (Sec 192, 196 IPC) by making Bismillah sign false papers. Offences under the latter Sections amount to obstruction of justice, and when committed by a public servant, call for not a mere reprimand but a more exemplary punishment. Yet no action has been taken against the police on this count.

3. ***Violation of the rights of the accused***: Under section 52 of POTA (Arrest) an arrested person has (1) 'the right to consult a legal practitioner as soon he is brought to the police station', (2)

'person arrested shall be permitted to meet the legal practitioner representing him during the course of interrogation of the accused person'. Obviously, none of the safeguards has been followed in cases of S.A.R. Gilani and Afsan Guru as both were illegally arrested.

IV. Nature of Evidence

1. Call records: The prosecution used call records from AirTel and Essar to show that the three accused men were in touch with each other and one of the dead militants, around the time of the attack on parliament. However, there are problems in these records, including double entries, the fact that computer printouts of the call records were not certified, and that the two prosecution witnesses were not technical people. A major problem is that what was presented as call records was not the actual computer generated code but records from the billing system, which is an alterable text record.

The Judges did not address this aspect at all — instead they accepted the call records on the presumption that they pertained to the relevant period, and emphasised that there was no evidence to suggest that the computers had not been working properly (a condition in Sub-section 2 of Section 65 (b) of the Indian Evidence Act). As for the double entries, they are explained away as a technical flaw, and in any case, not such as to affect the capacity of the computer to process information correctly. (Annexure 16, p. 269/ para 295)

However, the evidence of telecommunications engineer Farhan given to the Sessions Court, which was not challenged at the time, shows that the double entries were undoubtedly doctored. In this case, the second entry swapped the dialed and dialing numbers but showed that both calls were made at the same time. Since the call records show the location from where a call is made and to where, this is impossible. It is not clear how the Judges came to their conclusion about 'technical flaws'.

One must note that the entire case hinged on the telephone records of 9811489429. We must reiterate that the SIM card of this number was never found, and that there are doubts pertaining to whether it was ever sold to Afzal. In fact, the number came into use a month before the shopkeeper claims to have sold it to Afzal. In our opinion, the question is not of whether the computers were working properly during this period, but of whether they could have been and were doctored, and this has not been addressed. The only evidence, going by the Judgment itself that this number belonged to Afzal is his confession (given to the police). In other words, it is clearly the provisions of POTA – admissibility of evidence given to the police — that forms the lynchpin here for conviction of Afzal.

2. Condoning the non-sealing of evidence: One of the defence arguments pertained to the potential for tampering of evidence since certain critical evidence such as the slips on which phone numbers were listed or the I-cards were not sealed at the time of recovery. Potentially, the police could have put in slips bearing the numbers they wanted to frame. The Judges justified the failure to seal the evidence on the grounds that they furnished leads for future investigation. In any case, they argued, the phone numbers found on the body of the deceased terrorist Hamja (which the defence had implied were planted) were the same as those found on the bodies of the other terrorists, Raja and Rana.

3. Problem of recoveries: Despite accepting the illegality of arrests, the Judges do not concede that this vitiates the prosecution story of recoveries (of evidence). The Judges dispense with the problem caused by lack of independent witnesses at the time of arrest and recovery by citing 2000 (vii) A.D. (SC) 613, *Government of NCT of Delhi vs. Sunil* to the effect that the police must be trusted unless evidence could be proved to the contrary. It is not at all clear why the same police, who carried out arrests illegally, should have suddenly become honest when carrying out recoveries.

The police claimed to have recovered SIM card no. 9810446375 from Afsan at the time of her arrest. The prosecution argued on the basis of the call records that 9810446375 was in touch with a satellite phone and with what they term as Afzal's phone, 9811489429.

But given that the basis for saying that 9810446375 belonged to Shaukat is only his confession, this recovery is seriously doubtful. There are similar doubts about the other recoveries.

V. Confessions

It is in the Court's acceptance of the confessions made by Afzal and Shaukat that we see the challenge posed by POTA to the very concept of a fair trial. The fact that Gilani refused to confess was also held against Afzal and Shaukat, when they claimed that their confessions were not voluntary. Despite discrepancies between the two confessions, the Judges held that this did not vitiate the confessions in toto. The judges also note that when the confessions were recorded by the DCP, 'there is nothing on record that the atmosphere was not free from threat or inducement.' But surely, the police do not leave trails of evidence regarding torture. In fact, the judges themselves concede that Gilani's brother, Bismillah was 'forced' to sign false papers. A delegation of Delhi University teachers, who met Gilani, soon after his arrest, noted in a public letter that he had been tortured. The gravest danger of POTA is that it gives free rein to police torture in order to extract suitable 'confessions'. That Gilani did not succumb to the torture in no way detracts from the fact that Shaukat and Afzal did.

In a positive vein, however, the Judges note that confessions made to police against co-accused, in the absence of any other evidence, are not valid, thus exonerating Gilani and Afsan Guru (p. 350/ para 377).

VI. Acquittal of S.A.R Gilani and Afsan Guru

In dismissing the conversation between Gilani and his brother as non incriminating (see report, page 287-8), the Judges have clearly exercised common sense. As they point out, if the charge rested on Gilani's brother asking him what he had done, surely this would have meant the brother had prior knowledge too, and this was not even the police case. They also find that apart from this conversation, and apart from having been in telephonic touch with Shaukat and Afzal, whom he knew because they were also from Baramullah like him, there was no evidence against Gilani.

In the case of Afsan Guru, the Judges held that being in the house when meetings were held was not sufficient to impute knowledge of a conspiracy to her. As for the conversation she had with Shaukat on the 14th night (which according to the police showed that she was frightened and therefore aware of the conspiracy), by itself this is not incriminating (see report, page 288). The interception also had problems in that there are clear discrepancies between the duration of the conversation shown by the call records and the tape provided by the prosecution. Yet despite noting this, the Court does not call prosecution methods to account.

VII. Waging War Against the Government of India

While all concerned – prosecution, defense and Judge – agreed that the attack on parliament was a terrorist act, attracting the provisions of POTA, the defense disagreed that it constituted 'waging war on the Government of India' (Sec 121 of the IPC), since wars are normally waged between states, involve greater use of force, etc.

The High Court, however, felt that 'Insurgency is treated to be an act of waging war against the Government of India'. According to the Court, the point was not the numbers of people involved or the firepower they had, but their intention to overthrow government or challenge its sovereignty. The various judgments it cites to substantiate this stand, however, are all taken from situations of rebellion against kingship or colonialism. Indeed, in a democracy, it is not possible to equate 'insurgency' with 'waging war' — insurgency may even be seen as a democratic right when all other institutions of democracy have failed, unlike a situation when howsoever terrible the king, people have no rights. In a democracy, people also have every right to want their own form of sovereignty, as they define it. Democracy demands that insurgency be addressed politically and not just as an act of war that needs to be militarily or legally defeated.

In this case, the High Court also concluded (page 205/ para 216) that the firepower used was sufficient to constitute war. 'The fire power was awesome. Enough to engage a battalion. Had the terrorists succeeded the entire building with all inside would have perished. The foundation of the country would have shaken. The act was clearly an act of waging war against the Government of India.' Fortunately, some of us have more faith than the learned judges in the foundations of India, and do not think that they would have been so easily shaken. In a democracy, the people are sovereign, and the physical parliament building is only a symbol of this sovereignty. While an attack on parliament is extremely erious, it can by no means be construed as an attack on the sover-nty of the Indian people.

ost problematically, the judges have used the decision of ernment of India to station troops along the border, the snapping of ties and the subsequent tension to argue that for Afzal and Shaukat the punishment under Sec 121 should be enhanced from life imprisonment to death. The decision to escalate hostilities was an independent decision of the Government of India and not an inevitable consequence of the attack itself. The Government could as easily have downplayed the incident, especially as the Pakistani Government had officially condemned the attack. How then, can Afzal and Shaukat be held responsible for the 'clouds of war' and much less, be given a death sentence for this? Ironically, moreover, since in the end there was no war, Afzal and Shaukat are being given an enhanced death penalty for something that they did not will, and which never happened.

VIII. Punishment : the problems with the death penalty

The Sessions Judge had given Shaukat and Afzal the death penalty under Sec 302 IPC read with 120 B IPC (conspiracy to murder), Sec 3(2) POTA (committing a terrorist act) and life imprisonment etc. under other sections. The Delhi High Court upheld the sentences imposed by the Special Judge, POTA for the various offences, except for the offence u/s 121 of the Indian Penal Code (waging war against the state) in which the Special Judge had imposed the sentence for life imprisonment. The High Court enhanced the life sentence to that of death on the grounds of the serious national consequences flowing from the act. As mentioned above, this seems to us a flawed and legally incorrect approach.

Further, the judges play with semantics to argue that the definition of a terrorist act in POTA Sec 3(1) to include 'any act or **thing**' includes help in procuring explosives, which is a 'thing'. Therefore even though Shaukat and Afzal did not carry out the attack themselves, the Judges hold both Shaukat and Afzal liable under Sec 3(2) POTA (committing a terrorist act) which can carry a death penalty. It is, however, no-one's case that Shaukat helped in the procurement of explosives.

PUDR views the death penalty as a barbaric form of punishment, and a violation of the right to life. Moreover, its imposition is both politically and legally unsound. We believe that it gives a potentially dangerous form of power in the hands of the State, and is an anachronism in a democracy that is grounded in principles of egalitarian jurisprudence. Being irrevocable, death penalty leaves no scope for redemption since a death conviction once carried out cannot be undone. In most cases, death penalty comes across as an arbitrary punishment since the baseline 'rarest of rare' is ambiguous. In this case we see that the High Court while exonerating Gilani and Afsan Guru, upheld the death sentence on Mohammad Afzal and Shaukat Hussain and enhanced their punishment to death under Section 121 IPC. Given the way in which the debilities and injustices of trial under POTA apply, sustaining and enhancing the death sentence of the latter seems more a measure to balance the acquittal of Gilani and Afsan Guru, than required by the facts of the case itself.

PUDR demands

1. A fair trial, which we believe, is not possible under POTA
2. Rejection of the death penalty
3. Action against police officers commensurate with the illegalities they have committed

ANNEXURE 18

A Wife's Appeal for Justice

By Tabassum

Kashmir Times, 21 October 2004

I am the wife of Mohammad Afzal, the man accused of conspiring to attack the Indian Parliament on December 13, 2001. Afzal has been condemned to death by the Sessions Court Judge, S.N. Dhingra and his death sentence has been confirmed by the Hon'ble High Court of Delhi. Now the case has come up before the Hon'ble Supreme Court of India.

All over India people have condemned the attack on Parliament. And I agree that it was a terrorist attack and must be condemned. However, it is also important that the people accused of such a serious crime be given a fair trial and their story be fully heard before they are punished. I believe that no one has heard my husband's story and he has so far never been represented in the court properly.

I appeal to you to hear our story and then decide for yourselves whether justice has been done. Afzal and my story is the story of many young Kashmiri couples. Our story represents the tragedy facing our people.

In 1990 Afzal was attracted to the movement led by the JKLF, like thousands of other youth. He went to Pakistan for training and stayed there for a little while. However, he was disillusioned by the differences between different groups and he did not support pro-Pakistani groups. He stayed there only three months without getting any training. Afzal returned to Kashmir and he went to Delhi to pursue his studies. He always wanted to study and before he joined the movement he was doing his MBBS.

My husband wanted to return to normal life and with that intention he surrendered to the BSF. The BSF Commandant refused to give him his certificate till he had motivated two others to surrender. And Afzal motivated two other militants to surrender. He was given a certificate stating that he was a surrendered militant. You will not perhaps realise that it is very difficult to live as a surrendered militant in Kashmir but he decided to live with his family in Kashmir. In 1997 he started a small business of medicines and surgical instruments in Kashmir. The next year we were married. He was 28 years old and I was 18 years.

Throughout the period that we lived in Kashmir the Indian security forces continuously harassed Afzal and told him to spy on people they suspected of being militants. One Major Ram Mohan Roy of 22 Rashtriya Rifles tortured Afzal and gave him electric shocks in his private parts. He was humiliated and abused.

The Indian security forces used to regularly take Afzal to their camps and torture him. They wanted to extract information from him. One night the Indian security forces came to our home and abused all of us and took away Afzal to their camp; another time he was taken to the STF (State Task Force) camp Palhalan Pattan.

Some days later they took him to the Humhama STF camp. In that camp the officers, DSP Vinay Gupta and DSP Darinder Singh demanded Rs. one lakh. We are not a rich family and we had to sell everything, including the little gold I got on my marriage to save Afzal from the torture.

Afzal was kept in freezing water and petrol was put into his anus. One officer Shanti Singh hanged my husband upside down for hours naked and in the cold. They gave electric shocks in his penis and he had to have treatment for days.

You will think that Afzal must be involved in some militant activities that is why the security forces were torturing him to extract information. But you must understand the situation in Kashmir, every man, woman and child has some information on the movement even if they are not involved. By making people into informers they turn brother against brother, wife against husband and children against parents. Afzal wanted to live quietly with his family but the STF would not allow him.

You should also know that the STF force is notorious in Kashmir for extorting money from the people and they have become so infamous that when Mufti Sayed became the Chief Minister he promised in his election manifesto to disband the entire force. The STF is known for human rights violations including killing people in their custody and brutal, senseless, inhuman torture.

It was under these conditions that forced Afzal to leave his home, family and settle in Delhi. He struggled hard to earn a living and he had decided to bring me and our four-year old son, Ghalib, to Delhi. Like any other family we dreamed of living together peacefully and bringing up our children, giving them a good education and seeing them grow up to be good human beings. That dream was cut short when once again the STF got hold of my husband in Delhi.

The STF told my husband to bring one man Mohammad to Delhi from Kashmir. He met Mohammad and one other man Tariq there at the STF camp. He did not know anything about the men and he had no idea why he was being asked to do the job. He has told all this to the court but the court chose to believe half his statement about bringing Mohammad but not the bit that he was told to do so by the STF.

There was no one to represent Afzal in the lower court. The court appointed a lawyer who never took instructions from Afzal, or cross examined the prosecution witnesses. That lawyer was communal and showed his hatred for my husband. When my husband told Judge Dhingra that he did not want that lawyer the judge ignored him. In fact my husband went totally undefended in the trial court. Whenever my husband wished to say something the judge would not hear him out and the judge showed his communal bias in open court.

In the High Court one human rights lawyer offered to represent Afzal and my husband accepted. But instead of defending Afzal the lawyer began by asking the court not to hang Afzal but to kill him by a lethal injection. My husband never expressed any desire to die. He has maintained that he has been entrapped by the STF. My husband was shocked but he had no way of changing his lawyer while being locked up in the high security jail.

It was only after the High Court judgement was pronounced he got to know about the way the lawyer had represented him. Afzal refused to accept the same lawyer for his appeal in the Supreme Court. I had no way of getting Afzal a lawyer. I do not know anyone in Delhi. Finally Afzal wrote to the Defence Committee set up for Mr. Geelani. I am annexing his letter. And the Defence Committee helped Afzal to get a senior lawyer, Mr. Sushil Kumar. However, the Supreme Court cannot go into the evidence and so I do not know what will happen.

I appeal to you to ensure that my husband is not condemned to death and he is ensured a fair trial. Surely your conscience will not allow you to be a party to the death of a fellow human being who has not been represented in the court and who has not had a chance to tell his story. The police have made him falsely confess before the media even before the trial started. They humiliated him, beat him, tortured him and even urinated in his mouth. I feel deep shame to talk about these things in public but circumstances have forced me. It has taken a lot of courage for me to put all this on paper but I do so for the sake of my child who is now six years old.

Will you speak out at the injustice my husband has faced? Will you speak out on my behalf? I am of course fighting for my husband's life, for the life of my son's father. But I also speak as a Kashmiri woman who is losing faith in Indian democracy and its ability to be fair to Kashmiri Muslims.

INDEX

Annexures not included

Aaj Tak TV, 20
ABM Treaty, 8
Adams, John Quincy, xii
Advani, Lal Krishna (Union Home Minister), 14, 27, 43
Afghanistan, 53,
  attack on, 6-8, 100
Afsan Guru, 25, 27, 29, 31, 38, 40, 41, 47, 54, 58, 61, 62, 63, 68, 70, 71, 72, 74, 75, 76, 84, 101
Afzal, Mohammad, 13, 21, 22, 30, 38, 39, 40, 41, 44, 45, 46, 54, 55, 56, 57, 60, 61, 62, 63, 68, 72, 74, 75, 78, 79, 80, 83, 84, 85, 86, 90, 91, 92
  and media "confession", 18-20, 23, 24, 81, 89
  trial of, 26, 45, 47, 71, 93-6
  sentencing of, 28
  confession of, 30, 31, 33, 41, 42, 43, 44, 46, 53, 54, 55, 56, 60, 63, 78, 85, 86-93
  "chotu", 62, 77
AIRTEL, 40, 42, 74, 86
Aligarh Muslim University, 16, 21
All India Committee for Geelani, 26, 34n, 36n, 66
Al-queda, xvi, xvii, 8, 15, 100
Ambassador car (attack vehicle), 38, 39, 42, 44, 52-3, 55, 87
Amicus, 93, 94
Amnesty Internatinal, 18
Annan, Kofi, 4-5, 34n
anti-German hysteria, ix
Arifa, Qurat-ul-am-, wife of Geelani, 72, 73
arms and ammunitions, 31, 40, 57, 86, 97
Arnold, General Hap, x
Ashok Chand, DCP, 88-9
Asian Age, 36n, 37n
attack on Parliament, *see* December 13
Azadpur market, 39, 40, 56, 57, 61

Bansal, Neeraj, *see* Amicus
Baruah, Amit, 35n
Bharatiya Janata Party (BJP), 9, 10, 101, 102
Bharatiya Majdoor Sangh (BMS), 9, 10
Bill of Rights, 51
Bin Laden, Osama, 7, 41
Bismillah, 72, 73, 93
Blair, Tony, xii, xvi
Blum, William, 34n
Bullock, Alan, 105n
"Burger", 54
Bush, George, xii, xvi, 6, 51
Butani, 105n
Butler Commission, 100

call records, *see* telephone calls
Castlereagh, Prime Minister, xiv
Chaturvedi, Swati, 20-1
Chatterjee, Ruksh, 105n
chemicals, *see* explosives
Chennault, General, xi
Chief Justice of India, 26
Churchill, Winston, xii, xv, xvi
Chomsky, Noam, 35n
  on First Seminole war, xii-xiv

on 13 December, xvii, 2, 5
on 9/11, 5-6
on terrorism, 8, 34n
commission of inquiry, 2, 4, 5, 31, 52, 59, 98-103
common minimum programme, 103, 106n
Counterpunch, 34n
Curtiss, Adam, 15, 34n, 36n

December 13,
attack of, 1, 23, 24, 27, 32, 45, 52-3, 54, 60, 67, 70, 82, 83, 84, 85, 88, 97, 98
and 9/11, 2-3, 5, 12
and NDA, 8-13, 102
and Emergency, 13
and High Court Judgment, 13, 30
Delhi airport, 39, 53
Delhi Assembly, 39
Delhi Police, 17, 22, 24, 26, 27, 29, 31, 33, 40, 41, 42, 43, 44, 45, 46, 49, 50, 52-3, 54, 55, 58, 59, 60, 61, 71, 73, 74, 75, 76, 77, 78, 79, 80, 85, 86, 87, 88, 89, 90, 97, 98
Delhi University, 17, 26, 63, 68, 103
Dhingra, S. N., Special Judge, 43, 49, 50, 51, 65, 66, 68, 69-70, 73, 94
Dil Se, 27
disclosure statements, 41, 93, 97
of Afzal, 44, 87, 88
of Shaukat, 87, 88
of Geelani, 75
Du Boff, Richard, 34n

Economic and Political Weekly, 34n, 35n
Encyclopaedia Britannica, 105n
expert witnesses, 64, 65, 66, 76, 81
explosives, explosive material, 38, 39, 40, 41, 42, 53, 57, 82-3, 87, 105n

fabrication, concoction of evidence, 45, 46, 47, 48, 49, 51, 59, 70, 71, 78, 88, 93, 97
Fahrenheit 9/11, 6
false witnesses, 46, 50, 80-5
fast-track trial, 25, 31
fear,
freedom from, xii,
and umbrella of power, xiv,
and frightened population, xvii
resort to, ix, 3
manipulation of, x, xv
Fernandes, George, 9
Frontline, 34n, 35n

Gaddis, John Lewis, xii-xv
Gandhi, Indira, 13
Geelani, Syed Abdul Rehman, 15, 16, 17, 18, 22, 23, 24, 26, 28, 29, 30, 31, 38, 40, 41, 45, 47, 54, 62, 63, 64, 65, 66, 67, 68, 69, 70, 71, 72, 74, 75, 81, 83, 88, 89, 101
Geneva Convention, 7, 8
Germany, rise of Nazism in, ix, x, 98
Ghazi Baba, 22, 38, 39, 42, 54, 58, 86, 92, 96
Gonzalvis, Colin, 47
(*The*) *Guardian*, 35n, 36n
Guantanamo Bay, 7, 100
Gujarat, communal carnage in, 20
Gupta, Vinay, DCP, 94
Guru, Shaukat Hussain, 14, 17, 21,

22, 23, 26, 28, 31, 33, 38, 39, 40, 41, 49, 54, 56, 57, 58, 60, 61, 62, 63, 68, 71, 74, 75, 76, 79, 83, 84, 85, 88, 89, 90

Haksar, Nandita, 14, 18, 22, 27, 28, 34n, 36n, 37n, 43, 47, 50-1, 67, 95, 99-100, 103n, 105n, 106n
half-brother, Geelani's, 64-6, 67
hawala money, 41
Heidegger, Martin, x
Herman, E. & D. Peterson, 34n
hideouts, 21, 31, 38, 39, 41, 42, 44, 46, 81, 84, 87
High Court in Delhi, 13-14, 15, 27, 28, 29, 30, 31, 45, 46, 47, 57, 58, 60, 63, 67, 68, 69, 70, 71, 72, 74, 76, 80, 81, 87, 89, 90, 99, 101
(*The*) *Hindustan Times*, 16, 17, 20, 21, 27, 37n
(*The*) *Hindu*, 17, 26, 27, 35n, 36n, 37n, 106n
"Home Ministry" sticker, 39, 42
human rights, 2, 4, 5, 51, 100
human rights activists, 25, 87, 99, 101
Human Rights Watch, 34n
Hurriyat Conference, 99

IC-814, 16, 22, 53, 54
Id, *Eid*, 62, 65, 70, 77, 91
identity cards, 39, 40, 42, 52
IMEI number, 60
Indian Express, 26, 37n
intelligence agencies, 17, 21, 47
INTERPOL, 42
investigating agency, *see* Delhi Police
Iraq, invasion of, xvi, 55, 100
Inter Services Agency of Pakistan (ISI), 38, 41, 53, 55, 101

Jackson, Andrew, xii-xiv
J&K Police, 72, 73, 74, 76, 77, 80, 104n
Jaish-e-Mohammad (JeM), 15, 16, 18, 21, 23, 27-8, 38, 42, 53, 55, 60, 92, 104n
Jaiswal, Kamini, 47,
Jawaharlal Nehru University, 26
jehad, jihadists, xvi, 38, 86
Jethmalani, Ram, 47, 48, 69, 72, 93, 96, 101, 104n, 105n
Jewish-Bolshevik conspiracy, x
Jha, Prem Shanker, 26-7
Jordanian student, 17
Jowher, Zakia, 35n
Jyoti, Archana, 37n

Kak, Sanjay, 65, 66, 67, 103n
Kandahar, 54
Kashmiri language, 64-6, 104n
Ken Commission, 100
Kennedy, John F., 16
Khalsa College, 72
Klemperer, Victor, ix, x
Kothari, Rajni, 26
Kyoto Protocol, 8

landlords, 25, 43, 45, 62, 82, 83, 84, 93
laptop computer, 26, 38, 39, 40, 41, 58, 74, 79, 87, 93
Laskar-e-Toiba (LeT), 14, 18, 38, 42, 53, 56, 60, 92
liberation of Kashmir, *see* jehad
London School of Economics (LSE), 16, 21

Lygo, Ian, 35n

magnetic red light for VIPs, 39
Malhotra, V. K., 101
Malik, Neeraj, 37n
Mamdani, Mahmood, 35n
Masood Azhar, 23, 38, 41, 54, 55
militants, *see* terrorists
Milli Gazatte, 36n
Mitra, Chandan, 37n, 106n
mobile phones, 31, 39, 40, 41, 42, 45, 52, 58, 61, 62, 63, 74, 79, 80, 93
  98114-89429, 40, 41, 60, 75, 79, 80, 83
  98100-81228, 40, 71, 73
  98115-73506, 40, 41, 60, 75
Mody, Anjali, 37n
Mohammad, 38, 53, 54, 55, 56, 75, 91, 92, 95
Mohammad Abdullah, 18
Monbiot, George, 34n
Moore, Michael, 6
motorcycle, 39, 42, 54, 85
Musharraf, General Pervez, 10, 13, 43, 55
muslims, attack on, 11

Nagaraj, Vijay, 105n
Nagasaki, bombing of, xi
Narain, Nandita, 37n
(*The*) *Nation*, 34n
Navbharat Times, 36n
Navalakha, Gautam, 25
Nepal, 53
9/11, xvi, 1, 3, 8, 15, 23, 100, 103n
Nuremburg Tribunal, xvii

Outlook Magazine, 37n

Pancholi, N. D., 25
Pandey, Devesh K., 17
Pakistan, 10, 23, 24, 40, 41, 42, 43, 55, 80, 94
  High Commission of, 20-21
  war effort on, 11, 12, 14, 20, 82, 98
Parliament, 11, 39, 52, 53, 55, 61
Parliament complex/building, 1, 52-3, 54, 56, 57, 69, 70
Patil, Shivraj, 103
Patnaik, Utsa, 35n
Patranobis, Suthirtho, 16
Patriot Act, 8
Pearl, Daniel, 55
Peer, Basharat, 18, 25, 27, 36n, 74
Peoples Union for Civil Liberties, 66
Peoples Union of Democratic Rights (PUDR), 49, 50, 60, 63, 71, 74, 75, 79, 82, 83, 89
Pilger, John, 102, 106n
(*The*) *Pioneer*, 37n, 106n
Powell, Colin, 13
Prakash, Sampat, 65, 66, 67
Prevention of Terrorism Act (POTA), also POTO, 22, 24, 33, 41, 42, 43, 46, 48, 50, 51, 54, 63, 74, 75, 78, 82, 86, 87, 88, 89, 90, 101, 102
Puri, Balraj, 66

Qazi, Javed Ashraf, 55-6

Rajbir Singh, ACP, 18, 20, 23, 27, 81, 88, 89
Ramakrishnan, Nitya, 29, 47
Ramzan, 68,
Rashid, 64-5, 67
Rashtriya Sahara, 16
Rashtriya Swayamsevak Sangh (RSS), 9

Rediff.com, 104n, 106n
Revolutionary Democracy, 35n, 36n, 105n
Reichstag Fire, 98
Robinson, Mary, 5, 34n
Roy, Arundhati, 8, 34n, 101, 106n
Roy, Ashim, 35n
Roy, Ram Mohan, 94

Sangh Parivar, 9, 11, 12
satellite phone, 39, 40, 42, 80
Seminar, 36n, 37n, 103n, 105n
Sengupta, Suddhabrata, 37n
September 11, *see* 9/11
Shab-e-kadr, 68
Shanti Bhusan, 47, 49, 78, 98-9, 104n
Sharma, Neeta, 21
Sharma, Rajnish, 17
Shiv Sena, 101
shopkeepers, vendors, 25, 43, 45, 50, 82, 83, 93
SIM cards, 41, 61, 75, 79, 83
Singh, Darinder, DSP, 94
Singh, Jaswant, 54
Singh, Kumar Sanjay, 43
Singh, Shanti, 94
Socialist Alliance, 34n
South Asean Citizens Wire, 34n, 35n, 105n
Special Cell/Branch, *see* Delhi Police
Special Court, also Sessions Court, 14, 25, 27, 29, 30, 31, 35n, 41, 43, 45, 47, 49, 63, 64-70, 71, 90, 91, 93, 101, 102, 105n
Spaatz, General Carl, x
(*The*) *Statesman*, 36n
Srinagar, Kashmir, 40, 41, 58, 61, 62, 66, 71, 72, 73, 77, 78, 85, 87, 104n
statement u/s 313, 43, 46, 61, 96
  of Afzal, 43, 46, 47, 62, 77, 79, 85, 86, 90, 91, 93, 95
  of Shaukat, 77, 78
  of Geelani, 72, 75, 89
State Task Force, J&K, 90, 91, 94, 95, 105n
Steins, Graham, 9-10
Subramaniam, Vidya, 35n
Sujata mixer, 38
Supreme Court of India, 27, 32, 37n, 102, 104n

Tabassum, 94-5, 105n
TADA, 63
Taliban, 7
Tariq Ahmed, 38, 42, 86, 91, 92, 95, 96
Tehelka, 105n
telephone calls, conversations, 25, 26, 42, 45, 58, 60, 61, 62, 63, 64, 65, 68, 73, 74, 75, 76, 80, 84, 85, 87, 104n
terrorists, 3, 4, 10, 13, 14, 17, 18, 21, 22, 23, 24, 26, 28, 29, 30, 31, 38, 39, 40, 41, 42, 43, 44, 45, 46, 51, 52-3, 54, 55, 56, 57, 60, 69, 70, 75, 80, 82, 83, 84, 85, 86, 92, 96, 97
terrorism, 44, 98
  threat of, xvi, xvii, 101
  and preventive measures, 4-5;
  UN resolution on, 8
  and Islam, 23, 82
Thakur, Sujit, 16
Thomson, A.C., 34n
(*The*) *Times of India*, 23, 33n, 35n, 36n, 104n
Times News Network, 34n, 104n
time of arrest, 61, 71, 73, 74, 76, 77, 78
truck, Afsan Guru's, 40, 57, 58, 76, 77, 79

UK Embassy in Delhi, 39

United Progressive Alliance (UPA), 103
US Embassy in Delhi, 39

Vajpayee, Atal Behari, Prime Minister of India,
on Parliament attack, 1-2
on Zee film, 14, 27
Varadrajan, Siddharth, 104n
Venkatesan, V., 35n
Venkateswaran, Sujata, 105n
Vice-President of India, 39, 52

Wahi, Tripta, 36n
weapons of mass destruction, xvi, xvii, 8
Weeks, William Earl, xii-iv

Zakir Hussain College, 16
Zee film, 14, 27, 69
Znet/ Zmag, 34n, 35n, 106n